Ingeborg M. Niesler|Angela K. Niebel-Lohmann

# ATLAS OF FLOWERING PLANTS

## Visual Studies of 200 Deconstructed Botanical Families

SCHIFFER
PUBLISHING

4880 Lower Valley Road · Atglen, PA 19310

**Other Schiffer Books on Related Subjects:**
*The Sinister Beauty of Carnivorous Plants*, Matthew M. Kaelin,
ISBN 978-0-7643-5098-6

*Coastal Garden Plants: Florida to Virginia*, Roy Heizer,
ISBN 978-0-7643-4181-6

*Coastal Garden Plants: Maine to Maryland*, Roy Heizer,
ISBN 978-0-7643-4402-2

Originally published as *Bildatlas der Blütenpflanzen*
© 2017 Haupt Bern
Translated from the German by Simulingua, Inc.

Library of Congress Control Number: 2020943396

"Schiffer," "Schiffer Publishing, Ltd.," and the pen and inkwell logo are registered trademarks of Schiffer Publishing, Ltd.

Design and layout by pooldesign, CH-Zurich
Type set in Academy Engraved/Helvetica
ISBN: 978-0-7643-6133-3
Printed in China

Published by Schiffer Publishing, Ltd.
4880 Lower Valley Road
Atglen, PA 19310
Phone: (610) 593-1777; Fax: (610) 593-2002
E-mail: Info@schifferbooks.com
Web: www.schifferbooks.com

For our complete selection of fine books on this and related subjects, please visit our website at www.schifferbooks.com. You may also write for a free catalog.

Schiffer Publishing's titles are available at special discounts for bulk purchases for sales promotions or premiums. Special editions, including personalized covers, corporate imprints, and excerpts, can be created in large quantities for special needs. For more information, contact the publisher.

We are always looking for people to write books on new and related subjects. If you have an idea for a book, please contact us at proposals@schifferbooks.com.

## 35 The Plant Families

On a New Year's Day walk on January 1, 2004, I found a fallen poplar tree that had thick buds already developing on its branches. I broke off a few of the branches and put them on my new flatbed scanner at home and scanned them. No photos could have been better! Then the buds were dissected and each step was documented with a scan.

Out of botanical curiosity about what "everything looks like" in plants, I thus created a "virtual herbarium" with the intention of making it possible to read as much morphological information on the plant on one page as is presented in the drawn herbarium collections of earlier times—but created using the modern technique of scanning.

In the meantime, about 1,700 of these virtual herbarium specimens have been brought together in this collection of about 200 flowering-plant families: first, plants from our own gardens, then plants that are relevant for teaching, and finally material from the greenhouses of the Loki-Schmidt-Garten (Botanical Garden) in Hamburg. Naturally, this is still not much in terms of the total number of flowering plants, but this fund of plants made it possible to prepare overview tables for a variety of purposes in a relatively short time; among other things, for all the plant families that are arranged in this book according to the Angiosperm Phylogeny Group (APG) III classification.

This book was created in the hope that these representations of plants in the form of a "scanned herbarium" would appeal to and be useful to a wide variety of viewers. Enjoy reading and observing!

Hamburg, Spring 2017
*Ingeborg M. Niesler & Angela K. Niebel-Lohmann*

To provide a better understanding of the family tables and the accompanying texts, a brief overview of the general structure of flowering plants is first given here. This includes an introduction about the plants' habit and about their form of growth, their leaves, their leaf forms and arrangements, and their roots, and, above all, the structure of the flower—that is, the floral envelope or perianth (calyx and corolla); the arrangement and structure of the ovary, stamens, and stigmas, as well as nectaries, fruits, and seeds; and germination. The systematic overviews of the orders and the respective families belonging to the orders are given referring to the APG III system of 2009, so that at times some newer classifications were also adopted.

Whenever possible, the family name will also always be provided in English in the text or tables. An alphabetical list of English family names with the associated page reference can be found on page 258. The plant families are listed in alphabetical order to make them easier to look up. Botanical terms are explained in the glossary.

Materials and methods: Fresh flowering-plant material, mainly from the Loki-Schmidt-Garten greenhouse collection in Hamburg, was placed on a flatbed scanner (Sano Scan 5000F, Epson Perfection V370 Photo), covered with black velvet, and enlarged, using a millimeter (mm) standard measure. It proved a good idea to cover the plants with black velvet, in order to counteract the emergence of the "parallel shadows" that tend to arise if you have a bright background, which sharply distracts from the actual "herbarium" information. Depending on the size of the section, the image was scanned in various dots per inch (dpi) numbers (Canon maximum: 1,200 dpi; Epson maximum: 4,800 dpi). The habit of the plants was also documented in photos (Panasonic Lumix DMC-FX01), and some details with SEM photos (SEM Philipps 505, XL 20).

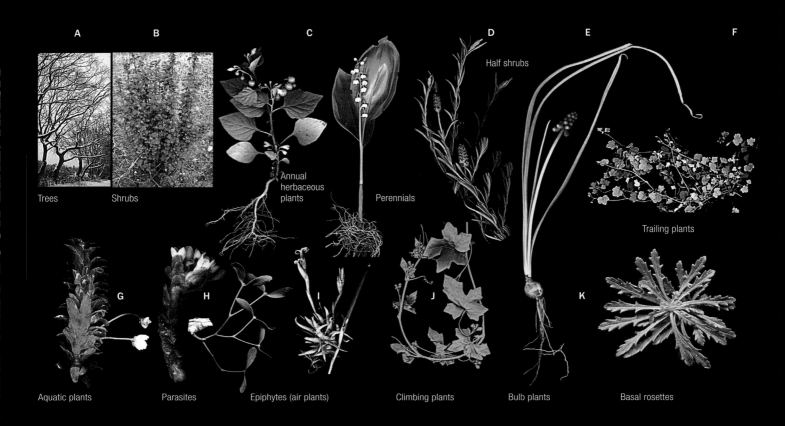

A | B | C | D | E | F

Half shrubs

Trees  Shrubs

Annual
herbaceous
plants

Perennials

Trailing plants

G | H | I | J | K

Aquatic plants    Parasites    Epiphytes (air plants)    Climbing plants    Bulb plants    Basal rosettes

A: *Aesculus hippocastanum* (horse chestnut), Sapindaceae. B: *Ribes sanguineum* (red flowering currant), Grossulariaceae. C: *left*, *Solanum nigrum* (black nightshade), Solanaceae; *right*, Convallaria majalis (lily of the valley), Asparagaceae. D: *Lavandula stoechas* (Spanish lavender), Lamiaceae. E: *Muscari botryoides* (small grape hyacinth), Asparagaceae. F: *Cymbalaria muralis* (Kenilworth ivy), Plantaginaceae. G: *Elodea canadensis* (Canadian waterweed), Hydrocharitaceae. H: *left*, *Cytinus* sp., Cytinaceae; *right*, *Viscum album* (mistletoe), Santalaceae. I: *Tillandsia loliacea*, Bromeliaceae. J: *Bryonia dioica* (red bryony), Cucurbitaceae. K: *Erinus alpinus* (alpine balm), Plantaginaceae.

**Trees** I Woody plants, at times over 50 meters tall, which grow only one trunk; the tree crown can branch out broadly. Many phylogenetically old families develop tree-shaped plants (fig. A).

**Shrubs** I Woody plants that branch out directly above the surface of the earth (fig. B).

**Half shrubs** I Half shrubs are plants that grow like a shrub above the surface of the earth, thus having woody stems, but their external annual growth withers between growing seasons (fig. D).

**Perennials** I Perennial herbaceous plants (fig. C).

**Herbaceous plants** I Annual to biennial herbaceous plants (fig. C, *left*) and perennials (fig. C, *right*).

**Bulb plants** I The bulbs, which usually consist of fleshy cataphylls with a compressed stem, serve as an underground storage organ that regrows leaves and flowers during each growing season. In this process the older cataphylls dry out like onion skins and thus form a protective husk against the environmental conditions (fig. E).

**Trailing plants** I Mostly perennial plants, these grow by trailing along the earth surface, where they can grow roots at the nodes and form new plants (fig. F).

**Basal rosettes** I Usually belong to the perennial plants, with a compressed stem and spiral leaf arrangement. As a rule, they grow long, upright receptacles, which grow anew during each growing season (fig. K).

**Climbing plants** I Annual-biennials; most, however, are perennial plants, herbaceous or woody. Instead of using supporting stems, they can grow upward toward the light by growing shoots, leaves, or roots on various supports (fig. J).

**Epiphytes** (air plants) I Are predominantly distributed in the tropical climate zones of the Earth. Their seeds, spread by wind or animals, usually germinate on woody bedding in higher, lighter regions of their site. Since they do not penetrate into the support or root in the soil, they adapt in various ways to be able absorb water and nutrients (fig. I).

**Parasites** I The herbaceous parasites as a rule tap into the roots of their host plant and thus connect into the host plant's nutrient and water cycle; as a result, growing their own leaves is often superfluous. Parasites with woody stems (such as mistletoe) use holdfasts to grow into the usually likewise woody host plant and thus connect into the water cycle of the host, but they grow their own green, perennial leaves; therefore, we speak of half (or hemi-) parasites (fig. H).

**Flowering aquatic plants** that grow exclusively in the water have many adaptations to their liquid support, such as floating leaves (fig. G).

A: *Nuphar lutea* (yellow water-lily), Nymphaeaceae, stem transverse. B: *Philodendron gonzalesii*, Araceae, shoot transverse. C: *Nymphaea* species (water lily), Nymphaeaceae, shoot transverse. D: *Aristolochia durior* (Dutchman's pipe), Aristolochiaceae, woody shoot transverse. E: *Carex pendula* (drooping sedge), Cyperaceae, shoot transverse. F: *Sambucus nigra* (black elder), Caprifoliaceae, half-shoot transverse. G: *Tilia plathyphyllos* (bigleaf linden), Malvaceae, shoot transverse. H: *Physostegia virginiana* (obedient plant), Lamiaceae, decussation-induced square-shoot transverse with marrow parenchyma. I: *Lamium album* (white deadnettle), Lamiaceae, shoot transverse. J: *Phragmites communis* (common reed), Poaceae; *right*, stalk transverse; *center*, the same, longitudinal in the node area; *left*, view of the node with ends of the leaf sheath. K: *Ornithogalum osmynellum*, Hyacinthaceae, compressed stem longitudinal. L: *Evonymus europaeus* (European spindletree), Celastraceae, winged stem; *left*, transverse; *right*, frontal. M: *left*, *Epiphyllum* sp.; *right*, *Disocactus* sp., Cactaceae, leaflike spreading succulent stem transverse. N: *left*, *Semele androgyna*, Asparagaceae; *right*, *Phyllanthus speciosus*, Euphorbiaceae. O: *above*, *Scutia buxifolia*, Rhamnaceae, stem and stem thorn longitudinal; *below*, *Zizyphus jujuba*, Rhamnaceae; *left*, stem thorn lateral; *right*, younger stem with stem thorn longitudinal. P: *Passiflora* sp., Passifloraceae, stem tendril. Q: *Humulus japonicus* (Japanese hops), Cannabaceae. R: *Rebutia* species, Cactaceae, succulent stem longitudinal. S: *Polygonatum multiflorum* (Solomon's seal), Liliaceae, rhizome. T: *Fragaria vesca* (wild strawberry), Rosaceae. U: Stem of a palm tree transverse, Arecaceae, detail.

Stems are the supports for the plant appendages. Woody plants (figs. D, G, L, U) at times grow stems that are several meters in diameter. Their annual growth can be seen in the annual rings in figs. D and G. They also show a difference between monocotyledonous and dicotyledonous plants: whereas the vascular tissues of the latter form closed rings with increasing age (xylem: water-conducting tissue inside; phloem: nutrient conduits on the outside; compare fig. G), the solitary vascular bundles of the former are distributed through the cross section of the stem as "spots" (compare figs. B, U). The grasses and other monocotyledons with a hollow stalk are the exceptions. In these, the vascular bundles are inevitably arranged in a ring (fig. J). Metamorphoses are shown in figs. K (compressed stem longitudinal), N (flat, leaflike flowering stems), R (stem thorns), Q (twining stem), S (rooted stem growing horizontally in the ground), and T (runner). In bulb plants and rosettes above all, the stem is compressed (fig. K). The long, mostly hollow stalks of the sweetgrasses (fig. J) have growth zones in the lower node area, which make it possible if, for example, the stalk has been bent over, for it to grow vertically upward again. Green stems that grow like leaves (figs. M, N), so-called **phylloclades**, also carry out photosynthesis thanks to their chloroplast-like features. Another kind of stem that grows underground is the **rhizomes**; they have roots that grow downward (fig. S). These grow new flowering stems during each growing season. **Succulent stems** (fig. R), which some plants grow in dry, desertlike habitats, store water in special, usually central tissues in order to survive dry periods. **Stem tendrils** (figs. P, Q) are used to attach the stem to various supports so that they can grow higher up toward the light. **Runners** (fig. T) help promote the vegetative propagation of plants that usually grow close to the ground. **Stem thorns** (fig. O) are protective mechanisms and represent reduced manifestations of the stem. Unlike prickles, the stem thorns are connected to the central vascular tissues. Nothing is known about the function of "winged" stems (fig. L), which are relatively rare.

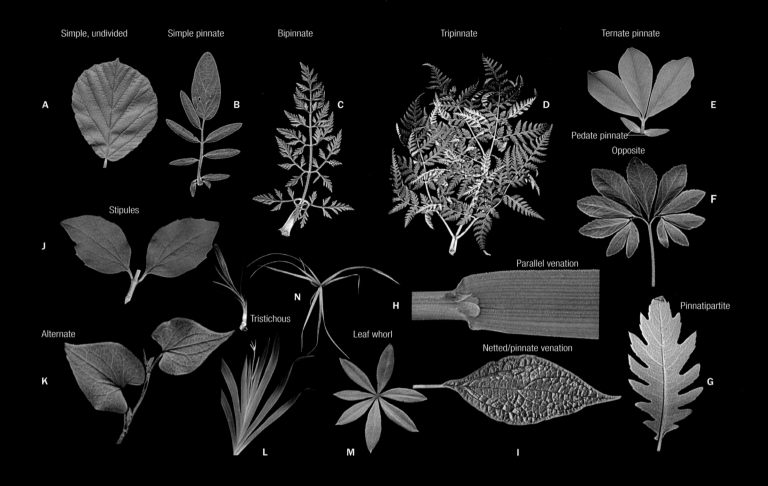

Simple, undivided   Simple pinnate   Bipinnate   Tripinnate   Ternate pinnate

A   B   C   D   E

Pedate pinnate

Opposite

Stipules

J

F

Parallel venation

N

H

Pinnatipartite

Tristichous

Alternate   Leaf whorl

K

Netted/pinnate venation   G

L   M   I

A: *Hamamelis mollis* (Chinese witch hazel) Hamamelidaceae. B: *Anthyllis vulneraria* (kidney vetch), Fabaceae. C: *Daucus carota* (wild carrot), Apiaceae. D: *Myrrhis odorata* (sweet cicely), Apiaceae. E: *Baptisia tinctoria* (yellow wild indigo), Fabaceae. F: *Hellborus*

*niger* (Christmas rose), Ranunculaceae. G: *Bocconia frutescens*, Papaveraceae. H: *Briza media* (quaking grass), Poaceae. I: *Parietaria officinalis*, Urticaceae. J: *Philadelphus coronarius*, Hydrangeaceae. K: *Saururus cornuus*, Saururaceae. L: *above, Clivia gardenii,*

Amaryllidaceae; *below, Bellamcanda chinensis,* Iridaceae. M: *Galium odoratum* (sweet woodruff), Rubiaceae. N: *Cyperus* sp., Cyperaceae.

The shape and arrangement of its leaves are just as characteristic of a plant as its flowers are. Simple undivided leaves (fig. A), with a blade that corresponds to the upper leaf, can be symmetrical or asymmetrical, but also oblong, round, cordiform (heart shaped), or pointed, or combinations of these. The margin can be smooth or have different forms (serrated, notched, etc.). The leaf may develop a more or less long stem; however, most monocotyledons have no stem, and the leaf blade usually merges into a (stem-clasping) leaf sheath. Stipules (fig. B) can develop at the base of the stem. The leaf upper side or leaf underside (or both) may be more or less hairy. This is interpreted as an adaptation to extreme habitats (such as UV protection in high-alpine plants).

The venation—that is, the course of the veins (vascular bundles)—is likewise characteristic: most monocotyledons show a macroscopic so-called parallel venation (fig. H), with ligules at the transition from leaf blade to leaf sheath. This is in contrast to most dicotyledons: their leaves can be recognized by the so-called netted/pinnate venation (fig. I).

If one leaf is attached per node, and the leaf at the next node points in the opposite direction, then this is an alternate leaf arrangement (fig. K). Two leaves that face each other at a node are called "opposite" (fig. J). If two leaves are opposite at a node, and this arrangements turns by 90° from node to node, respectively, we speak of a decussate leaf arrangement; that is, leaf pairs are arranged at right angles to the next pair above. If there are three or more leaves on a node, we speak of a whorl of leaves (fig. M). If the leaves are arranged more or less exactly in two rows opposite each other, we speak of a distichous leaf arrangement (fig. L); if there are three such rows, of a tristichous leaf arrangement (fig. N). The leaf blade can also be divided again: fig. B shows a simple pinnate leaf whose "stalk" between the pinnate leaflets is called a "rachis." If each of these leaflets is once again pinnately compound, you have a bipinnate or twice-pinnate leaf before you (fig. C); if each of these leaflets is again pinnately compound, a tripinnate leaf (fig. D). The leaf in fig. E is ternate and pinnate, the leaf in fig. F is referred to as pedate or foot-shaped pinnate, and the leaf in fig. G is pinnatipartite.

A: *Rebutia* sp., Cactaceae; *above*, habits; *below*, transverse. B: *Ulex europaeus* (common gorse), Fabaceae, stem and leaf spines. C: Lithops bromfieldii, Aizoaceae; *above*, leaf pair frontal; *below*, each with one leaf one detached, longitudinal. D: *Crassula portulacacea* (jade plant), Crassulaceae, succulent leaf; *above*, underside; *center*, leaf transverses; *below*, upper side. E: *Drosera rotundifolia* (round-leaved sundew), Droseraceae; *right*, *Drosera capensis*, leaf. F: *Sarracenia purpurea*, Sarraceniaceae, pitcher plant pitfall trap. G: *Dionaea muscipula* (Venus flytrap), Droseraceae, leaf; *at left*, half open; *below*, one half; *right*, closed. H: *Cephalothus folicularis*, Cephalothaceae; *left*, pitfall trap lateral; *right*, lid and rear inner part; *below*, detail of inner glandular tissue (light spots: glands). I: *Clematis vitalba* (common clematis), Ranunculaceae, simple pinnate leaf. J: *Ledum palustre* (marsh Labrador tea), Ericaceae. K: *Allium schoenoprasum* (chives), Liliaceae, round leaf; *left*, transverse; *right*, habit. L: *Ulmus laevis* (European white elm), Ulmaceae, unfurling foliage leaf. M: *Lathyrus latifolius* (broadleafed sweet pea), Fabaceae, leaf tendrils. N: *Passiflora herbetiana*, Passifloraceae, pinnapartite leaf below extra-floral nectaries.

Metamorphosis occurs not only in the stem, but also in the leaves: thus, for example, cacti transform their leaves into spines (fig. A). These, as well as the leaves of some shrubs that are reduced to spines (fig. B), should likely be interpreted as a defense against herbivores. Succulent leaves of most Aizoaceae and Crassulaceae (figs. C, D) are evolved to store water for dry periods. The pair of leaves fused to the tips in fig. C (*above left*) is sunk into the ground up to the patterned tip, which is to be understood as protection against evaporation, herbivores, and mechanical injury.

Some plants that grow in particularly nutrient-poor habitats have reshaped their leaves into "animal-catching traps" (figs. E–H). The leaves of the sundew species, which are provided with sticky stalked glands (fig. E), use the secretion of the stalked glands to catch insects that land on them. When this happens, the leaf slowly wraps itself around the insect in response to the stimuli from its movement. Then the plant's digestive secretions supply it with useful elements from its prey. The leaf tips of the Venus flytrap species are transformed into snapping or valve traps. On the inner surface of each side, you find three longer hairs that trigger the "closure stimulus" after being touched only twice. Glandular cells are formed around the trigger hairs (reddish coloring), which ensure that the prey is digested after it is caught. The trapping leaves of the Sarraceniaceae and Cephalotaceae have been transformed into "pitchers" (figs. F, H) containing a watery digestive secretion. The likewise transformed leaf tip exerts an optical decoy function with its patterning, while the margin of the "pitcher" is usually so smooth that the visitors slip down inside into the deadly liquid.

Leaf tendrils (figs. I, M) serve to hold on to supports, in the same way the stem tendrils do. Instead of using tendrils, the clematis can wind its rachis (fig. I) around supports.

On plants with relatively small leaves that occur in exposed, windy habitats, the leaf underside may be densely hairy and the leaf margin may be rolled up (fig. J), which limits excessive evaporation from the stomata. Even the robust bud scales (= lower leaf) in fig. L also have a protective function against the effects of the weather. They are reduced leaves, which often are also provided with sticky, sealing substances. Round leaves as in fig. K are primarily known from the subfamily Allioideae. Here, only the underside of the leaf shows outward. Various plant families have "extrafloral" nectaries at the base of the leaf and underneath the blade (fig. N).

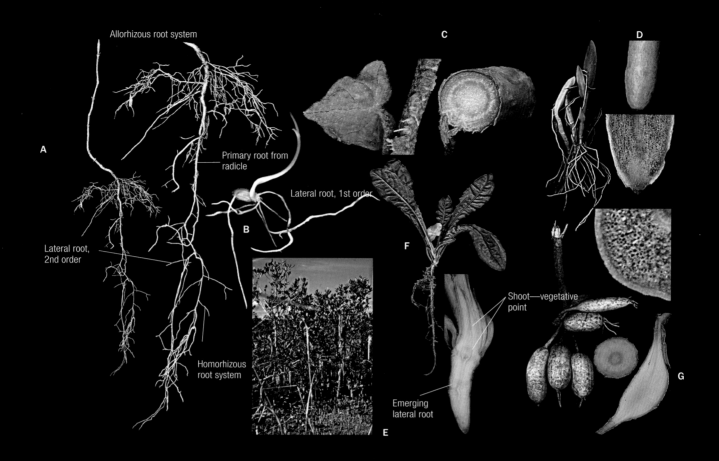

Allorhizous root system

A

Primary root from radicle

Lateral root, 1st order

B

Lateral root, 2nd order

Homorhizous root system

C

D

F

Shoot—vegetative point

Emerging lateral root

E

G

A: Young dicotyledon woody plant. The radicle develops into the primary root, which grows lateral roots of various orders. B: *Triticum aestivum* (wheat), Poaceae. In monocotyledon plants, the radicle is replaced early on by equivalent roots, resulting in so-called homorhizous root system. C: *Hedera helix* (English ivy), Araliaceae, aerial roots. D: *above left, Diaphananthe rudila*, Orchidaceae, habit with aerial roots; *above right, Phalaenopsis* species aerial root tip, Orchidaceae; *center*, aerial root longitudinal; *below*, a quarter of an aerial root, transverse. E: *Avicennia marina* (mangrove), Acanthaceae, "breathing roots," which protrude from the bottom at low tide. F: *Taraxacum officinale* (dandelion), Asteraceae, taproot; *left*, habit; *right*, area between leaves and taproot longitudinal. G: *Dahlia* sp. (dahlia), Asteraceae, tubers; *left*, habit; *center*, root tuber transverse; *right*, longitudinal.

Roots are the first organs that emerge from the seed during germination. They serve not only to anchor the plant in the soil, but, above all, to absorb water and nutrients from the soil. The root cap or calyptra, which is covered by a protective cap, is able to grow down among the often-sharp-edged particles of the soil due to its mucus-producing outer cells, which are constantly being reproduced. The root hair zone, which comes after the division and differentiation zone, is one of the most important areas of the plant for absorbing water and nutrients.

Monocotyledon and dicotyledon plants have different root systems: while in the dicotyledons the radicle as a rule becomes the primary root (fig. A; allorhizous root system), which can branch a variable number of times, in the monocotyledons the radicle is replaced relatively quickly by so-called homogeneous (fig. B; homorhizous roots). These different root systems also represent adaptations to different habitats: while plants with allorhizous root systems usually penetrate deep into the soil, plants with homorhizous root systems take root in a wider perimeter of soil, which is why, for example, grasses are almost exclusively planted on dikes. The grasses take root in the soil evenly and thus also hold it down. Roots can also contribute to a plant's "breathing" in habitats with alternating moisture levels (fig. E). They can also be used for climbing, such as with the aerial roots of ivy (fig. C). Epiphytic orchids, which do not take root in the ground, have to absorb all available nutrients and water from the air with their "aerial roots" (fig. D). For this reason, the roots have an appropriately specialized tissue on their exterior, the so-called velamen radicum. Finally, the roots of many plants form storage organs (fig. G), in which nutrients are stored during each growing season to enable the new growth.

THE MOST-IMPORTANT INFLORESCENCES

A: Young dicotyledon woody plant. The radicle develops into the primary root, which grows lateral roots of various orders. B: *Triticum aestivum* (wheat), Poaceae. In monocotyledon plants, the radicle is replaced early on by equivalent roots, resulting in so-called homorhizous root system. C: *Hedera helix* (English ivy), Araliaceae, aerial roots. D: *above left, Diaphananthe rudila,* Orchidaceae, habit with aerial roots; *above right, Phalaenopsis* species aerial root tip, Orchidaceae; *center,* aerial root longitudinal; *below,* a quarter of an aerial root, transverse. E: *Avicennia marina* (mangrove), Acanthaceae, "breathing roots," which protrude from the bottom at low tide. F: *Taraxacum officinale* (dandelion), Asteraceae, taproot; *left,* habit; *right,* area between leaves and taproot longitudinal. G: *Dahlia* sp. (dahlia), Asteraceae, tubers; *left,* habit; *center,* root tuber transverse; *right,* longitudinal.

The flowers grow either as usually terminal **single flowers** or in characteristic inflorescences. In **racemose inflorescences**, the petiolate flowers are directly attached to the stem (fig. A). In **panicles**, the inflorescence axis has multiple branches (fig. B). In **spicate** inflorescences, the sessile flowers are attached directly to the receptacle (fig. C). A **spadix** is distinguished by the fact that the sessile (without petiole) flowers are also attached directly to the receptacle, but the stem is thickened, unlike in a rachilla (fig. D). A **dichasia** is the typical inflorescence for plants with an opposite leaf arrangement. A petiolate bud node with two opposite bracteoles grows from the axil of a bract; from the bracteole axil likewise, a petiolate flower will grow, which has two bracteoles (fig. E). In a **simple umbel**, the petiolate flowers grow out from one point (fig. F). In **compound umbels**, all the umbellule stalks grow out from a point that has involucral bracts underneath. Each umbel in turn has petiolate flowers, which also grow out from a point with involucral bracts underneath. To increase the visual effect on flower visitors, the peripheral perianth is often enlarged (fig. G). Unlike with the dichasia, with the **scorpioid cymose inflorescence**, the **rhipidium**, the **drepanium**, and the **bostryx**, only one subsequent bud grows out of the axis of the bracteole in a variously oriented arrangement (fig. H). Spikelets are the typical partial inflorescences of grasses, which may be composed of different arrangements (fig. I). **Capitula** are inflorescences on compressed receptacles and are typical of the aster family (thus the German name, *Korbblütler*: "basket blooms"!); the tongue-shaped ray flowers are as a rule female, the central tubular flowers hermaphroditic (fig. J). The capitula of the Asteraceae can also consist exclusively of hermaphroditic tubular flowers (fig. K) or ray flowers (fig. L).

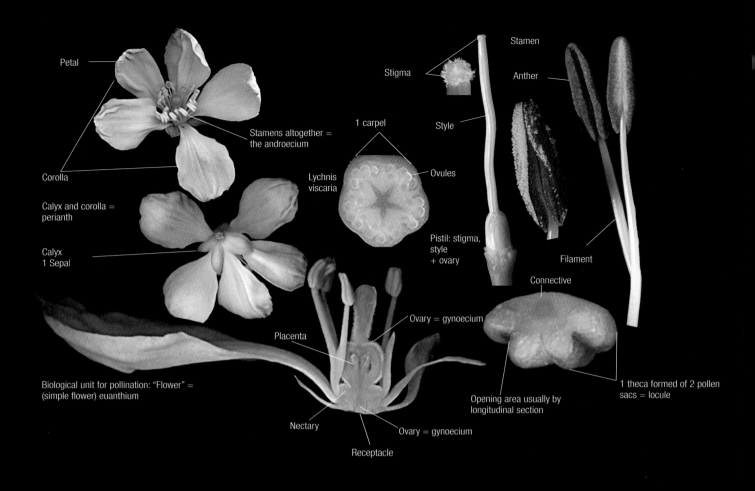

Petal

Stamens altogether = the androecium

Corolla

Calyx and corolla = perianth

Calyx
1 Sepal

Biological unit for pollination: "Flower" = (simple flower) euanthium

1 carpel

Lychnis viscaria

Placenta

Nectary

Receptacle

Stigma

Style

Ovules

Pistil: stigma, style + ovary

Ovary = gynoecium

Ovary = gynoecium

Stamen

Anther

Filament

Connective

Opening area usually by longitudinal section

1 theca formed of 2 pollen sacs = locule

*Left and center*, *Poncirus trifoliata* (hardy orange), Rutaceae, *right*, *Hemerocallis* sp. (daylily), Xanthorrhoeaceae: stigma, ovary lateral, stamen.

*Below center*, transverse view of *Lychnis viscaria* ovary (sticky catchfly), Caryophyllaceae.

The flowers of angiosperm plants can have very different structures. In a hermaphroditic flower, which grows on a principal axis, the receptacle initially originates from the floral envelope. Hermaphroditic flowers make up the majority of flower types; here, *Poncirus trifoliata* and *Hemerocallis* sp. as examples of stamens and ovaries.

Flowers are thus called hermaphrodite if both sexes (male = androecium and female = gynoecium) are represented in one flower. As a rule, the flower organs are arranged in circles (whorls). The involucral bracts may have the same (in most monocotyledons) or a different structure (in most dicotyledons). In various manifestations, the lowest whorl forms the **calyx**, which has individual **sepals** that are usually coarse and green but can also be vividly colored. The coarse form is due to its function as an outer perianth, which has a protective function for all the organs it envelops in the budding stage.

Most commonly, we find a whorl of five in most dicotyledons, and a whorl of three in most monocotyledons, thus:

3 or 5 sepals,
3 or 5 petals,
2 whorls of 3 or 5 stamens, and
in the center a whorl of mostly fused carpels.

A: *Ranunculus repens* (creeping buttercup), Ranunculaceae; *above*, flower frontal; *below*, the underside. B: *Baptisia tinctoria*, Fabaceae, faded blossom. C: *Arbutus unedo* (strawberry tree), Ericaceae; *left*, flower frontal; *right*, the underside. D: *Lychnis coronaria* (rose campion). Caryophyllaceae; *above*, blossom lateral; *below left*, calyx splayed out; *right*, a petal. E: *Camassia* sp., Asparagaceae, flower frontal. F: *Asparagus* sp., Asparagaceae; *above*, flower frontal; *below*, the underside. G: *Vriesea tequendame*, Bromeliaceae; *above left*, flower frontal; *below*, a petal; *right*, next to it, flower lateral; *far right*, sepals. H: *Linum usitatissimum* (common flax), Linaceae, an opening bud. I: *Lamium purpureum* (red dead-nettle), Lamiaceae, bud.

The **corolla** whorl emerges from the calyx, either in the form of individual petals—with a different structure than the calyx—or as **tepals**, if the petals either do not differ or differ only slightly from those of the outer whorl. If a typical calyx and petals are present, we speak of a **perianth** (most dicotyledon plants; figs. A–D), in contrast to a **perigone** (many monocotyledon plants) in which both outer whorls are more or less the same (fig. F). One of the few families of monocotyledon plants that grow a calyx and a corolla is the family that includes the pineapple (Bromeliaceae); among these, both whorls often show distinctive color differences (fig. G), which is obviously due to the fact that they are predominantly pollinated by birds.

The petals may be free (figs. A: actually "honey petals," B, D) or fused (fig. C). The same applies to the sepals. In some families, the petals are free but the calyx is fused (figs. B, D). The usually delicate petals form the so-called **display apparatus**, which serves as a visual-enticement signal for pollinators / flower visitors and thus is adapted to each guest in its shape, symmetry, color (and smell) (coevolution). In many cases, there is an additional contrasting color field or pattern on the base of the petals, a so-called **nectar guide**, which is intended to signal the way to the nectar "bar."

Also characteristic is the way the buds are covered by the floral envelope: in spiral arrangement (fig. H) or overlapping like roof tiles (imbricate; fig. I).

A B C E

a!

G D F

* Radial symmetry, many potential axes of symmetry

↑ Zygomorphic symmetry, only one potential axis of symmetry

⊥ Bilateral symmetry only 2 potential axes of symmetry

a! a! Asymmetric, no axis of symmetry!

A: *Hepatica nobilis* (common liverwort), Ranunculaceae, radial symmetry flower. B: *Pseudofumaria lutea* (yellow corydallis), Papaveraceae, zygomorphic symmetry. C: *Lunaria annua* (solder dollar or annual honesty), Brassicaceae, bilateral symmetry. D: *Raphanus sativus* ssp. *sativus* (radish), Brassicaceae, bilateral symmetry. E: *Canna indica* (Indian shot or edible canna), Cannaceae, asymmetric flower. F: *Calathea lutea*, Marantaceae, asymmetric flower. G: *Leucanthemum vulgare* (oxeye daisy), Asteraceae, peripheral ray flowers, zygomorphic; the tubular flowers of the disc show radial symmetry.

The symmetry of a flower reveals itself in the frontal view of the flower. If you can pass several symmetry axes through the center of the flower and then obtain the same image on both sides, this is called **radial** symmetry (fig. A; fig. G, *above left*). If only one axis of symmetry can be passed through the center of the flower, you have a **zygomorphic** flower before you (fig. B). If two axes can be passed through the center of the flower at a 90° angle, this is **bilateral** symmetry (figs. C, D). In some families of monocotyledons (Cannaceae, Marantaceae), it is not possible to pass an axis of symmetry through the center of the flower; here, you have an **asymmetric** flower before you (figs. E, F).

In some inflorescences that give the impression that they are a "flower" (fig. G, *above right*), such as in the aster family (Asteraceae; fig. G), the peripheral flowers may differ in structure and symmetry from those that are in the center of the inflorescence. The peripheral, mostly female flowers of the Asteroideae subfamily are usually tongue or ray shaped, with only one axis of symmetry; that is, zygomorphic (fig. G, *below*), while the hermaphroditic tubular flowers in the center are radial (fig. G, *above left*).

Like the flower color, symmetry is a feature that appeals to pollinators and was developed within the framework of so-called coevolution.

Nectar guides          Masked flowers                                    Spurs

A  B  G  H  I  C  D  E  F  J  K  L  M  N  O  P  Q  R  S

A: *Digitalis purpurea* (common foxglove), Plantaginaceae, flower frontal, nectar guide below. B: *Lobelia* sp., Campanulaceae. C: *Jovellana viola*, Calceolariaceae; *above*, frontal; *right*, lateral; *below*, lower lip. D: *Primula* sp., Primulaceae, flower with long styles. E: *Tropaeolum majus* (garden nasturtium), Tropaeolacea, flower frontal. F: *Aframomum melegueta* (grains of paradise), Zingiberaceae, flower frontal. G: *Antirrhinum orontium* (field snapdragon), Plantaginaceae, flower frontal. H: *Asarena procumbens*, Plantaginaceae, flower frontal. I: *Linaria vulgaris* (yellow toadflax), Plantaginaceae, flower frontal. J: *Utricularia calycifida* (carnivoros bladderwort),
Lentibulariaceae, flower frontal. K: *Silene cucubalus* (bladder campion), Caryophyllaceae; *left*, flower lateral; *right*, longitudinal: calyx inflated, androgynophore. L: *Symphytum azureum* (comfrey), Boraginaceae, corolla unfurled: scales in corolla throat. M: *Omphalodes scorpioides* (navelwort), Boraginaceae, corolla longitudinal with scales in corolla throat. N: *Narcissus pseudonarcissus* (wild daffodil), Amaryllidaceae; *left*, flower frontal; *right*, longitudinal; paracorolla. O: *Aconitum lycoctonum* (wolf's bane), Ranunculaceae, two spurs under the "helmet." P: *Viola* sp., Violaceae; *left*, stamen with nectar-secreting appendage; *center*, flower frontal; *right*, lateral; *beneath*
*it*, flower longitudinal. Q: *Impatiens njamnjamensis*, Balsaminaceae; *above*, flower frontal; *center*, longitudinal; *below*, lateral: calyx spur. R: *Aquilegia vulgaris* (common columbine), Ranunculaceae; *above*, flower frontal; *center*, lateral; *below*, spur longitudinal; one spur at left. S: *Pseudofumaria lutea* (yellow corydalis), Papaveraceae; *left*, flower lateral; *right*, longitudinal with the stamen appendage protruding into the spur.

As a rule, the male sex organs (**androecium**) emerge from the outer floral envelope in the form of **stamens**. A typical stamen has a **filament** that supports the anther. The anthers are usually composed of two **thecas**, each theca consisting of two **pollen sacs** that contain the **pollen**. Most of the thecas are on different sides (compare with Table: Structure of a Hermaphroditic Flower, p. 16)

The main way that the pollen sacs open up is that long cracks form between the two pollen sacs in a theca, but they can also open up through pores or valves. The filament grows in a sterile area between the thecas in one-half of the anther, the so-called **connective**.

For the pollen from one plant to reach the stigma of another of the same species, as a rule, vectors (wind, water, animals) have to act as transporters. To induce animal pollinators to transport the pollen, there have been a number of developments in the course of evolution that promote this process (such as development of flower scent; attraction by means of color / color contrasts; by the size, shape, and symmetries of the flower; and, primarily, by offering a food supply, usually as liquid nectar or food particles, but also as pollen or fatty oil).

A: *Adenanthera pavonia* (coral tree), Fabaceae; the extended connective supports a food particle intended for visitors. B: *Globba winitii*, Zingiberaceae; the flower's only fertile stamen (the two basal tips are staminodes) is as long as the style, which is also about three times as long as the flower; the lateral outgrowths evidently grow from the connective area. C: *Stenocarpus sinuatus* (firewheel tree), Proteaceae; the four flower stamens have widened filaments and have the appearance of petals. D: Melastomataceae; the stamens of this family are extremely diverse and often have outgrowths of connective that increase the visual impact and at times can serve as food particles. E: *Akebia × pentaphylla*, Lardizabalaceae; the stamens of the male flowers open outwards (extrorse). F: *Theobroma grandiflorum*,

Malvaceae; the stamens often appear clustered. G: *Remusatia vivipara*, Araceae; stamens joined with the synandrium. H: *Bacopa* sp., Plantaginaceae; sometimes the stamens do not let us recognized individual sacs. I: *Fremontodendron californicum*, Malvaceae; the stamens, which are fused basally to the filaments, form in the bud before they extend and splay out; androecia twine in a globose structure. J: *Convolvulus tricolor*, Convolvulaceae; before the stamen opens and releases the white pollen, the thecas show a blue coloration that is even patterned with white dots. K: The Commelinaceae very often display a widened connective and thecas, which face up or down, as well as hairy filaments. L: *Androlepis skinneri*, Bromeliaceae; the connectives form outgrowths here on the rear side of the stamens, which

might serve to attract visitors or act as a food particles. M: *Aristolochia litoralis*, Aristolochiaceae; the stamens are fused with the style into a so-called gynostemium. N: *Bulbine frutescens*, Asphodeloideae, subfamily of the Xanthorrhoeaceae; the long hairy stamens form a striking contrast to the petals. O: *Anthurium digitatum*, Araceae; unlike in fig. G, here the stamens are almost normal and grow in quadruplicate hermaphroditic flowers. P: *Dianella tasmanica*, Asphodelaceae; the stamens open through pores and have orange-yellow bodies just below the thecas that increase the visual impact.

The coloration of the filaments, thecas, or appendages usually contrasts with the petals and is also developed as an optical signal for the respective pollinators.

A: *Ruta graveolens* (common rue), Rutaceae. B: *Prunus spinosa* (sloe), Rosaceae.
C: *Chaenomeles japonica* (Japanese quince). D: *Psiguria triphylla*, Cucurbitaceae.

The female sex organ, the **gynoecium**, is in the center of the flower. It consists of a **pistil** (**fused carpels**); its tip supports the receptive fertile area, the **stigma**, usually on a style. The seed-bearing petal surface, which is covered by the fusion and thus protected, supports the **ovules**, which are attached to the **placenta** (**ovary**) on small stalks, the **funiculi**.

The ovary may be in a **superior** (fig. A), **medial** (fig. B), or **inferior** (fig. C; fig. D, *left*) arrangement, which is also related to the structure and position of the nectary. Superior ovaries are, so to speak, arranged uppermost in the flower whorls. Medial ovaries are often surrounded by a **hypanthium** (fused area of calyx/corolla/filaments), the inside of which usually acts as a nectary.

The number of carpels either can be indicated by the number of style arms or reveals itself through a transverse view of the ovary. The stigma is the part of the female sex organ that uses hair, papillae, or sticky surfaces to collect external pollen of the same species. The pollen grains begin to germinate on the stigma in a pollen tube, which usually grows between the papillae or hairs, through the style to the ovules. Here the genetic material in the pollen grains combines with that of the ovules, redivides, and causes the respective ovule to develop into a mature seed capable of germination.

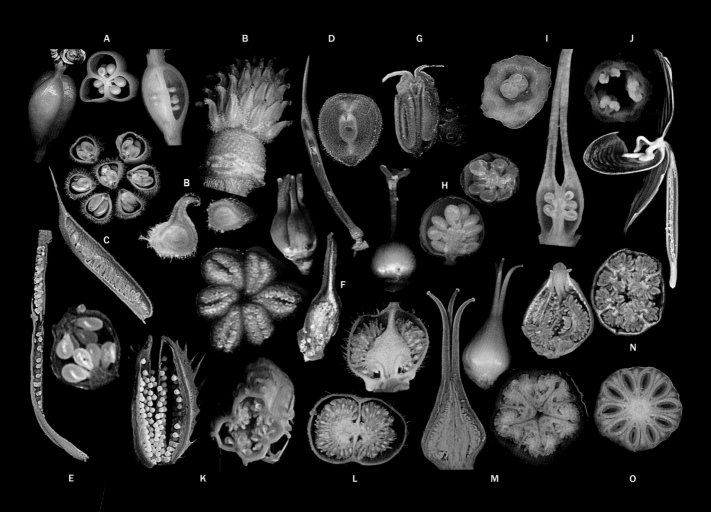

A B D G I J

B

H

C

F

N

E K L M O

OVARY PLACENTATION

A: *Belamcanda chinensis*, Iridaceae; *left*, ovary lateral; *center*, transverse; *right*, longitudinal. B: *Eranthis hyemale* (winter aconite), Ranunculaceae; *above*, ovary of a flower; *below*, a solitary carpel transverse; *left*, the same, longitudinal. C: *Aquilegia vulgaris* (common columbine), Ranunculaceae; *above*, ovary of a flower, transverse; *below*, longitudinal. D: *Phaseolus vulgaris* (common bean), Fabaceae; *left*, ovary, longitudinal; *right*, transverse. E: *Chelidonium majus* (greater celandine), Papaveraceae; *left*, ovary, longitudinal; *right*, transverse.

F: *Butomus umbellatus* (flowering rush), Butomaceae; *above*, ovary of a flower; *left*, the same, transverse; *right*, a solitary specimen, longitudinal. G: *Aegopodium podagraria* (goutweed), Apiaceae; *left*, ovary, longitudinal; *right*, transverse. H: *Talinum* sp., Talinaceae; *left*, ovary, lateral; *center*, longitudinal; *above right*, transverse. I: *Staphylea pinnata* (European bladdernut), Staphyleaceae; *above left*, ovary, transverse with surrounding nectary; *right*, next to it, longitudinal. J: *Paphiopedilum philippinesse*, Orchidaceae; *above left*, ovary, transverse;

*right*, next to it, flower longitudinal. K: *Argemone mexicana*, Papaveraceae; *left*, ovary, longitudinal; *right*, transverse. L: *Asarena erubescens*, Plantaginaceae; *above*, ovary, longitudinal; *below*, transverse. M: *Hypericum patulum*, Hypericaceae; *left*, ovary, longitudinal; *center*, lateral; *right*, transverse. N: *Parnassia palustris* (marsh grass of Parnassus), Parnassiaceae; *left*, ovary, longitudinal; *right*, transverse. O: *Linum usitatissimum* (common flax), Linaceae, ovary transverse.

The number of carpels in the gynoecium can vary between just one and many. The carpels may either be fused just with themselves—that is, **apocarpous** (at the suture [seam]; figs. B, C, D)—or fused together or united; thus, **syncarpous** (or coenocarpous). If they are fused together, there are essentially two possibilities:

- The splayed carpels may be fused in a whorl just at the margins (figs. E; K; J, *above*: **parietal placentation**) or
- All carpels are more or less bent inward in a whorl along the margins and fused together at the contact surfaces and margins in the center (fig. L: **axile placentation**).

The contact surfaces of the carpels form septums. The growth of these partitions may also be inhibited, resulting in unchambered, so-called **paracarpous** ovaries (fig. N).

The seed-bearing placentas are found mainly on the margins of the carpels (**parietal placentation**). In a few cases, the placenta covers the entire surface of the underside of the carpel (fig. F); this then is so-called **laminar placentation** (lamina = leaf surface). If the carpels are fused internally, this can also cause the contact surfaces of the septums to disappear, so that a column remains in the center with placentas and ovules in a ring around it (fig. H). However, there may be only one hanging ovule per carpel (fig. G).

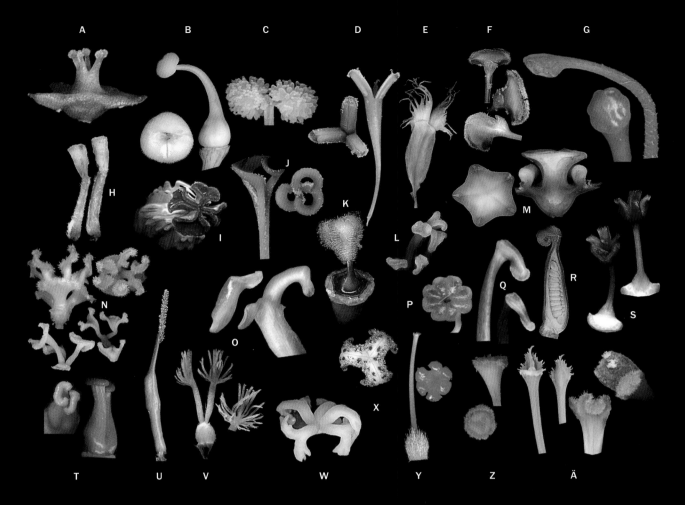

A: *Adoxa moschatellina* (moschatel), Adoxaceae; the five stigmas form a kind of little corolla. B: *Aeginetia indica*, Orobanchaceae; the capitate stigma reveals bifurcation only in the lateral view. C: *Argyraea nervosa* (Hawaiian baby woodrose), Convolvulaceae, two-headed stigma. D: *Belamcanda chinensis*, Iridaceae; unlike most Iridaceae with petaloid style arms, this stigma with three style arms is structured in a relatively normal way. E: *Iris japonica* (fringed iris), Iridaceae; here the style arms are developed differently than the petaloid form in fig. D; the actual stigma is the scaly indentation below the fringed tips. F: *Costus scaber*, Zingiberaceae; the funnel-shaped stigma is ciliate on the margin. G: *Grevillea* sp., Proteaceae; the stigma is oriented in one direction.

H: *Annona muricata*, Annonaceae; the style arms of the very numerous carpels are developed like a leaf scale. I: *Argemone mexicana*, Papaveraceae; unlike the mostly commissural stigmas of indigenous poppy plants, here the arched, bilobate stigmas are folded into a bowl shape. J: *Billbergia amoena*, Bromeliaceae; unlike most Bromeliaceae, which often show style arms twisted in helical form, here the stigmas are twisted slightly and are almost horizontal. K: *Codonopsis vinciflora*, Campanulaceae; the five style arms are not splayed before the female phase. L: *Chaenomeles japonica* (Japanese quince), Rosaceae; the five almost spoonlike style arms stand on free styles of the inferior ovary. M: *Napoleonaea vogelii*, Lecythidaceae; *right*, ovary, lateral;

*left*, style/stigma surface: the receptive fertile style arms are located in the red-colored areas in this five-pointed disciform stigma. N: Various Begoniaceae stigma tips. O: *Calathea peruviana*, Marantaceae. P: *Sin ningia bulbosa*, Gesneriaceae. Q: *Polygala myrtifolia*, Polygalaceae. R: *Paeonia cambessedesii*, Paeoniaceae. S: *Orchidantha maxillarioides*, Lowiaceae. T: *Bergenia cordifolia*, Saxifragaceae. U: *Bougainvillea × buttiana*, Nyctaginaceae. V: *Turnera scabra*, Turneraceae. W: *Carica papaya*—papaya, Caricacea. X: *Tricyrtis hirta*, Liliaceae. Y: *Ryania angustifolia*, Flacourtiaceae. Z: *Roridula gorgonias*, Roridulaceae. Ä: *left, Pterodiscus* sp.; *right, Proboscidea parviflora*, Pedaliaceae.

The **stigma**, the receptive fertile area for external pollen of the same species, usually has sticky papillae that can hold the pollen in various ways. Thus, the pollen grains, with the germinating pollen tube between the stigma papillae, can grow through the sterile area (the **style**) to the ovules. Here, they unite their genetic material with that of the ovules, to combine and redivide (fertilization/recombination). The sterile style may grow longer or shorter. In most cases, the number of style arms also indicates the number of fused-together carpels. The style arms can also be fused into a structure.

Septal nectaries      Perigone

A   B   C   D   E   F   G

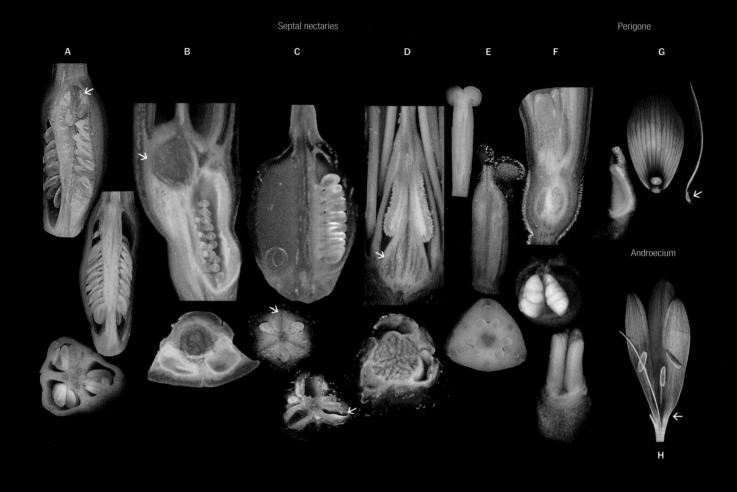

Androecium

H

A: *Gladiolus* sp., Iridaceae. B: *Tapeinochilus* sp., Zingiberaceae. C: *Ornithogalum* sp., Hyacinthaceae. D: *Puya* sp., Bromeliaceae. E: *Tulipa gesneriana* (garden tulip), Liliaceae. A–E: *above*, longitudinal each time, and transverse (*below*). F: *Alpinia shimadai*, Zingiberaceae; *above*, longitudinal; *center*, frontal; *below*, lateral G: *Fritillaria imperialis* (crown imperial), Liliaceae. H: *Colchicum laetum* (autumn crocus), Colchicaceae.

The "visitors' bar," the **nectary**, is located between the androecium and the gynoecium but sometimes is also part of the gynoecium. There, glands produce nectar in portions not intended to satiate the visitor to the flower, but rather just to create a taste for more, so that the visitor goes to as many flowers with the same nectar on offer as possible, thus ensuring the pollen is transferred.

### Nectaries of monocotyledon plants

Most monocotyledons have so-called septal nectaries. In these, the three carpels in the center of the ovary are fused to the margins/septa, where they grow nectar-producing glandular tissue on the inner surfaces (fig. C). Sometimes it is also positioned below the ovary (figs. C, D) or above it (figs. A, B). In a series of transverse views of the ovary, these margins appear above the actual nectary as mostly yellow-colored fused areas (fig. C). In such cases, the nectar is secreted into the flower area through small, slit-shaped openings. In some ginger plants (Zingiberaceae), there are usually one to two stalk-shaped nectaries attached to the inferior ovary, inside at the base of the flower (fig. F). Some Liliaceae grow nectaries in slightly bulging basal interior areas of the tepals (fig. G). The autumn crocus can produce nectar in slightly yellow-colored zones at the base of the stamen; this will be captured in the hairy and contrast-colored basal perigone area (fig. H).

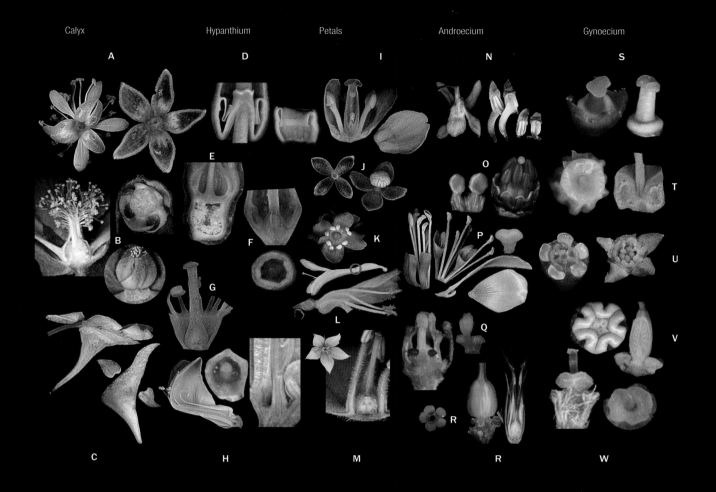

A    D    I    N    S
E    J    O    T
B    F    K    P    U
G    Q
L    V
C    H    M    R    W

A: *Tilia plathyphyllos*, Malvaceae. B: *Malva sylvestris*, Malvaceae. C: *Impatiens parviflora* (small balsam), Balsaminaceae. D: *Passiflora mixta*, Passifloraceae. E: Cactaceae. F: *Colletia hysterix*, Rhamnaceae. G: *Prunus laurocerasus* (cherry laurel), Rosaceae. H: *Robinia viscosa* (clammy locust), Fabaceae. I: *Berberis julianae*, Berberidaceae. J: *Nepenthes dormesianum*, Nepenthaceae. K: *Adoxa moschatellina* (moschatel) L: *above, Lonicera caprifolium* (Italian honeysuckle); *below*, *Lonicera xylosteum* (European fly honeysuckle), Caprifoliaceae. M: *Lysimachia punctata* (yellow loosestrife), Primulaceae. N: *Viola odorata* (sweet violet), Violaceae. O: *Greyia radkoferi*, Melianthaceae. P: Various Ranunculaceae. Q: Various Lauraceae. R: *Linum grandiflorum*, Linaceae. S: *Viburnum bodnantense*, Caprifoliaceae. T: *Cavendishia callista*, Ericaceae. U: *right, Spiraea media* (spirea), Rosaceae; *left, Sedum craigii*, Crassulaceae. V: *Cobaea scandens* (cup and saucer vine), Polemoniaceae. W: *Cornus mas* (cornelian cherry), Cornaceae.

The dicotyledons show the widest variety of nectary formation. Nectar can be produced and offered in more or less visually eye-catching glands, which are found both on the upper side of the sepal and inside, in the area of the hypanthium (fused zone of the calyx, corolla, and filaments), on petals (honey leaves), in the stamen area, or in basal growths on the gynoecium. The visitor always has to use its beak or proboscis to dive into the bottom of the flower to get its "rewarding gulp" for the visit (this way, in any case the insect will brush against the stamen with its pollen, and the stigma; it will shed the pollen it brought along and take new pollen back along with it). The red circle in fig. L shows "nectar robbing": a hole pierced in the corolla by a bumblebee to get to the nectar—the bumblebee's proboscis is too short for the long corolla tube.

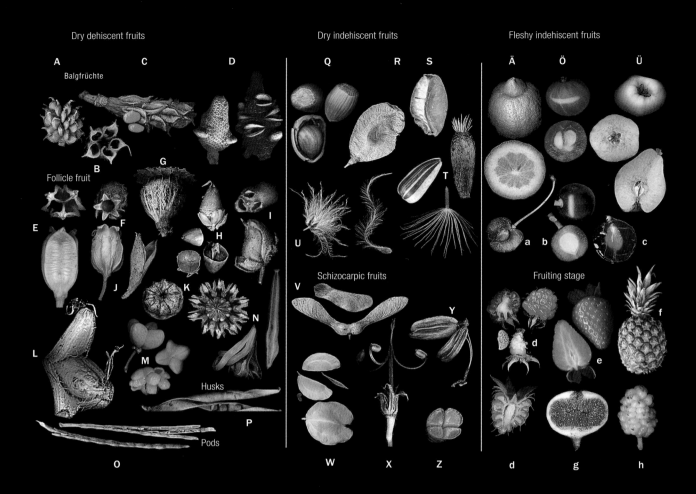

Dry dehiscent fruits  Dry indehiscent fruits  Fleshy indehiscent fruits

FRUITS

**Dry dehiscent fruits**
Balgfrüchte — A, C, D
Follicle fruit — B, E, F, G, H, I, J, K, L, M, N
Husks — P
Pods — O

**Dry indehiscent fruits**
Q, R, S, T, U
Schizocarpic fruits — V, W, X, Y, Z

**Fleshy indehiscent fruits**
Ä, Ö, Ü, a, b, c
Fruiting stage — d, e, f, g, h

A: *Ranunculus repens* (creeping buttercup), Ranunculaceae, follicles lateral. B: *Aquilegia vulgaris* (common columbine), Ranunculaceae, follicles opened at the suture. C: *Magnolia* × *soulangeana* (saucer magnolia), Magnoliaceae, opened follicles with seeds hanging out. D: *Banksia* sp., Proteaceae; follicle opened after a fire (*right*). E: *Tulipa gesneriana* (Didier's tulip), Liliaceae; loculicidal capsule, which opens at the back part of the carpels; *above*, frontal; *below*, lateral. F: *Lychnis flos-cuculi* (ragged robin), Caryophyllaceae; capsule openings with teeth; *above*, frontal; *below*, lateral. G: *Papaver orientale* (Oriental poppy), Papaveraceae; pore capsule lateral; the pores are formed below the commissural stigma. H: *Plantago major* (broadleaf plantain), Plantaginaceae, pyxidium. I: *Antirrhinum majus* (snapdragon), Plantaginaceae; pore capsule; *above*, frontal; *below*, lateral. J: *Buddleja davidii* (butterfly bush), Scrophulariaceae; septicidal capsule that opens at the fused sutures. K: *Cephalophyllum*

*fulleri*, Aizoaceae; hygrochastic capsule; *left*, closed frontal; *right*, opened due to effect of water. L: *Musa basjo* (hardy banana) Musaceae, fleshy capsule. M: *Euonymus europaeus* (European spindletree); *left*, lateral; *center*, frontal; *below*, opened. N: *Impatiens parviflora* (small balsam), Balsaminaceae; fleshy capsule opens when touched. O: *Alliaria petiolata* (garlic mustard), Brassicaceae, pod. P: *Lathyrus latifolius* (everlasting pea), one-leaved husk that opens at the back and suture. Q: *Corylus avellana* (common hazel), Corylaceae, nut. R: *Ulmus laevis* (European white elm), Ulmaceae, samara. S: *Triticum aestivum* (common wheat), Poaceae, caryopsis. T: *left*, *Helianthus annuus* (sunflower); *right*, *Arctium lappa* (greater burdock); *center*, *Solidago canadensis* (Canada goldenrod), Asteraceae, achenium. U: *Clematis vitalba* (common clematis), winged nutlet for wind dispersal. V: *Acer platanoides* (Spitz maple), bilocular winged schizocarp fruit. W: *Thlaspi arvense* (field pennycress), Brassicaceae, small pod: *Geranium molle*

(dovesfoot cranesbill), Geraniaceae, single mericarps that detach from the central column. Y: *Aegopodium podagraria* (goutweed), Apiaceae, cremocarp. Z: *Lamium album* (white dead-nettle), Lamiaceae, four nutlets (= mericarps from 2 carpels). Ä: *Citrus limon* (lemon), Rutaceae, berry. Ö: *Ribes rubrum* (currant), Grossulariaceae, berries. Ü: *Cydonia oblonga* (quince), Rosaceae, pome. a: *Prunus avium* (cherry), Rosaceae, drupe or stone fruit. b: *Prunus laurocerasus* (cherry laurel), Rosaceae, drupe. c: *Vitis vinifera* (common grape vine), Vitaceae, berry. d: *Rubus idaeus* (red raspberry), Rosaceae, drupelet or bramble fruit. e: *Fragaria vesca* (garden strawberry), Rosaceae, nut fruit or accessory fruit. f: *Pineapple comosus* (pineapple), Bromeliaceae, sorosis. g: *Ficus domestica* (fig), Moraceae, drupelet. h: *Morus alba* (white mulberry), Moraceae, multiple fruits.

There are fruits that are eaten by animals and thus have their seeds pass through the animal's gut; we call this dispersal system "endozoochory." Fruits can also be structured so that they cling to an animal's exterior (epizoochory seed dispersal); this is what happens, for example, with the devil's claw or grapple plant of different *Harpagophytum* species (Pedaliaceae) or burr fruits (such as *Agrimonia eupatoria*).

A: *Ricinus communis* (castor bean plant), Euphorbiaceae, seeds with caruncles (= elaiosomes); *left*, lateral; *right*, next to it, longitudinal. B: *Arachis hypogaea* (peanut), Fabaceae; *left*, seed lateral; *right*, a split cotyledon (germ layer) with recognizable radicle and true leaves. C: *above*, *Alcaea rosea* (hollyhock), Malvaceae, seeds with structured testa lateral; *below*, *Alyssum saxatile* (basket of gold), Brassicaceae, smooth testa. D: *Rubus idaeus* (red raspberry), Rosaceae, seeds with woody endocarp. E: *Nuphar lutea* (yellow water lily), Nymphaeaceae, seed with yellowish floating "swimming belt"; *left*, longitudinal. F: *Nymphaea alba* (white water lily), Nymphaeaceae, seeds with large-celled air-filled floating swimming belt; *left*, longitudinal. G: *Oryza sativa* (rice), Poaceae, caryopsis; *left*, longitudinal; *right*, lateral.

H: *Zea mays* (maize or corn), Poaceae, caryopsis; *left*, lateral; *right*, longitudinal. I: *Sorghum bicolor* (sorghum), Poaceae; *above*, longitudinal; *below*, lateral. J: *Poncirus trifoliata* (hardy orange), Rutaceae; *above*, seed lateral; *below*, longitudinal. K: *Magnolia × soulangiana* (saucer magnolia), Magnoliaceae; *left*, the seed is enveloped by an aril (arrilus); *center*, seeds with aril longitudinal; *right*, seeds without aril. L: *Paulownia tomentosa* (empress tree), Paulowniaceae, seeds with winged membranes. M: *Alsomitra macrocarpa*, Cucurbitaceae, winged seeds. N: *Epilobium parviflorum* (small balsam), Onagraceae, seeds with winged hairs. O: *Pseudofumaria lutea* (yellow corydalis), Papaveraceae, seed with elaiosomes (here: food particles for ants). P: *Bistorta officinalis* (meadow bistort), Polygonaceae; *left*, longitudinal; *right*, lateral.

Q: *Passiflora herbetiana* (native passionfruit), Passifloraceae; *below*, seeds with aril; *above*, without aril. R: *Hedychium horsfieldii*, Zingiberaceae; *left*, seed with aril; *right*, aril removed. S: *Theobroma cacao* (cacao tree), Sterculiaceae; *above*, seeds with aril; *below*, aril removed. T: *Freesia laxa*, Iridaceae, seed with elaiosome; *left*, longitudinal; *right and above*, lateral. U: *Euonymus europaeus* (European spindletree), Celastraceae, seed with aril; *left*, longitudinal; *right*, lateral. V: *Punica granatum* (pomegranate), Lythraceae; *left*, seed with fleshy aril; *center*, aril removed; *right*, seed, longitudinal. W: *Strelitzia reginae* (strelitzia or bird of paradise), Strelitziaceae, seed with fringed elaiosome. X: *Litchi chinensis* (lychee), Sapindaceae.

Seeds, like fruits, may have additional "dispersal devices," such as more or less fleshy, visually eye-catching arils (various families; figs. K, Q, R, S, U, V, X). Small and more or less fleshy elaiosomes (Violaceae, Papaveraceae; fig. O) induce small animals (such as ants) to collect seeds with such elaiosomes, which are of as much the same size as possible, and to take the seeds to their nests. The floating tissue on the seeds of various aquatic plants is developed to disperse the seeds by water (figs. E, F), while the winged hairs or membranes serve to disperse the seeds by wind (figs. L, M, N).

A    B    C    D    E    F

Homorhizous root system:
Radicle is replaced early on by
homogenous roots.

Allorhizous root system: Radicle
becomes the primary root.

A: *Triticum aestivum* (wheat), Poaceae, seedling with primary leaf and already a homorhizous root system. B: *Lepidium sativum* (garden cress), Brassicaceae; *above*, swollen seed with emerging radicle; *below*, seed coat and cotyledon; *right*, seedling with cotyledons; radicle, which becomes the primary root, with root hair zone. C: *Fagus sylvatica* (European beech); *left*, a single nut fruit; *center*, seedling lateral; *to the right*, germinating nut fruit with radicle; *above far right*, cotyledons frontal, not yet unfurled; *below the same*, unfurled with true leaf bud. D: *Quercus robur* (English oak), Fagaceae; *left*, nut fruit longitudinal with seed; *right*, seedling with primary leaves and remains of the cotyledons in the root area; *left*, next to it, detail. E: *Acer platanoides* (Norway maple), Aceraceae; *above*, winged schizocarp fruit; *below*, a locule longitudinal; *center*, seedling lateral with cotyledons and true leaves; *below*, cotyledons and true leaves frontal. F: *Trichodiadema* sp., Aizoaceae; *above*, SEM image of a germinating seed; *center*, seedling lateral with fused succulent cotyledons and true leaf pair; *right*, seedling frontal.

It is water that initially plays the main role in germination. The presence of water causes the seed coat (testa) and the seed ready for germination to "swell" until the seed coat opens at a predetermined place; the radicle emerges (fig. F) and can penetrate into the soil to ensure the necessary water and nutrient supplies to the seedling as soon as possible. Then the cotyledons stretch out and finally become green due to the effect of light (fig. B). The shape of the cotyledons is usually simpler than that of the subsequent true leaves, but they can already appear relatively specialized in shape and structure (as on the beech seedling in fig. C). Often, the cotyledons also serve as a nutrient reservoir (then they do not turn green), which the growing plant can use to feed itself (figs. A, D). The fused and slightly succulent cotyledons of some succulent plants may be a particularly early adaptation to their dry habitats.

## Nomenclature and systematic classification of angiosperm plants
*(Code of Botanical Nomenclature, Utrecht 1952)*


**Division**, phylum, divisio: -phyta (such as chlorophytes: green plants)
  Subdivision, subphylum, subdivisio: -phytina
    **Class**, classis: -opsida, but also: Monocotyledonae
      Subclass, subclassis: -idae
        Cohort, cohors: -iidae
        **Order**, ordo: -ale suborder, subordo: -inales
          **Family**, familia: -aceae, such as Asparagales (asparagus family) subfamily, subfamilia: -oideae, such as Allioideae
          Tribe, tribus: -eae subtribe, subtribus: -inae
            **Genus**: such as Allium (onion, leek)
              Subgenus section, subsection
                Subsection, subsectio
                Series
                  **Species**, such as *Allium cepa* L. (common onion)
                    Genus name + epithet = species name, often incorporating an abbreviation of the name of the author who first described this species
                    Subspecies
                      Variety, varietas
                      Subvariety, subvarietas
                        Form, forma line, linea
                        Clone

The above-listed structure of the hierarchical classification of the plant kingdom gives an overview of how the attribution is done. The essential groupings (following APG III, according to genetic comparison) are printed in bold.
In this book, the angiosperm division or phylum will be the first to be presented in a listing of the existing orders and subsequently in a listing of the families belonging to the orders. After this, about half the existing families will be presented in alphabetical order.

# ORDERS OF THE ANGIOSPERMS

## Early angiosperms

Amborellales

Nymphaeales

Austrobaileyales

Chloranthales

Canellales

Piperales

Laurales

Magnoliales

Acorales

## Monocotyledons

Alismatales

Petrosaviales

Dioscoreales

Pandanales

Liliales

### Commelinids

Asparagales

Arecales

Poales

Zingiberales

Ceratophyllales

## Eudikotyledons

Ranunculales

Sabiales

Proteales

Trochodendrales

Buxales

Gunnerales

**Core Eudicotyledons**

Dilleniales
Saxifragales
Vitales
Zygophyllales

**Rosids**

**Eurosids I**

Celastrales
Malpigiales
Oxalidales
Fabales
Rosales
Cucurbitales
Fagales
Geraniales
Myrtales
Crossosomatales
Picraniales

**Eurosids II**

Sapindales
Huerteales
Malvales
Brassicales
Berberidopsidales
Santalales
Caryophyllales
Cornales

**Asterids**

Ericales
Garryales
Gentianales
Lamiales
Solanales
Boraginales
Aquifoliales
Asterales
Escalloniales
Bruniales
Apiales
Paracryphiales
Dipsacales

| Order | Families |
|---|---|
| Amborellales | Amborellaceae* |
| Nymphaeales | Cabombaceae*, Hydatellaceae, Nymphaeaceae* |
| Austrobaileyales | Austrobaileyaceae, Schisandraceae* incl. Illiciaceae, Trimeniaceae |
| Chloranthales | Chloranthaceae |
| Canellales | Canellaceae, Winteraceae* |
| Piperales | Aristolochiaceae*, Hydnoraceae, Piperaceae*, Saururaceae* |
| Laurales | Calycanthaceae*, Gomortegaceae, Hernandiaceae, Lauraceae*, Monimiaceae, Siparunaceae |
| Magnoliales | Annonaceae*, Degeneriaceae, Eupomatiaceae, Himantandraceae, Magnoliaceae*, Myristicaceae |
| Acorales | Acoraceae |
| Alismatales | Alismataceae* incl. Limnocharitaceae, Aponogetonaceae, Araceae*, Butomaceae*, Hydrocharitaceae*, Juncaginaceae, Posidoniaceae, Potamogetonaceae, Ruppiaceae, Scheuchzeriaceae, Zosteraceae |
| Petrosaviales | Petrosaviaceae |
| Dioscoreales | Burmanniaceae, Dioscoreaceae*, Nartheciaceae, Taccaceae* |
| Pandanales | Cyclanthaceae*, Pandanaceae*, Velloziaceae* |
| Liliales | Alstroemeriaceae*, Colchicaceae*, Corsiaceae, Liliaceae*, Luzuriagaceae, Melanthiaceae*, Petermanniaceae, Philesiaceae*, Smilacaceae* |
| Asparagales | Amaryllidaceae* incl. Agapanthaceae now Agapanthoideae and Alliaceae now Alloideae, Asparagaceae* incl. Agavaceae now Agavoideae and Hyacinthaceae now Hyacinthoideae and Ruscaceae now Ruscoideae, Hypoxidaceae, Iridaceae*, Lanariaceae, Orchidaceae*, Xanthorrhoeaceae* incl. Asphodelaceae now Asphodeloideae and Hemerocallidaceae now Hemerocallidoideae |
| Arecales | Arecaceae* |
| Poales | Bromeliaceae*, Cyperaceae*, Eriocaulaceae, Juncaceae*, Poaceae*, Rapateaceae, Restionaceae*, Typhaceae incl. Sparganiaceae now Sparganioideae, Xyridaceae |
| Commelinales | Commelinaceae*, Haemodoraceae*, Pontederiaceae* |
| Zingiberales | Cannaceae*, Costaceae*, Heliconiaceae*, Lowiaceae*, Marantaceae*, Musaceae*, Strelitziaceae*, Zingiberaceae* |
| Ceratophyllales | Ceratophyllaceae |
| Ranunculales | Berberidaceae*, Circaeasteraceae*, Eupteleaceae, Lardizabalaceae*, Menispermaceae*, Papaveraceae*, Ranunculaceae* |
| Sabiales | Sabiaceae |
| Proteales | Nelumbonaceae, Platanaceae, Proteaceae* |
| Trochodendrales | Trochodendraceae* |
| Buxales | Buxaceae* incl. Didymelaceae, Hapthantaceae |
| Gunnerales | Gunneraceae*, Myrothamnaceae |
| Dilleniales | Dilleniaceae* |
| Saxifragales | Altingiaceae*, Cercidiphyllaceae, Crassulaceae*, Daphniphyllaceae, Grossulariaceae*, Haloragaceae, Hamamelidaceae*, Paeoniaceae*, Saxifragaceae* |
| Vitales | Vitaceae* |
| Zygophyllales | Krameriaceae, Zygophyllaceae* |
| Celastrales | Celastraceae* incl. Hippocrateaceae now Hippocrateoideae and Brexiaceae, Lepidobotryaceae, Parnassiaceae* |
| Malpigiales | Achariaceae, Chrysobalanaceae, Clusiaceae*, Erythroxylaceae*, Euphorbiaceae*, Hypericaceae*, Linaceae*, Malpighiaceae*, Ochnaceae, Passifloraceae*, Phyllanthaceae*, Picodendraceae, Podostemaceae, Rhizophoraceae, Salicaceae*, Violaceae* |
| Oxalidales | Brunelliaceae, Cephalotaceae, Connaraceae, Cunoniaceae, Elaeocarpaceae*, Huaceae, Oxalidaceae* |
| Fabales | Fabaceae*, Polygalaceae*, Quillajaceae, Surianaceae |

| Order | Families |
|---|---|
| Rosales | Barbeyaceae, Cannabaceae*, Dirachmaceae, Elaeagnaceae, Moraceae*, Rhamnaceae*, Rosaceae*, Ulmaceae*, Urticaceae* incl. Cecropiaceae |
| Cucurbitales | Anisophyllaceae, Begoniaceae*, Coriariaceae*, Corynocarpaceae*, Cucurbitaceae*, Datiscaceae |
| Fagales | Betulaceae*, Casuarinaceae, Fagaceae*, Juglandaceae* incl. Rhoipteleaceae, Myricaceae*, Nothofagaceae, Rhoipteleaceae, Ticodendraceae |
| Geraniales | Francoaceae, Geraniaceae*, Ledocarpaceae, Melianthaceae* |
| Myrtales | Combretaceae*, Lythraceae* incl. Punicaceae now Punicoideae and Sonneratiaceae now Sonneratioideae and Trapaceae now Trapoideae, Melastomataceae* incl. Memecylaceae, Myrtaceae*, Onagraceae*, Penaeaceae incl. Oliniaceae, Vochysiaceae |
| Crossosomatales | Crossomataceae, Geissolomataceae, Stachyuraceae, Staphyleaceae*, Strasburgeriaceae |
| Picraniales | Picramniaceae |
| Sapindales | Aceraceae*, Anacardiaceae*, Burseraceae, Meliaceae*, Nitrariaceae, Rutaceae*, Sapindaceae*, Simaroubaceae |
| Huerteales | Dipentodontaceae, Gerrardinaceae, Tapisciaceae |
| Malvales | Bixaceae*, Cistaceae*, Cytinaceae*, Dipterocarpaceae, Malvaceae* incl. Bombacaceae now Bombacoideae and Sterculiaceae now Sterculioideae and Tiliaceae now Tilioideae, Muntingiaceae, Neuradaceae, Sarcolaenaceae, Thymelaeaceae* |
| Brassicales | Bataceae, Brassicaceae*, Capparaceae*, Caricaceae*, Cleomaceae*, Koeberliniaceae, Limnanthaceae, Moringaceae, Resedaceae*, Salvadoraceae, Tovariaceae, Tropaeolaceae* |
| Berberidopsidales | Aextoxicaceae, Berberidopsidaceae |
| Santalales | Balanaphoraceae, Loranthaceae, Misodendraceae, Olacaceae, Opiliaceae, Santalaceae* incl. Viscaceae |
| Caryophyllales | Aizoaceae*, Amaranthaceae* incl. Chenopodiaceae now Chenopodioideae, Anacampserotaceae*, Basellaceae*, Cactaceae*, Caryophyllaceae*, Didieracee, Droseraceae*, Drosophyllaceae*, Frankeniaceae, Molluginaceae, Montiaceae*, Nepenthaceae*, Nyctaginaceae*, Phytolaccaceae*, Plumbaginaceae*, Polygonaceae*, Portulacaceae*, Simmondsiaceae*, Talinaceae*, Tamaricaceae |
| Cornales | Cornaceae* incl. Nyssaceae now Nyssoideae, Curtisiaceae, Grubbiaceae, Hydrangeaceae*, Loasaceae* |
| Ericales | Actinidiaceae*, Balsaminaceae*, Clethraceae*, Ebenaceae, Ericaceae*, Fouquieraceae, Lecythidaceae*, Marcgraviaceae*, Myrsinaceae*, Pentaphylacaceae*, Polemoniaceae*, Primulaceae*, Roridulaceae*, Sapotaceae*, Sarraceniaceae*, Styracaceae, Theaceae*, Theophrastaceae* |
| Garryales | Eucommiaceae, Garryaceae incl. Aucubaceae |
| Gentianales | Apocynaceae* incl. Asclepiadaceae* now Asclepiadoideae*, Gelsemiaceae*, Gentianaceae*, Loganiaceae, Rubiaceae* |
| Lamiales | Acanthaceae*, Bignoniaceae*, Byblidaceae, Calceolariaceae*, Gesneriaceae*, Hydrostachyaceae, Lamiaceae*, Lentibulariaceae*, Linderniaceae*, Martyniaceae*, Myoporaceae*, Oleaceae*, Orobanchaceae*, Paulowniaceae* Pedaliaceae*, Phrymaceae*, Plantaginaceae*, Schlegeliaceae*, Scrophulariaceae*, Stilbaceae, Verbenaceae* |
| Solanales | Convolvulaceae* incl. Cuscutaceae, Hydroleaceae, Montiniaceae, Solanaceae* incl. Nolanaceae, Sphenocleaceae |
| Boraginales | Boraginaceae* incl. Codon, Cordiaceae*, Ehretiaceae incl. Lennonaceae, Heliotropiaceae, Hydrophyllaceae*, Wellstedtiaceae? |
| Aquifoliales | Aquifoliaceae*, Cardiopteridaceae, Stemonuraceae |
| Asterales | Argophyllaceae*, Asteraceae*, Calyceraceae, Campanulaceae* incl. Lobeliaceae, Goodeniaceae*, Menyanthaceae*, Pentaphragmataceae, Rousseaceae, Stylidiaceae* |
| Escalloniales | Escalloniaceae |
| Bruniales | Bruniaceae, Columelliaceae incl. Desfontainiaceae |
| Apiales | Apiaceae*, Araliaceae*, Griseliniaceae, Myodocarpaceae, Pennantiaceae, Pittosporaceae* |
| Paracryphiales | Paracryphiaceae |
| Dipsacales | Adoxaceae*, Caprifoliaceae*, Diervillaceae, Dipsacaceae*, Linnaeaceae, Morinaceae, Valerianaceae* |

All families marked with an asterisk (*) are shown in the plates. According to APG III (2009), as amended.

# THE PLANT FAMILIES

**A–I:** *Acanthus spinosus.* A–C: Flower A: lateral. B: From below. C: From above. D: Calyx. E: Flower, frontal. F: Flower opened longitudinal; *right*, ovary. G: Leaf. H: Ovary, transverse. I: Fruit, lateral; *center*, seeds.

**J–L:** *Porphychroma poliana.* J: Unripe fruit. K: Seeds. L: Stamens.
**M:** *Strobilanthes cusia* stamens
**N:** *Justicia candicans* stamens
**O–U:** *Thunbergia alata.* O: Flower, frontal; underneath, from below. P: Flower, lateral, without calyx; *right*, enlarged.

**Q:** Dissected flower, longitudinal. R: Stigma, lateral. S: The same, frontal. T: Stamen; *left*, from behind; *right*, frontal.
**U:** ovary; *above*, lateral; *left*, transverse; *right*, longitudinal.
**V:** *Brillantaisia sp.* Fruit.

**Subfamilies** | Acanthoideae, Nelsonioideae, Thunbergioideae, Avicennioideae

**Genera** | about 250; species: about 4,000. Well-known genera: *Acanthus, Fittonia, Justicia, Pachystachys, Ruellia, Thunbergia.*

**Distribution** | Most species originated in the tropics, subtropics, and temperate zones; centers of plant diversity in the Indo-Malay region, Africa, Central America, Brazil
**Habit** | Mostly a perennial, rarely annual herbaceous plants, rarely epiphytes; rarely lignified, then shrubs, half shrubs, or small trees (mangroves: *Avicennia*), some are clockwise-twining climbing plants. Some are spiny, with the spines emerging from reduced foliage leaves or modified bracts or bracteoles.

**Leaves** | Usually in a basal rosette or opposite, rarely alternate or whorl arrangement. Anisophylly occurs. Blade: simple, rarely compound (fig. G). Leaf margin: smooth, notched, dentate, serrated. Cystoliths appear in nsome species.

**Flowers** | Single flowers ranging to dichasia; the hermaphroditic flowers as a rule are pentamerous (figs. A–C, E, O), mostly with five sepals, rarely four; petals fused in a funnel shape, same length or uni-, bi-, trilabiate, mostly zygomorphic (fig. E), rarely resupinate. Bracts often colored or green; each flower has two bracteoles. Five former stamens reduced to two or four fertile ones (figs. L–N). Stamens free or fused in pairs (figs. L, N). Ovaries superior, bilocular (figs. H, U). Ornithophily (nectar-eating birds, hummingbirds), entomophily (Hymenoptera, day- and night-flying moths), chiropterophily (bats).

**Fruits** | Mostly loculicidal capsule fruits, opening through two valves, seed dispersal often through exploding mechanism. Rarely drupes. Two or many seeds per locule; there are hygroscopic suction hairs on some seeds, which serve to absorb water.

**Use** | The family includes many ornamental and indoor plants, such as the **black-eyed susan vine** (*Thunbergia alata*) (figs. O–U). An insecticide is harvested from the leaves of the **Malabar nut** (*Justitia adhatoda*); besides this, the plant's contained substances have an expectorant and bronchodilator effect, and therefore extracts are used for treating asthma and hay fever.

***Andrographis paniculata*** is used both in Ayurvedic medicine and traditional Chinese medicine ("Indian echinacea"). Extracts of *Acanthus ebracteatus* can be used as a cough suppressant. Extracts of the roots of *Acanthus mollis* are used to treat diarrhea.

**Characteristics** | Ancient Greek: *acanthos* = the spiny one. The leaves of *Acanthus spinosus* (fig. G) were used as models for the leaf ornaments on Corinthian columns. The seed coat (testa) may have hairs or scales or be slimy; the funicules may be studded with a growth developed to help eject the seed.

**A–K:** *Actinidia chinensis*. A: Leafy shoot with flower; top view. B: Leaf underside. C: Denticulate leaf margin. D: Flower, frontal. E: Flower from underneath. F: Androecium. G: Flower, longitudinal. H: Young fruit, transverse. I: Young fruit, longitudinal. J: Ripe fruit, transverse. K: Ripe seeds; *right*, seeds, longitudinal.

**Genera** I 3; species: about 360. *Saurauia* (about 300 species), *Actinidia* (55–60 species), *Clematoclethra* (1 species).

**Distribution** I Tropical Asia and Americas, temperate East Asia and northern Australia

**Habit** I Trees, shrubs, lianas (fig. A)

**Leaves** I Alternate, spiral; leaf blade simple, herbaceous, rarely leathery; leaf margin smooth, serrated, or denticulate (fig. C); stomata without secondary cells. Stipules very small or absent.

**Inflorescences** I Mostly lateral, cymose inflorescences, paniculate dichasia, spicate, fascicled; single flowers

**Flowers** I Radial, hermaphroditic or functionally unisexual, then dioecious, usually pentamerous, cyclic, (2–) 5 (–8) persistent, free sepals, bud husks overlap like tiles (imbricate); corolla with (3–) 5 (–9), contorted or imbricate petals, which are free or basally fused (figs. D, E); 10–240 stamens (figs. D, F, G), in a spiral or two whorls; filaments free or fused with the petals, poricidal anthers, two-celled pollen, at times in tetrads, tricolorporate; gynoecium: ovary superior (fig. I), synocarpous, 3–5 (-many) carpels, usually one style per carpel, fused or spreading (fig. I); style can be preserved as the fruit ripens, thus the name *Actinidia* (Greek *actis* = rays). Between 10 and very many ovules per locule.

**Fruits** I Berries (fig. J) or loculicidal leathery capsules. Fleshy arils present (pulp).

**Use** I The fruit-bearing **kiwi** (*Actinidia deliciosa*; figs. A–I) is the best-known representative of the family. The fruits contain a lot of vitamins C and E as well as folic acid. The enzyme actinidain, a proteinase, contained in the fruit can cause contact allergies. The fruit of the **variegated-leaf hardy kiwi** (*Actinidia kolomikta)* and the **hardy kiwi** (also: **tara vine**, *A. arguta*) are also edible.

**Characteristics** I Aboveground organs often have simple or branched trichomes and have crystal idioblasts.

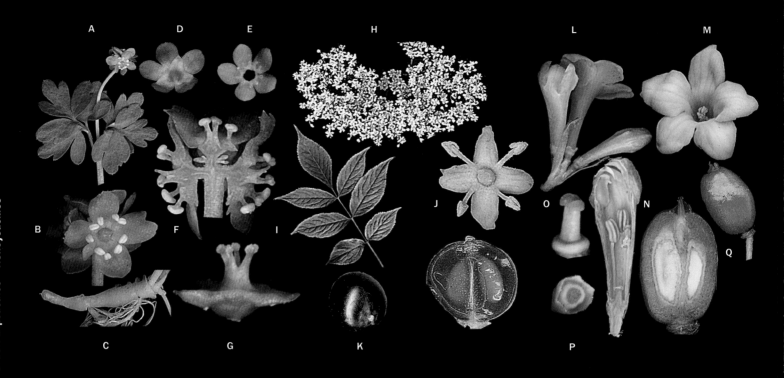

A–G: *Adoxa moschatellina*. A: Habit. B: Lateral inflorescence. C: Rhizome. D: Flower from below; calyx. E: Fused perianth. F: Inflorescence, longitudinal. G: Ovary, lateral.

H–K: *Sambucus nigra*. H: Top view of inflorescence. I: Simple pinnate leaf. J: Top view of flower. K: *Left*, ripe fruit; *right*, the same, longitudinal.

L–Q: *Viburnum × bodnantense* (= *V. farreri × V. grandiflorum*). L: Partial inflorescence. M: Top view of flower. N: Flower, longitudinal. O: Stigma and nectary. P: Calyx, nectary, and ovary, transverse. Q: Ripe fruit; *left*, longitudinal; *right*, side view.

**Genera** | 4; species: about 220. *Adoxa* (3–4 species), *Sinadoxa* (1 species), *Sambucus* (10 species), *Viburnum* (about 200 species)
**Distribution** | Temperate to subtropical latitudes of the Northern Hemisphere
**Habit** | Shrubs, trees, perennials
**Leaves** | Opposite (fig. A), leaf blade simple or compound (fig. I); leaf margin smooth, serrated, or denticulate, stipules very small or absent

**Inflorescences** | Terminal cymose inflorescences, often in umbrella-shaped panicles (fig. H), spicate, umbellate, or capitate (fig. F)
**Flowers** | Radial, hermaphroditic, tetramerous, or pentamerous (figs. B, J); five fused sepals, usually five stamens (*Sambucus*, *Viburnum*), rarely divided, then apparently eight or ten (*Adoxa*; fig. B); the tripetalous-pentapetalous ovary is half inferior (fig. G) or inferior (fig. N).

**Fruits** | Berries, berrylike drupes
**Use** | The **black elder**, common in central Europe (*Sambucus nigra*), is used for food and as a dye. Since all parts of the plant contain poisonous cyanogenic glycosides, which are destroyed to a large extent by heating, the fruit is edible only after it is cooked.

**Characteristics** | Representatives of this species-rich family were formerly assigned to the honeysuckle, elder, or viburnum families. The **moschatel** (*Adoxa moschatellina*; figs. A–G) got its name from its special scent. This was also the reason that people used to place this herb among their stored clothing.

**A–F:** *Aizoon sp.* A–C: Flower. A: Male phase. B: Female phase. C: longitudinal. D: Almost-ripe fruit, transverse. E: Fruit. F: The same, longitudinal.
**G–H:** *Sesuvium sp.* G: Flower, frontal. H: The same, longitudinal.

**I–M:** *Gibbaeum dispar.* I: Plant with flower. J: Flower, frontal. K: The same, longitudinal. L: Capsule. M: Opened capsule.
**N:** *Trichodiadema mirabile. Left,* leaves with pair of foliage leaves; underside at right.

**O:** *Titanopsis schwantesii* habit
**P:** *Sceletium* sp. Upper part of plant with flower, green/dry leaves.
**Q:** *Lithops lesliei. Left,* pair of leaves, frontal; *right,* leaf, longitudinal.

**R:** *Mesembryanthemum sp.* Upper surface of leaf.
**S:** *Fenestraria rhopalophylla. Left,* top view of leaf; *right,* longitudinal.

**Subfamilies** | Aizoideae, Mesembryanthemoideae, Ruschioideae, Sesuvioideae, Tetragonioideae
**Genera** | About 122; species: more than 2,200
**Distribution** | Tropics and subtropics of the Southern Hemisphere, southern Africa; in coastal areas up to southern Europe returned to the wild, United States to Chile. Introduced into Asia and New Zealand, meanwhile has been classified there as nonnative or neophytes
**Habit** | Shrubs to perennials. Predominantly perennials, but also annuals. The shrub species can grow to over 1 meter tall. Especially well known are the "living stones," small, stubby perennials (fig. I), which can survive long periods in dry regions without rain.
**Leaves** | Mostly opposite; the simple, entire leaves without stipules are more or less succulent; they have water storage tissues in bladder cells of the epidermis, which can at times be over 1 mm long, or in central water storage tissues. These plants sometimes grow only one pair of leaves in each growing season, while some plants are sunk into the ground up to the tip of the leaf (window leaf or *Monstera*; figs. Q, S).
**Inflorescences** | Single flowers ranging to dichasia or thyrses
**Flowers** | Radial, hermaphroditic, mostly pentamerous (tetramerous, pentamerous, octamerous, pentacarpellate calyx, ± free; the free petals and stamens usually resulting from multiplication by so-called secondary *dédoublement* or splitting in two. The ovary, which grows from 5–6 to 10 carpels, is superior to inferior (figs. H, C, K); the style arms are free.
**Fruits** | Mostly 5–6(–8–10) multilocular capsules, rarely berry or nut fruit. The capsules open at the plant's location when it rains (hygrochastic capsules); this lets the seeds be washed out by single drops.

**Use** | Some ornamental plants: **Hottentot fig** (*Carpobrotus edulis*) with edible fruit and leaves, **New Zealand spinach** (*Tetragonia tetragoniodes*) with edible leaves
**Characteristics** | Many species have more or less thin-walled bladder cells in the leaf epidermis that make them look "as if coated with ice crystals" (hence "ice plant family"; fig. R). The flowers develop their very striking colors from betalains. The primary pollinators are insects. The flowers usually open at full light: Carpobrotus or "midday flowers."

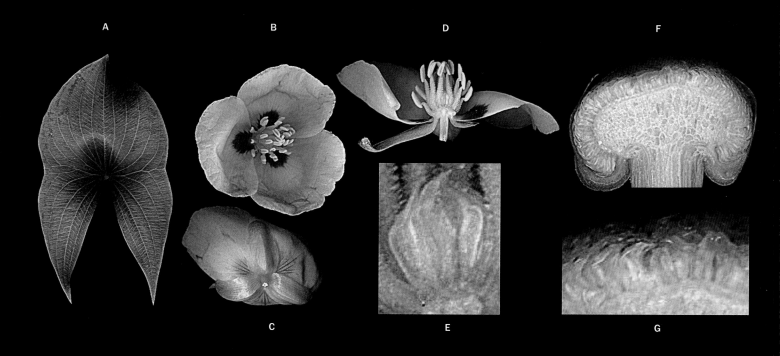

A–G: *Sagittaria montevideo*. A: Leaf. B: Flower, frontal. C: The same, from below. D: The same, longitudinal. E: Detail from D; ovaries, longitudinal. F: Unripe fruiting stage. G: Detail from F; ovaries with seeds.

**Genera** I 15; species: about 100
**Distribution** I Worldwide in tropical and subtropical regions
**Habit** I Usually perennial, rarely annual marsh and aquatic plants. Perennial species usually grow rhizomes; some grow turions as overwintering organs (exception: *Damasonium* plants grow root tubers).
**Leaves** I Basal, spiral, distichous (in two opposite rows) or in rosettes; leaf blade: simple, linear, lanceolate, ovate, rhombic; the base may be sagittate, hastate (fig. A), or truncate; floating leaves or erect-growing underwater leaves; leaf margin smooth or undulate; venation: parallel main veins, reticulate secondary veins
**Inflorescences** I Racemose inflorescence botryoid, paniculate, umbellate
**Flowers** I Radial, hermaphroditic or unisexual (*Sagittaria*; figs. B, D), including on a single plant, rarely subdioecious; perianth, trimerous, stamens mostly three to many, basally attached or free, outward-opening (extrorse); pollen mostly pantoporate; the ovary, comprising 3–∞ carpels, is superior; all carpels fused only with themselves (apocarpous) or fused only with others at the base
**Fruits** I Nutlet, stone (drupe) fruit or follicles with one to several seeds
**Use** I The common **European water plantain** (*Alisma plantago-aquatica*) is an ornamental plant. **Sword plants** (*Echinodorus* sp.) and **arrowhead**s (*Sagittaria* sp.) are popular aquarium plants.
**Characteristics** I The plants contain a milky sap. Earlier, the rhizomes and leaves (*herba et radix alismatis*) were used as laxatives; however, since they are toxic, at least when fresh, this is not recommended; these active ingredients can be present in differing concentrations.

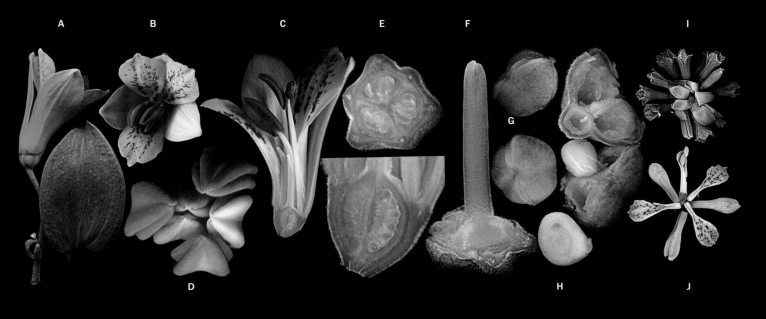

A–I: *Bomarea edulis*. A: Flower lateral with leaf. B: Top view of flower. C: Flower, longitudinal. D: Two whorls with three stamens each, frontal. E: Ovary; *above*, transverse; *below*, longitudinal. F: Style/stigma, lateral. G: Fruit; *left*, lateral and top view; *right*, opened with seeds. H: Seeds, longitudinal.

I–J: *Bomarea spec*. **cf.** *multiflora*. I: Inflorescence. J: Top view of blossom.

**Genera** I 4: *Alstroemeria, Bomarea, Drymophila, Luzuriaga*; species: 170
**Distribution** I Temperate to tropical regions of the Neotropics, Australia, and New Zealand
**Habit** I Mostly a perennial, herbaceous plants, rarely more or less woody plants, some climbing plants
**Leaves** I Alternate, spiral, distichous; leaf blade undivided, resupinate, linear to lanceolate; leaf margin smooth; venation: parallel (fig. A)
**Inflorescences** I Racemose or umbellate (fig. J), solitary (figs. A–C)
**Flowers** I Radial to slightly zygomorphic, hermaphroditic, perigone, trimerous; two whorls of three free stamens; the tricarpellate fused ovary is inferior (fig. F) or superior
**Fruits** I Capsule or berry
**Use** I Some varieties of the Peruvian lilies are used as ornamental plants (such as *Alstroemeria versicolor*). Their starchy underground plant parts are eaten raw or cooked. Likewise, in Central America, the starchy root tubers of *Bomarea edulis* are cooked as "white Jerusalem artichokes" and eaten mashed as a substitute for potatoes.
**Notes** I The family was named after Claus Alstroemer (1736–1794), a student of Linnaeus.

ALSTROEMERIACEAE

41

A–I: *Liquidambar styraciflua*. A: Branch with female inflorescences. B: Autumn leaf coloration. C: Branch with female flowers (lower bud) and male flowers. D: Female inflorescence; *left*, frontal; *above*, longitudinal; *below*, solitary female flower. E: *Left*, male flower with husk; *right*, husk removed. F: Unripe fruiting stage. G: *Left*, fruiting stage, longitudinal; *right*, transverse. H: Ripe fruit. I: Seeds.

**Genera** I 3: *Altingia* (10 species), *Liqudiambar* (3 species), *Semiliquidambar* (3 species)
**Distribution** I Eastern North America, Central America, eastern Mediterranean region (Turkey, Syria), east to Southeast Asia
**Habit** I At times very large, deciduous or evergreen trees
**Leaves** I Alternate or helical, leaf blade simple and undivided, lanceolate, ovate, obovate, or palmate divided (figs. A, B); leaf margin: entire, notched, serrated, denticulate.

Reticulate or net venation; stipules small and deciduous, bud scales present.
**Inflorescences** I Globose or capitulate
**Flowers** I Unisexual, monoecious, the male flowers have 4–10 stamens (fig. E); in female flowers (fig. D) the ovary, fused from two carpels, is inferior; pollination is by wind (anemophilous).
**Fruits** I Capsule aggregate fruits that open with two valves (figs. F–H); winged seeds (fig. I)

**Use** I The **American sweetgum** (*Liquidambar styraciflua*) is the best-known species. Like other members of the family, it has an aromatic resin (name: Latin *liquidus* = liquid, Arabic: *ambar* = amber), which is discharged when the bark is lacerated. The indigenous inhabitants of North America used to use it as a "sweet gum" like chewing gum. The **Oriental sweetgum** (*Liquidambar orientalis*) for a long time supplied false styrax (true styrax/storax comes from *Styrax officinalis*, which was used

as a coveted incense in ancient times). *Altingia excelsa* supplies a high-quality timber, which is traded under the name "Rasamala."
**Notes** I In the past, the three genera were considered to be part of the Hamamelidaceae (witch hazel family). The genus *Altingia* was named in honor of Willem Arnold Alting (1724–1800), who was governor of the Dutch East Indies, now Indonesia.

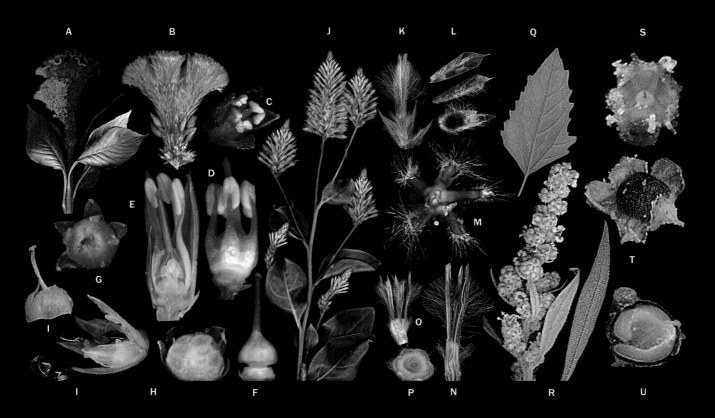

AMARANTHACEAE

**A–I:** *Celosia argentea* **var.** *Cristata*. A: Habit. B: Inflorescence. C: Flower, frontal. D: Stamens, lateral. E: Flower, longitudinal. F: Ovary with nectary, lateral. G: Young fruit, frontal. H: The same, transverse. I: Capsule.

**J–P:** *Ptilotus exalatus*. J: Habit. K: Flower, lateral, with bracts and bracteoles. L: Bract (*below*) and bracteoles. M–O: Flower. M: Frontal. N: Longitudinal. O: With bract, lateral. P: Nectary.

**Q–U:** *Chenopodium album*. Q: Leaf underside. R: Inflorescence with bracts of the partial inflorescences; *right*, bract underside with bladder hairs. S: Flower, frontal, T: Ripe fruit. U: Seeds, longitudinal.

**Genera** I 76; species: 2,050–2,500
**Distribution** I Worldwide
**Habitat** I Chenopodiaceae: saline soils, sea coasts
**Habit** I Shrubs, half shrubs, annual or perennial herbaceous plants, also succulent leaves and stems (Chenopodiaceae), rarely trees or lianas
**Leaves** I Usually alternate, rarely opposite, leaf blade variable; leaf margin: entire (figs. A, Q, R) or denticulate, often with bladder hairs (Chenopodiaceae); venation: reticulate venation; stipules absent, bud scales present
**Inflorescences** I Mostly glomerate thyrses or dichasia, spicate
**Flowers** I Radial, hermaphroditic, or unisexual, inconspicuous; perianth absent or simple; bracteoles and bracts herbaceous or scarious (figs. K, O); flowers of (1–3–) 5 (–8) tepals, (1–) 5 (–8) stamens, anthers with 2–4 pollen sacs (figs. C–D), pollen pantoporate; discs in some species with appendages (pseudostaminodes), the ovary fused from (1–2–) 3 (–6) carpels is superior (fig. F) with 1 (–2) ovules
**Fruits** I Propagation method: seeds often remain encased in a perianth, which becomes enlarged, hard, or fleshy. Rarely (operculum) capsules (figs. G–I) or berries.
**Use** I Some important crop plants such as **spinach** (*Spinacea oleracea*) and various cultured forms of the **beet** (*Beta vulgaris*), such as Swiss chard, sugar beets, and fodder beets. Some foxtail species (such as *Amaranthus caudatus*, *A. cruentus*) and **quinoa** (*Chenopodium quinoa*) play a role in human nutrition. Dye plants, such as **garden orache** (*Atriplex hortensis*)—a blue dye is harvested from the seeds.
**Characteristics** I Many succulent species and halophytes—for example, **glasswort** (*Salicornia europaea*)—are adapted to habitats with saline soil. Abnormal lateral growth may occur.

# AMARYLLIDACEAE

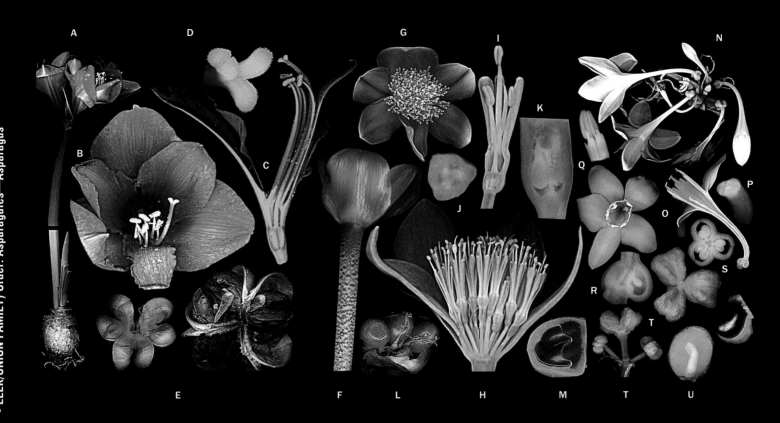

**A–E:** *Hippeastrum* **sp**. A: Inflorescence; *below*, bulb and side bud. B: Single flower, frontal. C: Flower, longitudinal. D: Stigma. E: Opened fruit; *left*, from below; *right*, frontal.

**F–M:** *Haemanthus coccineus*. F: Inflorescence, lateral. G: The same, frontal. H: The same, longitudinal. I: Single flower, longitudinal. J: Ovary, transverse. K: The same, longitudinal. L: Fruits. M: Seeds in fruit.

**N–U:** *Eucharis* **sp**. N: Inflorescence. O: *Left*, single flower frontal; *right*, longitudinal. P: Stigma. Q: Stamens. R: Ovary, longitudinal. S: The same, transverse. T: Fruiting stage. U: Seeds; *right*, frontal; *left*, longitudinal.

**Subfamilies** I Amaryllioideae, Agapantoideae, Allioideae
**Genera** I 73; species: about 1,600
**Distribution** I Worldwide, concentrated in warm temperate, subtropical to tropical zones
**Habit** I Perennial geophytes with a bulb (fig. A), rarely a rhizome (*Clivia*)
**Leaves** I Basal, alternate, rarely opposite; leaf blade variable (tubular, grooved, flat, linear, lanceolate to elliptic); leaf margin: entire; venation: parallel venation
**Inflorescences** I Umbellate

inflorescences (figs. G, H, N), single or in the axilla of a membranous bract or surrounded by six petallike spathes, simulating a single flower (fig. G)
**Flowers** I Radial, six tepals, three each in two whorls (fig. B, O), also basally fused; 4–6 free stamens (fig. I); the ovary, fused from three carpels (figs. J, K, R, S), is superior or inferior. Placentation: axile; three stigmas. Septal nectaries occur. More or less conspicuous secondary corollas may increase the visual effect for visitors to the flower (*Narcissus, Hymenocallis*

*narcissiflora, Eucharis*; fig. O).
**Fruits** I Trivalved capsules (fig. E) or berry (*Clivia*)
**Use** I Many ornamental plants (*Agapanthus, Hippeastrum, Narcissus*). The "**knight's star lily**" (*Hippeastrum* sp.) is falsely known as amaryllis commercially. Many vegetables: **common onion** (*Allium cepa*), **leek** (*A. porum*), **garlic** (*A. sativum*), and **wild garlic** (*A. ursinum*).
**Characteristics** I Alkaloids are widespread. The **Belladonna lily**

(*Amaryllis belladonna*) was formerly used as a dart poison because of the poisonous alkaloids in the bulb. Two to three grams of the bulb are deadly to humans. Apart from propagating by means of daughter bulbs, some species are also capable of vegetative propagation by means of bulbils (such as *Allium vineale*).

A–H: *Amborella trichopoda.* A: Foliage leaf. B: Inflorescence. C: Female single flower, frontal. D: The same, from below.
E: Flower, longitudinal. F: Staminode. G: Solitary carpels. H: Carpels, transverse.

**Genera** | 1; only species: *Amborella trichopoda*
**Distribution** | New Caledonia
**Habit** | Small evergreen shrub or tree
**Leaves** | Alternate, spiral to distichous; leaf blade simple; leaf margin: smooth (fig. A); lobed, serrated, reticulate venation; stipules absent
**Inflorescences** | Cymose (fig. B)

**Flowers** | Transition from foliage-like spathes to flowers, stamens, and carpels. Single flowers acyclic, dioecious; male flowers 5–11 tepals with 10–14 fertile, leaflike stamens, free, introrse, open with a slit; female flowers 5–8 tepals, staminodes, ovary superior of 5–8 free carpels (figs. G, H); these are incompletely closed at the tip; marginal placentation, hypanthium present.
**Fruits** | Aggregate fruits of one-seeded stone fruits
**Use** | —
**Characteristics** | The characteristic of this basal species within the angiosperms is their lack of tracheas in the xylem (water-conducting tissue).

AMBORELLACEAE

45

ANACAMPSEROTACEAE

**A–I:** *Anacampseros rufescens*. A: Two leaf pairs, frontal. B: All-cell succulent leaf, transverse. C: Habit lateral with flower buds. D: Flower bud with membranous bracteoles. E: Opened bud, frontal. F: Stigma. G: Androecium and ovary, transverse. H: Detail of ovary, transverse. K: The same, longitudinal.

**Genera** | 3: *Anacampseros*, *Grahamia*, *Talinopsis*; species: about 40
**Distribution** | Africa, America, Australia
**Habitat** | The succulent species grow in drier habitats.
**Habit** | Small shrubs, perennial herbaceous plants with at times thick trunks
**Leaves** | Spiral to opposite, simple, cylindrical to round, all-cell succulents with axillary hair tufts, bristles or scales
**Inflorescences** | Few-flowered thyrses, at times parchment-like bracteoles (figs. C, D)
**Flowers** | Radial, hermaphroditic, two succulent sepals, five petals, 5–25 stamens; the tricarpellate ovary is superior, one style with three style arms (fig. F).
**Fruits** | Unilocular capsules
**Characteristics** | The thick stems are often mucilaginous, a basal stalk, sometimes thickening into tubers as it approaches the roots; a hood forms out of the perianth.
**Notes** | The three genera were united into the family Anacampserotaceae only in 2010.

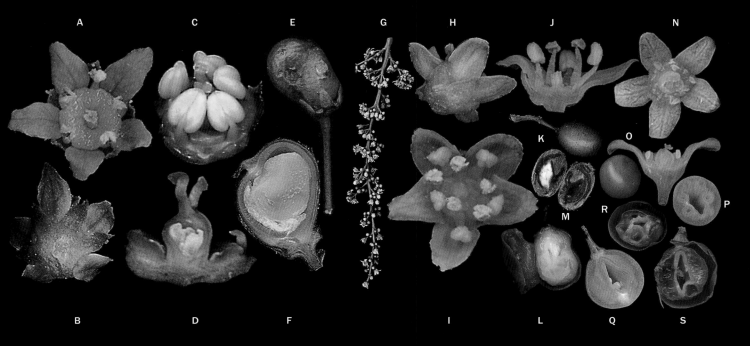

**A–F:** *Cotinus coggygria.* A: Flower, frontal. B: The same, from below C: Opened bud. D: Ovary, longitudinal. E: Ripe fruit, lateral. F: The same, longitudinal, with already green cotyledons.

**G–M:** *Harpophyllum caffrum.* G: Inflorescence. H: Single flower from below. I: The same, frontal. J: The same, longitudinal. K: Unripe fruit. L: Ripe fruit open. M: Seeds, longitudinal.

**N–S:** *Schinus molle.* N: Flower, frontal. O: The same, longitudinal. P: Unripe fruit, transverse. Q: The same, longitudinal R: Ripe fruit from below, transverse. S: The same, longitudinal.

**Subfamilies** I Anacardioideae, Spondioideae

**Genera** I 81; species: about 800. Well-known genera are *Anacardium*, *Cotinus*, *Mangifera*, *Pistacia*, *Rhus*, and *Toxicodendron*.

**Distribution** I Worldwide, tropical subtropical, also temperate regions

**Habit** I Trees, shrubs, evergreen or deciduous; rarely half shrubs, lianas, or perennial herbaceous plants

**Leaves** I Mostly alternate, rarely opposite or whorled, often clustered at the branch ends, aromatic and fragrant, simple and undivided or odd-pinnate; rarely can be abruptly pinnate, sessile, or petiolate. Leaf margin: entire, serrated, denticulate, notched. Stipules are absent.

**Inflorescences** I Cymose umbels, paniculate or racemose inflorescences (fig. G), terminal or lateral, rarely single flowers, rarely cauliflorous

**Flowers** I Radial, hermaphroditic, unisexual, monoecious, dioecious, gynodioecious or polygamo-monoecious, relatively small (figs. A, I, N), ternate to quinate, simple or compound perianth; 3–5 basally fused sepals, 3–5 (–8) free, rarely basally fused petals, usually (1–) 2 whorls, each containing (1–) 5 (–10) stamens (figs. C, I), all fertile; or up to nine staminodes present; 1–2–5 (–6)-carpellate ovary is usually superior (figs. D, O), rarely half inferior or inferior; 1 style with 1–5 (–6) stigmas.

**Fruits** I Mostly drupes (figs. E, K, R), but also aggregate fruits, samaras

**Use** I **Cashew** (*Anacardium occidentale*): The pear-shaped, about 10 cm long and 5 cm wide swelling peduncles/receptacles (hypocarps) are eaten as a fruit. In their Brazilian homeland, these sweet-sour-tasting fruits are consumed fresh and made into preserves or soft drinks. The kidney-shaped, oil-rich seeds are found at the end of the fruit; these are eaten roasted as cashew nuts. The pericarp contains the poisonous cashew seed oil. It is used, among other things, for producing artificial resin or as a lubricating oil. **Mango** (*Mangifera indica*): up to 1,000 cultivated varieties. Used as a fruit or to make preserves, ice cream, or chutneys. Mango seed oil is extracted from the seeds; this is used in the cosmetics industry and to make margarine and chocolate. The fruit peels contain urushiol (a derivative of catechol), which is among the strongest contact allergens.

**Brazilian peppertree** (*Schinus therebinthifolius*): The pink drupes are sold commercially as a pepper-like spice under the name "pink pepper." They are added to pepper mixtures for the visual effect. In Florida, the species is considered an invasive neophyte that spreads uncontrollably; as a result, there are efforts to combat its spread.

**Characteristics** I Name: in Greek, *ana* = upward, *kardi* = heart: the "heartnut tree." The plant has resin ducts. Wood, leaves, and fruit are frequently aromatic (turpentine-like) but often cause contact dermatitis, and some species are poisonous. In dry habitats, the plants have succulent stems.

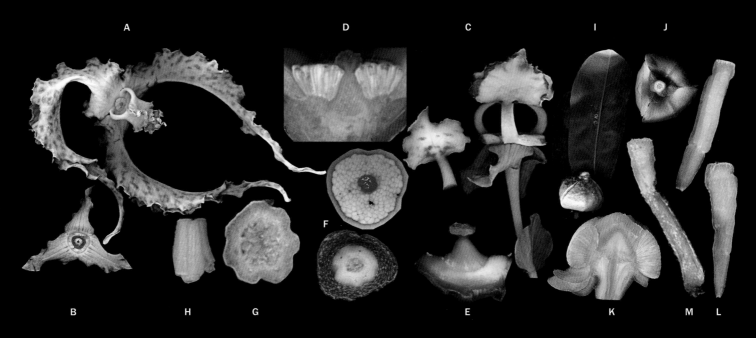

A–H: *Monodora crispata*. A: Flower, frontal. B: Calyx with androecium and gynoecium. C: Inner petals form a corolla above the ovary; *left*, single leaf. D: Androecium and gynoecium, longitudinal. E: Ovary with nectary, lateral. F: Androecium and gynoecium; *above*, frontal; *below*, withered. G: Ovary, transverse. H: Solitary stamen.

I–M: *Annona muricata*. I: Bud and foliage leaf. J: Bud from below. K: Bud, longitudinal. L: Stamens. M: Carpel.

**Subfamilies** I Anaxagoreoideae, Ambavioideae, Annonoideae, Malmeoideae

**Genera** I 131; species: about 2,200. Well-known genera are *Annona*, *Cananga*, *Monodora*, *Rollinia*, *Stelechocapus*

**Distribution** I Pantropical, ranging to temperate North America

**Habit** I Trees, shrubs, lianas

**Leaves** I Alternate, usually distichous, rarely helical, evergreen or deciduous; simple, entire, stipules absent

**Inflorescences** I Subterminal or intercalary, solitary or fascicle, rarely on lateral shoots

**Flowers** I Hermaphroditic, rarely unisexual, flower organs mostly in spiral arrangement, often patelliform or cup shaped, hanging (fig. A), often trimerous (fig. B: exception among the Magnoliales); 2–3–4 often-fused sepals; 3–6–12 mostly free petals; 3–6 or more stamens (figs. D, F), connective often with appendage. The ovary, consisting of one or more carpels, is superior (figs. G, E, M); cantharophily: pollination by beetles.

**Fruits** I Aggregate berry fruit of 1–8 (–12) berries that are fused with the receptacle. Also woody indehiscent fruit. Seeds with arils.

**Use** I Edible fruits of *Annona* species (Haitian *anon* = custard apple), such as the **cherimoya** (*Annona cherimola*): these plants, native to the Andean valleys of Colombia, Bolivia, and Ecuador, are cultivated throughout South America today. It is said to grow the most delicious fruit of the entire family. The sour-tasting flesh of the **soursop** (*Annona muricata*) and the shape of fruit, which can weigh up to 4 kg, have given the plant its name of "soursop." Since the fruits are sensitive to pressure, they are usually eaten locally. The fruit is used to make soft drinks, preserves, and ice cream. The fruit of the **three-lobed pawpaw** (*Asimina triloba*) grow solitary or in bundles. Due to its shape, texture, and taste, the fruit is also called the "Indian banana." Weighing up to 500 grams, this is the heaviest (and largest) of North American fruit. *Cananga* essential oil is harvested from the heavily fragrant flowers of the **ylang-ylang** (*Cananga odorata*). This oil is used in aromatherapy and is often the floral note in perfumes (such as in Chanel No. 5). The grated seeds of the **calabash nutmeg** (*Monodora myristica*) are used as a nutmeg substitute and are added to soups, stews, or cakes, especially in West Africa. The plant was brought to the Caribbean through the slave trade, where it is now established.

**Characteristics** I Leaves and seeds of many species contain insecticidal substances. The seeds are usually poisonous.

**A–E:** *Astrantia major.* A: Inflorescence with single umbel. B: Single umbel from below (husk). C: Palmate pinnate leaf. D: Male flower, lateral, 4 stamens not attenuated. E: Female flower, lateral.

**F–J:** *Aegopodium podagraria.* F: Ternate pinnate leaf. G: Compound umbel from below. H: Single blossom, frontal. I: Ovary; *left*, transverse; *right*, longitudinal. J: Ripe cremocarp.

**K–O:** *Orlaya grandiflora.* K: Compound umbel from below with enlarged ray flowers. L: Flower. M: Ray flower with asymmetric, enlarged petals. N: Tripinnate leaf. O: Ovary, longitudinal.

**Genera** | More than 200; species: more than 2,500

**Distribution** | Worldwide

**Habitat** | Temperate highlands, open grasslands, moist and dry brushwood and meadows, roadsides, brownfields to alpine regions, even shallow standing waters; calciphilous; avoids calcareous soil

**Habit** | Predominantly perennials, annuals to perennials; can grow to over 5 meters tall, also grows in a semispheric bushy form, can also be a creeper, and thistle-like. The stems often have sharp-edged grooves, which are gnarled and may be hollow (such as *Heracleum mantegazzianum*).

In some genera, underground runners cause almost lawn-like growth, such as of *Aegopodium podagraria* (goutweed).

**Leaves** | Mostly alternate, usually divided and range to tripinnate (figs. C, F, N); can have glandular hairs, rarely thickly fleshed. The petiole may also be inflated and clasp the stem. Leaves, petioles, and even the stems can be more or less densely hairy. Plants such as the water dropwort species (*Oenanthe* sp.) may have differently structured aquatic leaves.

**Inflorescences** | Simple, frequently compound umbels that have bracts that can be designated as involucral bracts (umbels) and involucel bracts (umbellule); these may also be colored to increase the visual effect. The flowers may grow up to 150 corymbs, which can be of unequal length.

**Flowers** | Mostly radial, mostly hermaphroditic, but also unisexual (fig. E), then monoecious or dioecious. The often-enlarged ray flowers increase the visual effect of the umbels; in this case they are zygomorphic (fig. K; fig. M, first plate; fig. B, second plate; p. 50). Calyx often greatly reduced or even absent. Petals free, enveloped in the bud stage (fig. D, first plate), often with heart-shaped margins; can be ciliate at the margin, mostly white, but also pink or yellowish. Five stamens (fig. L, first plate), also enveloped in the bud stage; two carpels, rarely single petaled due to atrophy, with two styles/stigmas forming the inferior ovary. The ovary is supported by a nectar-secreting glandular tissue (stylopodium; fig. I, *right*, first plate: upper lighter area). Pollination by insects (entomophily, especially beetles [cantharophily], flies, gnats, butterflies, bees).

A–C: *Scandix pecten-veneris*. A: Habit. B: Umbellules from below with pentapetalous involucel. C: Fruit with a long beak; *left*, longitudinal; *center*, lateral; *right*, transverse.

D–G: *Myrrhis odorata*. D: Umbellule with flowers and fruits. E: Single umbellule from below. F: Tripinnate leaf. G: Fruit; *left*, lateral; *right*, transverse.

H–L: *Levisticum officinale*. H: Bipinnate leaf. I: Compound umbel, frontal. J: Umbellule from below. K: Bud; *above*, closed; *below*, petals removed. L: Fruit; *left*, ripe with splayed-out mericarps; *above center*, unripe, transverse; *below center*, unripe lateral; *right*, longitudinal.

**Fruits** | Schizocarpic, cremocarp, sometimes called "double achene." Two single-seeded, five-ridged (ridge = carina) mericarps, which are attached to a dichotomous carpophore; when ripe they become loosened at the joint surface (commissure); the style may remain as a short to long beak on the fruit (fig. C, second plate). The smooth, round, or more or less furrowed, winged (fig. L, second panel), also coarsely hairy fruits (fig. O, first panel) are traversed by oil passages ("valleys" in cross section), which contain substances that are distinctly characteristic and have an odor.

Calcium oxalate occurs.
**Use** | The variety of substances contained, mainly essential oils, makes it possible to use these plants in a wide variety of ways. Leaves as aromatic herbs: **lovage** (*Levisticum officinale*), **parsley** (*Petroselinum crispum*), **dill** (*Anethum graveolens*), **coriander** (*Coriandrum sativum*), **sweet cicely** (*Myrrhis odorata*). Even the young leaves of the often-unpopular **goutweed** (*Aegopodium podaria*) can be eaten. The seeds of **caraway** (*Carum carvi*) and **anise** (*Pimpinella anisum*) are used as flavoring ingredients for alcoholic drinks.

Storage organs (root tubers) such as **carrots** (*Daucus carota*) and **celery** (*Apium graveolens*) are eaten as vegetables. For medicinal and healing purposes, we harvest the gum-resinous ingredients by cutting into the lower parts of the stem or root base.
**Characteristics** | This family also includes highly toxic plants, such as the **poison hemlock** (*Conium maculatum*), which was administered, mixed together with other poisonous plants, as the "cup of hemlock" in antiquity (for example, to Socrates). The **giant hogweed** (also called the **Hercules bush,** *Heracleum*

*mantegazzianum*), which comes from the Caucasus region, has an inflorescence that grows over 3 meters tall and can produce tens of thousands of single flowers per plant. It spreads as an invasive plant. Due to the substance (furanocoumarins) contained in all parts of the plant, it causes skin damage upon contact and in combination with UV light (such as large blisters).
**Notes** | The family, now designated as Apiaceae or Umbelliferae, was formerly also called Ammiaceae.

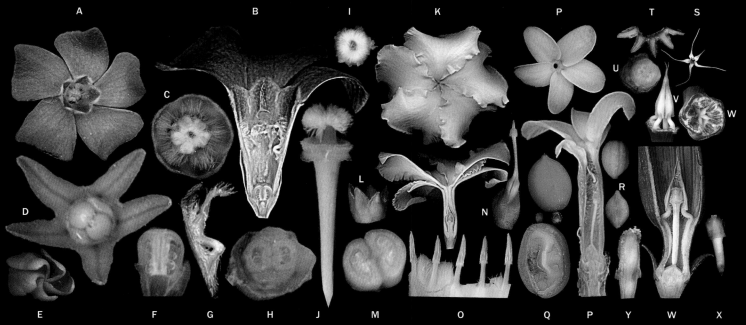

A–J: *Vinca minor*. A: Flower, frontal. B: The same, longitudinal. C: Detail, flower center. D: Calyx with ovary/nectary. E: Opening bud, frontal. F: Ovary, longitudinal. G: Kinked stamen. H: Ovary, transverse. I: Stigma from above. J: The same, lateral.

K–O: *Tabernaemontana coronaria*. K: Flower; *above*, frontal; *below*, longitudinal. L: Calyx. M: Ovary, transverse. N: Gynoecium. O: Stamens from the corolla.
P–R: *Alyxia ruscifolia*. P: *Above*, flower, frontal; *below*, longitudinal. Q: Fruit lateral; *below*, longitudinal. R: Seeds.

S–Y: *Strophanthus intermedius*. S: Flower, frontal. T: Calyx splayed out. U: Ovary, transverse. V: Stamens; *left*, lateral; *right*, enlarged flower center. W: Lower part of flower, longitudinal. X: Stigma, lateral. Y: The same, longitudinal.

**Subfamilies** | Apocynoideae, Asclepioideae, Rauvolfioideae, Perioplocoideae, Secamonoideae subfamily Apocynoideae
**Genera** | More than 77; species: more than 450
**Distribution** | Worldwide
**Habit** | Trees, shrubs, herbaceous plants, lianas, succulents; even to be found in semideserts
**Leaves** | opposite, alternate, leaf blade undivided, stipules may be present or absent.
**Inflorescences** | Panticulate, dichasia

**Flowers** | Radial, hermaphroditic, the rotated bud position (fig. E) often still traceable in the slightly spiraled, opened corollas; tetramerous-pentamerous, corolla mostly fused in a tubular or funnel shape (fig. B); five free or fused stamens, also fused with the ovary, often with kinked filament (fig. G); the bicarpellate ovary is usually superior, and nectaries are usually at the base of the ovary, formed on the carpel sutures as scaly (yellow) outgrowths (fig. D).
**Fruits** | Berries, drupes, capsules, seeds also with a tuft of hair

**Use** | The bast fibers of *Apocynum pictum* and *A. venetum* are used to manufacture ropes, mats, clothes, and paper. The roots contain apocynin, a substance that can be used medicinally. The poisonous milky sap of the **desert rose** (*Adenium obesum*) is used in Africa as a dart poison. A seed extract of *Strophanthus* species was used in Africa as a dart poison for hunting elephants. It contains the cardiac glycoside strophanthin, which formerly was administered for treating heart disease. Ornamental plants include **periwinkle** (*Vinca* sp.), **oleander** (*Nerium oleander*), and the **Madagascar palm** (*Pachypodium lameri*). Alkaloids derived from extracts of the **Madagascar periwinkle** (*Catharanthus roseus*) are used to combat certain cancers.
**Characteristics** | Many species are poisonous. Many contain a clear, milky sap.

APOCYNACEAE

# APOCYNACEAE

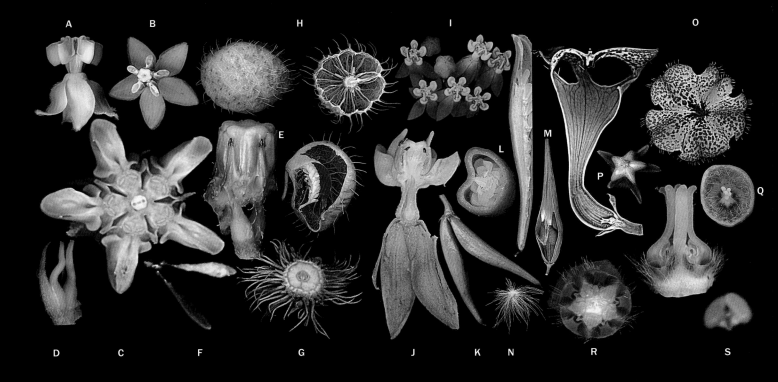

**A–H:** *Gomphocarpus fructicosus*. A: Flower, lateral. B: The same, frontal. C: Flower in the stamen area, transverse section. D: Gynoecium. E: Stamens with corpuscles and lower part of the ovary, lateral. F: Two partial stamens with corpuscle. G: Ovary, transverse. H: Ripe fruit; *left*, top view; *right*, transverse; *below*, disected, longitudinal. **I–N:** *Asclepias curassavica*. I: Partial inflorescence, frontal. J: Single flower, longitudinal. K–L: Unripe fruit. K: Lateral. L: *Left*, transverse; *right*, longitudinal. M: Ripe opened fruit. N: Seed winged hairs. **O–S:** *Ceropegia elegans*. O: *Right*, flower from above; *left*, longitudinal. P: Bud. Q: Androecium and gynoecium, lateral; *right*, in flower. R: The same, stamen area, transverse section. S: Two partial stamens with corpuscle.

**Genera** I More than 170; species: about 2,900
**Distribution** I Worldwide, mostly in tropical and subtropical regions
**Habit** I Shrubs, lianas, stem succulent plants, perennials, also climbing plants; rarely trees
**Habitat** I Some species grow in semideserts.
**Leaves** I Mostly opposite, simple undivided, stipules may be present or absent.
**Inflorescences** I Cymose, racemose
**Flowers** I Radial, hermaphroditic, pentamerous, calyx basally fused, corolla often with secondary corolla (from petals and stamens, compare fig. B); five stamens with only short threads; the thecas of the two adjacent stamens are usually connected via a so-called V-shaped translator. This has a corpuscle at its pointed end, where visitors to the flower usually pinch their legs and pull out the pollinium (figs. F, S) and transport it to the next flower ("pinch-trap flower"). Stamens and carpels are often fused into a so-called gynostegium (figs. B, E); the bicarpellate ovary is superior.
**Fruits** I Often pairs of follicle fruits
**Use** I All parts of the **bush banana** (*Marsdenia australis*) are edible; it is the most important bush plant for the Aborigines. The seed hairs of the **common milkweed** (*Asclepias syriacus*), which cannot be spun, were formerly used as padding material. During long treks through the Kalahari (Botswana), the Khoisan people traditionally chew bitter pieces of the stem succulent *Hoodia gordonii* due to its hunger- and thirst-suppressing properties. After the substances the plant contains were patented to market them as appetite suppressants, the Khoisan were granted—in a protracted process—a small share of the profits for their indigenous knowledge about the plant's use. Unfortunately, this "share" is an absolute exception in the field of biopiracy! Some ornamental plants, such as the **wax plant** (*Hoya carnosa*) and **Madagascar jasmine** (*Stephanotis floribunda*).
**Characteristics** I In many cases, the plants have a clear, milky sap, which may also be white in some *Gomphocarpus* species. The German name *Seidenpflanzen* (silk plants) refers to the long, silky seed hairs of *Asclepias* species; these serve to disperse the seeds by helping them fly away. The Greek god of healing, Asclepius, was the godfather of the name, since the plants were formerly used in folk medicine. *Stapelia* species belong to the so-called carrion flowers, which attract carrion-seeking flies with their stench and red-flesh-colored flowers. Often, their flowers are also hairy like an animal carcass, so that the deceived flies even lay their eggs there, which then perish.

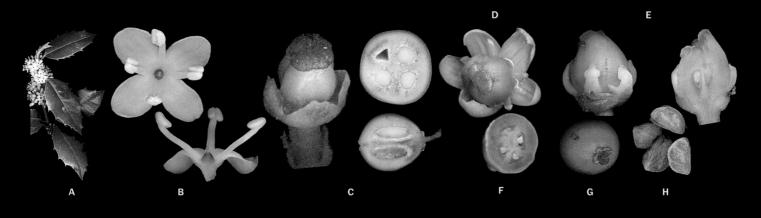

**A–C:** *Ilex aquifolium*. A: Leaf arrangement on branch with inflorescences. B: *Above*, male flower frontal; *below*, longitudinal. C: *Left*, female flower; *right above*, young fruit, transverse; *right below*, the same, longitudinal.

**D–H:** *Ilex integra*. D: Female flower with reduced stamens. E: *Left*, flower lateral, petals removed; *right*, longitudinal, husk removed. F: Ovary, transverse. G: Ripe fruit, frontal. H: Seeds.

**Genus** | 1: *Ilex*; species: about 400
**Distribution** | Worldwide
**Habit** | Evergreen or deciduous shrubs, trees up to 25 meters tall
**Habitat** | Often as undergrowth in deciduous forests
**Leaves** | Alternate, simple, usually leathery, the margins spiny, denticulate, or entire

**Inflorescences** | Cymes
**Flowers** | Radial, predominantly unisexual (figs. B, C), mostly tetramerous to pentamerous, usually white-fused corolla; 4–5 stamens, filaments in the male flowers basal with fused corolla (fig. B, *above*). The usually tetracarpellate ovary is superior, style reduced, stigma sessile,

sticky, flat, and four-lobed; female flowers can have reduced stamens (staminodes) (fig. E).
**Fruits** | Multiseeded drupes (fig. G)
**Use** | Ornamental shrubs; the leaves of *Ilex paraguariensis* are used to make **mate tea**; also used as a hardwood.

**Characteristics** | The fruit and leaves of the English holly (*Ilex aquifolium*) are poisonous; 20–30 fruits are lethal to adults (ingredients: triterpenes, saponins).

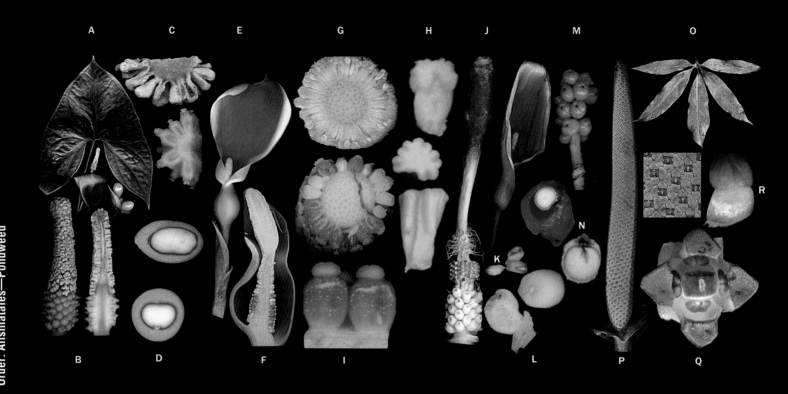

**A–D:** *Nephthytis afzelii.* A: Leaf; *below*, spadix with spathe and fruit. B: Spadix; *left*, lateral; *right*, longitudinal. C: Spadix, transverse; *above*, with stamens; *below*, ovary, transverse. D: Fruit; *above*, longitudinal; *below*, transverse.

**E–I:** *Remusatia vivipara.* E: Spadi (area of male flowers visible) with spatha and male spadix. F: Spadix, longitudinal. G: Male zone, transverse. H: Stamen; *above*, open: *center*, transverse; *below*, unopened. I: Spadix, female zone; *above*, transverse; *below*, ovaries, lateral.

**J–N:** *Arum maculatum.* J: *Right*, spadix with spathe; *left*, without. K: Stamen. L: Ovary; *left*, longitudinal; *top*, frontal. M: Fruiting stage. N: *Above*, fruit transverse; *below*, seeds, longitudinal.

**O–R:** *Anthurium digitatum.* O: Leaf. P: Spadix, lateral; *right*, detail. Q: Hermaphroditic flower; *center*, ovary, four stamens, four tepals. R: Stamen.

**Subfamilies** | Gymnostachydoideae, Orontioideae, Lemnoideae (floating on water: abnormal features!), Monsteroideae, Pothoideae, Lasioideae, Zamioculcadoideae, Aroideae
**Genera** | 106; species: more than 4,000
**Distribution** | Worldwide; concentration in the tropics
**Habit** | Very small to large, mostly perennial, herbaceous plants: geophytes, epiphytes, lithophytes, climbing plants, with aerial roots, rhizomes, tubers, or bulbils
**Leaves** | Alternate or basal, evergreen or deciduous, simple, entire, lobed, lanceolate, cordiform, sagittate (fig. A), pinnate, petiole often with basal leaf sheath
**Inflorescences** | Multiflowered

spadixes, surrounded by a usually conspicuous spathe (figs. A, E, J)
**Flowers** | Unisexual (fig. C) or hermaphroditic (fig. Q), dioecious or monoecious, then in zones on the spadix: above, male flowers; below, female flowers (figs. B, F, J). Perianth inconspicuous, small, bimerous to trimerous, or absent; usually 4–6 free stamens (figs. H, K, R). Ovary (fig. I) fused from three carpels.
**Fruits** | Berries (figs. D, M, N) mostly free on the spadix
**Use** | The starchy rhizomes of the **taro plant** (*Colocasia esculenta*) and **giant taro plant** (*Alocasia macrorrhiza*) are cooked like potatoes. The glucomannan-containing tubers of the **konjac root** (*Amorphophallus konjac*) are used as thickening and gelling agents in Japan (E 425). Since

the human body cannot digest these tubers, the products are marketed as diet foods (pasta, rice). Glucomannans, with a high water-binding capacity, suggest the feeling of "satiation." The fleshy inside ripe spadix of the **windowlea**f or **Swiss cheese plant** (*Monstera deliciosa*) is said to taste like pineapple-banana. Houseplants: **flamingo flower** (*Anthurium* sp.), **philodendrons** (*Philodendron* sp.), **calla lily** (*Zantedeschia* sp.), **peace lily** (*Spathiphyllum* sp.), **windowleaf** (*Monstera* sp.), and **dumbcane** (*Dieffenbachia seguine*). Take care: If you touch the latter plant, it can "shoot" calcium oxalate needles and other substances from special ringed cells into the skin, causing itching and eczema. If taken internally, it causes

burning and swelling of the tongue and mouth area, so that you cannot talk for some time. In the 17th century, *Dieffenbachia* was administered as a punishment to fleeing slaves in America (name: "dumb cane").
**Characteristics** | The **titan arum** (*Amorphophallus titanum*) has the largest "deceptive flowers" (= the flower's biological lure). The spadix emits a scent of carrion; this attracts carrion beetles and rover beetles, which lay eggs on the spathe. Pollination occurs by the pollen the insects bring with them. However, the hatching larvae cannot find any food and die.

**A–F:** *Hedera helix*. A: Aerial roots. B: Leaf. C–D: Flower. C: *Left*, frontal; right, lateral. D: Longitudinal. E: Fruiting stage with rhomboid leaves. F: Fruit; *left*, unripe, transverse; *right*, ripe, frontal; *below left*, transverse; *right*, longitudinal.

**G–N:** *Pseudopanax arboreus*. G: Compound umbel. H: Flower, frontal. I: Calyx. J: Opened bud with stamens. K: Flower, longitudinal. F: Ovary, longitudinal. M: The same, transverse. N: Palmate pinnate leaf.

**O–Q:** *Hydrocotyle ranunculoides*. O: Foliage leaf. P: Inflorescence; *above*, frontal; *below*, longitudinal. Q: Single blossom, frontal.

**Genera** | More than 40; species: more than 1,000
**Distribution** | Worldwide
**Habit** | Trees, shrubs, but also herbaceous plants
**Habitat** | In forests, ditches, bogs
**Leaves** | Alternate, with or without small stipules, simple, leathery, scutate, lobed or compound (fig. N). In common ivy (*Hedera helix*), heterophyllous leaves occur: the ordinary foliage leaves are mostly lobed (fig. B), while the leaves of the inflorescences have a pointed rhomboid form (fig. E).
**Inflorescences** | Umbels (figs. E, G), verticils, spikes
**Flowers** | Radial; hermaphroditic or unisexual; often small, whitish or greenish (figs. C, H), (tetramerous-) pentamerous; calyx present (fig. I) or reduced; five stamens, often fused with the disc lying on the inferior ovary. Five fused carpels with usually one ovule each form the usually half-inferior ovary, style often fused.

**Fruits** | Berries (fig. F), drupes or schizocarpic fruits
**Use** | Ornamental plants, such as **Japanese angelica tree** (*Aralia elata*) and **Hercules club** (*A. spinosa*). The most important useful plant is **ginseng** (*Panax ginseng*); the ginseng root cluster is used in dried form for many medical-pharmaceutical purposes. Leaf extracts of ivy are used as cough and anticonvulsant medicines.

**Characteristics** | Climbing plants such as common ivy (*Hedera helix*), with aerial roots, climb more than 5 meters high (fig. A). Ivy overgrowth may cause "light competition" for the supporting plant. The aerial roots can penetrate into cracks in masonry and then cause damage to a building facade. Contact dermatitis can occur if ivy is cut without wearing protective gloves. The fruit is very poisonous.

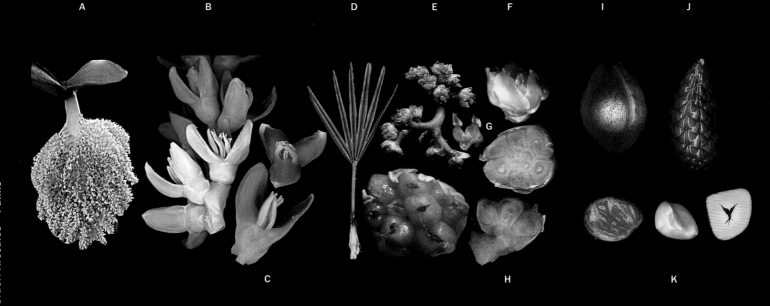

A  B  D  E  F  I  J

G

C  H  K

**A–C:** *Phoenix reclinata*. A: Male inflorescence. B: The same, detail. C: Male flower; *above*, frontal; *below*, longitudinal.

**D–H:** *Chamerops humilis*. D: Palmate divided leaf. E: Partial inflorescence; *below*, parts enlarged. F: Female flower, lateral. G: Reduced stamens. H: Partial inflorescence; *above*, transverse; *below*, longitudinal.

**I:** *Cocos nucifera* ripe fruit, floating fibers partially removed so that seeds are visible

**J:** *Raphia sp.* fruit
**K:** *Phytelephas macrocarpa. Left*, seed, lateral; *center*, testa removed; *right*, seed transverse.

**Subfamilies** I Calamoideae, Nipoideae, Coryphoideae, Ceroxyloideae, Arecoideae
**Genera** I 183; species: about 2,600
**Distribution** I Worldwide in the tropics and subtropics.
**Habit** I Treelike, single or more rarely multiple trunks, aboveground or underground creepers, some climbing plants, adventitious roots take over the function of the dying-off primary root, no secondary lateral growth
**Leaves** I Alternate, spiral arrangement, rarely distichous, almost undivided, bifid, fan-shaped (palmate; fig. D), costa-palmate, or pinnate, bipinnate, usually petiolate, occasionally spiny; the leaf base sometimes has a separate structure and can grow a corolla shaft, often filled with fibers. On the climbing palms, backward-facing barbed bristles can grow on the leaf veins. The terminal leaflets can be transformed into a twining tendrils.
**Inflorescences** I Heavily branched, paniculate or spicate, surrounded by a spathe
**Flowers** I Mostly radial, female (fig. F), polygamous, monoecious, dioecious. Some bloom repeatedly or can die after blooming (hapaxanthic), trimerous; three free or fused sepals, three petals, usually six stamens (fig. G), occasionally some reduced to staminodes; three free or basally fused carpels form the superior ovary. Entomophily, anemophily.
**Fruits** I Drupes, berries
**Use** I Edible seeds in about 100 species, such as the **coconut palm** (*Cocos nucifera*; fig. I). Edible fruits: the **date palm** (*Phoenix dactylifera*) or **Salak palm** (*Salacca zalacca*); the latter's fruit tastes like lychees. Palm oil is harvested from the pulp of the **African oil palm** (*Elaeis guineensis*), and palm kernel oil is harvested from the pits (seeds). Because they are so extensively used in nutrition, technology, and biodiesel and cosmetic production, the cultivation area for oil palms has increased worldwide, at the expense of the rainforests. The **peach palm** (*Bactris gasipaes*) is used in tropical America; the cone-shaped vegetable (the divisible tissues at the tip of multistemmed shoots) is eaten as heart of palm. Sago is harvested from the starchy stems of the **sago palm** (*Metroxylon sagu*); it is used in New Guinea to make a flat bread. Rattan furniture is manufactured using the long shoots of some **rotang palms** (*Calamus* species). The trunks of many palm trees are used for lumber. The pits of the **vegetable ivory palm** (*Phytelephas macrocarpa*; fig. K) are used as a vegetable substitute for ivory. The leaves of the **carnauba wax palm** (*Copernicia prunifera*) provide carnauba wax. The fruit of some **raffia palms** (*Raphia* sp.; fig. J) are used as fish poisons.
**Characteristics** I Palm trees are record holders in the plant kingdom: they form the largest inflorescences and grow the most flowers, such as the cabbage or gebang palm (*Corypha* sp., up to 7.5 meters in length and several million flowers), the longest leaves (*Raphia regalis*, up to 25 meters long), and the largest and heaviest seeds (sea coconut palm, *Lodoicea maldivica*, up to 50 cm in length and weighing 22 kg).

ARGOPHYLLACEAE

**A–F:** *Corokia* × *virgata*. A: Leafy branch with flowers. B: Flower, frontal. C: The same from below. D: The same, longitudinal.
E: Opened bud with still closed stamens, style/stigma. F: Ovary, transverse.

**Genera** | 2: *Argophyllum* and *Corokia*; species: 20

**Distribution** | Australia, New Zealand, New Caledonia, Polynesia, Rapa Iti Island

**Habit** | Trees, shrubs

**Leaves** | Alternate, simple, also evergreen, underside hairy (fig. A), mostly entire or slightly denticulate, petiolate, without stipules

**Inflorescences** | Racemose, axillary tufts

**Flowers** | Radial, hermaphroditic, mostly six free or basally fused sepals (fig. C), six free petals (fig. B), rarely fused, six free stamens (figs. B, E). The tricarpellate-pentacarpellate ovary is half inferior to inferior (fig. D), one style with three style arms; there is a six-lobed nectary on the ovary,

enveloping the style (figs. B, D).

**Fruits** | Capsule fruit (*Argophyllum*), drupes (*Corokia*)

**Use** | The **zigzag shrub** (*Corokia* × *virgata*) is sometimes available as an ornamental plant because of its angled branches and its winter hardiness. There are several varieties of the hybrid of *C. buddleioides* × *C. cotoneaster*.

**Characteristics** | The hairs are T shaped.

# ARISTOLOCHIACEAE

**A–I:** *Aristolochia clematitis.* A: Partial inflorescence. B: Flower in female phase, longitudinal. C: Flower in male phase, longitudinal. D: Gynostemium, frontal; the marginal stigma is ready to be pollinated. E: The same, lateral; anthers still closed. F: Anthers opened. G: Fruit. H: The same, transverse. I: Seeds.

**J–K:** *Aristolochia durior.* J: Flower, frontal. K: The same, longitudinal.

**L–N:** *Aristolochia grandiflora.* L: Bud, lateral. M: Open flower, frontal. N: Various surfaces of the perianth going toward the gynostemium.

**Genera** I about 4; species: about 480. Well-known genera: *Aristolochia* (Dutchman's pipe) and *Asarum* (wild ginger).

**Distribution** I Worldwide, various climate zones

**Habit** I Perennials, trees, lianas

**Leaves** I Alternate, spiral arrangement, simple, entire, cordiform, or palmate divided, soft leaved, petiole present. Venation: reticulate, palmate, or pinnate; glands may be present. Stipules are absent.

**Inflorescences** I Cymose, racemose or spicate, terminal or axillary (fig. A), simple or branched, single flowers rare, may be cauliflorous

**Flowers** I Radial or strongly zygomorphic (figs. B, C, K, L), hermaphroditic, trimerous, inflorescence simple of only one whorl of bell-shaped or campanulate fused sepals, or doubly articulated into calyx and corolla; 4–6 (–36) stamens, free or fused together with the style into a column (gynostemium; figs. D, E). The ovary, fused from 4–6 carpels, is inferior or half inferior. Entomophily.

**Fruits** I Mostly capsule; rarely nuts, berries, schizocarpic fruit, follicles

**Use** I In the Middle Ages, the flowering herb of the **European birthwort** (*Aristolochia clematitis*) was used as a labor-inducing remedy to accelerate birth (Greek *aristos* = very good, the best; *lockelus* = to do with giving birth); also used as an abortifacient. Today it is no longer in use, since we now know the carcinogenic and kidney-damaging effects of aristolochic acid. It is still used as a homeopathic remedy.

**Characteristics** I Deceptive flowers, "lobster-pot" trap (*Aristolochia* sp.). The lobster-pot-shaped flowers in the genus *Aristolochia* usually have a carrion-like odor, which, together with the often-reddish-brown flower color, attracts diptera (flies). The flies slide down the guide tube formed by the fused calyx and are prevented from climbing out by the upward-pointed trapping hairs (fig. B). Only after pollination do these barrier hairs wilt, the flower slants downward, and the pollen-covered animals can leave their prison—and then immediately fall into the next flowers they encounter. The flowers of *Aristolochia arborea* form a small capitulum inside, which is interpreted as a false fruiting body of a fungus of the genus *Marasmius* (*fungus mimesis*). The flowers are supposed to smell like mushrooms and attract female fungus gnats, which usually deposit their eggs in the fruiting bodies of the fungus.

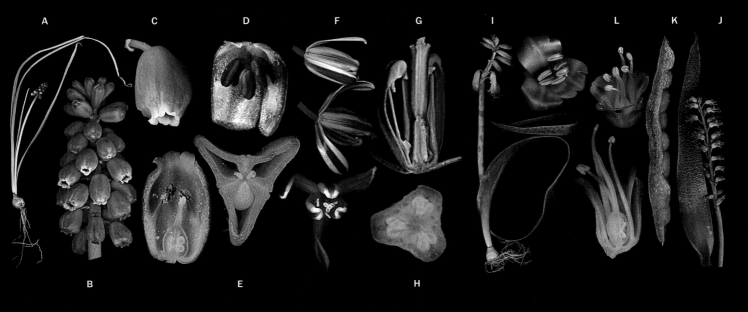

A–E: *Muscari botryoides*. A: Habit. B: Inflorescence. C: Flower, lateral, with bract; *below*, longitudinal. D: Unopened stamens from the bud, filaments fused with corolla. E: Ovary, transverse.

F–H: *Albuca nelsonii*. F: *Above and center*, opening flowers; *below*, flower, frontal. G: Flower, longitudinal. H: Ovary, transverse.

I: *Lachenalia aloides*. *Left*, habit; *above right*, flower, frontal.

J–K: *Lachenalia unicolor*. J: Habit. K: Leaf, transverse. L: *Above*, flower, lateral; *below*, the same, longitudinal.

ASPARAGACEAE

**Subfamilies** | Aphyllanthoideae, Brodiaeoideae, Scilloideae, Agavoideae, Lomandroideae, Asparagoideae, Nolinoideae. In the following, five of the seven subfamilies are presented. The subfamily of the Scilloideae shown here more or less includes the family of the former hyacinth family.
**Genera** | 70; species: about 1,000
**Distribution** | Old World; concentrated in the winter rain areas of the Capensis (Cape region in South Africa) and the Mediterranean
**Habit** | Perennial geophytes with bulbs, rarely with rhizomes
**Leaves** | Alternate, spiral arrangement, in basal leaf rosette; leaf blade simple, entire, linear (fig. A) to lanceolate (figs. I, J), parallel venation, sessile; some are marked with several colors (fig. I); occasionally have warts (figs. J, K) or hairs.
**Inflorescences** | Terminal, mostly racemose (fig. B), rarely spicate, occasionally capitiform
**Flowers** | Radial, rarely zygomorphic, hermaphroditic, trimerous, six free tepals, with three in two similar or different whorls (fig. F) or fused into a tube (fig. C); two whorls of three stamens, free or fused with the perianth (fig. D); the three carpels are usually fused to the superior to half-inferior ovary (figs. E, H); septal nectaries present; one style with three style arms. Usually entomophilous, occasionally ornithophilous.
**Fruits** | Capsule fruit
**Use** | Ornamental plants of numerous varieties from many genera: **Spanish bluebell** (*Hyacinthoides*), **garden hyacinth** (*Hyacinthus orientalis*), **grape hyacinth** (*Muscari*), **star of Bethlehem** (*Ornithogalum*), **puschkinia** (*Puschkinia*), **pineapple lilies** (*Eucomis*), and **wood hyacinths** (*Scilla*). The bulbs of the **tassle grape hyacinth** (*Muscari comosum*) are eaten on Crete and in southern Italy. Due to their intense fragrance, hyacinths were formerly cultivated in France for the production of perfumes.
**Characteristics** | The underground plant organs can have a milky sap. Toxic cardiac glycoside bufandienolides (which are also produced in the skin of true toads of the genus *Bufo*) occur, for example, in the bulbs of **climbing onion** (*Bowiea volubilis*) and the **sea squill** (*Drimia maritima*). These were formerly used medically, but this is obsolete today due to the plants' toxicity.

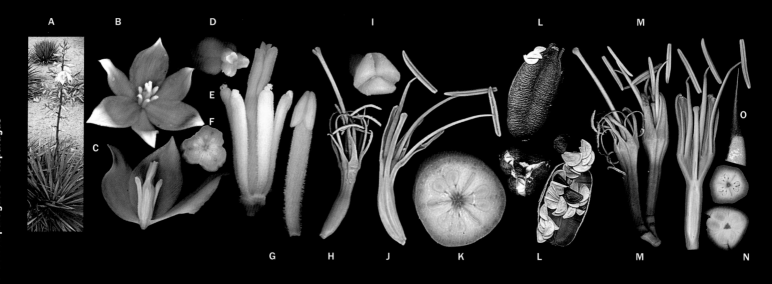

**A–G:** *Yucca filamentosa*. A: Habit. B: Flower, frontal. C: Blossom, longitudinal. D: Stigma. E: Ovary and stamens. F: Ovary, transverse. G: Solitary stamen, frontal.

**H–K:** *Agave seamanniana*. H: Flower, lateral. I: Stigma. J: Blossom, longitudinal. K: Ovary, lateral. L: Ripe fruit; *above*, lateral; *center*, top view; *right*, longitudinal.

**M–O:** *Agave weberi*. M: Flower, lateral; *right*, longitudinal. N: Ovary, transverse, with nectary at the sutures and in the center. O: Leaf spine.

**Genera** | 18; species: over 600. Well-known genera: *Agave*, *Beschorneria*, *Furcraea*, *Yucca*.
**Distribution** | Almost worldwide; main focus the Neotropics
**Habit** | Tree shaped, shrubby, also perennial herbaceous plants with rhizomes or bulbs, xerophytes, many succulents, rarely epiphytes
**Leaves** | Alternate, spiral arrangement, often as a leaf rosette; blade: simple, linear, parallel venation, evergreen; leaf tip can end in a spine.
**Inflorescences** | Racemose, paniculate, multiflowered, perennial, also hapaxanths
**Flowers** | Radial (fig. B), mostly hermaphroditic or functionally unisexual, poly- or monocarpous, six

tepals in two whorls of three each; tepals free or fused at the base in tubular form; two whorls each consisting of three stamens (fig. E), which can protrude from the perigone tube (figs. H, J, M). The ovary, fused out of three carpels, is superior or inferior (figs. F, K, N); septal nectaries are present; one style with three style arms.
**Fruits** | Capsule (fig. L), berries
**Use** | Young inflorescences of the **Spanish dagger** (*Yucca gloriosa*) are prepared like asparagus; the bulb of the **common camas** (*Camassia quamash*) is also edible. The Mexican national drink "pulque" is made by fermenting the juice of various agave species, while mezcal, an alcoholic

beverage, is extracted from the agave "hearts." Tequila is made exclusively from the **blue agave** (*Agave tequilana*). To harvest agave syrup, agave buds that are about to flower are cut off. The sweet, sugary plant sap flows out of the cut for about half a year; it becomes slightly syrupy after filtration and evaporation. The **Spanish dagger** (*Yucca gloriosa*) and **sisal** (*Agava sisalana*) as well as **henequen** (*Agava fourcroydes*) provide plant fibers. Since the **spider plant** (*Chlorophytum comosum*) is a popular office plant, in Germany it is also known as "clerk grass." Hostas (*Hosta* sp.) are used as a ground cover.
**Characteristics** | Many agave plants are known as "century plants"

because it takes several decades for them to flower; after that, they die. The German name *Agave* comes from the Greek and means "noble" or "sublime." The name of yucca "palm" for the popular ornamental plant is misleading because this is not a palm tree (see family Arecaceae). The upright, stemlike habit of the plants in combination with a tuft of leaves at the top led to the similar name. The yucca flowers are pollinated by yucca moths, whose females specifically transfer the pollen to the stigmas during egg laying. The hatched moth larvae eat up just a small part of the developing seeds, so that the reproduction of the yuccas is not endangered.

A–F: *Cordyline australis*. A: Habit, in New Zealand in natural habitat. B: Inflorescence C: Solitary flower; *left*, lateral/from below; *center*, frontal; *right*, longitudinal. D: Young fruiting stage. E: Young fruit; *above left*, lateral, *below*, longitudinal; *right above*, transverse. F: Unripe seed.

**Genera** I 141; species: about 178
**Distribution** I Australia, New Zealand, Madagascar, India, South America
**Habit** I Woody, shrubby, or treelike plants (fig. A), secondary lateral growth, perennial herbaceous, rarely lianas, some xerophytes, rhizomes sometimes thickened with nodes, plants with milky sap
**Leaves** I Alternate, spiral, distichous, arranged in rosettes, leaves are narrow, grasslike to broad and lanceolate, entire, with parallel venation

**Inflorescences** I Racemose, spicate, paniculate (fig. B)
**Flowers** I Radial, hermaphroditic (fig. C), trimerous out of two whorls each with three tepals fused into a tube; these can have a similar or different structure; in the latter case, the inner petals are fringed, six stamens fused with the perigone (fig. C). The ovary, fused out of three carpels, is superior (fig. E); septal nectaries are present; one style with three style arms.
**Fruits** I Capsule or berries (fig. E)
**Use** I Ornamental plants; outdoors,

however, only in frost-free regions, especially variegated varieties (such as *Cordyline fruticosa*). The rhizomes of some species are eaten as "root" vegetables, such as that of the **renga lily** (*Arthropodium cirratum*) and the **cabbage tree** (*Cordyline australis*). From the seawater-resistant leaf fibers of the cabbage tree, the Maoris made ropes, fishing rods, or baskets, among other things.
**Characteristics** I The Aborigines chewed the water-bearing leaf bases of *Lomandra longifolia* during times of water shortages, using the seeds

to make a bush bread.
**Notes** I In the past, the representatives of the subfamily were classified in a separate family, the Laxmanniaceae.

ASPARAGACEAE

61

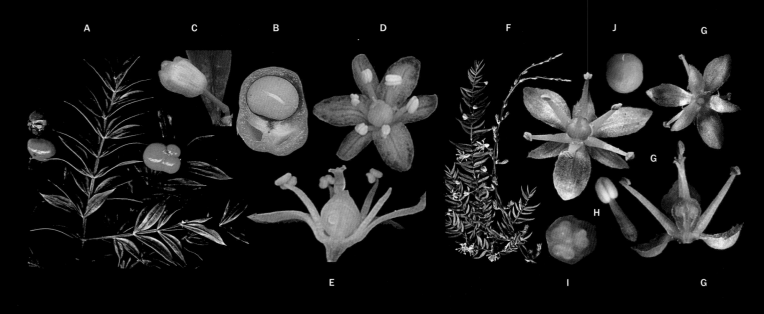

**A–E:** *Asparagus madagscarius*. A: Branch with phylloclade and fruit. B: Fruit, transverse. C: Bud, lateral. D: Flower, frontal. E: Blossom, longitudinal.

**F–J:** *Asparagus* **sp**. F: Branch with phylloclade and flowers. G: *Left,* flower, frontal; *top right,* underside; *below,* flower, longitudinal. H: Unopened stamen of a bud. I: Ovary, transverse. J: Fruit.

**Genera** I 2; *Asparagus* with about 200 species, *Hemiphylacus* with five species; the latter endemic to Mexico
**Distribution** I Worldwide; center of plant diversify in Cape region
**Habit** I Small shrubs, perennial herbaceous plants with rhizomes, lianas
**Leaves** I Alternate, blade often severely reduced, often scalelike; therefore the growth of phylloclades (figs. A, F), which take over the photosynthesis, is widespread. Leaves, if any, are simple, entire, and parallel veined.

**Inflorescences** I Single or in different inflorescences
**Flowers** I Radial, hermaphroditic or unisexual, monoecious or dioecious, flowers small, often only a few millimeters to 1 cm long; greenish, yellowish, white; six tepals of three pieces in two whorls (figs. D, G), two whorls of three stamens each, free (fig. G) or basally fused with the perigone (fig. E), female flowers with staminodes. The ovary, fused from three carpels, is superior (figs. D, E, G); septal nectaries are present, one style with three style arms.

**Fruits** I 1–6 seeded berries (*Asparagus*; figs. A, J), leathery capsules with 3–6 seeds (*Hemiphylacus*)
**Use** I The best-known and economically most important representative is **garden asparagus** (*Asparagus officinalis*). Its young shoots (Greek *apharagos* = young shoots) are eaten cooked, either green (harvested aboveground) or white (cut underground). The ingredient L-asparagine combined with a high potassium content (> 200 mg / 100 g) is responsible for the diuretic effect of

asparagus. The sulfur-containing aspartic acid and its breakdown products lead to the typical strong smell of your urine after eating asparagus. In parts of southern Europe, the shoots of **wild asparagus** (*Asparagus acutifolius*) are eaten as a vegetable side dish.
**Characteristics** I The **bridal creeper** (*Asparagus asparagoides*) is considered an unpopular wild plant in Australia.
**Notes** I The former family of the Asparagaceae corresponds today only to the subfamily Asparagoideae.

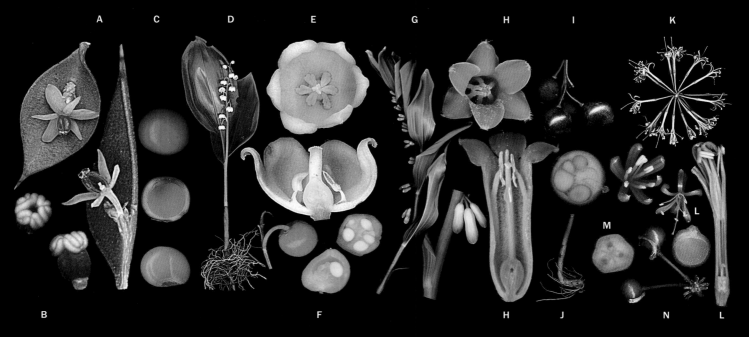

A C D E G H I K

B F H J N L

**A–C:** *Ruscus aculeatus* flower on phylloclade; *left*, frontal; *right*, longitudinal. B: Androecium; *above*, frontal; *below*, lateral. C: Fruit; *above*, lateral; *center*, transverse; *below*, seeds.

**D–F:** *Convallaria majalis*. D: Habit. E: *Above*, flower, frontal; *below*, longitudinal. F: *Left*, fruit, lateral; *center*, longitudinal; *right*, transverse.

**G–J:** *Polygonatum multiflorum*. G: Habit; *bottom right*, buds. H: *Above*, flower, frontal; *below*, longitudinal. I: Fruit; *above*, lateral; *below*, transverse. J: Rhizome, lateral.

**K–N:** *Dracaena surculosa*. K: Umbellate inflorescence. L: Blossom; *left*, opening; *center*, frontal; *right*, longitudinal. M: Ovary, lateral. N: Unripe fruit, lateral; *right*, longitudinal.

**Genera** I 24–30; species: 475–700. Well-known genera: *Aspidistra, Beaucarnea, Convallaria, Dasylirion, Dracena, Polygonatum*
**Distribution** I Worldwide, temperate, tropical and subtropical zones
**Habit** I Tree-shaped perennial plants with atypical lateral growth, shrubs, small shrubs, lianas, perennial herbaceous plants with rhizomes (figs. D, J) or tubers
**Leaves** I Alternate or opposite, spiral, distichous, whorled. Blade: linear to broad, oval-lanceolate (figs. D, G). Leaves are simple, entire, parallel veined, and occasionally greatly reduced, scaly. The formation of phylloclades (fig. A) is widespread; these take over the photosynthesis.

**Inflorescences** I Mostly racemose (fig. D) or single
**Flowers** I Radial, mostly hermaphroditic, rarely unisexual, then either monoecious or dioecious (fig. A), trimerous, six tepals of three each in two whorls, ± the same, free or fused in a bell or campanulate shape (figs. E, H); mostly (1–) 2 whorls of three stamens each, free or basally fused with the perigone (figs. E and H, respectively, *below*), in *Ruscus*, male flowers with three anthers (fig. B), female flowers with staminode tube. The ovary, fused out of three carpels, is superior (figs. E, H).
**Fruits** I Mostly berries (figs. C, F, I, N), rarely capsule fruit
**Use** I Many ornamental plants: lily of

the valley, bowstring hemp, dragon tree, lily turf, David's harp, May lily, aspidistra. The saponin-containing roots of *Nolina palmeri* can serve as a substitute for soap. Because of its characteristic scent, the **lily of the valley** (*Convallaria majalis*) serves as a perfume plant. Fibers can be harvested from the leaves of various *Sanseveria* species. **Mondo grass** (*Ophiopogon japonicus*) is used in Chinese medicine.
**Characteristics** I The **cast iron plant** or **bar room plant** (*Aspidistra elatior*) can also cope very well with little light and with drafts; therefore it worked well as a houseplant, especially in shoemaker shops or butcher shops, where the customer

traffic meant that doors are opened frequently. The lily of the valley, especially the flowers and fruit, is classified as toxic because of the cardiac glycosides the plants contain. When people collect wild garlic leaves in the spring before they flower, deadly mix-ups with the edible wild garlic occur from time to time. The vascular stigmas, which remain on the rhizomes of the **Solomon's seal** (*Polygonatum multiflorum*), are reminiscent of foot corns and were therefore used in the Middle Ages to treat them.

A–E: *Tussilago farfara*. A: *Above*, inflorescence, frontal; *below*, longitudinal. B: Tubular flower; *above*, frontal; *below*, lateral. C: Ray flower, lateral. D: Achenes with flight hairs. E: Inflorescence capitulum or head.

F–H: *Centaurea cyanus*. F: *Above*, inflorescence, frontal; *below*, from underneath/lateral. G: Tubular flowers, frontal; *below*, lateral; style already grown through the anther tube. H: Fruit.

I–M: *Taraxacum officinale*. I: Inflorescence before fruiting, upper involucral leaves closed. J: Inflorescence, frontal. K: Ray flower, lateral. L: Anther tube with stigma ready to be pollinated. M: Fruiting stage.

**Subfamilies** | Asteroideae with tubular and ray flowers, Liguliflorae with ray flowers, Tubuliflorae with tubular flowers

**Genera** | More than 1,500; species: more than 25,000

**Distribution** | Worldwide, except in Arctic regions

**Habit** | Evergreen shrubs, half shrubs, (rhizome) perennials, epiphytes, rarely trees (rosette trees), rarely aquatic plants

**Habitat** | (Mountain) forests, grasslands, shrublands.

**Leaves** | Alternate, rarely opposite, without stipules, leaf blade simple and undivided to multiply pinnate, petiolate or sessile (compare plate II, p. 65)

**Inflorescences** | The capitulum or calathium is characteristic (figs. A, F, J); composite capitula also occur. A large number of flowers may grow on a variously shaped receptacle (globose, disciform, patelliform, etc.), which may be "naked" (fig. E) or may have chaff or bristles; at times there may be over 100 single flowers. Depending on the subfamily, there are capitula with radial tubular flowers (Tubuliflorae), which are pentamerous and gamosepalous, or capitula with marginal, usually female zygomorphic pentamerous ray flowers, which surround the central tubular flowers in rows (Asteroideae; fig. A); capitula with hermaphroditic zygomorphic ray flowers (Liguliflorae; fig. J) are also possible.

**Flowers** | Radial: tubular flowers; zygomorphic: ray florets. All gamosepalous, the calyx may consist of bristles, scales, or variously structures hairs and are usually preserved as a pappus on the fruit. Five stamens adhering to the anthers form a tube, the contents of which open inward; the style, which usually has papillae, grows through the tube and pushes the pollen upward in front of it (secondary pollen presentation). Only after this pollen has been collected by the flower visitors do the two style arms unfold and are then ready to be pollinated on their upper side. Some species of Tubuliflorae have enlarged (sham) ray flowers, which are then sterile (fig. F).

**Fruits** | Achenes, indehiscent fruit developed from two carpels, with or without petiolate or sessile pappus; it simply falls to the ground or can be spread by the wind.

**Use** | Many medicinal and healing plants. Many plants are used for human nutrition, such as **lettuce** (*Lactuca sativa*), **black salsify** (*Scorzonera hispanica*), **salsify** (*Tragopogon porrifolius*), **Jerusalem artichoke** (*Helianthus tuberosus*), and the **common sunflower** (*Helianthus annuus*); their leaves, roots, tubers, or seeds can be consumed. The fleshy receptacle of the **artichoke** (*Cynara cardunculus*) is eaten. The Jerusalem artichoke is also used for producing bioenergy and alcohol.

**Characteristics** | Milky sap is excreted from special tubes. The Jerusalem artichoke is considered an aggressive neophyte in some regions.

ASTERACEAE

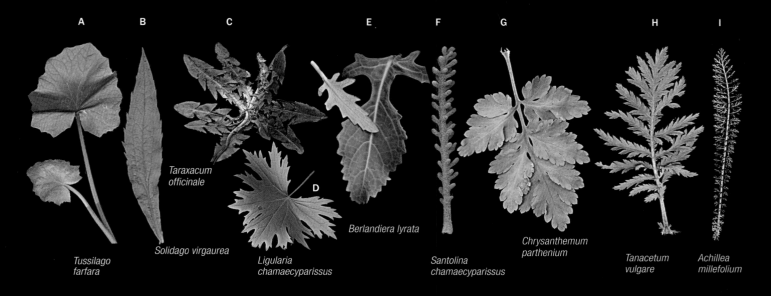

A: *Tussilago farfara*

B:

Solidago virgaurea

*Taraxacum officinale*

D

Ligularia chamaecyparissus

Berlandiera lyrata

Santolina chamaecyparissus

Chrysanthemum parthenium

Tanacetum vulgare

Achillea millefolium

**Asteraceae leaf blade.**
**A:** *Tussilago farfara*, simple and undivided. **B:** *Solidago virgaurea*, simple and undivided. **C:** *Taraxacum officinale*, undivided, runcinate. **D:** *Ligularia chamaecyparissus*, cordiform and denticulate. **E:** *Berlandiera lyrata*, pinnatipartite. **F:** *Santolina chamaecyparissus*, simple pinnate. **G:** *Chrysanthemum parthenium*, unipinnate or bipinnate. **H:** *Tanacetum vulgare*, bipinnate. **I:** *Achillea millefolium*, bipinnate.

**Variety of leaves** | The alternate, rarely opposite or spiral rosettes leaves, without stipules, of the aster family are extremely variegated. The petiolate or sessile blade can be simple and undivided (figs. A, B, D, E) or runcinate (fig. C), as well as simple to bi- or tripinnate. But it can also be disciform, in which case it then can fall off early (caducous) or can even be succulent, and thus stores water in dry habitats. The leaves are simple, and venation is pinnate or palmate; in most cases, articulated sap tubes conduct white or yellow milky sap, which can cause symptoms of poisoning in grazing animals. Alternatively, the leaves have schizogenous resin ducts, which makes them glandulous and glutinous. In addition to smooth leaf surfaces, there are also leaves with villous, woolly, or felted hairs leaves (fig. F). The hairs may also be limited to the underside of the leaf. In the thistles with usually more or less pinnatipartite leaves, the leaf margins may have pointed thorns.

BALSAMINACEAE

**A–E:** *Impatiens parviflora.* A: Flower; *above*, lateral; *left below*, frontal: male phase; *right*, next to it, frontal: female phase. B: Stamens; *left*, frontal; *center*, lateral; *far right*, from underneath. C: Gynoecium with five stigmas, frontal. D: Dissected flower; *at the very bottom*, calyx spur; *left*, frontal; *right*, lateral. E: *Left*, fruit, lateral; *right*, capsule with seeds.

**F:** *Impatiens kilimanjari. Left*, flower frontal; *right*, lateral.
**G:** *Impatiens paucidentata. Left*, flower lateral; *right*, frontal.
**H:** *Impatiens niamniamensis. Left*, flower, lateral; *right*, frontal.
**I:** *Impatiens Novette.* Leaf with extrafloral nectaries; *left*, detail.

**Genera** I 2, *Impatiens* and *Hydrocera*; species: more than 1,000
**Distribution** I Eurasia, Africa, North America
**Habitat** I Waysides, humid forests, along riverbanks
**Habits** I Herbaceous plants, at times 2 meters tall
**Leaves** I Opposite, whorled, usually no stipules
**Inflorescences** I Single, racemose
**Flowers** I Zygomorphic, hermaphroditic; three sepals, the rear one usually with a spur; five paired fused petals; five stamens, which usually form an "anther cap" over the stigma/ovary (fig. B) and, after having released the pollen, become detached with all filaments at the base. The pentacarpellate ovary has five delicate, threadlike style arms (fig. C).
**Fruits** I When touched, the fleshy capsule fruit spring open (fig. E); drupes.
**Use** I Cultivated forms of the **African impatiens** (*Impatiens walleriana*) are grown as summer flowers.
**Characteristics** I The **Himalayan balsam** (*Impatiens glandulifera*) was brought to Europe in the 19th century as a garden ornamental plant. Due in part to its high seed production (over 4,000 per plant), the exploding pods (seeds travel up to 7 meters distant), the seeds' stickiness, and their high germination capacity (80% successful), the species was able to spread widely throughout Europe and is today considered as invasive neophyte. In addition, the **small balsam** (*Impatiens parviflora*) spreads in forests. There, the plant occupies a niche that has not been occupied by any other plant in central Europe since the Ice Ages. Therefore, it is questionable whether it is among the invasive neophytes.

A B C D E F G

**A–D:** *Basella alba*. A: Inflorescence. B: Single flower, longitudinal. C: Dissected bud with still-closed stamens. D: Gynoecium with three style arms.

E: Unripe fruit; *above*, top view; *center*, longitudinal; *below*, transverse.
F: Fruiting stage.
G: *Above*, opened fruit; *bottom left*, fruit transverse.

**Genera** I 4; species: 20
**Distribution** I Pantropical, mostly in the Americas
**Habit** I Perennial herbaceous plants, climbing plants, basal stems sometimes thickened
**Leaves** I Mostly alternate, rarely opposite, undivided, often fleshy, margin mostly smooth, without stipules
**Inflorescences** I Spicate, paniculate, racemose. The usually three bracts fall off early.
**Flowers** I Radial, hermaphroditic or unisexual, two bracteoles below the flowers, hypanthium present; the two sepals may be petallike, fused at the base, also fused with the petals; position rotated 180° to the bracteoles; greenish, whitish, reddish, often becoming dark to black as the fruit ripens; (4–) 5 (–13) petals, at most basally fused, similar to sepals; (4–) 5 (–9) stamens (fig. C), at times basally fused with the petals; three fused unilocular carpels form the superior ovary with a style and always three stigmas (fig. D); a ring-shaped nectary is present.
**Fruits** I Nut fruits (fig. G) with persistent perianth
**Use** I The leaves of **Malabar spinach** (*Basella alba*) are edible and are eaten in the tropics as vegetables; cooked, they are a bit slimy. The red juice of the fruit is used as ink and a dye in China. The **Madeira vine** or **mignonette vine** (*Anredera cordifolia*), which originated in South and Central America, is eaten as a tuber and leafy vegetable and is an ornamental plant. The **ulluco** (*Ullucus tuberosus*) is an important food plant in South America; the tubers are eaten in many ways (raw, cooked, roasted) and when dried will keep a very long time.

# BEGONIACEAE

**A–C:** *Begonia pavonina*. A: Female flower, frontal; *right*, lateral. B: Gynoecium; *above*, transverse; *below*, longitudinal. C: Male flower.

**D–E:** *Begonia rex*. D: Male flower, frontal; *beneath*, female flower, longitudinal. E: Gynoecieum, lateral; *below*, ovary, transverse.

**F–J:** *Begonia felicifolia*. F: *Above*, male flower; *beneath*, female flower. G: Female flower, lateral. H: Ovary; *above*, longitudinal; *below*, transverse. I: Androecium, lateral. J: Stigmas, frontal.

**K–O:** *Begonia boliviensis*. K: Flower; *left*, male; *right*, female. L: Androecium, lateral. M: Gynoecium. N: Female flower, longitudinal; detail: stigmas. O: Ovary; *left*, transverse; *right*, longitudinal.

**Genera** | 2, *Begonia* and *Hillebrandia*; species: 1,400–1,500

**Distribution** | Tropics and subtropics, mostly in South America

**Habitat** | In humid undergrowth, on roadsides, also in sunny areas

**Habit** | Mostly perennial herbaceous plants with rhizomes and tubers, shrubs, half shrubs, also succulents, rarely a root climber

**Leaves** | Alternate, spiral arrangement, distichous, basal rosettes; leaf blade usually simple, hairy, or glabrous; petiolate, stipules present

**Inflorescences** | Cymes, dichotomous, with bracts

**Flowers** | Radial, zygomorphic, monoecious, diclinous, only one type of involucral bracts, 2-4-5-10 involucral bracts. Male flowers: often 2–4 involucral bracts (figs. C, D); many stamens, sometimes basally fused. Female flowers: 2–5 (–10) involucral bracts (figs. A, K), (1–) 3 (–8) carpels are fused to an inferior ovary that often has triangular wings (figs. B, M); 15–50 ovules per locule, staminodes may be present, usually a short style with very differently structured style arms.

**Fruits** | Loculicidal capsule fruit, rarely berrylike

**Use** | There are many varieties of the **South African wild begonia** (*Begonia dregei*) that are cultivated as ornamental plants. The **painted-leaf begonia** (*Begonia rex*) is often easy to propagate from pieces of the leaves. The succulent *Begonia cucullata*, originating from South America, is used as a pot or indoor plant in cooler regions, and as an outdoor and balcony plant in warmer regions. Begonia hybrids with double flowers are popular.

**Characteristics** | Asymmetrical leaves with sometimes conspicuous markings; the leaf structure and stigma forms are characteristic of each species. In the tropical forests the begonia species usually have only a narrowly limited distribution area. A problem for the survival of the species (such as *B. octopetala*) is the ongoing destruction of rainforests. Only one species within the family does not belong to the genus *Begonia*: *Hillebrandia sandwicensis*.

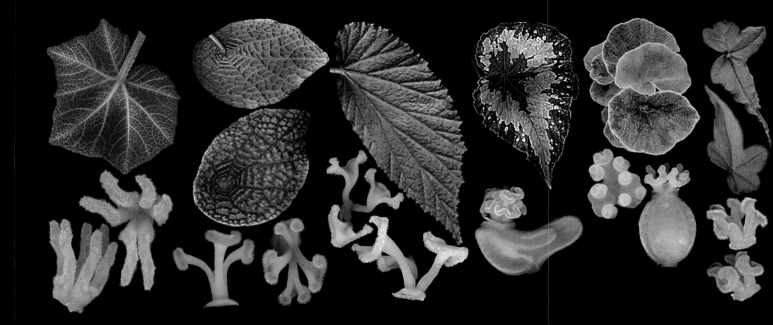

**Leaves and stigmas**

A: *B. palesta*
B: *B. felicifolia*
C: *B. malabarica*

D: *B. rex*
E: *B. venosa*
F: *B. partita*

Begonias are mainly cultivated as houseplants because of their striking, very different leaves. The asymmetric leaves and the style arms are major distinguishing characteristics within the family. On the leaves, the shape, the margin, and surface markings on the top and underside of the leaf, as well as the coloring, are all extremely variable: there are smooth, barely hairy (*B. rex*, *B. partita*) to extremely hairy leaves (*B. venosa*); leaves characterized by prominent leaf veins (*B. felicifolia*); and leaves that are green on top but have red hairs on their underside (*B. palesta*). While there are hardly any differences among the stamens in the male flowers, usually with four involucral bracts, the mostly 3 (–4) two-lobed/branched stigmas in the female flowers are attenuated with 4–5 involucral bracts (fig. B.; *B. palesta*), half round (fig. B.; *B. felicifolia*), flat and triangular (fig. B; *B. malabarica*), undulating (fig. B; *B. rex*), or more or less spiraling (fig. ; *B. venosa*, *B. partita*). Usually the stigmas are yellow in color; light green is rather rare.

BERBERIDACEAE

**A–G:** *Mahonia aquifolium*. A: Flower, frontal. B: Flower, longitudinal. C: Stamen; *left*, still closed; *right*, opened with open valves. D: Nectary leaf. E: Ovary, transverse. F: Fruiting stage. G: Fruit, transverse.

**H–M:** *Berberis julianae*. H: Flower, frontal. I: Flower, longitudinal. J: Fruit, lateral. K: Fruit, longitudinal. L: The same, transverse. M: Leaf spines.

**N–Q:** *Nandina domestica*. N: Top view of flower. O: Bud, longitudinal. P: Ovary and stamen. Q: Fruit; *left*, lateral; *center*, longitudinal; *right*, transverse. R: Seeds.

**Genera** I More than 14; species: more than 700

**Distribution** I East Asia, eastern America, mainly in the northern temperate latitudes, but also in tropical mountains (such as the Andes)

**Habit** I Shrubs with long and short shoots, some xerophytes, perennial herbaceous plants with rhizomes as overwintering organs

**Leaves** I Mostly alternate, distichous, leaves herbaceous or leathery, mostly petiolate, simple entirely or oddly pinnate (*Mahonia*), ovate to roundish, scutate, smooth leaf margin smooth, serrated, or spiny-dentate

**Inflorescences** I Racemose, paniculate, spicate, rarely single

**Flowers** I Radial, hermaphroditic (figs. A, B, H, I), mostly trimerous, double perianth, usually 3 (–4) petallike sepals; 6–12 petals in 2–4 whorls; often have nectary leaves; usually six stamens in two whorls (figs. A, C), nectaries present (fig. D); one superior carpel (figs. B, I, O, P) with many ovules. Entomophily.

**Fruits** I Follicles (*Epimedium*), berries (*Berberis*: fig. J; *Mahonia*: fig. F), rarely nutlets (*Achlys*) or capsule fruits

**Use** I The red fruits of the **common barberry** (*Berberis vulgaris*) are edible; they are used to make preserves, dried in muesli and in Persian rice dishes. The fruits have a high vitamin C content, which makes them very sour. Barberries are good bee pasture plants, and the inner bark can be used as a yellow dye. Some species are used medicinally. Many ornamental plants (such as *Mahonia aquifolium*, *Berberis darwinii*, *B. julianae*, *B. thunbergii*). The rhizomes and roots of the **mayapples** (*Podophyllum peltatum*, *P. hexandrum*) produce—in addition to other toxins—a resin (podophyllin) that has cytostatic properties and is therefore used in cancer therapy. You can rub yourself with the leaves of the **vanilla leaf** (*Achlys triphylla*), which smell of vanilla—they supposedly repel mosquitoes and other insects.

**Characteristics** I The stamens are very sensitive: in response to a tactile stimulus, they move inward toward the style and in the process press the sticky pollen onto any flower visitor (fig. C). Since barberries act as intermediate hosts for the dreaded grain black and stem rust (*Puccinia gramminis*), a fungus that infests all crop species and causes crop failures, as happened in the United States in the early 20th century, barberries were extensively eliminated from the main wheat-growing areas. All barberries produce the poisonous alkaloid berberine in the vegetative organs, and some also in the seeds. The **heavenly bamboo** (*Nandina domestica*), which originated in Asia, is considered an invasive plant in the US.

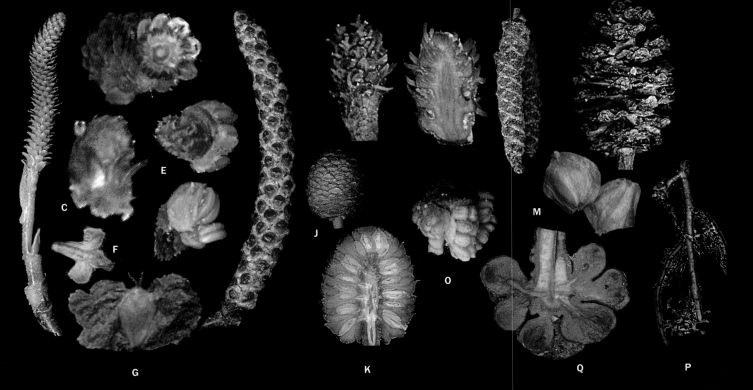

**A–G:** *Betula pendula.* A: Female inflorescence. B: The same, transverse. C: Bract of the female inflorescence with four flowers. D: Male inflorescence. E: *Above*, single male flower lateral; *underneath*, top view. F: Fruit scale. G: Seeds.

**H–Q:** *Alnus glutinosa.* H: Female inflorescence. I: The same, longitudinal. J: Unripe female cone. K: The same, longitudinal. L: Ripe cone. M: Seeds. N: Male inflorescence. O: Single male flower. P: Piece of root with root tuber. Q: Root tuber, longitudinal.

**BETULACEAE/BETULOIDEAE**

**Genera** | 6; species: about 110–200. Alders (*Alnus*), birches (*Betula*), hazelnuts (*Corylus*), hornbeams (*Carpinus*), American hop hornbeam (*Ostrya*), and hazel-hornbeam (*Ostryopsis*).

**Distribution** | Northern Hemisphere, temperate regions, mountainous regions in the tropics

**Habitat** | Alders often grow in boggy areas or along the banks, birches often in sandy soils.

**Habit** | Trees, shrubs

**Leaves** | Alternate, spiral, bifarious-trifarious, leaf blade simple, margin serrate, denticulate to almost smooth, petiolate, stipules usually fall off early.

**Inflorescences** | Catkins, cones

**Flowers** | Diclinous, monoecious, male flowers in hanging catkins (figs. D, N), stamens often cleft, female flowers in catkin-like ears (fig. A) or cone-like inflorescences (figs. H–K); two carpels fused into an inferior bilocular ovary with 1–2 ovules. Wind pollination.

**Fruits** | Nuts, naked or covered with a shell. Alternatively, they sit in the axil of scales that resulted from the fusing of the bracts and the prophylls (fig. L); also winged (figs. G, M).

**Use** | The bark of **birch** species is used for tanning (Russia leather) or to extract tar (*Oleum Betulae empyreumaticum*); birch branches are also tied together to make brooms.

**Characteristics** | Predominantly wind pollinated. Due to their high pollen production, hazel, alder, and birch trees are significant hay fever allergens. In the nodules that form in the alder's (*Alnus glutinosa*) root zone live atmospheric-nitrogen-binding bacteria (*Frankia alnii*; fig. Q). Due to their good nitrogen supply, in the autumn **alder** trees do not have to move the nitrogen from their leaves for reuse in the trunk and therefore do not display any autumn colors. The wood can be used to make furniture. The leaves and the bark, combined with iron ions, can be used to make a black ink.

71

BETULACEAE/CORYLOIDEAE

**A–G:** *Corylus avellana.* A: Young plant growing from attached nut. B: Leaf underside. C: Young fruiting stage. D: Ripe nut; *above left,* from underneath; *right,* next to it, lateral; *left below,* opened; *right,* next to it, seeds longitudinal. E: Male inflorescence. F: Male flower; *above,* frontal; *left,* from beneath; *right,* next to it, from above. G: Female inflorescence; *left,* lateral; *center,* longitudinal; *right,* dissected flowers; *far right,* single flower.

**H–N:** *Carpinus betulus.* H: Unfurling leaf with buds. I: Male inflorescence. J: Male flower; *left,* from beneath; *right,* next to it, frontal. K: Female inflorescence. L: Female single flower. M: Old single flower without bract. N: Fruit on bract with wingnuts or samara for flying.

**Genera** I 4, hornbeams (*Carpinus*), hazel (*Corylus*), American hop hornbeam (*Ostrya*), and *Ostryopsis*; species: about 50

**Distribution** I Temperate zones of the Northern Hemisphere, southeastern Europe, West Asia

**Habitat** I Basins, also soils with good groundwater access, deciduous forests, brushwood, hedgerows

**Habit** I Deciduous trees, shrubs

**Leaves** I Distichous, alternate, simple, stipules lanceolate to a point or caducuous, leaf margins (double) serrated to denticulate (figs. B, H).

**Inflorescences** I Catkins, cones; *Carpinus* has female flowers in dichasia.

**Flowers** I Diclinous, monoecious, male flowers usually in hanging catkins (figs. E, I), female flowers in catkin-like ears or small cones, the female cones of the hazel (*Corylus*) remain surrounded by bud scales, with only the style arms protruding (fig. G). Wind pollinated.

**Fruits** I Nut fruits, enclosed in a pericarp of three fused bracteoles or bracts. In the hornbeam (*Carpinus betulus*), this serves as wings, to allow flight.

**Use** I The nut fruits of the **common hazel** (*Corylus avellana*) and also the **Turkish hazel** (*Corylus colurna*) both are eaten raw and processed to make desserts; the oil is also harvested. The Turkish hazel (*Corylus colurna*) is also planted as a roadside and park tree; the **American hop hornbeam**

(*Ostrya carpinifolia*), as an ornamental plant. **Notes** I The Corylaceae are at times still treated as a separate family but primarily are included as the Coryloideae subfamily of the Betulaceae (birches).

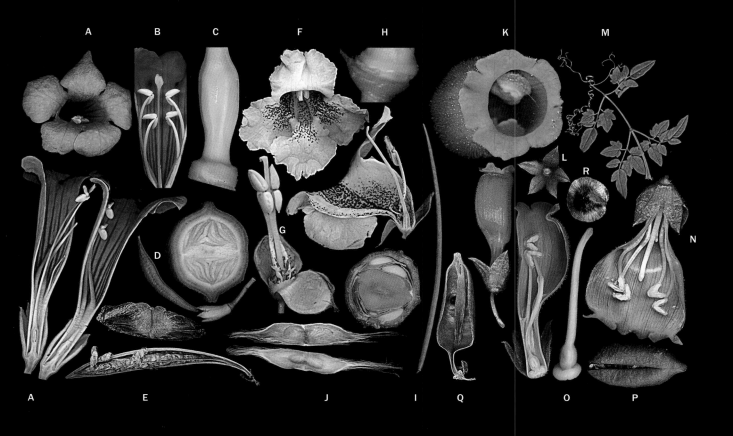

**A–E:** *Campsis radicans.* A: *Above,* flower frontal; *below,* lateral. B: From a bud; stamens and style/stigma. C: Gynoecium, *below,* with nectary. D: Unripe fruit; *left,* lateral; *right,* transverse. E: *Above,* winged seed; *below,* fruit lateral.

**F–J:** *Catalpa speciosa.* F: *Above,* flower frontal; *below,* lateral. G: Stamens and style/stigma. H: Lower part of the gynoecium, with nectary. I: Unripe fruit, lateral. J: The same; *right,* transverse; *left,* unripe seeds with flying hairs.

**K–R:** *Eccremocarpus scaber.* K: *Above,* flower, frontal; *below,* lateral. L: Calyx. M: Leaf with tendrils. N: Unfurled flower. O: *Left,* flower, longitudinal; *right,* gynoecium, with nectary. P: Fruit. Q: The same, lateral. R: Seeds.

**Genera** | 110; species: about 800
**Distribution** | Worldwide in the tropics
**Habit** | Mostly trees, lianas; also perennial herbaceous plants
**Leaves** | Opposite, leaf blade simple, up to fourfold pinnate, often glands or tendrils on the basal petiole
**Inflorescences** | Panicles, cymes, also cauliflory, usually descending-valvate bud position
**Flowers** | Zygomorphic, pentamerous, the 2–5-lobed calyx is usually basally fused, also bilabiate; corolla campanulate to funnel form; usually 4 (–5) stamens; can be two plus two staminodes or four plus one staminodes; both thecas can also spread apart; the bicarpellate, usually bilocular superior ovary, is basally enveloped by a nectary-ring protuberance; the style usually supports a bilobate stigma, which may have a delicately pronounced leaf shape. The flowers are pollinated by insects, bats, or birds.
**Fruits** | Capsule, mostly loculicidal or septifragal; the usually flat seeds are often winged, sometimes with a tuft of hair or wing membrane. Most are anemochores, also hydrochores and zoochores.
**Use** | Ornamental plants, such as **hardy gloxina** (*Incarvillea delvayi*), **trumpet vine** (*Campsis radicans*), **Chilean glory flower** (*Eccremocarpus scaber*), or the **southern catalpa** and **northern catalpa** (*Catalpa bignonioides, C. speciosa*), are planted as park or roadside trees. They are considered to be slightly toxic. In tropical and subtropical regions, the **jacaranda** (*Jacaranda mimosifolia*) is planted as a roadside tree because of its flowers. The **sausage tree** (*Kigela africana*) is also cultivated as an ornamental plant. Its long, hanging, sausage-like fruits are used in traditional medicine in Africa. The hard-shelled capsule fruits of the **calabash tree** (*Crescentia cujete*) are used to make jars and the famous rumba shakers. The relatively soft wood of the **African tulip tree** (*Spathodea campanulata*) is used for cabinetmaking. The hard and durable ipé wood of *Handanthus heterophyllus* (formerly *Tabebuia*) is used in many ways.
**Characteristics** | Pinnately leaved species often with leaf tendrils, also disc-like holdfast tendrils. Glandular hairs or glandular scales occur. The large flowers have a tubular corolla that opens wide; thus, like a trumpet.

# BIXACEAE

A–F: *Cochlospermum vitifolium*. A: Flower, frontal. B: The same, from below. C: Ovary, transverse. D: Flower, longitudinal, involucral bracts removed. E: Stamen, with opening pore. F: Ovary, lateral.

**Genera** | 4; species: more than 20

**Distribution** | Pantropical

**Habit** | Shrubby, rarely herbaceous

**Leaves** | Alternate, spiral; leaf blade simple, lobed; leaf margin smooth or denticulate, also hairy, such as stellate hairs; more or less long stalked; stipules present

**Inflorescences** | Single, paniculate, cymose

**Flowers** | Radial, rarely zygomorphic; the five sepals usually fall off early, mostly five free petals; (3–) 50–150 free stamens, often open by means of apical pores or clefts (fig. E); 2–5 (–10) carpels are fused to a superior, often-hairy ovary (figs. C, F); one more or less long style supports one small apical stigma.

**Fruits** | 2–5 valved capsules, also spiny

**Use** | Ornamental shrubs, such as the **buttercup tree** (*Cochlospermum vitifolium*), also called "wild cotton," because the seed hairs can be used to fill pillows or mattresses. The roots of *C. tinctorium* are used in traditional West African medicine for liver disease, and root or leaf extracts are administered against malaria. The roots of various "snail shell" species (*Cochleospermum*) contain carotenoids and are used as yellow dyes. The bark fibers are sometimes used to make ropes. The annatto colorant from the seed shells of the **achiote** (*Bixa orellana*) are used as a coloring for food (E160b) and lipstick; hence the common name "lipstick tree." The indigenous inhabitants of Brazil use the coloring to protect themselves from sunlight or insects.

**Characteristics** | Many parts of the plant contain a red or yellow milky sap. The former Cochlospermaceae family has been transferred to the Bixaceae family.

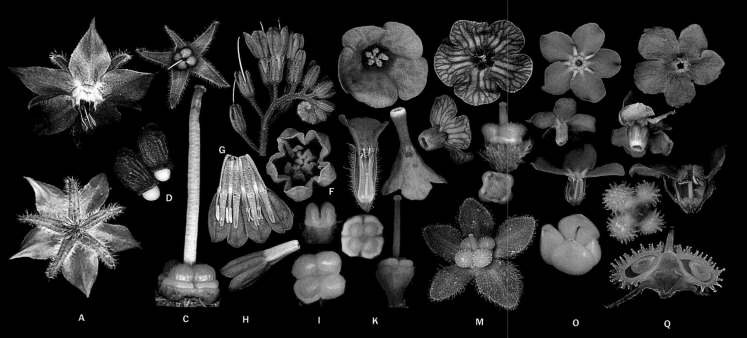

**A–D:** *Borago officinalis.* A: Flower from the front/below. B: Calyx/gynoecium. C: Gynoecium/nectary, lateral. D: Seeds with white fruit particles. **E–I:** *Symphytum azureum*; inflorescence, lateral. F: Flower, frontal. G: dissected corolla, with stamens and corolla throat scales. H: Corolla. I: Ovary, style/stigma removed; *left*, nectary.

**J–K:** *Pulmonaria mollis.* J: *Above*, flower, frontal; *below left*, lateral; *right*, corolla. K: *Above*, ovary/nectary, frontal; *right*, gynoecium lateral. **L–M:** *Cynoglossum creticum*; L: *Above*, flower, frontal; *below left*, corolla; *right*, gynoecium/nectary, lateral. M: *Above*, nectary; *below*, calyx/gynoecium.

**N–O:** *Myosotis sylvatica.* N: *Above*, flower, frontal; *below*, lateral; *center*, corolla. O: Mericarps.
**P–Q:** *Lappula echinata.* P: *Above*, flower, frontal; *below*, *longitudinal*; *center*, corolla. Q: *Above*, gynoecium, frontal; *below*, longitudinal.

**Genera** | 145; species: over 2,700
**Distribution** | Worldwide; concentration: Mediterranean region
**Habit** | Rarely are trees and shrubs; usually annual, biennial, or perennial herbaceous plants
**Leaves** | Alternate, without stipules, usually with stiff hairs (hence the German name, Raublattgewächse, or bristle-leaf family!); also leaf rosettes
**Inflorescences** | Scorpiod cymes, also cochleate (fig. E)
**Flowers** | Radial to slightly zygomorphic, hermaphroditic, pentamerous; five sepals free or fused at the base, often of unequal size. The corolla tube, fused from five petals, has invaginations that, as scales in the corolla throat, are also set apart visually from the mostly blue-colored petals (figs. G; N, *above*; P, *above*). Five stamens, often with basal appendages (fig. A, *above*). The bicarpellate fused ovary is superior; it is articulated by a false septum into four valves, in the middle of which the style stands, often surrounded by a nectar-producing glandular ring (fig. K).
**Fruits** | Four separate nutlets
**Use** | Ornamental plants: **Lungworts** (*Pulmonaria* sp.), **forget-me-nots** (*Myosotis* sp.), **comfrey** (*Symphytum* sp.), **hound's tongue** (*Cynoglossum* sp.), **borage** (*Borago officinalis*), the leaves and flowers of which are often used as a kitchen herb. Red dye extracted from the roots of the **dyer's alkanet** (*Alkanna tinctoria*) is used to dye wood, marble, medicines, wine, and cosmetics. The honeyworts are good plants for feeding bees (such as the **wax plant**, *Cerinthe major*).
**Characteristics** | Most of these plants contain liver-damaging pyrrolizidine alkaloids. Therefore, eating borage leaves ("cucumber herb") is not recommended. Some anthocyanin-containing flowers change their flower color during the course of anthesis: first red (acid), later blue violet (alkaline). This is caused by a change in the pH value in the cell sap (as in "red cabbage" and "blue cabbage"). The corolla throat scales in the flowers block free access to the nectar, so that anyone who is not a potential pollinator is unable to steal the nectar.

75

**A:** *Cardamine pratensis*. *Left*, flower, frontal; *right*, bud, lateral.
**B:** *Lunaria annua*. *From left*: ovary; petal, longitudinal; petal, sepal; the same, with outgrowth; silicula, lateral; replum, with two seeds.
**C:** *Iberis sempervirens*. *Above left*, inflorescence, frontal, with enlarged ray flowers; *right*, ovary, lateral; *underneath*, ray flower, frontal.
**D:** *Bunias orientalis*. *Above*, flower from beneath; *below*, ovary; *left*, longitudinal; *right*, lateral.
**E:** *Biscutella laevigata*. *Above*, flower, lateral; *below*, silicula.
**F:** *Thlaspi arvense*. *Left*, silicula, lateral; *right*, opened, with replum and seeds at left.

**G:** *Capsella bursapastoris*. *Above*, unripe silicula, lateral; *below*, silicula, with replum.
**H:** *Isatis tinctoria*. *Left*, fruit, lateral; *right*, longitudinal.
**I:** *Erysimum cheiri*. *Left*, pod, longitudinal; *right*, lateral.
**J:** *Raphanus sativus silique*. *Left*, longitudinal; *center*, lateral; *right*, transverse.

**Genera** | More than 330; species: more than 3,700
**Distribution** | Worldwide, temperate regions, also the Arctic
**Habitat** | Worldwide, temperate regions, also the Arctic
**Habit** | Half shrubs, mostly herbaceous plants, annuals to perennials, rarely succulents
**Leaves** | Alternate; in older plants without stipules, simple, pinnate, digitate, pinnatipartite, sinuate
**Inflorescences** | Racemose, double racemose, corymbose, mostly without bracts
**Flowers** | Bilateral, the ray flowers of the corymb are often enlarged to enhance the visual attraction (fig. C), then zygomorphic, hermaphroditice, tetramerous; two plus two sepals, the two outer sometimes enlarged (figs. A, B, E); four free petals, usually shaped like a plate or nail (unguiculate; fig. B, *center*); two short plus four long free stamens, which have nectar glands at the base in various arrangements; the bicarpellate fused ovary is superior; one style usually with capitate stigma, often remaining on the fruit as a beak.
**Fruits** | Pods (three times as long as they are wide) and silicula with replum and false septum (fig. B, *right*), sometimes articulated (fig. J)
**Use** | Vegetable and fodder crops: **cabbages** (*Brassica oleracea* ssp.), **oil seed rape** (*B. napus*), **radishes** (*Raphanus sativus* var. Sativus), **horseradish** (*Armoratia rusticana*), **arugula** (*Eruca vesicaria* ssp. Sativa), **sea kale** (*Crambe maritima*). Oil and spice plants: **mustard** (*Sinapis* sp.), **garden cress** (*Lepidium* sp.). Ornamental plants: **annual honesty** (*Lunaria annua*), **evergreen candytuft** (*Iberis sempervirens*), **common wallflower** (*Erysimum cheiri*), **stock** (*Matthiola incana*), and **purple rock cress** (*Aubrieta* × *cultorum*).
**Characteristics** | The enzyme myrsinase serves as a defense against herbivores. It splits the mustard oil glycosides typical of cruciferous plants into aggressively strong mustard oil and glucose. In the intact plant, both these substances are safely stored separately. If the plant is injured, such as when an animal tries to graze on it, the spicy mustard oil is released. The **true rose of Jericho** (*Anastatica hirochuntica*) is one of the so-called "resurrection" plants. This annual herbaceous plant bends its sprouts inward after they dry out, also enclosing the seeds. Like "tumbleweeds," the plants tumble along over the land during storms and gradually release the seeds. After moisture returns, the branches unroll again. This process is reversible. The resurrection fern, *Selaginella hierochuntica*, is often sold as the "rose of Jericho" in the trade or at Christmas markets. The **European sea rocket** (*Cakile maritima*) can grow in saline habitats (*optional halophyte*). The leaves can be eaten a salad. **Thale cress** (*Arabidopsis thaliana*) is used in genetics as a model organism.

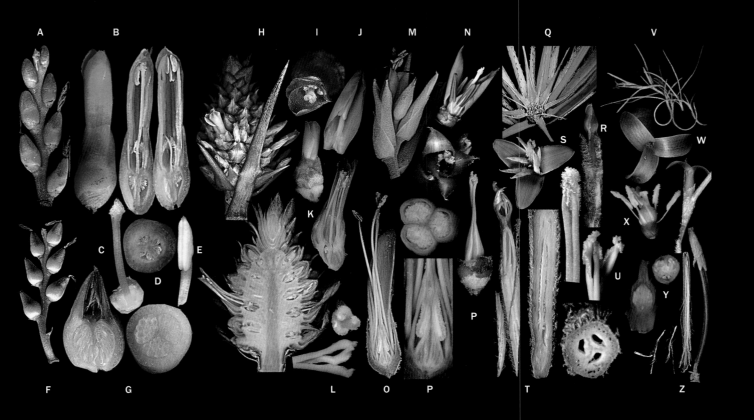

**A–G:** *Aechmea penduliflora*. A: Partial inflorescence. B: *Left*, flower, lateral; *right*, longitudinal. C: Style. D: Ovary, transverse. E: Stamen. F: Fruiting stage. G: Fruit; *left*, longitudinal; *right*, transverse.

**H–L:** *Ananas comosus*. H: Inflorescence, lateral; *below*, longitudinal. I: Flower, frontal; *below*, lateral. J: Petal with ligule. K: Flower, longitudinal. L: Stigma, frontal;

*below*, lateral.

**M–P:** *Puya floccosa*. M: Partial inflorescence, lateral. N: *Above*, open bud; *below*, flower, frontal. O: Flower, longitudinal. P: Gynoecium; *above*, transverse; *below*, longitudinal; *right*, lateral.

**Q–U:** *Bromelia karatas*. Q: Inflorescence. R: Bud, lateral. S: Flower, frontal. T: *Left*, flower, longitudinal; *center*,

ovary; *right*, nectary. U: Stigmas; *left*, lateral; *right*, splayed out.

**V–Z:** *Tillandsia usneoides*. V: Plant part, with flower. W: Flower, frontal; *right*, lateral. X: Androecium, lateral. Y: Ovary; *left*, longitudinal; *right*, transverse. Z: *Right*, fruit; *center*, longitudinal; *left*, seeds.

---

**Subfamilies** | Bromelioideae, Tillandsioideae, Pitcairnioideae
**Genera** | about 60; species: about 3,000. Well-known genera: *Pineapple*, *Aechmea*, *Billbergia*, *Bromelia*, *Tillandsia*, *Puya*, *Vrisea*.
**Distribution** | Neotropical
**Habit** | Usually xerophytes, succulents, epiphytes, lithophytes, terrestrial species; rarely deciduous, perennial herbaceous plants; rarely hapaxanthic; grows layers that generate vegetative propagation
**Leaves** | Alternate, spiral, rarely distichous, predominantly evergreen, often rosulate with compressed stems, mostly with leaf sheath, rarely petiolate. In the epiphytes, the rosettes grow as an external water reservoir

("water tank plants"), since the roots are predominantly a holdfast. The plant absorbs water through special suction scales on the water tank leaves and through adventitious roots. Leaf blade: linear, ligulate to triangular; parallel venation, leaf margin also with spines.
**Inflorescences** | Terminal or lateral, spicate or racemose (figs. A, H, M, Q); rarely single flowers (fig. V)
**Flowers** | Radial (fig. S), hermaphroditic, rarely unisexual, small, enveloped by intensely colored bracts (fig. Q), which attract birds and more rarely bats or butterflies. Three sepals, basally fused, three petals, mostly free; two whorls of three stamens (fig. X); ovary of three fused carpels, seldom superior, mostly half inferior or inferior

(figs. D, G, P, T); septal nectaries; one style with three style arms. The structure of the stigma (figs. C, L, U) varies widely.
**Fruits** | Capsules (fig. Z) from superior ovaries, berries from inferior ovaries, multiple fruits. The small seeds of the capsule fruits often grow characteristic appendages to allow wind propagation.
**Use** | In the **pineapple** (*Ananas comosus*), the entire inflorescence becomes fleshy (fig. H, *below*), so that this is where the multiple fruits grow. They are cultivated especially because of their vitamin C content. In the Philippines, people extract tear-resistant fibers from the leaves, which are made into textiles called piña fabric. **Spanish moss** (*Tillandsia*

*usneoides*) was formerly used as packaging material.
**Characteristics** | The family name goes back to the Swedish physician and botanist Olof Bromelius (1639–1705). The bromeliad epiphytes develop special communities of species (so-called phytotelmata) in the water-filled cavities in their "water tank leaves." Animals and aquatic plants live on the nutrients in the water-filled cavities, which are generated by decomposing fallen leaves and dead animals. The gray color of many species of *Tillandsia* is due to their shield hairs, which have been converted into water-absorbing suction scales.

## BUTOMACEAE

**FLOWERING RUSH FAMILY**
**Order: Alismatales—Arrowheads**

C

**A–E:** *Butomus umbellatus.* A: Umbellate inflorescence with upper part of a leaf, lateral. B: Inflorescence, frontal. C: Leaf, transverse. D: *Above*, flower, lateral/frontal; *below*, from underneath. E: Gynoecium; *above left*, lateral; *right*, next to it, transverse; *below left*, single carpel; *center*, frontal, with style arms; *right*, longitudinal.

**Genus** I 1; species: only one: *Butomus umbellatus*
**Distribution** I Habitat in temperate Eurasia and North Africa, naturalized in North America
**Habit** I Perennial herbaceous plant, rhizome-forming water and marsh plant
**Leaves** I Up to 1 meter long in basal rosettes, leaf blade grasslike, grooved, triangular (fig. C), submerged leaves ligulate, leaves with aerenchyma (fig. C)

**Inflorescences** I Cymes with up to 30 single flowers (figs. A, B)
**Flowers** I Radial, hermaphroditic, two perigone whorls of three tepals each (fig. D); the two whorls may have similar or different structures. The flower is green to white, or pink to purple to brownish colored, proterandrous; six plus three stamens (fig. D); six free, superior carpels (fig. E) with yellowish stigmas and laminar placentation (fig. E, *above right*); nectary at the base of the carpels (fig.

E, *above left*: drops of nectar); entomophily.
**Fruits** I Follicle fruits that grow on elongated pedicels. This arrangement lets the wind disperse the seeds better (= wind dispersal). They are then spread farther by water (= hydrochory).
**Use** I The starchy rhizomes are processed into flour or bread in parts of Russia. The stalks can be woven into mats, for instance.
**Characteristics** I The German name,

**Schwanenblumengewächse** (swan flower family), comes from the elongated style, shaped like a swan's neck (fig. E). The plant grows in shoreline reed beds along still and slowly flowing waters. In central Europe it has become rare in places; in North America, where it was introduced as an ornamental plant, it is now considered an invasive neophyte. The plant contains a clear, milky sap.

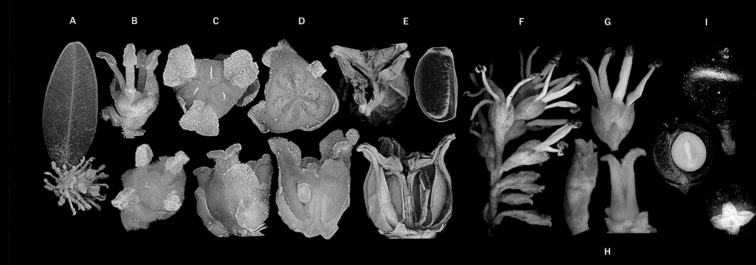

A B C D E F G I

H

**A–E:** *Buxus sempervirens*. A: Leaf and partial inflorescence, frontal. B: Male flower; *above*, lateral; *left below,* frontal. C: Female flower; *above*, frontal, with nectar drops; *below*, lateral. D: Female blossoms; *above*, transverse; *below*, longitudinal. E: *Above*, ripe fruit, frontal; *right*, seeds; *below*, ripe fruit, longitudinal.

**F–I:** *Sarcococca hookeriana*. F: Partial inflorescence. G: Male flower, lateral. H: Female flower; *left*, lateral; *right*, with husk removed: gynoecium. I: Ripe berry; *above*, lateral; *center*, longitudinal; *below*, from underneath.

**Genera** I about 4; species: more than 100

**Distribution** I Worldwide, but disjointed, from the temperate zones to the tropics. Eurasia, central and South Africa, North and Central America; main focus in East Asia

**Habit** I Trees, shrubs, half shrubs, herbaceous plants

**Leaves** I Alternate or opposite, evergreen, leaf blade leathery, ovate, entire, leaf margins smooth or denticulate

**Inflorescences** I Mostly racemose (such as *Buxus* with female terminal flowers and lateral male flowers; fig. A), or spicate in *Pachysandra* and some *Sarcococca* species (with male flowers at the top and female in the lower part of the inflorescence; fig. F); rarely solitary or in a thyrse

**Flowers** I ± radial, unisexual, mostly monoecious, rarely dioecious arrangement, small inconspicuous flowers, male flowers mostly with four involucral bracts and usually 4–6 stamens (figs. A, B, F, G), nectary in the center; female flowers (figs. A, C, F, H) with six spirally arranged involucral bracts and three carpels fused to a superior ovary (figs. C, D)

**Fruits** I Capsule (fig. E) or berries (fig. I)

**Use** I Ornamental plants: While **boxwood** (*Buxus*) and its varieties are planted in cottage gardens, borders, and hedges; **carpet box** (*Pachysandra* sp.) is planted as a ground cover; and **sweet box** (*Sarcococca* sp.) for its early fragrant flowers. Boxwood grows very slowly and the wood becomes extremely hard. It is used for lathing and, for example, to make woodwind instruments or violins. The toxic substances that boxwood contains are at times still used in homeopathy to treat rheumatism.

**Characteristics** I The plants form toxic alkaloid substances. Due to its early blooming period (March–April), wild bees and honeybees gladly fly into the pollen- and nectar-rich flowers of the **common boxwood** (*Buxus sempervirens*). Boxwoods are attacked by various fungal diseases, resulting in dieback, box fusaria, and boxwood blight.

A–F: *Cabomba aquatica*. A: Plant part with dichotomous leaves; *above*, shoot tip, frontal. B: Flower, frontal. C: Petal; the auricle on the base functions as a nectary. D: Young flower, husk removed. E: Ovary, transverse. F: Flower, longitudinal.

**Genera** | 2: *Cabomba* (5 species), *Brasenia* (1 species)

**Distribution** | Tropical to temperate America. Naturalized in Africa, East Asia, Europe, Australia.

**Habit** | Perennial, herbaceous aquatic plants that grow branched rhizomes on the bottom of a body of water

**Leaves** | Alternate, spiral, distichous or tetramerous, or opposite, either only floating leaves (*Brasenia*) or floating and differently structured underwater leaves (heterophyllous leaves in *Cabomba*). Leaf blade of the floating leaves entire, peltate. Leaf blade of underwater leaves divided, palmate with 5–7 incisions, which in turn are subdivided in forks into numerous linear segments (fig. A). Stipules are absent.

**Inflorescences** | Lateral between the nodes; solitary

**Flowers** | Hermaphroditic; more or less long pedicels position the blossoms on or above the water surface (entomophily in *Cabomba*, anemophily in *Brasenia*); perianth spiral arrangement or arranged in two whorls (fig. B), trimerous; three sepals, petaloid, free; three petals, yellow, purple, or white, with inwardly projecting "ears" (auricles) that function as nectaries (fig. C); 3–6 (*Cabomba*; fig. D), 12–18 (or more: *Brasenia*) stamens, free; ovary superior (fig. E); free carpels

**Fruits** | 4–7 mm long follicular fruits with leathery pericarp, which may also be combined into aggregate fruits

**Use** | Because of its submerged dichotomous leaves and high oxygen production, the **Carolina fanwort** (*Cabomba caroliniana*) is often used as an aquarium plant. Beginning with aquarium plants released into nature, it has been spreading worldwide as an invasive neophyte. In Australia, these plants clog water pipes, for example. It has now arrived in China and India, but also in Germany, Sweden, and other European countries. The leaf buds of the **watershield** (*Brasenia schreberi*) are eaten pickled or raw in China, and in Japan as salad. Flour is extracted from the rhizomes; they are also eaten cooked.

**Characteristics** | The submerged plant parts are covered with a gelatinous mucus.

**A–D:** *Pereskia saccharosa*. A: Flower on foliate branch. B: Flower from underneath. C: The same, longitudinal; *below*, detail: ovary, longitudinal. D: Sprout tip, lateral.
**E–H:** *Opuntia ficus-indica*. E: Sprout with flowers and buds. F: Flower, lateral. G: The same, longitudinal. H: Style arms.

**I–K:** *Rhipsalis* **sp**. I: Branch with flowers. J: Flower, longitudinal. K: Style arms.
**L–M:** *Rhipsalis mesembryanthemoides*. L: Sprout with flower, lateral. M: Berry; *left*, lateral; *above*, transverse; *below*, longitudinal.

**O–R:** *Mammilaria* **sp**. O: Habit, frontal. P: Flower, lateral, with mamilla; *below*, longitudinal. Q: Ovary, transverse. R: Style arms.

**Genera** | 110; species: about 1,500
**Distribution** | Deserts and semideserts of the US, Mexico, Andean countries; one species in Africa
**Habit** | Most are stem succulents, up to several meters tall; xerophytic trees, shrubs, dwarf shrubs
**Leaves** | Reduced to spines, supported on areoles, only *Pereskia* has "normal foliage leaves" (fig. A). Glochids (tufts with short spiny hairs) may also be present.
**Flowers** | Usually grow from the areoles, radial, predominantly hermaphroditic, large, rarely slightly zygomorphic, husk is multipetaled, helical, spiral, flowers of all colors except for blue; numerous stamens and carpels; the unchambered ovary with parietal ovules is inferior; style simple (figs. J, P), and there may be 3–5–7 or many mostly papillose style arms present (figs. R, K, H); can have disciform and thread-like stigmas.
**Fruits** | Many-seeded berries (fig. M)
**Use** | The fruits of some cacti are edible: **dragon fruit** (*Hylocereus undatus*), **pitahaya** (*Hylocereus monacanthus*), and the **prickly pear cactus** (*Opuntia ficus-indica*).
**Characteristics** | The plants form water-soluble betalains as flower and fruit pigmentation. The **queen of the night** (*Selenicereus grandiflorus*) produces heart-stimulating substances that have an effect similar to that of digitalis. The **peyote** (*Lophophora willamsii*) produces a variety of different alkaloids in its natural habitats as a defense against herbivores; these include mescaline, a psychoactive hallucinogenic substance. Cochineal insects (*Dactylopius coccus*) live on the **prickly pear cactus** (*Opuntia ficus-indica*) in the Americas. The red dye, carmine, produced by the females is bitter and serves as a defense against herbivores. The indigenous population used the dye on clothing and other textiles. It is approved as a food coloring (E120) but is also produced synthetically (cochenille red A E124). Prickly pear cacti were often planted as living fences (such as in Australia) and today are feared as invasive neophytes in many places. With few exceptions, almost all cacti are listed in appendix I of the Washington Convention on International Trade in Endangered Species of Wild Fauna and Flora. Cacti do not have thorns, but rather spines that grow by modification of their leaves.

A–E: *Calceolaria biflora*. A: Partial inflorescence. B: Flower, frontal. C: Young flower dissected; stigma and two stamens visible. D: Solitary stamen. E: Ovary, transverse.

F–K: *Calceolaria paralia*. F: Habit. G: Calyx. H: Ovary with capitate glandular hairs. I: The same, transverse. J: Flower, longitudinal. K: Stamen.

**Genera** I 2: *Calceolaria*, *Jovellana*; species: about 275

**Distribution** I Neotropical, North Island of New Zealand

**Habit** I Rarely shrubs, usually herbaceous

**Leaves** I Opposite, simple, leaf margin smooth or denticulate

**Inflorescences** I Dichasias

**Flowers** I Zygomorphic, hermaphroditic, tetramerous, four sepals (fig. G), of various sizes, also in two whorls; the fused corolla is "slipper shaped" (fig. B), bilabiate (the opening is referred to as the "mouth"), two stamens with splayed anthers (figs. C, D). The bicarpellate ovary is half inferior, and the carpels are of different sizes (fig. E, I); instead of nectar, flower excretes pollen and oil from oil-gland hairs, which cover the ovary (fig. H); one style with a capitate stigma.

**Fruits** I Capsule fruit

**Use** I Ornamental plants

**Characteristics** I In their origin habitats, the slipper flower blossoms are pollinated by oil-collecting bees of the genera *Centris* and *Chalepogenus*. Outside their natural distribution area, the flowers are visited by vigorous bumblebees when the "mouth" is closed; if it is open, other bees can also penetrate into the flowers.

**Notes** I The genera formerly belonged to the figworts (Scrophulariaceae) but were put into a separate family by Richard G. Olmstead by 2001.

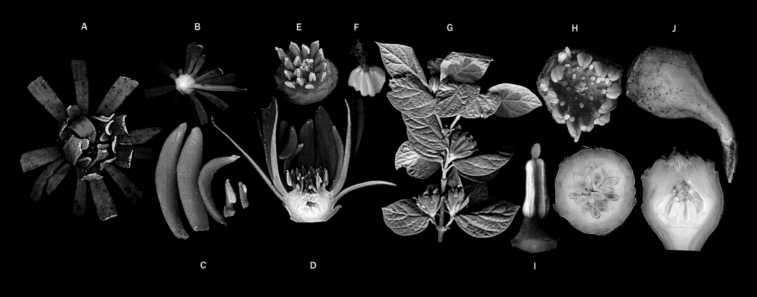

A–J: *Calycanthus fertilis*. A: Flower, frontal. B: The same from beneath. C: Transition from stamens to petals. D: Flower, longitudinal. E: Detail: top view of androecium and stigma. F: Dissected carpels. G: Leafy shoot with axillary flowers. H: Detail of central flower part, stamens to stigmas. I: Eternal view of stamen with food particles emerging from the connective. J: Young fruit; *above*, habit; *underneath left*, transverse; *right*, longitudinal.

**Subfamilies** I Calycanthoideae, Idiospermoideae

**Genera** I 5; species: 11. Well-known genera are *Calycanthus* and *Chimonanthus*.

**Distribution** I Temperate China, North America, northeastern Australia

**Habit** I Trees or shrubs with essential oils

**Leaves** I Opposite, evergreen or deciduous, leaf blade simple, entire, leathery, aromatic, stipules absent

**Inflorescences** I Single axillary

**Flowers** I ± radial, hermaphroditic, spiral arrangement; 15–30 involucral bracts; smooth transition between tepals and stamens (fig. C); recessed receptacle (hypanthium); fragrant; 15–55 stamens, of which 10–25 grow as petaloid staminodes among the fertile stamens. Flowers offer protein- and fat-rich food particles at the top of the staminodes (fig. I) in exchange for pollination. In the *Calycanthus*, the inner tepals hold beetles fast in the hypanthium, and the food particles found there and on the stamens (figs. C, D, H, I) are eaten by the beetles. After the anthers open, the beetles also eat the pollen.

Entomophily, especially by beetles. Superior ovary (1–3) usually grown from 5–45 carpels (fig. F), each supporting two ovules.

**Fruits** I Aggregate fruit; solitary achenes enveloped by the hypanthium (fig. J)

**Use** I The **sweetshrub** (*Calycanthus fertilis*) and the **spice bush** (*C. occidentalis*) are planted as ornamental shrubs. The bark, leaves, and roots of *C. fertilis* (figs. A–F) are used medicinally. Even though it has been found to contain alkaloids with strychnine-like effects, the aromatic bark of *C. fertilis* was used by Native Americans as a spice (Carolina allspice).

**Characteristics** I The family name refers to the petallike sepals (Greek *kalyx* = goblet or calyx, *anthos* = flower). The spirally arranged perianth, many stamens and carpels, and the flowing transition of the tepals to the stamens places the family close to the magnolia species.

# CAMPANULACEAE

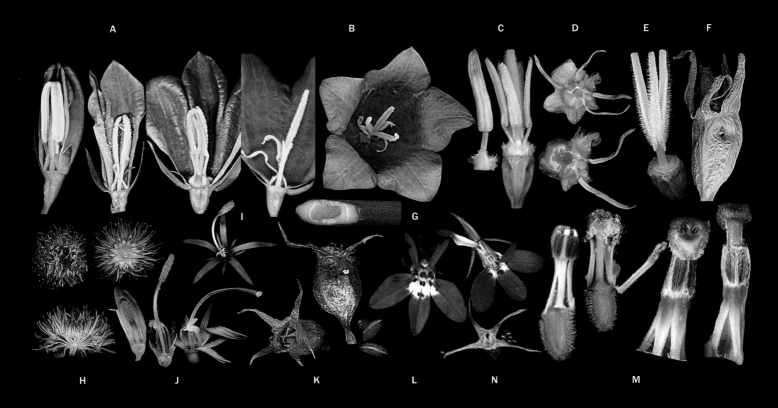

**A–G:** *Campanula persicifolia*. A: Bud at various stages. B: Flower, frontal, anthers emptied, stigmata splayed out. C: Androecium, from bud; *left*, stamen with filament. D: Flower: "nectar cover" or filament base, frontal; *below*, nectary. E: Gynoecium. F: Capsule with pore. G: Sprout with milky sap.

**H–K:** *Jasione laevis*. H: Inflorescence; *left*, frontal; *right*, from underneath; *below*, longitudinal. I: Flower frontally in male phase, pollen on the outside of the style. J: *Left*, opened bud; *center*, male-phase flower, longitudinal; *right*, female phase, lateral, stigma visible. K: Capsule; *left*, frontal; *center*, lateral; *right*, seeds.

**L–N:** *Lobelia erinus*. L: *Left*, flower, frontal; *right*, from above. M: *From left to right*: Stages of pollen release; *right*, stigmas ready to be pollinated. N: Capsule with seeds, frontal.

**Genera** | More than 80; species: more than 2,400

**Distribution** | Worldwide, temperate zones

**Habitat** | Open meadows, on roadsides

**Habit** | Predominantly herbaceous plants, rarely shrubs and half shrubs, mostly upright, rarely trailing

**Leaves** | Alternate, rarely opposite, mostly simple, stipules absent

**Inflorescences** | Cymose, racemose, but also capitiform and umbellate inflorescences (fig. H)

**Flowers** | Radial, in the related Lobeliaceae family zygomorphic and bilabiate, pentamerous, protandrous (male phase initially); the five sepals are usually free, while the petals are as a rule fused into a campanulate flower. The anthers on the stamens form a ring tunnel; the papillose style has to grow through this, with the pollen remaining stuck between the papillae (secondary pollen presentation; figs. I, J, M) until it is collected by visitors. Only then do the usually three style arms splay apart, and the stamens fold downward or remain fused together (Lobeliaceae; fig. M). The inferior ovary comprises usually two to five carpels. It supports a glandular nectar tissue; this is covered by the filaments, which broaden at the base and are hairy around the margins (nectar cover; fig. D), and the cover allows only a narrow proboscis access to the nectar. Predominant flower color is blue, but there are also red and white flowers.

**Fruits** | Mostly seed-rich capsule fruits that open apically by means of five or ten teeth (figs. K, N), or a lateral pore (fig. F); the site is already visible in the flower (fig. C, *right*). When ripe, it functions like a spreader to disperse the seeds.

**Use** | Many ornamental plants: **peach-leaved bellflower** (*Campanula persicifolia*), **sheep's bit scabious** (*Jasione laevis*), and **blue lobelia** (*Lobelia erinus*). In the winter, the leaf rosettes of the **rampion bellflower** (*Campanula rapunculus*) can be harvested like lamb's lettuce. Its thick, fleshy roots can be eaten as a vegetable.

**Characteristics** | Contains a milky sap (fig. G). The plants can also store inulin as an energy reserve.

Lobeliaceae often contain alkaloids. A feature of the **bearded bellflower** (*Campanula barbata*), which grows in high-alpine altitudes of up to 2,700 meters, is that the internal temperature of its flowers is higher than the external temperature, so that many smaller insects spend the cold nights there.

**A–F:** *Humulus lupulus*. A: Male flower. B: Female inflorescence; *left*, longitudinal; *right*, top view. C: Young fruiting stage. D: Young fruit on basal bract with yellow beads of resin. E: Young fruit, longitudinal. F: Ripe seeds.

**G–I:** *Humulus japonicus*. G: Male flower. H: Female inflorescence. I: Female single flower, lateral.

**J–N:** *Celtis australis*. J: Male flower, frontal. K: Female flower, lateral. L: Foliage leaf. M: Unripe fruit; *left*, longitudinal; *right*, lateral. N: Ripe fruit; *right*, seeds.

**Genera** | 2; with 3 species
**Distribution** | Predominantly in the Northern Hemisphere: North Africa, North America, but also Southwest Asia, southern Europe
**Habitat** | In brushwood, waste ground or ruderal habitat, riverside forests, alder marshes
**Habit** | Trees, perennials, perennial herbaceous plants without milky sap, also twining
**Leaves** | Alternating or opposite, distichous or spiral, leaf blade undivided, lobed, digitate, leaf margin serrated, stipules present; they can

also be fused.
**Inflorescences** | Paniculate, spicate-like, dioecious
**Flowers** | Single flowers also hermaphroditic and male, usually with resin glands (fig. D), inconspicuous, petals mostly absent, one whorl with five stamens, two carpels fused into a syncarpous superior ovary, usually two style arms on a short style (figs. I, K). Anemophily.
**Fruits** | Drupes, rarely small nuts
**Use** | **Hops** (*Humulus lupulus*) are used for flavoring beer. The young shoots, still growing underground and

before the leaves emerge, can be eaten as "hop asparagus." Later they become too bitter. The tough stems of **hemp** (*Cannabis sativa*) are used to make clothing or ropes. These varieties are usually free of THC (tetrahydrocannabinol). The resin is smoked as hashish, and the leaves and flowers as marijuana. The **Mediterranean hackberry** (*Celtis australis*) and the **common hackberry** (*C. occidentalis*) are planted as shade trees. The wood can be used to make musical instruments. The leaves of *Celtis* species are also

used as animal feed. The fleshy drupes of some hackberry species are said to be edible, and the seeds can be used in baking.
**Characteristics** | Hops have two-sided climbing hairs on their leaves and shoots, which can be used as barbs to hook firmly on to other plants and thus make the plants serve as a support for the hops.

A–F: *Canna indica*. A: Flower and buds, lateral. B: Flower, lateral; lower part next to it at right, longitudinal. C: Ovary; *left*, longitudinal; *right*, transverse. D: Fertile stamen, with a theca of both sides and secondary pollen presentation. E: Flower in its individual parts. F: Ripe fruit. G: Seeds.

**Genus** | 1: *Canna*; species: 10–20

**Distribution** | Origin exclusively in the Neotropics, but cultivated in many parts of the tropics today

**Habitats** | Humid forests, shorelines, and swamps

**Habit** | Perennial herbaceous plants with starchy rhizomes as overwintering organs

**Leaves** | Leaf arrangement: distichous to spiral arrangement; leaves simple, entire, ovate to oblong, pinnate nervation with parallel lateral nerves, rolled up on one side in bud state, with interleaved leaf sheaths

**Inflorescences** | Terminal, paniculate, bracts up to 15 cm long in the axil

**Flowers** | Asymmetrical, hermaphroditic, single flowers small, trimerous; three free sepals, mostly green, remain on the fruit; three petals basally fused into a tube (fig. B). What can be taken to be a conspicuous, often red or yellow, "flower" actually comprises transformed stamens (figs. B, E). Of the original two whorls, each with three stamens, only a half-fertile stamen remains, with one theca; this is fused with the style (fig. D). The others have been transformed into petaloid staminodes of various sizes, one of which is more or less sharply bent downward and forms a labellum (fig. A); three carpels are fused to an inferior ovary (fig. C). The style is petaloid. Pollen falls on the stigma, where the flower-visiting insects collect it: secondary pollen presentation (fig. D). Septal nectaries are present.

**Fruits** | Trilocular, walnut-sized capsule fruit (fig. F) with hard black seeds (fig. G); these are used to fill rattles.

**Use** | Many *Canna indica* hybrids are planted in tropical, subtropical, and temperate regions as ornamental plants; there are said to be over 1,000 different varieties. The rhizomes are edible when cooked. The starch harvested from them is marketed as "Queensland Arrowroot."

**Characteristics** | Like the seeds of the carob tree, *Canna* seeds have a constant weight. Therefore, the original inhabitants of South America used them for weighing gold. Despite the name "indica," the plants come from South America.

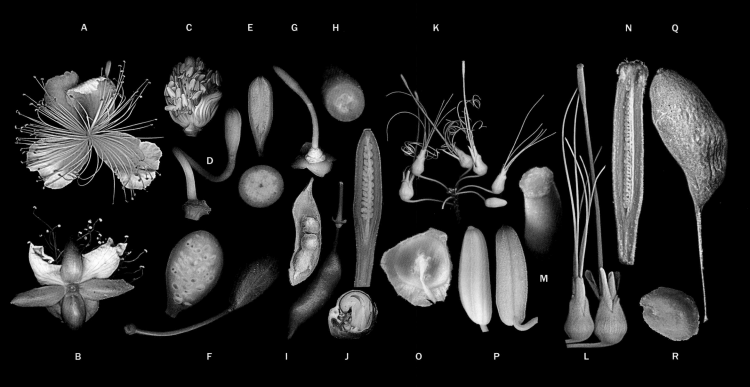

**A–F:** *Capparis spinosa*. A: Flower, frontal. B: The same, from underneath. C: Bud, husk removed, androecium and gynoecium tip. D: Ovary with gynophore. E: Ovary; *above*, longitudinal; *below*, transverse. F: Fruit; *left*, longitudinal; *right*, lateral.

**G–J:** *Capparis* **sp**. G: Ovary with gynophore. H: The same; *above*, transverse; *below*, longitudinal. I: Fruit; *left*, longitudinal; *right*, lateral. J: Seeds, transverse.

**K–R:** *Steriphoma paradox*. K: Partial inflorescence, lateral. L: *Left*, male, and *right*, female flower phases, lateral. M: Ovary and stigma, frontal. N: Ovary, longitudinal. O: Nectary, frontal. P: Stamen from both sides. Q: Fruit. R: Seeds.

CAPPARACEAE

**Genera** | 16; species: more than 450
**Distribution** | Worldwide, mostly tropical and subtropical, also on arid steppes
**Habit** | Mostly trees or shrubs, also lianas, many xerophytes, rarely herbaceous plants
**Leaves** | Mostly alternate, rarely opposite, leaf blade simple or compound, digitate, often evergreen; if stipules present, then small or spiny
**Inflorescences** | racemose, corymbose, umbellate, paniculate, with bracts, without bracteoles, 2–10 flowers or solitary
**Flowers** | Radial to zygomorphic, hermaphroditic, tetramerous; the lower axis often forms a ring-shaped, tubular or scale-shaped disc, four sepals, 0–4 petals, (1–) 4–8 or many stamens; the bicarpellate ovary is unilocular to multilocular; one apical style supports a capitate or bilobiate stigma. Androecium and gynoecium may be supported by a common stalk (androgynophore); often only the gynoceum is supported by a stalk (gynophore; figs. D, G).
**Fruits** | Pods (fig. I) to berry shaped, with or without replum, rarely capsule fruit or drupes
**Use** | The pickled flower buds of the **caper bush** (*Capparis spinosa*) are used in cooking as capers. **Crateva species** are cultivated for their fragrant flowers and edible berrylike fruits and are used in folk medicine. The fruits of the **shepherd's tree** (*Boscia albitrunca*) are eaten by the indigenous population of southern Africa, although they are not supposed to taste very good. A porridge or "witgat koffie" (for stretching coffee, with a taste that takes getting used to) is made from the roots. It is one of the most important fodder plants for wildlife and livestock. The bitter leaves of *Maerua angolensis* are eaten in times of need, and the leaves are also used as a laxative and as a remedy for various ailments. Powdered leaves can also be used as a fish poison. The fleshy roots of *Maerua oblongifolia* are eaten sweetened; they are supposed to recall the taste of coconut. *Steriophoma peruvianum* is used in homeopathy. In the genus *Steriphoma*, the stamens hang a long way outside the flower, so they are often cultivated as ornamental plants in greenhouses.
**Characteristics** | Simple or branched trichomes (hairs) are widespread. As with other crucifer plants, caper plants produce glucosinolates (mustard oil glycosides) as a defense against herbivores.

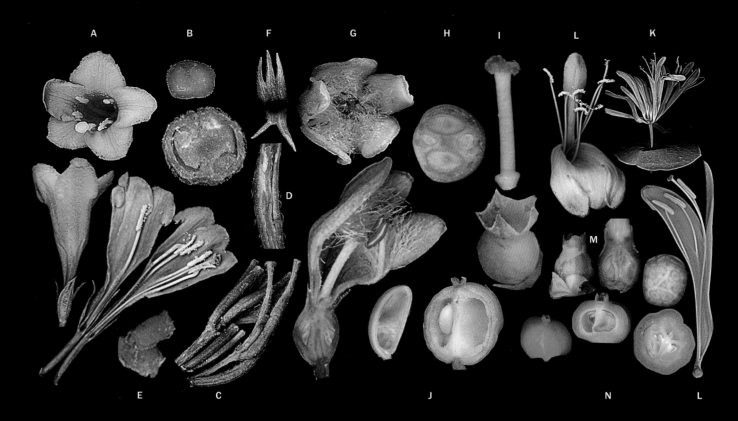

A–F: *Weigelia florida*. A: Flower; *above*, frontal; *below left*, lateral; *right*, longitudinal. B: Stigma, frontal. C: Young fruits. D: The same; *left*, transverse; *right*, partially longitudinal. E: Seeds. F: Calyx.

G–J: *Symphoricarpus rivularis*. G: flower; *above*, frontal; *below*, longitudinal. H: *Above left*, ovary, transverse; *below*, lateral with calyx. I: Style/stigma, lateral. J: *Right*, longitudinal fruit; *left*, seeds.

K–N: *Lonicera caprifolium*. K: Inflorescence, lateral, with bract of two fused leaves. L: Flower, frontal; *below right*, longitudinal. M: *Left*, ovary with calyx, lateral; *center*, longitudinal; *right*, transverse. N: Fruit; *left*, lateral; *center*, longitudinal; *right*, transverse.

# CAPRIFOLIACEAE

**Genera** | 5; species: 220
**Distribution** | Northern Hemisphere
**Habit** | Shrubs, lianas, perennials
**Leaves** | Opposite, basal rosettes, leaf blade undivided, without stipules; however, sometimes with small hairy bulges near the stipules
**Inflorescences** | Thyrses, capitiform verticles, capitulum
**Flowers** | Radial or zygomorphic, hermaphroditic, with or without spur, basally fused, tetramerous-pentamerous, pentamerous calyx, usually fused, also small-lobed (laciniate), corolla usually pentamerous, fused basally into a narrow, long tube (figs. A, L), with nectar guides or a short tube. Access to this may be restricted by dense hair (fig. G). One to five stamens, basal filaments fused with the corolla (figs. A, G, L); the inferior ovary comprises 2–3 fused carpels; stigma mostly capitate (figs. B, I).
**Fruits** | Berries, drupes, capsule fruits (figs. J, N)
**Use** | Many ornamental plants, such as **honeysuckle** (*Lonicera*), **snowberry** (*Symphoricarpos rivularis*), **weigelia** (*Weigelia florida*)
**Characteristics** | The nectar-rich flowers, heavily fragrant after 7:00 p.m., of **Italian honeysuckle** (*Lonicera caprifolium*) are pollinated by moths. The berries of some honeysuckle species, such as **black-berried honeysuckle** (*Lonicera nigra*), are fused together into so-called double berries. The red, currant-like berries of **European fly honeysuckle** (*Lonicera xylosteum*) are slightly toxic. **Himalayan honeysuckle** (*Leycesteria formosa*), which comes from that region, freezes back in the winter in central Europe, but it sprouts again and has the potential to spread like a weed.
**Notes** | After new revisions, the Diervillaceae, Linnaeaceae, Dipsacaceae, and Valerianaceae families are also included. However, in this book they are dealt with individually; see each family in turn.

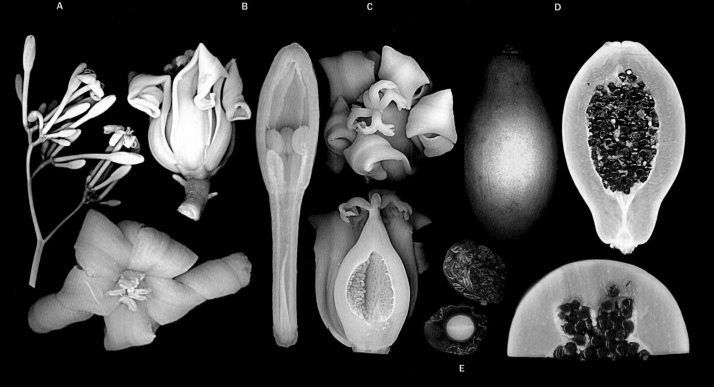

**A–E:** *Carica papaya.* A: Partial inflorescence, lateral; *below,* male single flower, frontal. B: *Left,* female flower, lateral; *right,* male flower, longitudinal. C: *Above,* female flower, frontal; *below,* the same, longitudinal, D: Ripe fruit; *above left,* lateral; *right,* longitudinal; *below,* transverse. E: Seeds; *above,* lateral; *below,* longitudinal.

**Genera** I 4–6; species: over 30
**Distribution** I Tropical America (and West Africa), main focus in South America
**Habit** I Small softwood trees containing milky sap in all parts of the plant; shrubs, rarely herbaceous plants
**Leaves** I Alternate, spiral, also crowded as palmlike tuft, leaf blade often with palmate lobes, digitate, often in tufts, without stipules
**Inflorescences** I Panicles, cymes, tufts

**Flowers** I Radial, rarely hermaphroditic, unisexual (figs. A–C), corolla more or less fused (the male flowers often more tightly fused); the mostly pentamerous, small calyx is more or less free-petaled; usually five plus five stamens, with the pentamerous corolla fused (fig. B), in two whorls; the tricarpellate-pentacarpellate ovary is superior and has five multiple cleft-style arms on a short style (fig. C).
**Fruits** I Berries (fig. D)

**Use** I The **papaya** (*Carica papaya*) is eaten fresh as a fruit or, when unripe, cooked as a vegetable (fig. D) and processed into fruit drinks or preserves. The milky sap from the unripe fruits contains the proteolytic enzymes papain and chymopapain, which are used, among other things, for tenderizing meat; otherwise used for tanning leather or for preparing wool and silk to prevent shrinkage during washing. The seeds, which taste like cress (fig. E), are said to be able to combat intestinal parasites.
**Characteristics** I The flowers, which usually open at night, are pollinated by moths. Although frost sensitive, papayas can attain tree size (up to about 6 meters tall); they barely lignify (become woody) and remain soft. For the sake of rapid growth in height, they do not develop hardwood, so the plants live only a short time.

# CARYOPHYLLACEAE

A–E: *Stellaria holostea*. A: Habit with inflorescence. B: Pair of leaves. C: flower, frontal. D: Calyx from below. E: Androecium/gynoecium, frontal.

F–H: *Lychnis coronaria*. F: flower, lateral. G: Fused calyx, unfurled. H: Petal.

I: *Dianthus barbartus*. Bud with outer calyx, lateral.

J–Q: *Silene dioica*. J: Female flower, frontal. K: Male flower, frontal. L: Female flower, longitudinal. M: Gynoecium with stamens reduced at the base; these function as a nectary. N: Male flower, longitudinal. O: Petals. P: Nectary of the male flower. Q: Capsule.

R–S: *Lychnis floscuculi*. R: Petal. S: Capsule.

T: *Stellaria holostea* capsule.

**Genera** | More than 85; species: about 2,200

**Distribution** | Worldwide in all climate zones, concentrated in the northern temperate latitudes

**Habitats** | In meadows, on riverbanks, on heaths, on dunes, in pine forests

**Habit** | Almost always herbaceous, can be villous (weak hairs), can be cushion plants

**Leaves** | Opposite or in whorls, leaf blade undivided, narrow and linear, often without stalk, often fused (figs. A, B)

**Inflorescences** | Often dichasia (fig. A), thyrses, bracts often present, membranous

**Flowers** | Radial, hermaphroditic or unisexual (figs. J, K), dioecious perianth single or double, tetramerous-pentamerous, calyx free (fig. D) or fused (fig. G), also with outer calyx (fig. I); 4–5–10 corolla or absent, often with paracorolla (figs. J, K) from corolla scales; petals with plates and claws (figs. H, O, R); one to ten stamens (fig. E) in two whorls, often only one whorl of stamens; the usually (bicarpellate, tricarpellate) pentacarpellate ovary is superior and unilocular; style mostly solitary (fig. L). Usually entomophily.

**Fruits** | Capsules that burst open through five or ten teeth (figs. Q, S), also capsules that open via a valve (fig. T), rarely berries or nuts

**Use** | Many ornamental plants, such as **sweet william** (*Dianthus barbartus*), **Chinese pinks** (*D. chinensis hybrids*), **maiden pink** (*D. deltoides*), **rose campion** (*Lychnis coronaria*), **snow-in-summer** (*Cerastium tomentosum*). The young, fleshy sprouts of the **seaside sandplant** (*Honkenya peploides*) can be eaten before they flower. **Rupturewort** (*Herniaria glabra*) is used in folk medicine as a diuretic. Because of their high saponin content, the roots and rhizomes of the **soapwort** (*Saponaria officinalis*) were formerly used for washing delicate laundry (such as wool).

**Characteristics** | "Trumpet-flowers"; the **red campion** (*Silene dioica*) is even triecious: there are hybrid male and female plants. The seeds are often poisonous, such as those of the **corncockle** (*Agrostemma githago*). The nodes are often thickened.

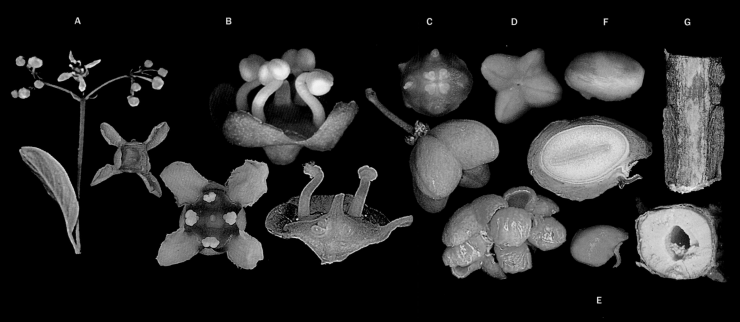

**A–G:** *Evonymus europaeus.* A: Dichasia inflorescence. B: Single flower; *left*, from underneath; *center above*, lateral; *center below*, frontal; *right*, longitudinal. C: Ovary, transverse. D: Ripe fruit; *above*, frontal; *below left*, lateral; *beneath it*, opened, E: Ripe seed with aril; *above*, longitudinal; *below*, lateral. F: Seeds without aril. G: Winged stem; *above*, lateral; *below*, transverse.

**Genera** | More than 90; species: about 1,300

**Distribution** | Tropical and subtropical regions, Europe to southern Sweden, Baltic region

**Habitat** | Forests, brushwood

**Habit** | Small trees, shrubs, also climbing or twining. The stem may be winged (fig. G).

**Leaves** | Opposite or alternate, leaf blade simple, even leathery, evergreen or deciduous, the stipules are usually small or absent.

**Inflorescences** | Cymose, racemose, fasciled (bundled), dichasia (fig. A)

**Flowers** | Radial, hermaphroditic, also diclinous, trimerous-pentamerous; the 3–5 sepals are basally fused or free; 3–5 petals, which may also be absent; 3–5 stamens in one whorl, rarely two whorls; the stamens of the inner whorl are then transformed into nectar-producing staminodes; alternatively, there is a usually flat disc; 2–5 carpels form the fused superior ovary (fig. B, *right*; fig. C); the style is usually short, with a two-to-five-lobed, capitate stigma.

**Fruits** | Loculicidal capsule, also nonopening, samara, berry, drupe; seeds can have vividly colored arils

(fig. D, *below*; fig. E).

**Use** | Ornamental plants, such as the **burning bush** (*Euonymus alatus*), **winter creeper** (*Euonymus fortunei*). The leaves of the **khat bush** (also "**Abbyssinian tea**," *Catha edulis*) are chewed as an intoxicant. Seeds of *Kokoona zeylanica* provide oil, which is used as lamp oil and to ward off leeches. Oil and yellow dye is made from the seeds of the **European spindle tree** (*Euonymus europaeus*); it also provides wood for carving. The name "spindle tree" makes it clear what the wood was used for: making spindles.

**Characteristics** | Many species have gumlike milky sap, triterpene derivatives in the bark, polyterpenes (gutta-percha); sometimes they also contain toxic alkaloids. The pink-colored capsule of the European spindle tree (*Euonymus europaeus*) is reminiscent in form and color of the headgear of some clergy; hence the German name, *Pfaffenhütchen* (priest's cap)!

# CIRCAEASTERACEAE

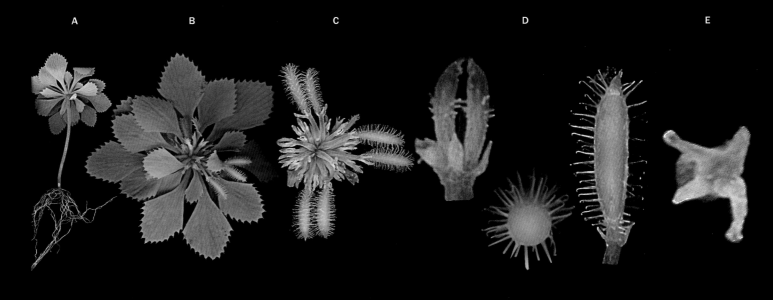

**A–E:** *Circeaster agrestis.* A: Entire plant, lateral. B: The same, top view. C: Inflorescence with male and female flowers, frontal.
D: *Left*, female flower, lateral; *center*, ovary, transverse; *right*, the same, longitudinal. E: Male flower.

**Genera** | 2; with 1 species each:
*Circeaster agrestis* and *Kingdonia uniflora*
**Distribution** | Northwest India, China
**Habit** | Annual (*Circeaster*) or perennial (*Kingdonia*); herbaceous plants up to 10 cm tall
**Habitat** | Between 2,100–5,000 meters altitude, in forests or on grassland
**Leaves** | Either one basal leaf (*Kingdonia*) or several (*Circeaster*), alternate, leaf blade spatulate or wedge shaped, leaf margin denticulate, dichotomous venation (fig. B), petiole present, stipules absent

**Inflorescences** | Axillary
**Flowers** | Radial, unisexual, monoecious (fig. C), heterodichogamy (*Kingdonia*), greatly reduced; sepals in *Kingdonia* are petaloid; petals very small, up to 1 mm (*Circeaster*) in diameter, and up to 8 mm (*Kingdonia*); 2 (–3) (*Circeaster*) or (4–) 5 (–8) (*Kingdonia*) petals, free, spiral arrangement; (1–) 2 (–3) (*Circeaster*) stamens or (3–) 5–8 (*Kingdonia*), alternating to the petals; one staminode (*Circeaster*) or 8–13 (*Kingdonia*); 1–3 carpels (*Circeaster*) or (3–) 7–9 (*Kingdonia*), free, superior
**Fruits** | Achenes

**Characteristics** | The two taxa of Circeasteraceae were formerly listed as representatives of Ranunculaceae. At times they were even placed in separate families (Circeastereaceae, Kingdoniaceae). Their connecting bifurcate leaf venation, atypical for angiosperms, makes them an interesting object for research for evolutionary systematists. The venation can be interpreted either as a very original feature (echoes of the leaves of the gymnosperms, ginkgos, or ferns) or as a reduction of more-complex structures. RNA studies revealed membership in a common family. In

the leaves of both species, there is no separation into palisade and spongy parenchyma. *Kingdonia* is said to have been named after the mother of the English plant collector Francis Kingdon-Ward (1885–1958).
*Kingdonia uniflora* is endemic to China, where also *Circeaster agrestis* is on the Red List of Endangered Plants.

**A–E:** *Cistus monspeliensis*. A: *Above*, flower, frontal; *below*, from underneath. B: Androecium/gynoecium, lateral. C: Ovary, longitudinal. D: Ripe fruit; *above*, transverse; *center/below*, lateral. E: Ripe seeds, whole and in various sections.

**F–H:** *Helianthemum nummularium*. F: *Above*, flower, frontal; *below*, from underneath. G: Gynoecium, lateral. H: Ovary; *above*, transverse; *below*, longitudinal.

**Genera** I 8; species: more than 170
**Distribution** I Worldwide, temperate to warm temperate regions, main concentration in the Mediterranean
**Habitat** I Deciduous forests, macchia, or shrubland
**Habit** I Dwarf shrubs, half shrubs, herbaceous plants, annuals to perennials

**Leaves** I Opposite or alternate; leaf blade: oblong, elliptic, also narrow, acicular, leathery, can be evergreen; also leaf rosettes, often with glands or glandular hairs, stellate hairs; stipules present or absent
**Inflorescences** I Cymes or mostly single flowers

**Flowers** I Radial, hermaphroditic, usually 3–5 sepals of unequal size (fig. F, *below*); five free petals, turned and crumpled in the bud; numerous free stamens; the usually 3–5–10 carpels are fused to a superior ovary; the style may be shorter or longer; the stigma is usually capitate.
**Fruits** I Capsule fruit

**Use** I Leaves of the **pink rock rose** (*Cistus creticus*) are used to make tea. The leaves and branches of the **gum rock rose** (*C. ladanifer*) provide labdanum resin.
**Characteristics** I The flowers of the **sunrose** (*Helianthemum nummularium*; figs. F, G) open only in sunshine and track the sun.

# CLEOMACEAE

A B C D G H J

E

E F L M

**A–E:** *Cleome sparkii.* A: Leafy branch with inflorescence. B: Left bud; *center,* flower, frontal; *right,* the same, lateral. C: The same, petals removed. D: Long pedicellate gynoecium (gynophore), lateral. E: Ovary; *left,* transverse; *right,* longitudinal.

**F–M:** *Cleome rutidosperm.* F: Habit. G: Leaf. H: Flower, frontal. I: Calyx. J: Androecium from a bud. K: One of the central petals. L: Ovary, transverse. M: Unripe seeds.

**Genera** I 10; species: about 300
**Distribution** I Tropical, subtropical America
**Habitat** I Also in deserts and steppes
**Habit** I Woody to herbaceous; can be trailing plants
**Leaves** I Alternate; leaf blade ternate to multifoliate; compound, petiolate; margins and veins often hairy

**Inflorescences** I Racemose or solitary, axillary
**Flowers** I Zygomorphic, hermaphroditic; four free sepals; four free petals, often arranged in a semiwhorl; six stamens, often long filaments (fig. C); the bicarpellate ovary is superior; one style with a capitate stigma.

**Fruits** I Pods (fig. E) with or without permanent replum.
**Use** I Ornamental plants, such as **spider flowers** (*Cleome/Tarenaya hasslerana, Cleome/Tarenaya spinosa*). The leaves and young shoots of **African cabbage** (*Cleome gynandra*) and also the young fruit of

**Rocky Mountain beeplant** (*C. serrulata*) are eaten as vegetables.
**Characteristics** I The gynophore (fig. D) lifts the ovary out of the flower.

A–F: *Clethra alnifolia*. A: Leafy branch with inflorescence. B: *Left*, flower from underneath; *right*, frontal. C: Flower, longitudinal. D: Solitary stamen; *left*, front view; *right*, from behind. E: Ovary, transverse. F: Fruit.

G–L: *Clethra arborea*. G: Racemose inflorescence. H: *Above*, flower from underneath; *below*, frontal. I: Flower, longitudinal. J: Solitary stamen; *above*, with view of the opening area; *below*, lateral from underneath. K: Young stamen. L: Young fruit; *above*, longitudinal; *below*, transverse.

**Genera** I 2; species: over 90
**Distribution** I Worldwide except Africa and Australia
**Habit** I Shrubs
**Leaves** I Alternate, spiral arrangement, tufted at the shoot tips, leaf blade undivided, usually evergreen, leathery or herbaceous plants

**Inflorescences** I Terminal racemiform (fig. G), panicles, single flowers
**Flowers** I Radial, hermaphroditic; calyx has five deep lobes that remain on the fruit; 5 (–6) sepals; five free petals, slightly sloping, basally fused at the highest; 10 (–12) stamens; anthers also splayed apart (fig. D), opening by pores (fig. J), often fused at the base with the petals; tricarpetallate superior ovary (figs. C, I) with nonterminal, axile placentation of ovules; one long style with trilobate/trifid stigma (fig. B, *right*; fig. H, *below*)
**Fruits** I Loculicidal trilocular capsule fruits (fig. F), seeds are sometimes winged.
**Use** I Ornamental shrubs, such as **summersweet** (*Clethra alnifolia*)

**Characteristics** I The bark on the branches is often hairy. Often has stellate hairs. *Clethra arborea* is also called the lily-of-the-valley tree, because the hanging flowers are reminiscent of the lily of the valley.

CLUSIACEAE

A–D: *Clusia* **sp**. A: Male flower, frontal. B: The same, lengthwise. C: Androecium and basal nectary. D: *Left and center*, closed stamen; *left*, lateral; *center*, from the front; *right*, opened stamen from the front.

E–H: *Garcinia mangostane*. E: Ripe fruit; *left*, frontal; *right*, lateral. F: Fruit, longitudinal. G: Aril from fruit: H: Seed; *left*, lateral; *right*, longitudinal, schizogenous oil glands.

**Genera** | 27; species: more than 1,000
**Distribution** | Worldwide, from the temperate zones to the tropics
**Habit** | Trees, shrubs, lianas, perennials
**Leaves** | Opposite, whorl arrangement, leaf blade simple, often evergreen, mostly without stipules

**Inflorescences** | Cymes, thyrses, solitary
**Flowers** | Radial, hermaphroditic or unisexual (figs. A, B: male flower), dioecious; bimerous-tetramerous to fourteenfold calyx and corolla; four to many stamens, often united in bundles or fascicles, tubes, or other synandria (fig. C: with annular nectary);

1–3–5–15 carpels form the superior ovary; style free or united; stigma lobate, radiate, scutate
**Fruits** | Mostly berries, septicidal or septifrage capsules, drupes. Seeds often with aril (fig. G).
**Use** | **Mangosteen** (*Garcinia mangostana*) are consumed as fruit or juice. A resinous gum ("gummi-

gutta") is harvested from the bark of *Garcinia* or *Clusia* species; this is used to produce a yellow pigment, as well as essential oils for cosmetics.
**Characteristics** | Resin ducts, schizogenous oil glands

**A–L: *Colchicum laetum*.** A: Habit. B: Sprout from rooted tuber. C: Transition from shoot to tuber, longitudinal. D: Flower, frontal. E: Stigmas; *right*, detail. F: Androecium around stigmas; basal areas of filaments excrete nectar. G: Tepal with opposing/ alternating stamen. H: Nectar-collecting area on basal tepal. I: Ovary; *left*, longitudinal; *above right*, transverse. J: Stamen, front view. K: The same, from behind. L: Apical area of the "petal tube."

**M–R: *Gloriosa lutea*.** M: Flower, frontal. N: Ovary; *left*, transverse; *right*, longitudinal. O: Stigmas. P: Opened fruit. Q: Seed with aril; *right* and *left* the same, longitudinal. R: Rhizome parts.

Classified into six tribes: Anguilariae, Burchardieae, Colchicae, Iphigenieae, Dipladenieae, Uvularieae

**Genera** | 15; species: about 284. Well-known genera: *Colchicum*, *Gloriosa*, *Sandersonia*, *Uvularia*.

**Distribution** | Temperate latitudes to tropics; not present in South America

**Habit** | Perennial herbs with underground stem tubers (figs. A, B), which may be covered by a tunic; rarely has rhizomes (fig. R) as overwintering organs.

**Leaves** | Basal rosette or alternate, arrangement is spiral to distichous; leaf blade: simple, undivided, entire, filiform, linear, lanceolate to ovate, usually parallel venation.

**Inflorescences** | Racemose or umbellate, solitary

**Flowers** | Radial (figs. D, M), hermaphroditic, rarely unisexual, trimerous; six tepals in two whorls of three, tepals free or—in *Colchicum*, for example—fused into a long tube; nectaries at the base of the tepals or the stamens (fig. H); six stamens in two whorls of three (fig. F), free or fused with the tepals (fig. G); superior ovary comprising 3 (–4) fused carpels (figs. I, N)

**Fruits** | Capsules (fig. P); seed can have an aril (figs. P, Q).

**Use** | A number of ornamental plants come from this family (*Colchicum*, *Gloriosa*, *Sandersonia*). **Colchine**, a toxic alkaloid extracted from the autumn crocus (*Colchicum autumnale*), is used medically to treat gout and other diseases. It is difficult to determine the dosage, since it is close to the lethal dose and there is no antidote! Deadly poisonings have occurred due to confusion with leaves of the wild garlic. Colchicine blocks formation of the spindle apparatus during cell division, so that although the chromosomes are doubled, no cell wall is formed between the daughter cells. Polyploid cells develop; this is lethal in animals and humans. In a plant kingdom, enlarged cells develop after treatment with colchicine; therefore, it is used in plant breeding, especially for wheat and strawberries. Young shoots of the **spreading bellwort** and the **perfoliate bellwort** (*Uvularia sessilifolia* or *U. perfoliata*) are said to be eaten cooked as substitutes for asparagus.

**Characteristics** | The family is named after the ancient kingdom of Colchis. This is a region that today is in Georgia, on the east coast of the Black Sea. In Greek mythology, it was said to have been the homeland of the poisoner-preparer Medea.

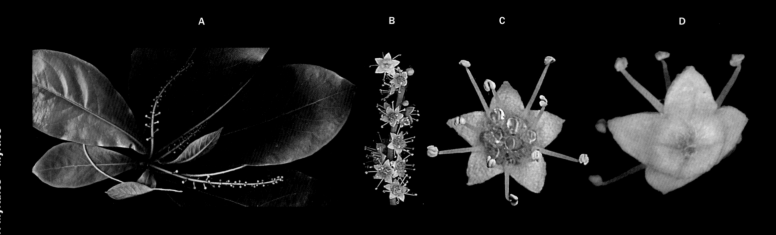

A–D: *Terminalia catappa*. A: Leafy branch with inflorescences. B: Part of an inflorescence. C: Flower, frontal, with droplets of nectar. D: Flower, underside.

**Genera** I 20; species: 400–500
**Primary distribution** I Pantropical, tropics, at times the subtropics
**Habit** I Trees up to 50 meters tall, shrubs, dwarf shrubs with rhizomes, lianas
**Habitat** I Forests, grasslands, mangrove swamps
**Leaves** I Opposite or alternate, also spiral and rosette arrangements, also crowded at the tips of the shoots (= terminal in *Terminalia*), leaf blade simple and undivided, also with glandular hairs; standing petioles may also be spiny, without stipules.
**Inflorescences** I Simple compressed or compound racemose; the inflorescence has bracteoles.
**Flowers** I Radial, hermaphroditic, rarely unisexual; 4–5 sepals (fig. D), also fused into a tube; 4–5 petals (fig. C) or they are reduced; stamens in 1–2 whorls of 4–5, usually of various lengths, rarely numerous; hairy filament bases with long hairs that also function as a display apparatus. The bicarpellate-pentacarpellate ovary is inferior, uniclocular with 2–5 ovules, from which often only one develops with a disc-shaped nectary on it, which can be hairy; it produces conspicuous drops of nectar (fig. C); simple style with a small, capitate stigma.
**Fruits** I Winged or fleshy fruits, drupes, accessory fruits
**Use** I Timber from *Terminalia* species, such as **limba** or **korina** (*Terminalia superba*). The fruit of the **myrobalan** (*Terminalia chebula*) are used for tanning. The edible core of the **tropical almond** (also **beach almond**, *Terminalia catappa*) is the so-called Indian almond. The dried leaves are used in aquariums to prevent diseases. The **Rangoon creeper** (*Quisqualis indica*) is used as an ornamental plant, and its fruits are used medically. The **bushwillow species** (*Combretum* sp.) are likewise used in traditional medicine, and the wood is used for firewood.

**Characteristics** I Some species that live in mangrove swamps grow viviparous fruits that already germinate on the mother plant, such as the **white mangrove** (*Laguncularia racemosa*). Since they grow in tidal areas, they also have so-called breathing roots. The fruits of the tropical almond can float. Climbing *Combretum* species twine counterclockwise. The plants can have domatia.

**A–C:** *Commelin tuberosa.* A: Flower; *above left,* frontal; *right,* longitudinal; *below left,* from underneath. B: Androecium/gynoecium. C: Staminodes.

**D–E:** *Callisia multiflora.* D: *Left,* flower from underneath; *upper right,* frontal. E: Opened bud, frontal, husk removed, stamens surround the stigma.
**F–J:** *Geogenanthus poeppigii.* F: *Above,* flower, frontal; *left below,* from underneath;

*at the bottom,* longitudinal. G and I: Stamens. H: Ovary, longitudinal. J: Staminodes.
**K–M:** *Tradescantia hirta.* K: Flower, lateral/frontal. L: Gynoecium and 1 stamen. M: Ovary, transverse.

**N:** *Tradescantia* **sp.** staminode
**O:** *Pollia condensata* stamen
**P:** *Cyanotis lanata* stamen
**Q:** *Tripogandra diuretica* stamen
**R:** *Commelina* **sp.** stamen

**Subfamilies** I Commelinoideae, Cartonematoideae
**Genera** I about 40; species: about 650. Well-known genera *Rhoeo, Tradescantia, Zebrina.*
**Distribution** I Tropical and subtropical
**Habit** I Mostly annual or perennial herbaceous plants or succulents, rarely epiphytes. Occasionally slightly woody at the base, mostly grow upright, but also creepers, climbers, or hanging plants. Rhizomes as overwintering organs.
**Leaves** I Alternate, spiral or distichous arrangement, distributed either in a basal rosette or along the stem; leaves entire, with leaf sheath, parallel venation
**Inflorescences** I The main axis of the inflorescence forms a flower at the tip and surmounts the secondary axes, which grow out beneath it, also ending in a flower (= cymose). Occasionally have bracts.
**Flowers** I Radial (fig. K) to more or less zygomorphic (figs. A, F); mostly hermaphroditic or unisexual; plants monoecious or dioecious, trimerous; sepals usually free or basally fused; three petals usually free, occasionally fused into a tube or unguiculate; two whorls of three stamens, all or 1–3 fertile (figs. J, O, P, R); the remainder may grow as staminodes, which serve to attract flower visitors by offering them small, nonfertile pollen grains to eat (figs. C, G, I, N; "feeding anthers"). Does not produce nectar; these are pure pollen flowers; filaments often with conspicuous hairs (figs. J, L, Q, P, R); the superior ovary (figs. B, H) usually consists of three fused carpels. Insect or self-pollination.
**Fruits** I Mostly capsule, rarely berries
**Use** I Many ornamental plants; in temperate northern Europe, most of them are not reliably winter hardy and can therefore be grown only as indoor plants. One exception are the **spiderworts** (*Tradescantia* × *andersoniana* hybrids).
**Characteristics** I The family is named after the Dutch botanist Caspar Commelijn (1667–1731). Most taxa form calcium oxalate raphides. Some species are considered to be aggressive neophytes, such as the **small-leaf spiderwort** (*Tradescantia fluminensis*), a popular pot plant that has overgrown and suffocated native vegetation in some places in New Zealand.

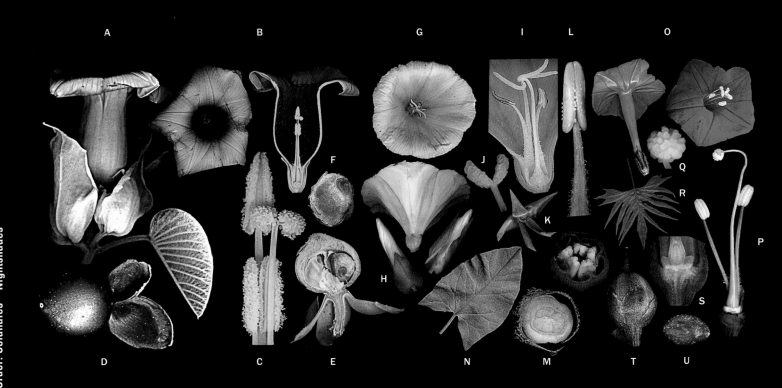

**A–F:** *Argyreia nervosa*. A: Part of a sprout with leaf and flower, lateral, with bracts. B: *Left*, flower, frontal; *right*, longitudinal. C: Stigmas and 2 stamens. D: Fruit, lateral. E: The same, longitudinal. F: Seeds.

**G–N:** *Convolvulus arvensis*. G: *Above*, flower, frontal; *below*, lateral. H: Bud with 2 bracts. I: Flower, longitudinal, detail. J: Stigma, lateral. K: Calyx. L: *Above*, stamen; *below*, androecium from bud, frontal. M: Ovary, transverse. N: Leaf.

**O–U:** *Ipomoea quamoclit*. O: Flower; *left*, lateral; *right*, frontal. P: Gynoecium and 2 stamens. Q: Stigma. R: Leaf. S: Ovary, longitudinal, with basal/lateral nectary. T: Fruit. U: Seeds.

**Genera** | More than 50; species: more than 1,500

**Distribution** | Worldwide in various habitats

**Habit** | Herbaceous or perennials, mostly twining, also woody in tropical latitudes

**Leaves** | Opposite, leaf blade: simple, without stipules, often large and sagittate. *Ipomoea quamoclit* has pinnatipartite leaves (fig. R).

**Inflorescences** | Branched, solitary on axils to paniculate, often with bracts (fig. A)

**Flowers** | Radial, calyx, and corolla pentamerous; bracts often implanted around the calyx (fig. H); large, funnel- to wheel-shaped, tortuous bud position (fig. H). The bicarpellate (-tricarpellate-pentacarpellate) ovary is superior, with an nectary, often-annular, underneath (fig. I, *right*; fig. S); the style can be simple or forcate; the stigma, simple, lobate, or capitate (fig. Q).

**Fruits** | Capsules (figs. D, E, T)

**Use** | Food sources: the root tubers of the **sweet potato** (*Ipomoea batata*); roots of some species supply drugs (such as *Ipomoea purga*, *Convolvulus scammonia*). The **Hawaiian baby woodrose** (*Argyreia nervosa*) is administered in Ayurvedic medicine. Its seeds ("Hawaiian babies") contain an LSD-like psychoactive substance, which causes symptoms such as ergot poisoning and may be fatal. There are many ornamental plants, such as morning glories (*Ipomoea* sp.).

**Characteristics** | Some members of the Cuscutaceae family are complete parasites and do not root in the soil. Some are unpopular wild plants.

A–J: *Cordia* **sp**. A: Part of a sprout with leaves and terminal flowers. B: Leaf margin of the underside, detail. C: Paniculate
florescence. D: *Above*, flower, frontal; *below*, lateral. E: Calyx. F: Ovary; *left*, lateral; *right*, next to it, longitudinal. G: Flower,
longitudinal. H: Ovary, transverse. I: Style arms. J: Young androecium, top view; *right*, above it, solitary stamen from behind.

**Genera** I 3; species: more than 300
**Distribution** I Tropics of South
America and Southeast Asia
**Habit** I Trees, shrubs, half shrubs,
rarely annual herbaceous plants, rarely
lianas
**Leaves** I Alternate, petiolate or
sessile, hairy, margin often denticulate
(fig. B), without stipules

**Inflorescences** I Umbellate, spicate,
corymbose (fig. C)
**Flowers** I Radial, hermaphroditic,
tetramerous-pentamerous-octamerous;
usually five fused sepals (fig. E);
usually five petals (fig. D) in tubular to
campanulate fusion; usually five
stamens, often with hairs beneath the
anthers (fig. J); the superior

bicarpellate ovary can develop two or
four locules.
**Fruits** I Drupes
**Use** I The hardwood of *Cordia
dodecandra* is often made into
furniture because it is termite resistant.
It is also used for making musical
instruments (tonewood). The fruits of
some tropical *Cordia* species are

edible. The roots and bark of *Cordia
africana* are used as a remedy; as a
decoction of leaves of other *Cordia*
species, it is likewise used.

**A–D:** *Coriaria nepalensis*. A: Racemose inflorescence. B: *Above*, flower from underneath; *below*, lateral. C: *Above*, flower, frontal; *below*, longitudinal. D: Unripe fruit; *above left*, frontal; *above right*, longitudinal; *below*, transverse.

**Genus** | 1; species: 5–30
**Distribution** | Warm temperate zones of Central and South America, Mediterranean region, East Asia
**Habit** | Trees, shrubs, half shrubs
**Leaves** | Opposite, whorled; leaf blade: simple, sessile, leathery, entire; also evergreen; no stipules

**Inflorescences** | Single, racemose
**Flowers** | Radial, hermaphroditic or unisexual, mostly pentamerous; five sepals, more or less spiral arrangement (fig. B, *above*); five petals, often smaller than the calyx; stamens in two whorls of five, longer than the petals; 5 (–10) mostly only basally

fused carpels form the superior ovary with usually five styles, each with one curved stigma
**Fruits** | Nutlike, achenes coated with a fleshy corolla (fig. D)
**Use** | The fruit of *Coriaria terminalis* and *C. sarmentosa* are edible. Some species are also used for tanning. An

insecticide, as well as a dye and ink, can be harvested from *Coriaria myrtifolia*. Various ornamental shrubs
**Characteristics** | The fruits of som species are poisonous and hallucinogenic.

**A–F:** *Cornus mas*. A: Inflorescence; leaves appear later. B: Partial inflorescence with bract-like bud scales. C: Flower, frontal; *left*, beneath it, from underneath. D: Gynoecium with basal nectar ring. E: *Above*, ripe fruit, lateral; *beneath it*, longitudinal. F: Seeds, transverse.

**G–L:** *Cornus sanguinea*. G: Paniculate inflorescence on foliate branch. H: Winter coloration of the stem. I: Flower from beneath. J: *Above*, flower, frontal; *left*, beneath it, longitudinal. K: Partial fruiting stage. L: Fruit, longitudinal.

**M–O:** *Cornus kousa*. Inflorescence framed by white bracts. N: Inflorescence, bracts removed. O: Single flower; *left*, frontal; *right*, longitudinal.

**Genera** | Cornoideae, 2 (*Alangium*, *Cornus*); species: about 85

**Distribution** | Temperate Northern Hemisphere, rarely tropical (Central and South America, Madagascar, Indo-Malaysian), and Southern Hemisphere (New Zealand)

**Habit** | Trees, shrubs, dwarf shrubs, rarely herbaceous plants

**Habitats** | Often in light deciduous forests

**Leaves** | Opposite, sometimes alternate, leaf blade simple, can be evergreen

**Inflorescences** | (Cyme) umbels, corymbs, often with bracts underneath (fig. M)

**Flowers** | Radial, hermaphroditic, also unisexual, then dioecious, small, often tetramerous flowers; calyx 4–5 laciniate, also absent; corolla 4–5-petaled, free, also absent; one stamen whorl of 4–5 stamens; the bicarpellate-tricarpellate-tetracarpellate ovary is inferior; from no locules to up to four locules; one style with lobate stigma; there is usually a circular nectar ring around the style (fig. C, *right*; fig. D; fig. O, *right*).

**Fruits** | Drupes, often with two ovules (figs. E, F); berries

**Use** | Ornamental shrubs, such as **blood twig dogwood** (*Cornus sanguinea*), **kousa dogwood** (*C. kousa*); also varieties with variegated leaves. The fruit of the **cornelian cherry** (*Cornus mas*) are edible. The hardwood is used to make spools and weaver's shuttles.

**Characteristics** | The cornelian cherry flowers before the leaves appear (fig. A). Often, four usually white, bright bracts grow below the inflorescence (fig. M). The branches of *Cornus sanguinea* turn red in winter (fig. H).

A–E: *Davidia involucrata*. A: Leaf. B: *Left*, inflorescence with 2 "handkerchief-like" bracts; *above right*, detail of inflorescence, composed of many male and female flowers. C: The same, longitudinal. D: *Above left*, female flower, frontal; *below*, ovary, transverse; *right*, next to it, female flower, longitudinal. E: Ripe fruit; *above*, lateral; *below*, transverse.

**Genera** | 5; species: 32
**Distribution** | Southeast Asia, North America
**Habit** | Trees, shrubs
**Leaves** | Spiral arrangement, simple, without stipules, mostly spiral arrangement, evergreen
**Inflorescences** | Capitiform, umbels, racemose
**Flowers** | Radial, hermaphroditic or unisexual, mostly pentamerous; calyx usually only as a denticulate or undenticulate margin or reduced; petals mostly small; 8–10–16 stamens; the unilocular ovary is inferior, with usually one ovule; the style is simple, with a two-column stigma.
**Fruits** | Drupes
**Use** | **Tupelo honey** (from the *Nyssa* species) is an American specialty. The fruit of the **water tupelo tree** (*N. aquatica*) and the **black tupelo tree** (*N. sylvatica*) are said to be edible. Because of their bright autumn foliage, they are also cultivated as ornamental plants.
**Characteristics** | A well-known specimen is the **handkerchief tree** or **ghost tree** (*Davidia involucrata*) (fig. B), which has relatively large, white involucral leaves/bracts that look like handkerchiefs hanging from the ends of its branches when it blooms.
**Notes** | The family was formerly categorized as a separate family, Nyssaceae (Davidiaceae), but was recently added to the Cornaceae as the Nyssoideae subfamily.

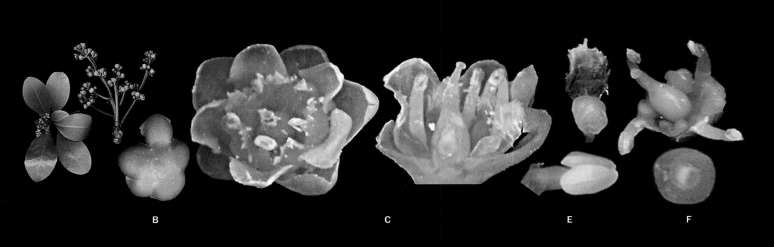

A–F: *Corynocarpus laevigatus*. A: Leafy sprout with inflorescence, frontal; *right*, next to it, paniculate inflorescence, lateral. B: *Left*, flower from underneath; *right*, flower, frontal. C: Flower, longitudinal. D: *Right*, flower with gynoecium/androecium and nectary scales, husk removed; *left*, next to it, solitary nectary scale with leaves. E: Solitary stamen. F: Ovary, transverse.

**Genus** | 1; species: 5
**Distribution** | Malay archipelago, Oceania
**Habit** | Evergreen trees, shrubs
**Leaves** | Alternate, spiral, leaf blade: simple, petiolate, entire, stipules are present or absent.

**Inflorescences** | Paniculate, racemose
**Flowers** | Radial, hermaphroditic, pentamerous, five free sepals, five free petals (fig. B), stamens in two circles of five, often alternate with nectary scales (fig. B, *right*; fig. C; fig. D, *left*); two carpels are fused into a superior ovary (fig. C; fig. D, *right*).
**Fruits** | One-seeded drupes
**Use** | The initially poisonous seeds in the fruit of the **karaka tree** (*Corynocarpus laevigatus*) can be consumed as flour after it is treated in various ways; the leaves are used to heal wounds. The wood is used for timber or firewood.
**Characteristics** | All parts of the plant are poisonous!

COSTACEAE

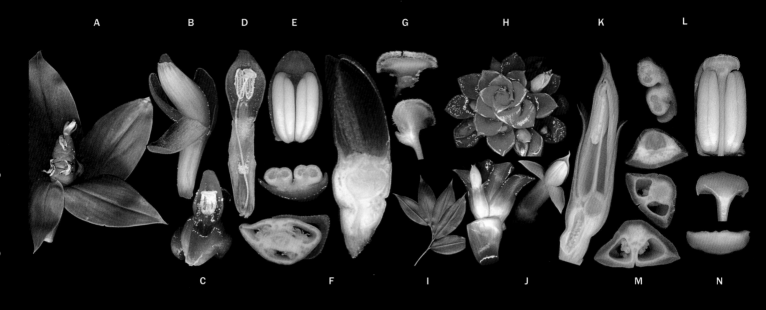

**A–G: *Costus scaber*.** A: Habit with cone-shaped inflorescence. B: Opening flower with calyx and corolla. C: Open flower, frontal. D: Flower, longitudinal. E: *Above*, stamen, top view; *below*, transverse. F: Ovary; *left*, transverse; *right*, longitudinal, with nectary. G: Stigma; *above*, frontal; *below*, lateral.

**H–N: *Tapeinochilos ananassae*.** H: Inflorescence. I: Foliage leaf. J: *Right*, flower lateral; *left*, opening bud. K: Flower, longitudinal. L: Stamen; *left*, transverse; *right*, top view, with style/stigma in center. M: Ovary, transverse; *below*, basal area; *center/above*, in the nectary area. N: Stigma, 2 different side views.

**Genera** | About 8; species: more than 100

**Distribution** | Almost worldwide in the tropics. Main focus in Neotropics, Pacific islands.

**Habit** | Perennial herbaceous plants with rhizomes as overwintering organs. Some succulents, climbing plants, epiphytes. They usually grow unbranched, spirally twining stalks, so-called pseudostems.

**Leaves** | Alternate, spiral, basal rosettes occur occasionally; leaf blade simple, entire, ovate to oblong, petiolate; at times the leaf sheath surrounds the stalk.

**Inflorescences** | Terminal, cone-shaped (figs. A, H), spicate, capitiform, cymose, often surrounded by strikingly colored bracts, rarely single flowers

**Flowers** | Hermaphroditic, zygomorphic, trimerous; three free calyxes and petals; one fertile stamen (figs. D–F, K, L), the five remaining transformed into staminodes, fused to a conspicuous labellum with a petaloid structure; usually much larger than the bracts and petals; three carpels are fused to an inferior ovary; many ovules per locule. Insect or bat pollination (entomophily and chiropterophily).

**Fruits** | Two-to-three-chambered capsules, rarely nuts

**Use** | The rhizomes of *Cheilocostus speciosus* (syn. *Hellenia speciosa*) are used medicinally in India. Some species are cultivated as part of botanical garden collections, such as the **pineapple ginger** (*Tapeinochilus ananassae*), which has waxy bracts that recall the shape of a pineapple and remain attractive for a long time.

**Characteristics** | In contrast to the Zingiberaceae, the Costaceae do not have an aromatic fragrance. Therefore, the name "ornamental ginger" is sometimes used for *Costus* plants. The Costaceae do not provide Indian costos root (*Sassurea lappa*); this species belongs to the Asteraceae.

**A–C:** *Cotyledon tomentosa*. A: Dichasial cyme inflorescence. B: Flower, frontal. C: *Above*, flower, longitudinal; *below*, transverse, with basal carpel scales.

**D–G:** *Echeveria pulvinata*. D: Inflorescence. E: Flower, frontal. F: Flower, longitudinal. G: *Left*, ovary, transverse; *right*, next to it, gynoecium, lateral, with carpel scales.

**H–K:** *Sempervivum arachnoideum*. H: *Left*, flower, frontal; *right*, next to it, flower from underneath. I: Petal with opposing and alternating stamen. J: Gynoecium; *lower left*, lateral / from underneath, with carpel scale; *above right*, top view. K: *Left*, ovary, transverse; *right*, the same, longitudinal.

**Subfamilies** | Sempervivoideae, Kalanchoideae, Crassuloideae
**Genera** | 34; species: more than 1,400
**Distribution** | Worldwide; concentrated in warm, dry regions, especially in Mexico and southern Africa
**Habit** | Rarely small trees (*Kalanchoe beharensis*) or with succulent trunks (*Tylecodon*), mostly perennial, rarely annual herbaceous plants
**Leaves** | Alternate, opposite or basal (cushion) rosettes, sessile. Leaf blade: simple, flat to cylindrical, entire, more or less succulent, stipules absent.
**Inflorescences** | Mostly thyrses, corymbs (fig. D), panicles, dichasia (fig. A)
**Flowers** | Radial (figs. B, E, H), hermaphroditic as a rule, usually protandrous, (trimerous-)pentamerous (-32)-fold; sepals, free or basally fused, much shorter than the petals (fig. H, *right*); these are free or fused into a tube, often with dorsal keel (fig. F); the same or double number of stamens are present, like petals, free, usually obdiplostemonous; as many carpels as petals, mostly free or basally fused, often with nectary scales (figs. C, G); superior ovary (figs. C, F). Insect or bird pollination (entomophily or ornithophily).
**Fruits** | Follicle fruits. Seed dispersal by wind and gravity.
**Use** | Many ornamental and houseplants, such as **kalanchoes** (*Kalanchoe blossfeldiana*), **stonecrops** (*Hylotelephium* sp.), **jade plants**, or the "**money plant**" (*Crassula ovata*), or **sedum**. The rhizomes of the **rhodiola** (*Rhodiola rosea*) are said to have a performance-enhancing effect. The **creeping stonecrop** (*Sedum rupestris*) is said to be edible as a kitchen herb.
**Characteristics** | The emperor Charlemagne ordered people to plant **houseleeks** (*Sempervivum tectorum*) on their roofs to ward off lightning strikes and fire. The latter did indeed work, because rooftops overgrown with houseleeks are more humid than ones without them. Sempervivum means "always alive." The **Goethe plant** (*Kalanchoe pinnata*) and other *Kalanchoe* species grow bulbils at the indentations of their leaf margins. They fall to the ground and grow roots. It was in the stonecrop family that a special metabolic pathway, Crassulacean acid metabolism (CAM), was first detected. In this process, the plants absorb carbon dioxide through the stomata during the night and store it in the form of malic acid or malate. During the day, the stomata remain closed and the malic acid / malate is converted into glucose in the normal Calvin cycle. As a result, plants growing in dry habitats lose less water during the hot daytime. Many other adaptations to dry habitats occur, such as succulence, hairiness as radiation protection (e.g., the cobweb houseleek, *Sempervivum arachnoideum*), or waxy layers.

# CUCURBITACEAE

**A–D:** *Psiguria triphylla.* A: Female flower; *above*, frontal; *below*, longitudinal. B: Male flower; *left*, lateral; *right*, longitudinal. C: Ovary, transverse. D: Leaf.

**E–J:** *Cucurbita pepo* **ssp.** *pepo.* E: Part of a sprout with ripening fruit; *below*, above it, male and female flower. F: Male flower, frontal. G: *Below*, female flower, longitudinal; *above*, male flower, longitudinal. H: Stigma/style. I: Stamens. J: Young fruit, transverse.

**K–P:** *Bryonia dioica.* K: *Above*, male flower, frontal; *below*, female flower, frontal. L: Detail of underside of flower: Calyx. M: 2 of 5 stamens. N: Female flower; *above*, lateral; *below*, longitudinal. O: Fruit, transverse. P: Seeds.

**Genera** | More than 115; species: more than 800

**Distribution** | Worldwide in the tropics, a few genera in temperate regions

**Habitat** | In semideserts

**Habit** | Perennials, often trailing herbaceous plants or climbers with stem tendrils, often with taproots, also tubers, can have thick trunks (*Pachycaulie*), are used for storage

**Leaves** | Alternate, petiolate, leaf blade simple or lobed, very rarely succulent, sometimes with water-storing cells; stipules are mostly absent or transformed into spines, some species with extrafloral nectaries.

**Inflorescences** | Cymose or single flowers

**Flowers** | Radial, unisexual with rudiments of the opposite sex, monoecious or dioecious, pentamerous; the flower often develops a cup-shaped or campanulate hypanthium with annular nectar glands; five sepals are usually fused; the five petals are mostly funnel form or campanulate, free or fused. The normally five stamens often have only one theca; the bicarpellate-tricarpellate ovary is inferior, bilobate to trilobate; one style with 2–3–5 style arms; its habits of male and female organs are very similar (for reasons of pollination!) (figs. H, I).

**Fruits** | Berries (fig. O), gourds (fig. E), also capsule fruit

**Use** | **Pumpkins** and **winter squash** (*Cucurbita pepo*), **zucchini** and **summer squash** (*C. pepo* subsp. *pepo convar giromontiina*), **muskmelons** (*Cucurbita melo*), **cucumbers** (*Cucumis sativus*); these all are eaten fresh, fried, pickled, candied, baked. The juice can also be fermented to make alcoholic drinks, as well as liqueurs and cordials. The seeds of many species are edible and nutritious. The hollowed-out fruit are also used as containers. Also medicinal use.

**Characteristics** | Stem tendrils, branched or unbranched, also transformed into spines; some plants use explosive dispersal of seeds: the **squirting cucumber** (*Ecballium elaterium*), exploding cucumber (*Cyclanthera brachystachya*).

A B C D F H J L M O

E G I K N P

**A–E:** *Dicranopygium atrovirens*. A: Bracts around the spadix. B: Spadix, female phase. C: *Above*, male-phase spadix, frontal; *below*, longitudinal. D: Male flower, lateral; *right*, frontal. E: *Left*, female-phase spadix; female flower, *above*, frontal; *below*, longitudinal.

**F–I:** *Asplundia* **sp**. F: Male-phase spadix. G: Detail of F; *below*, male flower, frontal. H: *Below left*, male-phase spadix, longitudinal; *right*, male flower, lateral; *above*, frontal. I: *Left*, female flower, frontal; *right*, the same, longitudinal.

**J–P:** *Cyclanthus bipartitus*. J: Female-phase spadix, lateral. K: *Left*, the same, frontal; *right above*, in male phase, frontal. L: *Above*, stamens from underneath; *below*, from above. M: Female-phase spadix, longitudinal. N: Female flower, longitudinal; *left*, stamens. O: Stamens. P: Spadix in male phase, longitudinal.

**Subfamilies** I Carludovicoideae, Cyclanthoideae

**Genera** I 12; species: about 230. Genera are *Asplundia*, *Carludovica*, *Chorigyne*, *Cyclanthus*, *Dianthoveus*, *Dicranopygium*, *Evodianthus*, *Ludovia*, *Schultesiophytum*, *Sphaeradenia*, *Stelestylis*, *Thoracocarpus*.

**Distribution** I Neotropical

**Habit** I Terrestrial perennial or epiphytic herbaceous plants, rarely lianas

**Leaves** I Alternate, spiral to distichous, petiole usually present, leaf sheaths open; leaf blade usually divided, either palmate or bifid

**Inflorescences** I Terminal or lateral spadix enveloped by 2–4 (–11) leaflike or petaloid spatha (fig. A)

**Flowers** I Radial, unisexual, monoecious, in dense groups, spiral arrangement, each group composed of either a fenake flower, which is surrounded by four male flowers (Carludovicodeae; fig. E), or of alternating whorls in a "disciform"

arrangement of male and female flowers (Cyclanthoideae; fig. J). The flowers have either four or no involucral bracts; each male flower consists of 10–20 (–150) stamens, which may be basally fused (fig. L, *center*). The female flowers contain four filament- or worm-shaped staminodes opposite the perianth, which can grow to be up to 10 cm long (figs. A, C, F) and can support the remnants of the anthers; the ovary, fused from four carpels, is inferior or

medial, four stigmas alternating with the tepals.

**Fruits** I Multiple fruits of fleshy berries

**Use** I The dried leaf fibers of *Carludovica palmata* are used to braid Panama hats.

**Characteristics** I *Carludovica palmata* is known by the common name "**Panama hat palm**," but it is not a representative of the palm family.

A  B    D  E      F      G        I        J

C                            H                        K

**A–E:** *Carex pendula.* A: Habit; *above*, male inflorescence; *below*, female. B: Leaf, transverse. C: Sprout, transverse. D: *Right*, male inflorescence; *left*, one of its flowers. E: *Left*, female inflorescence; *above right*, flower, 3 of its stigmas; *below*, young fruit; *below left*, utricule with ovary, longitudinal; *right*, transverse.

**F–H:** *Carex grayii.* F: Male and 2 star-of-Bethlehem-like female inflorescences with stigmas. G: *Left*, upper part of the male inflorescence; *right*, one of its flowers. H: *Left*, female flower; *center*, bract; *right*, utricule, longitudinal, with ovary and ovule.

**I–K:** *Carex hirta.* I: *Above*, inflorescence; *below*, detail. J: *Above*, young flower; older one below it. K: *Left*, ovary, transverse; *right*, fruit.

**Subfamilies** | Mapanioideae, Cyperoideae
**Genera** | about 100; species: about 5,500. Best-known and largest genera: *Carex, Cyperus.*
**Distribution** | Worldwide; concentrated in temperate and subpolar regions, especially in swampy, humid habitats
**Habit** | Mostly a perennial, rarely an annual, grasslike herbaceous plants; usually with triangular (fig. C), rarely articulated, stalks (but never thickened and gnarled). Stalks (unlike the sweetgrasses) are pithy, with underground, creeping rhizomes; the plants grow tufts or tussocks.
**Leaves** | Mostly alternate, often basal, ternate, with usually closed leaf sheath. Leaf blade: linear, filiform, bristly, grassy (fig. A), often keeled (fig. B), with parallel venation.
**Inflorescences** | Single spikes or arranged in many spicate, paniculate, or capitiform inflorescences (figs. D, E, F, I), surrounded by foliage-like bracts
**Flowers** | Radial, hermaphroditic or unisexual, then monoecious or dioecious; flowers small, inconspicuous; tepals reduced to bristles, hairs, scales; (1–) 3 stamens; the ovary, fused from (1–) 2 carpels, is superior; one ovule per flower. In the genus *Carex*, the flower or fruit is surrounded by a tubular organ (= utricle), which grows from the flower's husk (figs. E, H, K).
**Fruits** | One-seeded nut fruits

**Use** | Papyrus was made from the pith of *Cyperus papyrus* stalks; it was cut into strips, which were laid one atop the other and pressed. The gnarled and thickened runners of the **water chestnut** (*Eleocharis dulcis*), **yellow nutsedge** (*Cyperus esculentus*), and **nutgrass** (*Cyperus rotundus*) are edible. The latter two species are feared as aggressive neophytes in some places. Some sedge species are dried to make bedding for animals; for example, **lesser pond sedge** (*Carex acutiformis*) and **slender tufted sedge** (*C. acuta*). People used to use many of the reeds for weaving or braiding baskets, etc. The **lakeshore bulrush** (*Schoenoplectus lacustris*) is planted in constructed wetlands because it generates a particularly large amount of oxygen. Its rhizomes are edible. The cotton-like hairs of the **cottongrass family** (*Eriophorum* sp.) were formerly used to staunch bleeding wounds. In addition, people used them to make candle wicks and to stuff pillows.
**Characteristics** | The **crooked sedge** (*Carex curvula*) often forms the dominant plant community on acid soils in the alpine tier of the European Central Alps: the "Alpine grass heath." The plants are regularly attacked by a fungus (*Pleospora elynae*), which causes them to die away starting from the leaf tips, turn yellow by early summer, and crinkle up in a characteristic way.

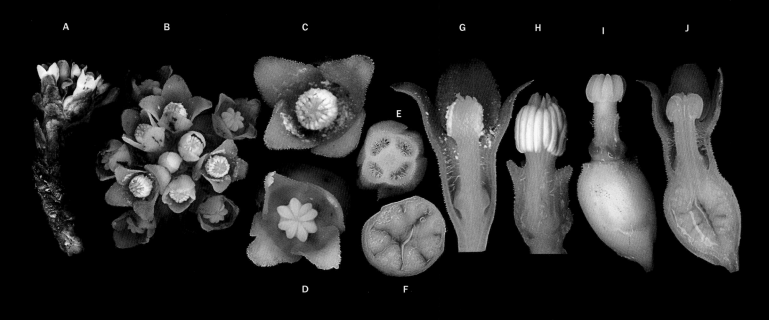

A–J: *Cytinus cf. hypocystis.* A: Inflorescence, lateral. B: The same, frontal. C: Male flower, frontal. D: Female flower, frontal. E: Male flower, transverse, in the nectar cover area. F: Ovary, transverse. G: Female flower, longitudinal. H: Androecium dissected from the perianth; the orange-colored nectary can be seen in the basal section. I: Gynoecium without perianth, lateral, with slightly more intensely colored nectary. J: Female flower, longitudinal.

**CYTINACEAE**

**Genera** | 2: *Cytinus, Bdallophyton*; species: about 8

**Distribution** | Mediterranean region, South Africa Cape region, Canary Islands, Madagascar, Mexico, Central America

**Habit** | Chlorophyll-free root parasites; except for the flower and fruit, they live underground and use haustoria to penetrate the host plant's roots and absorb nutrients from them.

**Leaves** | Foliage leaves are absent; only the inflorescence bracts, which are alternate or opposite, whorled, often reduced to membranous scales.

**Inflorescences** | Racemose, capitiform (figs. A, B)

**Flowers** | Radial, hermaphroditic or unisexual, then monoecious or dioecious; 4–9 sepals fused into a tube; petals absent, male flowers with 8–100 stamens (figs. E, G), often sessile without filaments, united into a column (figs. C, H). Female flowers: ovary consisting of 4–8 (–14) carpels, inferior (figs. F, J), with 25–100 ovules, parietal; the style is more or less long; most of the eight stigma surfaces are apically flattened; laterally angular (figs. D, I). Pollination probably by entomophily.

**Fruits** | Berries, seeds without endosperm

**Characteristics** | The Mediterranean species are often parasites on plants of the rockrose family (Cistaceae); others are found on aster family (Asteraceae) plants. The classification of this family is controversial; some authors consider it one of the Rafflesiales, which include only highly specialized full parasites.

**A–C:** *Dillenia philippinensis*. A: Flower, frontal. B: Calyx. C: Flower, longitudinal.

**D–G:** *Hibbertia dentata*. D: Flower, frontal. E: Flower from beneath. F: Flower, longitudinal. G: Gynoecium, frontal.

**DILLENIACEAE FAMILY**
Order: Dilleniales

# DILLENIACEAE

**Genera** I 12; species: about 400
**Distribution** I Pantropical, especially tropical Asia
**Habit** I Deciduous or evergreen trees, shrubs, lianas, rarely perennial herbaceous plants
**Leaves** I Usually alternate and spiral arrangement, rarely opposite or basal, leaf blade usually simple and lobed, leaf margin smooth or with winged stipules

**Inflorescences** I Cymose or racemose inflorescences or solitary
**Flowers** I Radial or zygomorphic, hermaphroditic, mostly pentamerous; usually (3–) 5 (–20) free sepals; usually (2–) 5 free white or yellow petals; (1–10) 15–150 free or fused stamens, either all fertile or at times sterile; usually (1–) 2–7 (–20) carpels, free or fused into a syncarp; superior ovary (figs. F, G)

**Fruits** I Mostly aggregate, follicle or nut fruits, rarely capsules or berries. Sepals are often retained. Seeds with arils.
**Use** I The **elephant apple** (*Dillenia indica*) is planted in Southeast Asia and the Caribbean islands as an ornamental tree for its large, white flowers and its sour-aromatic, edible sepals. Soap is made from the pulp.

The **guinea flower** (*Hibbertia scandens*) is used as a container plant.
**Characteristics** I The name honors the German physician and botanist Johann Jakob Dillen (1684–1747).

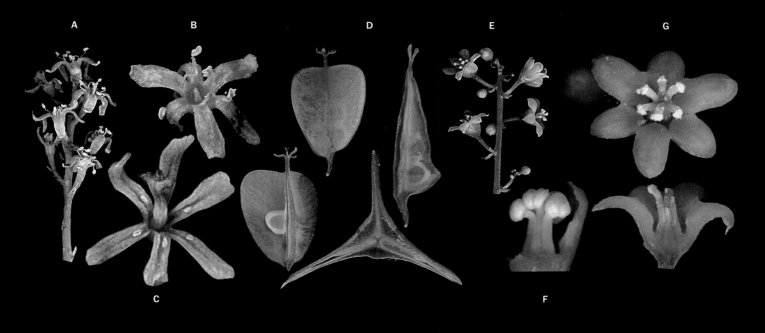

**A–D:** *Dioscorea elephantipes.* A: Inflorescence. B: Older male flower, frontal. C: Female flower, frontal. D: Young fruit; *above*, lateral; *left*, underneath, longitudinal; *right center*, across; *far right*, other longitudinal plane.

**E–G:** *Tamus communis*, E: Inflorescence. F: Unopened stamens, lateral. G: Flower; *above*, frontal; *below*, longitudinal.

**Genera** I 3: *Dioscorea*, *Stenomeris*, *Trichopus*; species: 600–870
**Distribution** I Worldwide, especially in the tropics, even in warm temperate regions
**Habit** I Perennial herbaceous climbers or lianas, rarely shrubs; rhizomes or tubers as overwintering organ
**Leaves** I Mostly alternate, spiral arrangement, rarely opposite, leaf blade often large, simple or compound, leaves sessile or petiolate, occasionally with extrafloral nectaries, margin is entire, feather venation with acrodromous and eamptodromous secondary veins.

**Inflorescences** I Great variety: panicular, spikes, racemose
**Flowers** I Radial, dioclinous, usually dioecious, but also monoecious; flowers are trimerous of six tepals in two whorls (figs. B, C, G); six stamens, three in two whorls; the ovary, consisting of three fused carpels, is medial to inferior; style short with three stigma lobes.
**Fruits** I Mostly capsule fruits, rarely berries or samaras (fig. D)
**Use** I The starchy tubers of about 40 *Dioscorea* species, called **yams**, have been used as a food source for a long time. The small underground tubers of

the **air potato** (*D. bulbifera*) are inedible. However, the plant grows edible tubers in the leaf axils, but these must be boiled to destroy the poisonous substances they contain. Steroidal saponins occur in all parts of the plant, and diosgenin, which is used to produce contraceptive hormones, is formed particularly in the yam tubers.
**Characteristics** I The family name Dioscoreaceae honors the Greek physician Pedanius Dioscurides, who shaped the art of healing for a long time in antiquity. His book *De Materia medica* ("On medical matters") was the standard work of ancient medicine.

The German name, **Schmerwurzgewächse** (wild yam family), is derived from the Old High German *smerte* = sharp, probably because of the high content of irritating calcium oxalates. The genus *Tacca*, with 5–16 species, is classified by some authors in the Schmerwurzgewächse or wild yam family. In accordance with APG III, here it is presented as its own family, Taccaceae (see under that family).

**A–C:** *Scabiosa columbaria*. A: *Above left*, capitulum, frontal, in male phase; *right*, next to it, underside; *below*, longitudinal. B: Single flower; *above*, frontal, in female phase; *below that*, lateral view. C: Not-quite-ripe fruiting stage; *below left*, single fruit, frontal, with 5 calyx bristles; *above right*, the same, lateral; *below right*, longitudinal.

**Genera** I 11-14; species: about 290.
**Distribution** I Europe (Mediterranean region) to eastern Asia, central to southern Africa.
**Habitats** I Mostly dry, open habitats.
**Habit** I Half-shrubs, herbaceous plants, annuals to perennials.
**Leaves** I Opposite or whorled leaf arrangement, without stipules.
**Inflorescences** I Capitiform inflorescences surrounded by involucral bracts or on a whorl of bracts (Fig. A right), ray flowers, often enlarged (Fig. A left, B below).
**Flowers** I Zygomorphic, hermaphroditic, protandrous, also purely female inflorescences can occur; tetramerous-pentamerous, corolla gamosepalous, bilabiate, calyx still flexible on the flowers, becoming bristly as fruit ripens (Fig. C). Outer calyx often as a membranous margin, cup-shaped; 2-4 stamens, the unicarpellate ovary usually has 1 hanging ovule.
**Fruits** I Nut-like (achenes) with retained calyx and outer calyx (Figure C); the fruits are often dispersed by sticking to the outside of an animal's coat.
**Use** I Ornamental plants. The dry, often hard fruits of some members of the teasel family were used in the past for "carding" (combing) shorn wool or for raising a nap on wool fabrics ("teaseling").

**Characteristics** I The achenes of the field scabious (Knautia arvensis) have an elaiosome, which encourages ants to carry away the fruit; this occurs in addition to dispersal by epizoochory. The 5 dark calyx bristles of the dove pincushion (Scabiosa columbaria, Fig. C) are hygroscopic, which is supposed to cause them to creep along the ground in humid conditions. Recently, the teasel family was assigned to the honeysuckle family (Caprifoliaceae).

A: *Drosera rotundifolia* habit

B–H: *Drosera capensis*. B: Racemose inflorescence, lateral. C: Leaf with capitate glandular hairs. D: Flower, frontal. E: The same, longitudinal. F: Calyx. G: Fruit, lateral. H: Capsule, frontal.

**Genera** | 3: *Drosera* (sundew), *Dionaea* (Venus flytrap), *Aldrovanda* (waterwheel); species: 110

**Distribution** | Worldwide

**Habitats** | Acid, moist to wet, nutrient-poor soils, such as hill moors and low-moor bogs, fresh water

**Habit** | Rosettes (fig. A); also submerged, rootless aquatic plants

**Leaves** | Whorled, leaf blade round or oblong, with sticky tentacles (figs. A, C), sensitive to stimuli, leaves that snap shut along the midrib, petiolate

**Inflorescences** | Often scorpioid cymes, racemose (fig. B)

**Flowers** | Radial, hermaphroditic, tetramerous-pentamerous; calyx tetramerous-pentamerous (fig. F); corolla usually pentamerous (fig. D); petals free, cordiform margin (fig. D); the tetracarpellate-pentacarpellate ovary is superior, 4–5 solitary style arms.

**Fruits** | Capsules (figs. G, H)

**Characteristics** | These plants capture insects by using sticky and snapping traps, in which the animals remain stuck. The plant digests them with secretions from glands. The Venus flytrap (*Dionaea muscipula*) is considered by many authors to be the fastest plant in the world; often just stimulating the three trigger hairs on the trap halves twice is enough to snap the trap shut. By using digestive secretions, the plant can consume everything except for the chitinous exoskeleton of the animals it preys upon (mostly insects).

DROSOPHYLLACEAE

A–I: *Drosophyllum lusitanicum*. A: Habit. B: Young leaf with glandular hairs, not yet unfurled. C: *Above*, flower, frontal; *beneath it at right*, lateral. D: Calyx; *left*, frontal; *at right*, next to it, solitary sepals. E: Unopened stamen from bud. F: Young fruit, transverse, cut higher and deeper. G: Gynoecium; *left*, lateral; *right*, longitudinal. H: Open capsule. I: Mature seeds.

**Genus** | 1; only species: dewy pine, *Drosophyllum lusitanicum*

**Distribution** | Spain, Portugal

**Habitat** | On slightly acidic to neutral soils, extremely dry stony/rocky sandy soils, very sunny habitats that tend to dry out

**Habit** | Half shrub, rarely over 1.5 meters tall

**Leaves** | Leaves are up to 30 cm long; the buds unfurl outward (fig. B). Sticky trap composed of two different kinds of glands: red-colored, immobile trapping glands with multicellular shafts that excrete a sticky secretion; and digestive glands, which can be colorless or red, occur 5–10 times more frequently, and excrete digestive secretions directly onto the leaf surface.

**Inflorescences** | Corymbs

**Flowers** | Pentamerous, calyx with tentacles, hairy (fig. D), five free yellow petals (fig. C); androecium: 10–20 stamens arranged in two whorls (fig. E); the pentacarpellate ovary with five free (filamentous) styles and capitiform stigmas (fig. G) is superior.

**Fruits** | Capsule (fig. H) with 5–10 black seeds, up to 2 mm in size (shiny) (fig. I), which remain able to germinate for several years

**Characteristics** | The plants trap insects, which they attract by a honey fragrance. Well-developed root system with taproot (habitats that dry out). Self-pollinator; the flowers open only for a few hours.

A  B  C  D  F  H
G
E  I

**A–B:** *Crinodendron patagua*. A: Flower; *above left*, frontal; *right*, next to it, from underneath; *below left*, lateral, front petals removed; *right*, next to it, longitudinal. B: *Above*, ovary, transverse; *below it*, longitudinal.

**C–I:** *Elaeocarpus sylvestris*. C: Inflorescence, frontal and lateral. D: *Above*, younger flower, frontal, petals removed; *below it*, older flower with petals. E: Flower from underneath, calyx. F: Single young petal. G: Flower, longitudinal. H: Nectary surrounding transverse section of ovary. I: Mature ovary, transverse.

**Genera** I 11–14; species: about 290

**Distribution** I Europe (Mediterranean region) to eastern Asia, central to southern Africa

**Habitats** I Mostly dry, open habitats

**Habit** I Half shrubs, herbaceous plants, annuals to perennials

**Leaves** I Opposite or whorled leaf arrangement, without stipules

**Inflorescences** I Capitiform inflorescences surrounded by involucral bracts or on a whorl of bracts (fig. A, *right*), ray flowers, often enlarged (fig. A, *left*; fig. B, *below*)

**Flowers** I Zygomorphic, hermaphroditic, protandrous; also purely female inflorescences can occur; tetramerous-pentamerous, corolla gamosepalous, bilabiate; calyx still flexible on the flowers, becoming bristly as fruit ripens (fig. C). Outer calyx often as a membranous margin, cup shaped; 2–4 stamens; the unicarpellate ovary usually has one hanging ovule.

**Fruits** I Nutlike (achenes) with retained calyx and outer calyx (fig. C); the fruits are often dispersed by sticking to the outside of an animal's coat.

**Use** I Ornamental plants. The dry, often-hard fruits of some members of the teasel family were used in the past for "carding" (combing) shorn wool or for raising a nap on wool fabrics ("teaseling").

**Characteristics** I The achenes of the **field scabious** (*Knautia arvensis*) have an elaiosome, which encourages ants to carry away the fruit; this occurs in addition to dispersal by epizoochory. The five dark calyx bristles of the dove pincushion (*Scabiosa columbaria*; fig. C) are hygroscopic, which is supposed to cause them to creep along the ground in humid conditions. Recently, the teasel family was assigned to the honeysuckle family (Caprifoliaceae).

**ELAEOCARPACEAE**

117

# ERICACEAE

**A–D:** *Ledum palustre.* A: Habit. B: Leaf, transverse. C: *Above*, flower, frontal; *below*, lateral. D: Fruit.

**E–H:** *Vaccinium myrtillus.* E: *Above*, flower, frontal; *below*, longitudinal; *left*, stamens. F: Gynoecium. G: Ovary, transverse. H: Fruit, frontal; *center*, longitudinal; *below*, transverse.

**I–K:** *Arbutus unedo.* I: *Above*, flower, frontal; *center*, nectar drops inside the corolla; *below*, longitudinal. J: Stamen; *above*, from the front; *center*, from behind; *below*, open. K: Young fruit; *left*, lateral; *center*, transverse; *right*, longitudinal.

**L–O:** *Macleania cordifolia.* L: *Above left*, corolla, lateral; *right*, bud; *below*, corolla, longitudinal. M: *Above*, flower, frontal; *below*, bud, frontal. N: Stamen; *left*, from the front; *right*, lateral. O: *Above*, ovary, longitudinal; *below*, transverse.

**Genera** | More than 125; species: more than 3,900

**Distribution** | Worldwide, except Australia. Main concentrations: East Asia, New Guinea.

**Habits** | Shrubs, half shrubs, mycorrhiza often occurs, climbing plants, also herbaceous plants.

**Habitat** | Often on mineral-poor acid soils, in tropical areas in the mountains, hill moors

**Leaves** | Spiral arrangement, opposite, whorled, leaf blade undivided, usually evergreen, usually without stipules, margin often rolled up, underside hairy (fig. B)

**Inflorescences** | Racemose, spicate, corymbose, paniculate, solitary

**Flowers** | Radial, sometimes slightly zygomorphic, hermaphroditic, rarely diclinous, tetramerous-septamerous; calyx usually free, may also be reduced to a margin (fig. F); corolla mostly fused, rarely free (fig. C); stamens inserted on outer margin of a disc (figs. E, F); they often open through apical pores (fig. J, *below*); often the connective forms "taillike" appendages on its rear side (fig. J); (4–) 5 (–10) fused carpels form the superior or inferior ovary. One style with a capitate, rarely slightly lobed stigma.

**Fruits** | Berries (fig. H), drupes, (septicidal) capsules (fig. D), nut fruits

**Use** | Some Ericaceae grow delicious fruits, such as **bilberries** (*Vaccinium myrtilis*) and **lingonberries** (*V. vitis-idaea*). In Scandinavia, people eat the fruit of the **black crowberry** (*Empetrum nigrum*). Fruit wine and preserves are made from the fruit of the **strawberry tree** (*Arbutus unedo*). This family supplies many ornamental plants: rhododendron species (about 1,200 species) and *Erica* species (over 500), such as the **winter heath** (*Erica carnea*), **cross-leaved heath** (*E. tetralix*), **redvein enkianthus** (*Enkianthus campanulatus*), and mountain laurel (*Kalmia latifolia*). Some plants have medical uses, such as **marsh tea** (*Ledum palustre*), which is used in homeopathic medicine, and wintergreen oil from the leaves of the **American wintergreen** (*Gaultheria procumbens*) is an analgesic and promotes circulation. **Scotch heather** (*Calluna vulgaris*) is a popular bee pasture plant that supplies us with heather honey.

**Characteristics** | One- to multicelled trichomes, also glandular scales; the stems are sometimes winged. Some plants contain toxic substances, such as the **bog rosemary** (*Andromeda polifola*).

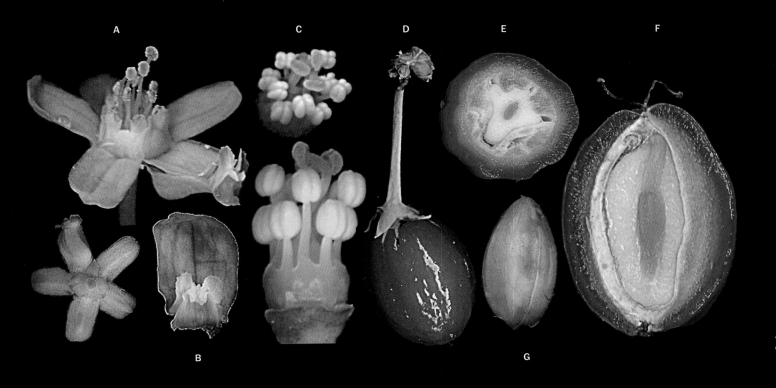

A B C D E F G

**A–G:** *Erythroxylum coca*. A: Flower, lateral; *below it*, from underneath. B: Single petal. C: *Above*, androecium surrounding style arms, frontal; *below*, lateral, perianth removed. D: Ripe fruit, lateral. E: Fruit, transverse. F: The same, longitudinal. G: Seeds.

**Genera** | 4; species: 240
**Distribution** | Pantropical, both in the tropics and subtropics
**Habit** | Trees, shrubs
**Leaves** | Alternate, rarely opposite, leaf blade simple, intrapetiolar stipules present (in front of the petioles)
**Inflorescences** | Terminal, axillary, in tufts
**Flowers** | Radial, hermaphroditic; five free sepals; five free petals, with

appendages or calluses on the inside (fig. B, *right*); two whorls of five stamens, can be of various lengths in the two stamen whorls (fig. C), also with fused filaments (fig. C); 3–4 fused carpels form the superior, trilocular to quadrilocular ovary. There are usually only 1 (–2) viable seeds; style free, with a capitiform stigma.
**Fruits** | Drupes (figs. D–F); the calyx and filaments are retained on the base of the fruit.

**Use** | Wood (the "ironwood" and "redwood" of *Erythroxylum areolatum*), dye made from the bark, essential oils; the leaves of **Erythroxylum coca** are used by indigenous people to produce cocaine.
**Characteristics** | Young stems often have scales; may be heterostylous. These plants are often given the common name "redwood" because the heartwood is reddish,

but this has no taxonomic meaning. Ironwood is also a collective name for (tropical) woods, which are characterized by the fact that their wood is very hard and heavier than water.

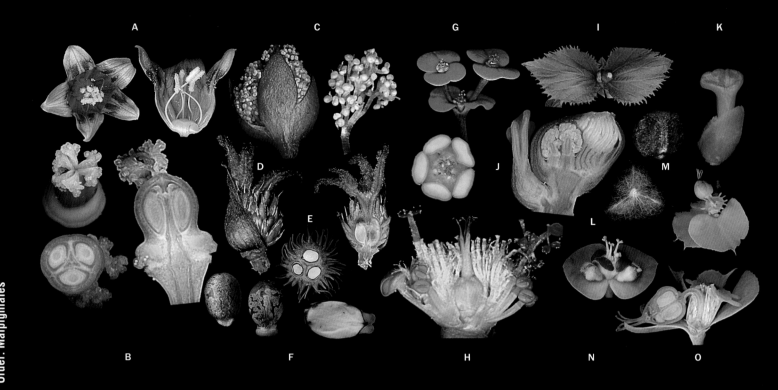

**A–B:** *Manihot esculenta*. A: *Left*, male flower, frontal; *right*, longitudinal, with nectary. B: female flower; *top left*, frontal; *below*, ovary, transverse; *right*, female flower, longitudinal, husk removed.
**C–F:** *Ricinus communis*. C: Male flower; *left*, lateral; *right*, without husk. D: Female flower; *left*, lateral; *right*, longitudinal. E: Fruit, transverse. F: *Left*, seed with caruncle; *right*, longitudinal.
**G–H:** *Euphorbia milii*. G: Partial inflorescence. H: *Above*, top view of cyathium, surrounded by 5 nectaries; *below*, longitudinal.

**I–M:** *Dalechampia spathulata* **var.** *Rosea*. I: Pleiochasium with bracts. J: Pleiochasium, longitudinal. K: Female flower with bract. L: Fruit. M: Seeds.
**N:** *Euphorbia* **sp.** cyathium
**O:** *Euphorbia segetalis* cyathium; *above*, lateral; *below*, longitudinal

**Genera** | 218; species: more than 5,700
**Distribution** | Worldwide
**Habit** | Perennials, herbaceous plants, also stem succulents
**Habitats** | On sandy beaches, bushy fields, rough pasture, mountain and water meadows, light forests, forest edges, brushwood
**Leaves** | Alternate or opposite, also spiral arrangement, leaf blade simple or palmate, stipules usually small or absent
**Inflorescences** | Triple- or multiradial pleiochasia change over into dichasia; one inflorescence (= cyathium), often surrounded by colored bracts: one central female flower is surrounded by up to five rows of male flowers; 4–5 often crescent-shaped or oblong-round (extrafloral) nectaries between the bracts and the male flowers create the image of a single flower.
**Flowers** | Radial, rarely zygomorphic, unisexual, monoecious or dioecious, receptacle also with nectary; calyx present or absent; 4–5 usually free petals; male flowers with one or more stamens, free or fused; female flowers with superior, mostly trilocular ovary of 2–3 fused carpels, each with 1–2 ovules; style free or fused
**Fruits** | Capsule, also winged, also mericarps, which detach themselves from the center column and usually burst open through two valves; seeds also have a caruncule (fig. F)

**Use** | Food, ornamental and medicinal plants, such as **cassava** (*Manihot esculenta*). Cassava is inedible when raw, but when the toxic cyanogenic glycosides have been removed through extensive pretreatment and cooking, it is edible. The **Para rubber tree** (*Hevea brasiliensis*) supplies both natural rubber and latex, as does *Manihot glaziovii*. The highly toxic seeds of the **castor bean plant** (*Ricinus communis*) provide castor oil. The seeds of the **candlenut tree** (*Aleurites moluccanus*) are edible after roasting. Biodiesel can be obtained from the seed oil of the **spurge tree** (*Jatropha curcas*). The **crotons** (*Codiaeum variegatum*) include many colorful ornamental plants that are popular houseplants.
**Characteristics** | Bracts can be vividly colored (fig. I), such as on the **poinsettia** (*Euphorbia pulcherrima*) or the **crown-of-thorns** (*Euphorbia milii*; fig. G). In adapting to the dry habitats of cacti in the New World, the spurge species of the Old World have developed comparable habits. Such external similarity of genetically different plants is called "convergence." Most of the plant parts contain a poisonous (!), skin-irritating milky sap; hence the German name *Wolfsmilch* (wolf's milk) for the genus *Euphorbia*.

**A–D:** *Pisum sativum.* A: Leaf with stipules/tendrils. B: *Left*, flower, frontal; *right*, from behind. C: Dissected flower, lateral, androecium and gynoecium separated. D: Nine fused stamens; *above*, the 10th free; *below*, ovary.

**E:** *Cytisus scoparius. Above,* flower, lateral; *below*, with furled stamens.
**F:** *Genista canariensis* calyx
**G:** *Robinia viscosa* calyx
**H:** *Trifolium pratense.* Opened calyx.

**I:** *Lathyrus latifolius.* Closed and open fruit; *center,* seeds.
**J:** *Anthyllis vulneraria.* Open ovary.
**K:** *Medicago lupulina* fruits
**L:** *Entada gigas.* Part of the loment, seeds below.

**Genera** I 730; species: more than 19,000
**Distribution** I Worldwide
**Habitats** I Chalky soils, in steppes and semideserts
**Habit** I Shrubs, trees, perennials. The sprout can also be winged.
**Leaves** I Mostly alternate, different pinnation, such as ternate (= "cloverleaf-like"), paired or unpaired, with or without tendrils, also with spiny leaves; the stipules are often conspicuous.
**Inflorescences** I Mostly racemose
**Flowers** I Zygomorphic: "butterfly blossoms," hermaphroditic; five sepals, mostly fused. The usually free corolla consists of the vexillary (= flag), the

two alates (= wing), and the carina (= keel; fig. C) of two petals. The stamens, numbering 4–7–10 to numerous, are multiply fused; in many native species with ten stamens, nine are fused to a filament tube, and the tenth, at the top, remains free (fig. D); one carpel forms the superior ovary, which may be multiseeded; usually a patelliform nectary develops around the base; the style may have a tuft on top; the stigma is usually small.
**Fruits** I Legumes (bursts open at the back and suture), straight or furled; also articulated, one-seeded nutlets
**Use** I Fodder plants and seeds as food: **garden peas** (*Pisum sativum*), **lentils** (*Lens culinaris*), **beans**

(*Phaseolus* and *Vigna* species), **soybeans** (*Glycine max*), **chickpeas** (*Cicer arietinum*), and **peanuts** (*Arachis hypogaea*). The low-alkaloid seeds are free of bitter substances in the cultivated varieties of the **blue, yellow**, and **white lupins** (*Lupinus angustfolius, L. luteus, L. albus*). These can be used as the so-called **sweet lupins**, for human nutrition.
**Characteristics** I The roots of legumes grow root tubers with nitrogen-bonding bacteria of the genus *Rhizobium* living in them. Because of this characteristic nitrogen enrichment, **bigleaf lupine** (*Lupinus polyphyllus*) is planted on nutrient-poor soils and plowed under before they bloom as

green manure. The fodder plants include **red clover** (*Trifolium pratense*), **white clover** (*T. repens*), **alsike clover** (*T. sativus*), **common bird's foot** (*Ornitopus sativus*), **garden vetch** (*Vicia sativa*), **common sainfoin** (*Onobrychis viciifolia*), and **birdsfoot trefoil** (*Lotus corniculatus*). Ornamental plants such as **clammy locust** (*Robinia viscosa*), **Scotch broom** (*Cytisus scoparius*), **sweet pea** (*Lathyrus odoratus*), **wisteria** (*Wisteria sinensis*), and the **common laburnum** or **golden chain tree** (*Laburnum anagyroides*).

FAGACEAE

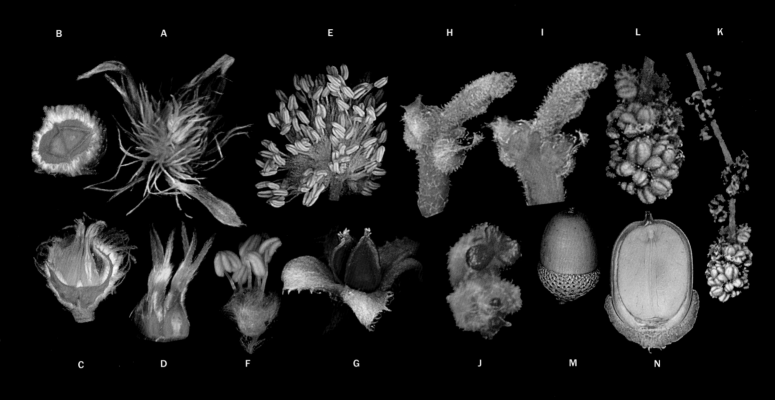

A–G: *Fagus sylvatica*. A: Female dichasia. B: The same, transverse. C: The same, longitudinal. D: Two single flowers, lateral. E: Male inflorescence. F: Male single flower. G: Cupule with 2 ripe fruits (beechnuts).

H–N: *Quercus robur*. H: Female dichasia. I: The same, longitudinal. J: The same, frontal, with stigma. K: Male inflorescence. L: The same, lower part of K, enlarged. M: Fruit (acorn) in cupule. N: The same, longitudinal.

**Genera** I 4–6; species: over 650
**Distribution** I Mostly Northern Hemisphere, temperate to tropical
**Habit** I Mostly trees, rarely shrubs
**Leaves** I Alternate, distichous or spiral, leaf blade usually simple, also notched margin, petiolate, often with stellate hairs, stipules present, usually caducous
**Inflorescences** I Male flowers in catkins, female in dichasias (figs. A, H)
**Flowers** I Radial, mostly unisexual, monoecious, 2–3 tepals, free or fused; male (fig. L) and female (figs. H–J) dichasia of the oak are uniflorous; female flowers (figs. A–D) of the European beech with two trimerous husk whorls and staminodes; 3–6 carpels are fused to an inferior ovary,

with two hanging ovules.
**Fruits** I Nuts encased in a woody, scaly, or spiny cupule (Cupulaceae: cupulum fruit), which can open through four valves (beech; fig. G) or is set solitary in the cupula (oak; fig. M). The seeds are often covered in hair.
**Use** I Durable wood, such as **oak**s (*Quercus* sp.) or **beech** (*Fagus* sp.). Oak bark is used for tanning and medicinally as an astringent. Some seeds are eaten raw or cooked, such as that of the **sweet chestnut** (*Castanea sativa*). Oak galls, which grow on oaks, can be harvested to make iron gall ink, which is indelible. Many beeches (also varieties such as the copper or weeping copper beech, cultivar "Purpurea endula") and oaks

(also American species, such as the northern red oak [*Q. rubra*] or swamp oak (*Q. palustris*]) are planted as ornamental trees in cities. In the meristem secondary bark of the **cork oak** (*Q. suber*), the phellogen (or cork cambium) is particularly productive. At the earliest when the trees are about 20 years old, the brittle and unelastic bark (so-called maiden cork) is removed. This cork is processed into granules, because it is not suitable for making a bottle cork. Only after another ten years, the tree has grown new layers of cork, about 5–8 cm thick, the so-called "female" cork. From this time on, for about 150 more years, each new layer of cork that grows can be peeled off from a

maximum of one-third of the tree.
**Characteristics**: It is possible to extract an oil from the seeds of the European beech (*Fagus sylvatica*). However, the oil can be harvested at most only every 5–8 years, since the tree lives through so-called mast and hunger years. During the mast years, the tree grows an especially large number of fruit, so that the animals that consume them can multiply rapidly due to the good food supply. In the subsequent "hunger" years, the tree grows only a few fruit, and the population that consumes them may collapse.

**A–E:** *Dovyalis caffra.* A: Leafy shoot with leaf spine. B: Partial inflorescence. C: Male single flower from underneath. D: The same, longitudinal. E: Exposed nectary at the base of the filaments.

**F–I:** *Ryania angustifolia.* F: Flower, frontal. G: Stigma. H: Gynoecium; *left*, longitudinal; *center*, lateral; *right*, transverse. I: Half nectary.

**J–M:** *Xylosma flexuosa.* J: Leafy branch with inflorescence. K: Partial inflorescence. L: Male flower, longitudinal. M: Bud; *left*, from underneath; *right*, lateral.

**Genera** | 89; species: more than 1,200
**Distribution** | Tropical, subtropical, rarely temperate
**Habit** | Trees
**Leaves** | Alternate, opposite or whorled, simple
**Inflorescences** | Axile or terminal, racemose, paniculate, rarely solitary
**Flowers** | Radial, hermaphroditic or unisexual, dioecious; (2–) 3–6–16 free

sepals, overlapping, also tortuous; petals isocarpic, small, and may be absent, also with inner basal, scaly outgrowth; many stamens, free (fig. D) or in bundles; the ovary, fused from 2–10 carpels, is superior (fig. H, *left*) to inferior; style free or fused, can be heavily branched; annular crooked nectary is also located in the hypanthium (fig. H, *left*).
**Fruits** | Capsules, berries, drupes,

indehiscent fruits; dry, also winged, seeds sometimes with aril, also hairy
**Use** | *Hydnocarpus kurzii* provides chaulmoogra oil, which has been successfully used against leprosy. *Dovyalis caffra* has edible fruits.
**Characteristics** | The receptacle is often deep set and cup shaped, with fibers or bundles of fibers released from effigurations (corona), also with various other nectary characteristics.

As a result of molecular findings, members of the old family Flacourtiaceae have today been predominantly assigned to the Salicaceae or Achariaceae.

Order: Malpighiales

FLACOURTIACEAE

GELSEMIACEAE

**A–D:** *Gelsemium sempervirens.* A: Leafy branch with flower and buds; *below*, detail. B: *Left*, flower, frontal; *right*, lateral.
C: Gynoecium with basal nectar ring in calyx. D: *Left*, ovary longitudinal; *right*, transverse.

**Genera** I 2–3: *Gelsemium, Mostuea, Pteleocarpa*; species: more than 10
**Distribution** I Mostly tropical: Africa, America, Asia
**Habit** I Shrubs, lianas
**Leaves** I Opposite, whorled, leaf blade simple and undivided, notched, denticulate or smooth margin, petiolate, also leathery. Stipules present or absent, leaf glands present.
**Inflorescences** I Cymose, paniculate, often with different bracts and bracteoles
**Flowers** I Radial, hermaphroditic, fragrant, tetramerous-pentamerous; white, yellow, red, blue; calyx fused; corolla fused (fig. B); 4–5 stamens; the bicarpellate and usually bilocular ovary is superior (fig. D); 1–2 styles often of different lengths or one style with five style arms (fig. C).
**Fruits** I Two valved capsule fruit, seeds hairy or winged
**Use** I Extracts from the underground plant parts of **yellow jessamine** (*Gelsemium sempervirens*) are used in homeopathy to treat diseases of the nervous system, especially in case of paralysis. This can occur if someone is poisoned with this poisonous plant. Ornamental plants.
**Characteristics** I Abnormal secondary lateral growth; alkaloids are often present.

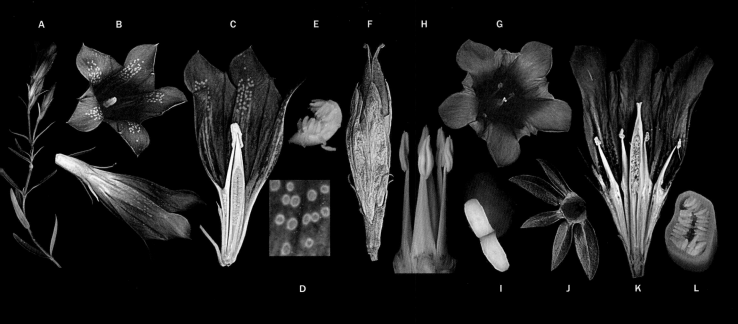

A   B   C   E   F   H   G

D   I   J   K   L

**—F:** *Gentiana pneumonanthe*. A: Habit. B: *Above*, flower, frontal; *below that*, lateral. C: Flower, longitudinal. D: Detail of the flower scan. E: Partial ovary, transverse. : Ripe fruit, lateral.

**G—L:** *Gentiana superior*, "Bella blue." G: Flower, frontal. H: Androecium. I: Stigma. J: Calyx. K: Flower, longitudinal. L: Ovary, transverse.

**Genera** | about 80; species: 00–1,600

**Distribution** | Worldwide

**Habit** | Rarely trees, herbaceous perennials, herbaceous plants; also ianas, rosette plants

**Habitat** | Many species grow in mountainous terrain.

**Leaves** | Mostly opposite, leaf blade simple and undivided, sessile and entire

**Inflorescences** | Single axillary, dichasias

**Flowers** | Radial, hermaphroditic, pentamerous, calyx usually fused into campanulate or tubular form (at least at the base); the white, yellow, pink, or blue corolla is campanulate, funnel form, or salver form; a dotted nectar guide is often found on each of the petals (figs. B, C, D); 5 (–12) stamens, which often open only when they tilt together over the stigma, when it is not yet ready for pollination (fig. C); the bicarpellate ovary is superior; one style with two stigma lobes (fig. I).

**Fruits** | Many-seeded capsules

**Use** | Due to the bitter substances contained in all parts of the plant, gentians were used as a remedy to stimulate the appetite and for digestive problems. Extracts distilled (mostly) from the roots of the **yellow gentian** (*Gentiana lutea*) are used to make herbal bitters and schnapps; the **purple gentian** (*G. purpurea*), **Hungarian gentian** (*G. pannonica*), and the **spotted gentian** (*G. punctata*) are also used. In earlier times, the **European centaury** (*Centaurium erythraea*) was a very valuable medicinal plant (called *Tausend Güldenkraut* or "thousand guilder" plant in German), and it remains so today. In America, the plant is cultivated for medicines for liver and gall bladder symptoms. Ornamental plants include, in addition to the gentian species, the **Texas bluebell** (*Eustoma grandiflora*) for cut flowers.

**Characteristics** | All parts of the plant are hairless; the flowers are usually open only in sunny, dry weather. In Europe, all gentians are protected plants.

# GERANIACEAE

A B C D E F G H I J K L M N O P Q

**A–B:** *Erodium cicutarium*. A: Flower, frontal. B: Partial fruit, detached.
**C–F:** *Geranium maderense*. C: Flower, frontal. D: Calyx. E: *Left*, ovary, transverse; *right*, gynoecium. F: Androecium, style/stigma.
**G–J:** *G. molle*. G: *Right*, flower, frontal; *left*, single petal. H: Ovary, transverse. I: *Left*, fruit, lateral; *right*, from underneath. J: *Above*, seed, lateral; *below*, longitudinal.
**K–M:** *Pelargonium sidoides*. K: *Below*, gynoecium, lateral; *above*, stigma, frontal. L: Flower, frontal. M: Androecium in calyx.
**N–P:** *P. carnosum*. N: Flower, frontal. O: Androecium and style/stigma, frontal. P: Calyx from underneath.
**Q:** *G. robertianum* from bud: *above*, stamens; *below*, androecium around style/stigma, lateral.

**Genera** I More than 10; species: more than 750
**Distribution** I Temperate, subtropical, in the Northern and Southern Hemispheres, main concentration in South Africa
**Habit** I Small shrubs, half shrubs, perennials, herbaceous plants, annuals to perennials
**Habitats** I Waste ground, roadsides, sandy soils
**Leaves** I Alternate or opposite, palmate, divided or pinnate, usually petiolate, also hairy, stipules present
**Inflorescences** I Cymose or solitary; often have bracts
**Flowers** I Radial to slightly zygomorphic (figs. A, C, L, N), hermaphroditic, rarely dioecious; pentamerous, calyx pentapetalous (figs. D, P), mostly free; the five sometimes slightly unguiculate (fig. G, *left*) petals are often of uneven length, the two longer ones with nectar guides (fig. L) or basally marked wings (fig. N); 5–10 stamens (figs. F, M, O, Q), also in 2–3 rows of uneven length, fused at the base, can have with nectar glands and be reduced to staminodes; the five carpels (fig. H) form a superior, beak-like, elongated ovary, which forms one axile ovule per locule; style with five style arms (fig. E, *right*; fig. K).
**Fruits** I Capsule fruits, schizocarpic fruits in one-seeded mericarps. These fruits have awn-like hygroscopic growths; these become detached from the central axil, which remains in place, and fall off (figs. B, I).
**Use** I The plants often have glandular hairs and often develop a typical scent: geranium oil can be distilled from leaves and stems of the **rose geranium** (*P. graveolens*). Scented geraniums, such as the *apple geranium* (*P. odoratissimum*) or the *peppermint geranium* (*P. tomentosum*). Pelargoniums (zygomorphic flowers) and geranium hybrids (radial flowers) are also popular ornamental plants for balconies and flower beds. Umckaloabo, a medicinal extract that stimulates the body's defenses, is harvested from the roots of the **South African geranium** (*P. sidoides*).
**Characteristics** I The beak-like style (figs. B, I), which remains on the fruit, has given its name to many species, such as **common stork's bill** (*Erodium cicutarium*), **Madeira cranesbill** (*Geranium maderense*), **dove's-foot crane's-bill beak** (*Geranium molle*), and **herb-Robert** (*Geranium robertianum*).

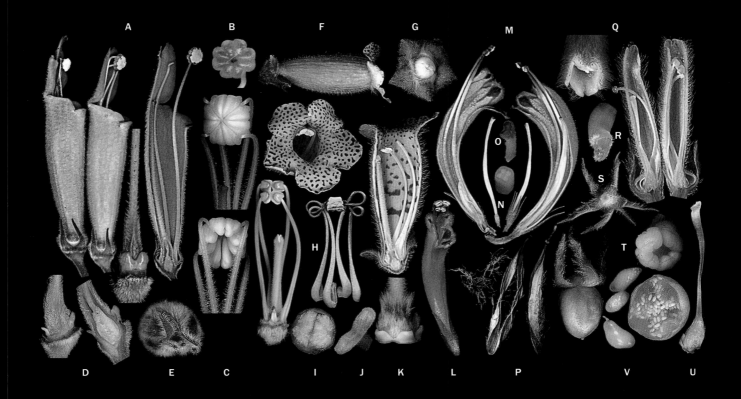

A B F G M Q

D E C I J K L P V U

**A–E:** *Sinningia bulbosa*. A: *Left*, flower, lateral, in male and female phase; *right*, longitudinal; *center*, gynoecium with nectary. B: Stigma. C: Stamens in front of stigma; *above*, frontal; *below*, from behind. D: *Left*, ovary, lateral; *right*, longitudinal. E: Bud, frontal: calyx.

**F–K:** *Kohleria warcewiczii*. F: *Above*, flower, lateral; *below*, frontal; *right*, longitudinal. G: Calyx. H: Androecium. I: Ovary, transverse. J: Stigma. K: Nectary.

**L–P:** *Aeschynanthus parasiticus*. L: Flower, lateral. M: The same, longitudinal. N: Ovary, transverse. O: Stigma. P: *Left*, fruit open with seed; *right*, lateral.

**Q–V:** *Columnea sanguinea*. Q: Flower; *above left*, frontal; *right*, longitudinal. R: Stigma. S: Calyx from underneath. T: Stamens. U: Gynoecium, longitudinal. V: Fruit; *left*, lateral; *right*, transverse; *center*, seeds.

**Genera** | More than 140; species: more than 3,000
**Distribution** | Worldwide in the tropics, several species in the temperate zones
**Habit** | Small trees, shrubs rarely annual herbaceous plants, epiphytes, rarely lianas, often with rhizomes, woody tubers, also grows runners
**Leaves** | Alternate, opposite, simple to pinnatipartite, elliptical, ovate, circular to cordiform, without stipules
**Inflorescences** | Racemose, paniculate, solitary in the leaf axils, lateral, cymose partial inflorescences
**Flowers** | Zygomorphic, hermaphroditic, rarely unisexual, then monoecious; pentamerous, usually five sepals, often hairy, as is the outer side of the corolla; this is a wheel-shaped to oblong tube, also bilabiate. The anthers of the usually four stamens often clubbed together in pairs (figs. C, L), at times exactly over the stigma (fig. C); the fifth stamen often reduced to a staminode (fig. H, *left*); the bicarpellate ovary is superior to inferior; style with two-to-four-lobed stigma (figs. J, R), often protruding laterally in protandrous species in the male phase to prevent self-pollination; nectary is annular or usually four-lobed (fig. K). Usually ornithophily, but also entomophily and chiropterophily.
**Fruits** | Mostly oblong capsules, berries. Seeds also with hairy tuft.
**Use** | Ornamental plants: **African violets** (*Saintpaulia ionanthes*), **gloxinia** (*Sinningia hybrids*), **Cape primroses** (*Streptocarpus × hybridus*) as houseplants. In times of need, the leaves of *Conandron ramondioides* are eaten after being cooked.
**Characteristics** | Leaves can be heavily hairy; hairs contain blue or red sap, forming resin and oil veins; domatia occur.

A–E: *Selliera radicans*. A: Habit. B: Flower; *above left*, lateral; *right*, next to it, underside; *below*, frontal. C: From bud: stigma, enveloped by the indusium and unopened stamens; *top*, frontal; *below it*, lateral. D: Flower, longitudinal; *below right*, ovary, transverse. E: Nectary at base of the style (see arrow).

**Genera** | 10–12; species: over 400
**Distribution** | Australia, Malaysia, some species in South America, Africa, New Zealand, Southeast Asia, Caribbean islands
**Habit** | Mostly evergreen herbaceous plants (fig. A), annuals to perennials, erect, rarely climbing, rarely spiny, rarely small trees or half shrubs
**Leaves** | Alternate, basal, rarely opposite, spiral, often sessile; simple leaf blade that is lobed, entire, serrated, or denticulate, without stipules
**Inflorescences** | Cymose, racemose, spicate, capitulate, corymbose, solitary
**Flowers** | Zygomorphic (fig. B), hermaphroditic; 3–5 sepals, free or fused, mostly small, also only annular, usually retained on the fruit; five petals, mostly basally fused, usually bilabiate, rarely unilabiate. Androecium: five stamens, free (fig. C) or basally fused with the corolla; the corolla is also sheathed in corolla ligules or fused together to form a tube, opening inward; the bicarpellate ovary is inferior to half inferior, rarely superior, with one to several axile ovules (fig. D); style with indusium (fig. C).
**Fruits** | Capsules, rarely drupes or small nut fruits; the seeds can be winged.
**Use** | Ornamental plants, such as the **blue fan flower** (*Scaevola aemula*) as a balcony plant; *Selliera radicans* is planted in moist rockeries.
**Characteristics** | Protandrous with secondary pollen presentation, in which the anthers are already open during budding, and the pollen is emptied into a style/indusium. As the stigma grows, it is pushed forward to the edge of the indusium, so that no self-pollination takes place. Visitors to the flower comb the pollen out of the style cup.

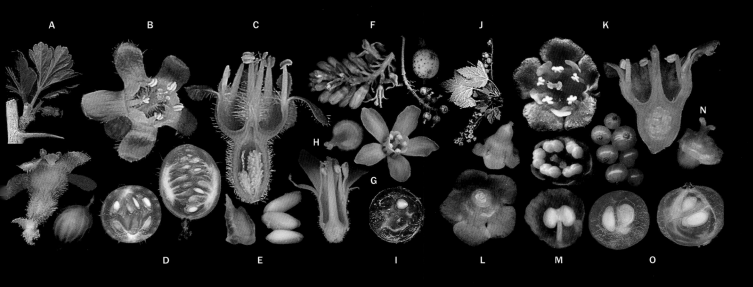

A    B    C    F    J    K

H    N

G

D    E    I    L    M    O

**A–B:** *Erodium cicutarium*. A: Flower, frontal. B: Partial fruit, detached.
**C–F:** *Geranium maderense*. C: Flower, frontal. D: Calyx. E: *Left*, ovary, transverse; *right*, gynoecium. F: Androecium, style/stigma.

**G–J:** *G. molle*. G: *Right*, flower, frontal; *left*, single petal. H: Ovary, transverse. I: *Left*, fruit, lateral; *right*, from underneath. J: *Above*, seed, lateral; *below*, longitudinal.

**K–M:** *Pelargonium sidoides*. K: *Below*, gynoecium, lateral; *above*, stigma, frontal. L: Flower, frontal. M: Androecium in calyx.

**N–P:** *P. carnosum*. N: Flower, frontal. O: Androecium and style/stigma, frontal. P: Calyx from underneath.
**Q:** *G. robertianum* from bud: *above*, stamens; *below*, androecium around style/stigma, lateral.

**Genus** | 1: *Ribes*; species: over 140
**Distribution** | Temperate zones of the Northern Hemisphere, a few in South America (the Andes)
**Habit** | Usually shrubs up to about 2 meters tall, divided into long or short shoots, mostly deciduous, rarely evergreen
**Leaves** | Alternate, spiral, rarely tufted, broad leaf base; leaf blade: simple, usually 3–5 lobes, usually curled when in the bud, petiolate, leaf margin: can be ciliate

**Inflorescences** | Racemose or umbellate
**Flowers** | Radial, hermaphroditic or unisexual; if unisexual, then dioecious; with well-developed hypanthium, tetramerous-pentamerous; sepals petaloid, relatively large and colored; petals smaller or absent; 4–5 stamens; may grow nectar glands; the two carpels are fused into a unilocular, mostly inferior, rarely half-inferior ovary with many ovules.

**Fruits** | The ovaries and receptacles form berries, also bristle glands.
**Use** | Many species are cultivated for their berries, such as **red currants** (*Ribes rubrum*). The young leaves of the **blackcurrant** (*Ribes nigrum*) can be added to vegetable soups, the summer leaves are dried to make tea, and the buds are used in the perfume industry. The **flowering currant** (*Ribes sanguineum*) is a popular ornamental shrub that is also a food source for wild bees.

**Characteristics** | Some species have spines. The **white currant** is a variety of the **red currant**, and both belong to the species *Ribes rubrum*. The **gooseberry** (*Ribes uva-crispa*) and **blackcurrant** were cross-bred with each other in the search for mildew-resistant berry bushes. This is how the **jostaberry** (*Ribes × nigridolaria*) was developed.

GROSSULARIACEAE

A–G: *Gunnera perpensa*. A: Habit with inflorescence in male phase. B: Male partial inflorescence. C: Two single male flowers. D: Inflorescence in female phase. E: *Left*, gynoecium, lateral; *at right*, longitudinal. F: Kidney-shaped leaf. G: Rhizome, longitudinal; dark-colored areas are colonies of symbiotic *Nostoc* bacteria.

**Genus** | 1: *Gunnera*; species: over 50
**Distribution** | South Pacific (western South and Central America), New Zealand, Southeast Asia, Africa, Madagascar. Primarily in the temperate latitudes to the tropics of the Southern Hemisphere, often in very wet, swampy habitats.
**Habit** | Mostly perennial herbaceous plants with rhizomes or runners. Rhizomes often have reddish, deeply lacerated and hairy cataphylls.
**Leaves** | Basal, alternate, leaf blade is circular or kidney shaped (fig. F), divided in palmate-lobed shape, from 7 mm to 3 meters (!) in diameter, with rough surface, rhubarb-like (although the rhubarb is not a close relation; it

belongs to the Polygonaceae family); with protruding hydathodes, often with a long, thick petiole that supports short spines and can be up to 5 meters tall. Leaf base cordiform, sagittate, or peltate. Leaf margin notched, serrated.
**Inflorescences** | The flowers, which grow in the foliage leaf axils or are pseudoterminal, are large (up to 1 meter tall), simple or compound, racemose or spicate (fig. A), with many inconspicuous, small, sessile flowers without bracts; the lower ones are often female, the upper ones male (figs. B, C). In between, they are hermaphroditic. Alternatively, all flowers can be unisexual.
**Flowers** | Rarely dioecious,

protandrous, distichous; two sepals; two petals; two stamens; two carpels form an inferior, unilocular ovary (figs. D, E). Involucral bracts, stamens, and carpels are in the transverse plane. Wind pollination.
**Fruits** | One-seeded drupes, usually green or red, rarely white or yellow
**Use** | Some garden ornamental plants that require warm temperatures and are not winter hardy in northern latitudes. In Chile, the petioles of the **giant rhubarb** (*Gunnera manicatum*) are peeled and eaten as a vegetable. The tannic acid-containing rhizomes are used for tanning.
**Characteristics** | Nitrogen-fixing *Nostoc* bacteria live in the rhizomes,

between the leaf bases, in a symbiotic relationship with the plants (fig. G: dark areas are *Nostoc* colonies). The giant rhubarb leaves obtain nitrogen from the bacteria, while the latter obtain sugars from the plant's photosynthesis. The genus *Gunnera* was named in honor of the Norwegian bishop and naturalist Johan Ernst Gunnerus (1718–1773). The plants are called "giant rhubarb" and "mammoth leaf" because of their very large leaves. The **Chilean rhubarb** (*Gunnera tinctoria*) is a dreaded, invasive neophyte in New Zealand.

**A–H:** *Anigozanthus flavidus.* A: Inflorescence, lateral. B: Bud, longitudinal.
C: Unopened stamens with orange-colored, contrasting connective appendages.
D: Open flower; *left*, frontal; *top right*, lateral. E: Riper stamen; *above*, from behind;
*underneath*, lateral. F: Flower, longitudinal. G: Ovary, transverse. H: Almost ripe fruit;
*left*, lateral; *above right*, transverse; *underneath*, longitudinal.

**I–J:** *Xiphidium caeruleum.* I: Habit. J: Flower, frontal.

**Subfamilies** I Haemodoroideae,
Conostyloideae
**Genera** I About 14; species:
about 116
**Distribution** I Australia, Cape region,
New Guinea, tropical Central and South
America. Tropical to warm temperate
latitudes.
**Habit** I Perennial herbaceous plants
with rhizomes or tubers as
overwintering organs
**Leaves** I Alternate, in rosette or in
distichous leaf arrangement, leaves
simple, linear to lanceolate, entire,
sessile, parallel venation, leathery,

occasionally xeromorphic
**Inflorescences** I Cymose or botryoid
(fig. A) or solitary
**Flowers** I Rarely radial, usually
zygomorphic, hermaphroditic,
trimerous; (3–) 6 uniformly shaped
tepals usually in two whorls; tepals
mostly free, rarely fused into a tube
(figs. A, B, D, F), then ending in six
petal tips (fig. D). The outer side of the
petals is heavily hairy; 1–2 whorls,
each with three stamens (fig. E),
usually free; the tubular flowers are
fused with the corolla (fig. C). The
flowers can have staminodes and

connective appendages (fig. C); the
three carpels are fused into a superior
to inferior ovary (figs. B, G); septal
nectaries are present. Pollination by
insects, birds, mammals.
**Fruits** I Capsules, schizocarpic fruits
(fig. H), nuts
**Use** I The **kangaroo paws**
(*Angiozanthus species*) are grown as
ornamental plants in frost-free areas.
The shape and hairiness of its flowers
are reminiscent of a kangaroo's paws.
**Characteristics** I The
representatives of this family contain a
characteristic red-colored sap,

especially in their underground parts.
A red pigment is harvested from the
rhizomes of such plants as
*Haemodorum corymbosum.* The
Aborigines used to roast and eat the
rhizomes of various species. The
flowers of the *Xyphidium caeruleum*,
which originated in the tropical
Americas, are pollinated by means of
"buzz pollination" by pollinating bees of
the genus *Euglossa.* To do this, the
bees use their flight muscles to
produce a sound at a frequency that
causes the anther to open up.

HAMAMELIDACEAE

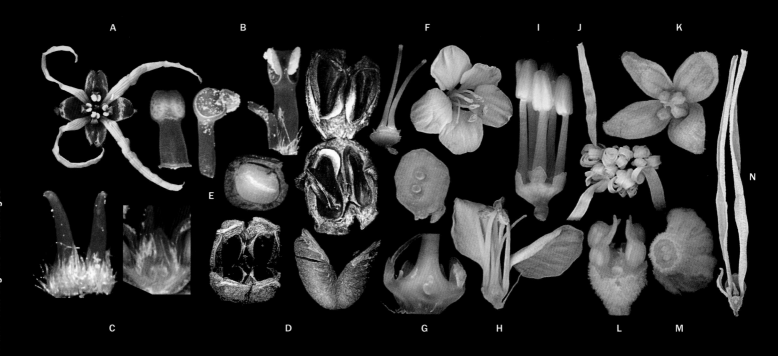

A–E: *Hamamelis mollis*. A: Flower, frontal. B: Stamen; *left*, unopened; *center*, opened with 1 valve; *right*, 2 open valves. C: Ovary; *left*, lateral; *right*, longitudinal. D: Fruit; *left*, frontal; *above*, longitudinal; *underneath*, lateral. E: Seeds, longitudinal.

F–I: *Corylopsis pauciflora*. F: *Left*, gynoecium, lateral; *right*, flower, frontal. G: Ovary; *above*, transverse; *below*, longitudinal. H: Flower, lateral; anterior petals and stamens removed. I: Androecium from a bud, lateral.

J–N: *Loropetalum chinensis*. J: Partial inflorescence, buds with unfurling petals. K: Flower, frontal, petals removed. L: Flower from a bud, lateral; petals and calyx removed. M: Ovary, transverse. N: Flower, longitudinal.

**Subfamilies** I Disanthoideae, Exbicklandoideae, Hamamelidoideae
**Genera** I 27; species: more than 800
**Distribution** I From the temperate zones to the tropics; concentration is in the subtropics.
**Habit** I Trees or shrubs, usually deciduous, also evergreen
**Leaves** I Usually alternate and distichous, rarely spiral, rarely opposite; leaf blade: simple, ovate; leaf margin: smooth or serrated, pinnate, at times with large stipules; petiole is present.
**Inflorescences** I Capitiform, spicate, paniculate, racemose
**Flowers** I Radial, hermaphroditic or unisexual, monoecious, single flowers small, usually tetramerous-pentamerous (figs. A, F, K); 4–5 sepals

are basally fused (figs. A, K); two, four, or five petals, free (fig. N), occasionally unguiculate (fig. H), or absent (such as *Parrotia*); 3, 4–5 (figs. A, F, I), 10–14, or 15–32 free stamens, all fertile or some reduced to staminodes; usually 2 (–3) superior to inferior carpels, free or fused. Entomophily and anemophily.
**Fruits** I Bivalved capsule fruits (fig. D), which often retain the calyx on them
**Use** I Because of the very early flowering of some trees (at times, some already in winter), these plants are often cultivated in gardens and parks, such as the **Chinese witch hazel** (*Hamamelis mollis*), **Japanese witch hazel** (*H. japonica*), and the hybrids of both species, the **hybrid witch hazel** (*H. × intermedia*). The flowers of the **winter hazels**

(*Corylopsis* sp.) usually have an intense fragrance, and the leaves display an interesting red color; the same is true of the **redbud hazel** (*Disanthus cercidifolius*). The much more demanding **witch alders** (*Fothergilla* sp.) bloom in the fall in many botanical gardens. Due to their high tannin content, the leaves and bark of the **American witch hazel** (*Hamamelis virginiana*) are used as an astringent, hemostatic, and anti-inflammatory remedy for injuries to the skin or mucus membranes. The leaves of the **Chinese fringe flower** (*Loropetalum chinense*) (figs. J–N) are said to have an cough-soothing and anti-inflammatory effect. The hardwood of some species is used; for example, Japanese wooden swords are made

from the heartwood of *Distylium racemosum*, and the wood of the **false parrot** (*Parrotiopsis jaquemontiana*) is used for making wooden sticks and handles.
**Characteristics** I Members of the witch hazel family usually have stellate hairs; they can also have schizogenous secretory canals, in which the plant produces its characteristic balsams (viscous mixtures of resins and essential oils). The long, slender petals of the **Chinese witch hazel** (fig. A) can withstand frost down to −10°C. They furl up in the cold; when the weather becomes warmer again, they can unfurl.

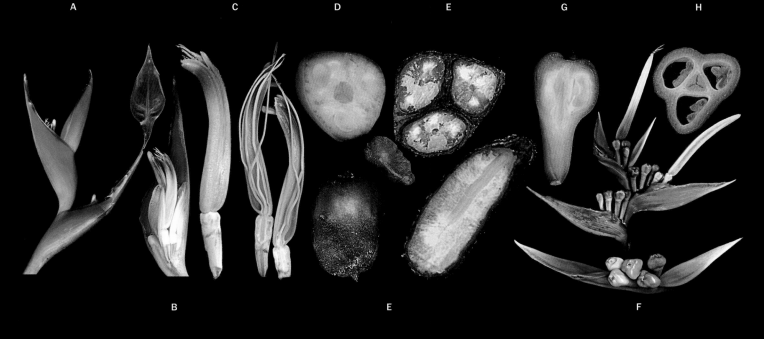

**A–E:** *Heliconia stricta*. A: Inflorescence, lateral. B: Bract with buds and flowers. C: Single flower; *left*, lateral; *right*, next to it, longitudinal. D: Ovary, transverse. E: Ripe fruit; *below left*, lateral; *right*, next to it, longitudinal; *underneath*, frontal.

**F–H:** *Heliconia aurantiaca*. F: Partial fruiting stage, lateral; *underneath*, frontal. G: Unripe fruit, longitudinal. H: The same, transverse.

**HELICONIACEAE**

**Genus** | 1: *Heliconia*; species: over 200
**Distribution** | America and some in the South Pacific Islands region
**Habit** | Perennial, evergreen herbaceous plants with rhizomes as overwintering organs, giant perennials up to 5 meters tall
**Leaves** | Alternate, distichous; leaf blade: simple, entire, mostly linear-lanceolate, up to 1 meter long; long, petiolate, parallel leaf venation, extending out from the strong midrib. Leaves are often deeply lacerated parallel to the lateral nervation.

Aboveground, the plant grows a banana-plant-like pseudo-stem out of the closely interleaved leaf sheaths.
**Inflorescences** | Terminal (figs. A, F), racemose, cymose, upright or hanging
**Flowers** | Zygomorphic, hermaphroditic; the small, inconspicuous single flowers are surrounded by large, conspicuously colored, cymbiform bracts (fig. B), hence the name "lobster claw." Trimerous; three calyxes and petals, basally fused into a tube up to one petal (fig. C); five fertile stamens with

basally fused tepals; one staminode. Three carpels are fused into an inferior ovary (figs. C, D). One ovule per locule; the long, thin style ends in a capitate or (bilobate) trilobate stigma; septal nectaries produce abundant nectar, which is diluted with rainwater. Predominantly ornithophily, but also chiropterophily.
**Fruits** | Red, blue, or orange drupes with 1–3 seeds (fig. E)
**Use** | In the tropics, the leaves of various species are used as packing material for foodstuffs. *Heliconia* are not frost hardy, and as a result they

only occasionally are commercially available as cut flowers in the cool temperate regions. However, some species are grown as ornamental plants in the tropics and subtropics.
**Otherwise**: The yellow-, red-, or orange-colored inflorescences are pollinated by hummingbirds and honey eaters. Flowers, which are pollinated by fruit bats at night, have greenish white inflorescences.

**A–E:** *Hydrangea macrophylla.* A: Inflorescence, frontal. B: *Center*, blossom, frontal; *left*, lateral / from underneath; *right*, longitudinal. C: Ripe fruit, lateral. D: The same, longitudinal. E: The same, frontal.

**F–I:** *Kirengeshoma palmata.* F: *Below*, flower and bud, lateral; *above it*, flower, frontal. G: Blossom, longitudinal. H: Calyx, frontal; *in the center*, ovary, transverse. I: *Left*, ovary, longitudinal; *right*, transverse.

**Genera** I 17; species: about 200
**Distribution** I The Americas, Southeast Asia
**Habits** I Trees, shrubs, half shrubs, lianas, perennial herbaceous plants
**Leaves** I Opposite, rarely alternate, leaf blade simple, also evergreen
**Inflorescences** I Cymes (corymbose; fig. A), cymose, often with bracts

**Flowers** I Radial, hermaphroditic (figs. B, F), also sterile flowers; a hypanthium may be present; calyx (fig. H) and corolla with 4–5 (–12) petals, corolla basally or completely fused (operculum). Stamens mostly in two whorls of five (4–12) or secondarily multiplied (up to 200). The bicarpellate to 12-carpellate ovary is inferior or half inferior; disc is present; style separate or fused.
**Fruits** I Loculicidal capsule fruits (figs. C–E), rarely berries
**Use** I Ornamental plants, such as the **big leaf hydrangea** (*Hydrangea macrophylla*), **panicle hydrangea** (*Hydrangea paniculata*), **climbing hydrangea** (*Hydrangea petiolaris*), **sweet mockorange** (*Philadelphus coronarius*), **yellow wax bells** (*Kirgeshoma palmata*), *Deutzia* species, and hybrids.
**Characteristics** I Cultivated varieties often display multiple petals.

A–C: *Elodea canadensis*. A: Habit. B: Shoot tip, longitudinal, with vegetation point. C: Male flower; *above*, frontal; *left*, underneath from below; *right*, lateral, 1 petal removed.

**Subfamilies** I Anacharidoideae, Hydrilloideae, Hydrocharitoideae, Stratiodoideae

**Genera** I 18; species: about 116. Well-known genera: *Elodea*, *Hydrocharis*, *Stratiotes*.

**Distribution** I Worldwide from the temperate latitudes to the tropics

**Habit** I Annuals or perennials, herbaceous freshwater or saltwater plants. Many species grow rhizomes on the bottom of the body of water; others grow roots at the nodes; many live submersed, while some float freely.

**Leaves** I Opposite, alternate or whorled, basal or distributed along the stalk, petiolate or sessile (figs. A, B); parallel venation

**Inflorescences** I Cymose or solitary

**Flowers** I Radial, rarely hermaphroditic, mostly unisexual, monoecious, dioecious (fig. D) or triecious, single flowers large and conspicuous or small, inconspicuous, reduced; two whorls of free tepals, trimerous (fig. C, *left*); involucral bracts sometimes absent, flowers can be enveloped by two free or one or two fused, sheathlike bracts; 1–2 or more stamens; the ovary, formed from 2–20 fused carpels, is inferior. The number of stigmas corresponds to the number of carpels. Hydrophily.

**Fruits** I Many-seeded capsule fruits; hydrochory

**Use** I Because of its effects, the **Canadian waterweed** (*Elodea canadensis*) is a popular aquarium plant and is used in school teaching as an object for investigating evidence of oxygen production during exposure to light.

**Characteristics** I The **Canadian waterweed**, originally native to North America and Canada, was introduced to Europe in the mid-19th century and spread rapidly. Presumably, only male plants were introduced, and as a result the plant can reproduce only vegetatively there. The related **western waterweed** (*Elodea nutallii*) has also been naturalized in Germany.

A    B    C    D

E

**A–E:** *Phacelia tanacetifolia*. A: Bipinnate foliage leaf. B: Cyme lateral. C: Single flower; *above*, with still-unopened stamens; *underneath*, frontal; *right*, next to it, longitudinal. D: Ripe fruit; *above*, lateral; *underneath*, transverse. E: Ripe seeds.

**Genera** | 15; species: about 200
**Distribution** | Worldwide
**Habit** | Annual to perennial herbaceous plants, rarely shrubs
**Leaves** | Alternate, rarely opposite; leaf blade: simple to multiply pinnate, mostly hairy and glandular, without stipules

**Inflorescences** | Scorpioid cymes, furled
**Flowers** | Usually radial, pentamerous, sepals usually free; the pentapetalous corolla may be campanulate, wheel form, or funnel form; the five stamens may have small outgrowths on their filaments; the

superior, bifoliate ovary may have 1–2 styles.
**Fruits** | Two-column capsule (fig. D)
**Use** | The **lacy phacelia** (*Phacelia tanacetifolia*) serves as source of food for bees, as a green manure plant for soil improvement, and as an ornamental plant. It has been

cultivated since 1832.
**Characteristics** | The Hydrophyllaceae are at times also treated as a subfamily of Boraginaceae.

A–G: *Hypericum patulum*. A: Flower, frontal. B: Flower from underneath. C: Flower, longitudinal. D: Style arms. E: Androecium, lateral. F: One bunch of stamens, lateral. G: Ovary, transverse.

H–O: *Hypericum perforatum*. H: Flower, frontal. I: The same from underneath. J: Young androecium from the bud. K: The same from underneath; it is possible to recognize single bundles. L: Gynoecium, lateral. M: Ovary, longitudinal. N: The same, transverse. O: Ripe three-valved capsule.

**Genera** | 9; species: more than 550
**Distribution** | Worldwide
**Habit** | Half shrubs, perennials
**Habitat** | Damp meadows, loamy soil, limestone cliffs, semiarid and nutrient-poor grasslands, shorelines, ditches, forests, brushwood
**Leaves** | Opposite, whorled, leaf blade often dotted with oil glands, also acicular, as well as evergreen and sessile
**Inflorescences** | Terminal, in pyramid form, paniculate

**Flowers** | Radial (figs. A, H), hermaphroditic; five free sepals (figs. B, I); five free petals; androecium (figs. E, J), numerous stamens in bundles (fig. F) of three or five, set opposed to the petals, which are sometimes equipped with nectary scales; 3–5 carpels form the superior ovary (fig. C), with usually separate styles (figs. D, L, M).
**Fruits** | Capsule fruit (fig. O), berries
**Use** | Ornamental plants, such as *Hypericum beanii* from China or *H. calycinum* as a ground cover. The

dark-dotted petals of the **common St. John's wort** (*Hypericum perforatum*) contain oil glands (as the leaves do likewise). These release a red dye when rubbed. The buds, when marinated in olive oil, yield St. John's wort or red oil, which is used to treat mood swings especially during the cold months. Very fair-skinned people should pay attention when taking this red oil, since it makes you light sensitive; you should not go out in sunshine or go to a tanning salon when taking red oil.

**Characteristics** | The round or angle-edged stems can be winged. The name "St. John's wort" comes from the blossoming time of the common St. John's wort, which is around St. John's Day (June 24).

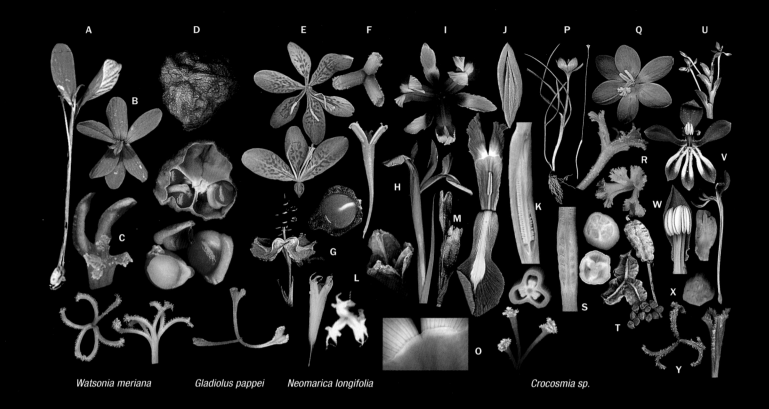

A    D    E    F    I    J    P    Q    U

H

M

K

B

C

G

L

O

R

V

W

S

X

T

Y

*Watsonia meriana*        *Gladiolus pappei*        *Neomarica longifolia*                    *Crocosmia sp.*

**A–D:** *Freesia laxa.* A: Plant, longitudinal. B: Flower, frontal. C: Stigma. D: Fruit; *above*, frontal; *center*, transverse; *below*, seeds.
**E–G:** *Belamcanda chinensis.* E: *Above*, flower, frontal; *below*, longitudinal. F: Stigma; *above*, frontal; *below*, lateral. G: *Left*, fruit; *right*, seeds, longitudinal.
**H–O:** *Iris sibirica.* H: Habit. I: *Above*, flower, frontal; *below right*, part of a flower, frontal. J: Equitant leaves, transverse. K: Ovary; *above*, longitudinal; *below*, transverse. L: Fruit, frontal. M: Fruit, lateral. O: Stigma.
**P–T:** *Crocus dalmaticus.* P: Habit. Q: Flower, frontal. R: *Above*, stigma, lateral; *below*, frontal. S: Ovary; *left*, longitudinal; *right*, transverse. T: *Above*, fruit, lateral; *below*, fruit, frontal, with seeds.
**U–Y:** *Lapaeirousia jaquinii.* U: Partial inflorescence. V: Flower, frontal; *right below*, longitudinal. W: Stamens. X: Ovary; *above*, longitudinal; *below*, transverse. Y: Stigma; *left*, frontal; *right*, lateral.

**Genera** | 73; species: 2,318. Well-known genera: *Crocus, gladiolus, iris.*
**Distribution** | Worldwide; center of plant diversity in South America, South Africa, and Australia
**Habit** | Rarely low half shrubs, mostly tuber or rhizome perennials, rarely annuals. The tubers may be surrounded by dry involucral bracts ("tunics"). There are a few myco-heterotrophic species (*Geosiris* sp.).
**Leaves** | Mostly distichous, sessile, linear, grassy (fig. P), scutate (fig. J), with open or closed leaf sheath, occasionally folded, mostly unifacial
**Inflorescences** | Cymose, spicate, racemose to paniculate, fan shaped or scorpioid, rarely solitary, terminal
**Flowers** | Radial or zygomorphic (*Gladiolus* sp.), hermaphroditic; flowers vary greatly in size and color; six tepals in two whorls of three; perigone is free or partially fused into a tube (figs. A, V); inner tepals often grow smaller; one whorl usually consisting of three stamens (figs. E, W); inferior ovary consisting of three fused carpels (figs. K, S, X); style also with three petaloid (fig. O), flattened or divided (fig. F, R, Y) style arms.
**Fruits** | Capsules, seeds can support an aril (fig. D, *below*) or be winged.
**Use** | Many ornamental plants, such as the **early crocus** (*Crocus tommasinianus*), **golden crocus** (*C. flava*), **yellow flag** (*Iris pseudocorus*), **garden montbretie** (*Crocosmia × crocosmiiflora*), and **tiger flower** (*Tigridia pavonia*). The **gladiolus** (*Gladiolus × hortulanus*) was created by cross-breeding various South African species. Due to its origin, however, this garden plant is very susceptible to frost and therefore must be dug up in the fall and overwintered frost-free. The **German iris** (*Iris × germanica*), a longtime cottage garden plant, was cultivated because of its fragrant rhizomes ("violet roots"). It was used as an expectorant remedy for colds, as a fixative in perfumery, and as an aromatic ingredient in various liqueurs. **Freesia hybrids** are used as cut flowers. The style arms of the *Crocus sativus* (saffron or autumn crocus) are used as a food colorant.
**Characteristics** | The **marsh gladiolus** (*Gladiolus palustris*) grows in calcareous, nutrient-poor moorland meadows. Since these habitats have become rare, this plant also is threatened with extinction and is therefore under strict protection. The iris was the model for the lily-shaped crest of the French noble Bourbon family (the fleur-de-lis). The Latin name of the "iris family" refers to the leaf form of some species (Latin *gladius* = sword, *gladiolus* = small sword).

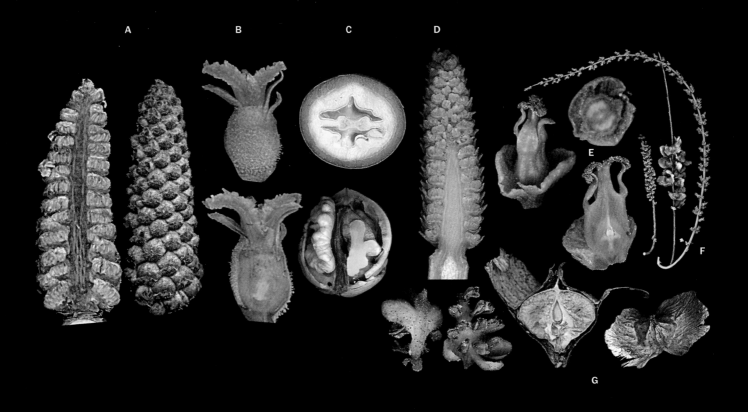

**A–C: *Juglans regia*.** A: Male inflorescence/catkin; *right*, lateral; *left*, longitudinal. B: *Above*, female flower, lateral; *beneath it*, longitudinal. C: *Above*, unripe fruit, transverse; *below it*, opened ripe nut fruit.

**D–G: *Pterocarya fraxinifolia*.** D: Male inflorescence, longitudinal; *beneath it, left*, single flower, frontal; *right*, next to it, lateral. E: Female flower; *above*, lateral; *right*, next to it, ovary, transverse; *beneath it*, longitudinal. F: Habit; *left*, male inflorescence; *center*, ripe fruiting stage; *right*, female inflorescence, lateral. G: *Right*, ripe fruit; *left*, longitudinal.

**Genera** | About 10; species: about 60
**Distribution** | Temperate to tropical America, Eurasia
**Habit** | Trees, rarely shrubs
**Leaves** | Alternate, rarely opposite or whorled, leaf-blade parapinnate or imparipinnate with 5–31 leaflets, rarely trifoliate or simple; the margin is smooth or serrated, buds naked or have bud scales; deciduous or evergreen, stipules absent.
**Inflorescences** | Catkins or spikes, hanging or upright, only one flower in each bract; flower is lateral or terminal on older or previous year's shoots.

**Flowers** | Mostly dioecious, monoecious, petals absent; bracts (and bracteoles) fused with the receptacle (figs. B, C); 3–40–100 stamens, sessile (figs. A, F); female flowers (figs. B, E) usually have four-lobed calyx, sometimes with solitary stamens.
**Fruits** | Nut fruit with green coats (figs. D, E) or winged (fig. K)
**Use** | Walnut is a popular wood for making furniture, including veneers; for example, the **English walnut** (*Juglans regia*), **black walnut** (*J. nigra*), and **Caucasian wingnut** (*Pterocarya fraxinifolia*) ("Caucasian

nutwood"). The seeds are edible and can be eaten raw (such as in muesli, in ice cream, or to make nut brittle). Unripe walnuts can be used for dyeing (using the green "shells"); they can also be used as a tanning agent.
**Characteristics** | Usually wind pollination. The plants have resin glands and glandular or bundled hairs. The small unripe single nuts of the **Caucasian wingnut** have two membranous wings that make them look like the heads of elephants. They are often used in handicraft work. The leaves contain a glycoside that

penetrates the soil after leaves fall. There it is transformed into juglone by splitting off the glucose. Juglone is poisonous to fish and has a mutagenic effect. Above all, this substance is phytotoxic and prevents the growth of other, competing plants within the tree's area of influence. Such mutual influences of plants upon each other are called "allelopatic effects."

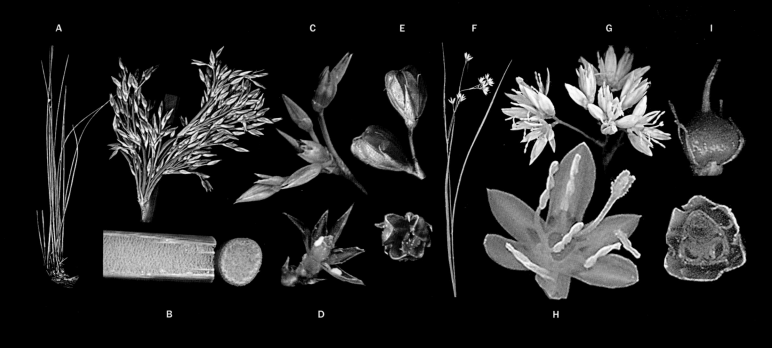

A–E: *Juncus effusus*. A: Habit. B: Stem; *left*, longitudinal; *right*, next to it, transverse. C: *Left*, inflorescence; *right*, partial inflorescence. D: Flower, lateral. E: Fruit; *below*, frontal; *above right*, lateral.

F-H: *Luzula nivea*. F: Habit. G: *Above*, partial inflorescence. H: Single flowers. I: Fruit; *above*, lateral; *below*, transverse.

**Genera** I 7; species: about 430. Well-known genera: *Juncus* (rushes) and *Luzula* (wood-rushes).
**Distribution** I Worldwide, especially in the temperate and arctic regions
**Habit** I Grassy herbaceous plants and perennials, usually with rhizomes, but there are also species that grow in tufted and cushion forms.
**Leaves** I Basal, (binate-)ternate, leaf blade mostly without nodes, cylindrical, stalklike, glabrous and rigidly erect, with a locular, foamlike pith (stellate parenchyma; *Juncus*) or grasslike and often hairy (*Luzula*; fig. F). Leaf sheaths open, with auricles (*Juncus*) or fused (*Luzula*); ligules often present

**Inflorescences** I Sympodial (i.e., without a main axis), capitiform, globose, umbellate, paniculate (= anthela, funnel shaped; fig. I), never in spikes
**Flowers** I Radial, hermaphroditic, rarely unisexual and dioecious; flowers, reminiscent of lily family, are small, inconspicuous; two times three tepals (fig. G), scarious, glumaceous (figs. D, J), light greenish to brownish black; usually six stamens in two whorls; superior ovary out of three fused carpels, with three papillose style arms. Mostly wind pollination, occasionally insect or self-pollination.
**Fruits** I Capsules (figs. E, H, L);

*Luzula*, three seeds with elaiosomes: myrmecochory; *Juncus*, multiple seeds
**Use** I The pith of the **common rush** (*Juncus effusus*) was formerly used to make wicks for lamps. The plant is used in Japan to manufacture the traditional tatami. These mats serve as a floor covering, including for practicing Japanese martial arts. Rushes can be used to weave baskets, bags, and other everyday objects. The **snowy wood-rush** (*Luzula nivea*) is an ornamental plant.
**Characteristics** I A "truism" about rushes (in German, a *Binsenweisheit* is a truism; *Binse* is the German word for rush) is that the absence of stem

nodes is normal; otherwise these are common among the Poales order. In Germany, one common name for the **field wood-rush** (*Luzula campestris*) is "rabbit bread," since not only ants but also other animals (rabbits) eat the food particles on the seeds. The leaf rosettes of the **hairy wood-rush** (*Luzula pilosa*), which grows in beech forests, serve the plant as a water collector.

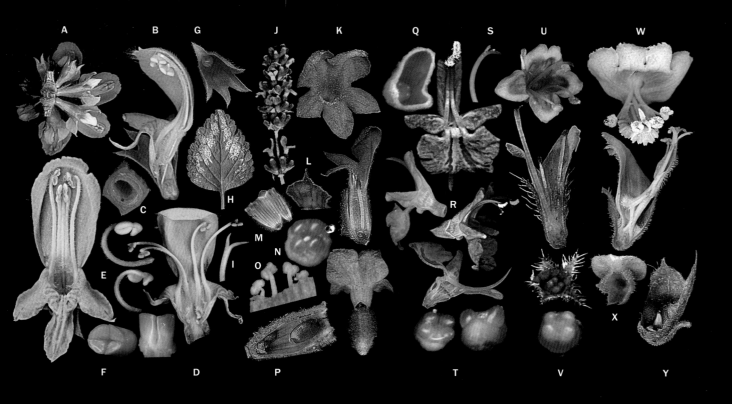

**A–I:** *Galeobdolone luteum*. A: Partial inflorescence from underneath. B: *Below left*, flower, frontal; *above right*, the same, longitudinal. C: Sprout, transverse. D: Blossom with corolla opened from the front. E: Stamen; *above*, from the front; *below*, from behind. F: Ovary; *left*, frontal; *right*, lateral, with nectary. G: Calyx, frontal. H: Foliage leaf. I: Stigma.

**J–P:** *Lavandula angustifolia*. J: Inflorescence. K: Flower; *above*, frontal; *center*, longitudinal; *below*, from behind. L: Bract of the flower. M: Calyx splayed out. N: Ovary, frontal, with nectar ring. O: Stamens, rear side. P: Fruit with seeds, longitudinal.

**Q–T:** *Rosmarinus officinalis*. Q: Calyx. R: *Above*, flower, frontal, corolla at left beneath it; *right*, flower lateral; *below*, longitudinal. S: Stigma. T: Ovary; *left*, frontal; *right*, lateral

**U–V:** *Mentha longifolia*. U: *Above*, flower, frontal; *below*, longitudinal. V: *Above*, ovary in the calyx; *beneath*, removed from it.

**W–Y:** *Ocimum basilicum*. W: *Above*, flower, frontal; *below*, longitudinal. X: Calyx, frontal. Y: Mericarp.

**Genera** | More than 230; species: more than 7,000

**Distribution** | Worldwide

**Habits** | Trees, shrubs, half shrubs, herbaceous plants, also lianas

**Habitats** | Grow mostly in open places, roadsides

**Leaves** | Opposite to decussate (four-sided stalks!; fig. C), leaves without stipules

**Inflorescences** | Dense cymes (whorled in the upper axils; fig. A), panicles

**Flowers** | Most strongly zygomorphic to slightly radial, hermaphroditic, (tetramerous-)pentamerous; calyx often more or less bilabiate and zygomorphic (figs. G, X); corolla usually with more or less distinct upper (2) and lower (3) lip, often ending in a tube; four stamens, didynamous, at times also just two stamens; the superior bicarpellate ovary is divided into four nutlets by one false septum; the nectaries are attached to its outer base either locally or encircle it completely; one central style with usually bilobate/laciniate stigma often also lying on the upper lip; only the two-armed stigma protrudes downward. Various pollination mechanisms.

**Fruits** | Four mericarps. Single seed. Nutlets, berries.

**Use** | Ornamental plants, medicinal herbs with essential oils: **mint** (*Mentha* species), **sage** (*Salvia officinalis*). Kitchen herbs: **oregano** (*Origanum vulgare*), **thyme** (*Thymus* species), **rosemary** (*Rosmarinus officinalis*). Today, valuable wood suppliers are included in the mint family, such as **teak** (*Tectona grandis*).

**Characteristics** | Many species have specially formed stamens; also widespread are the connective levers of the stamens (*Salvia officinalis*), which usually lie close to the upper lip and fold the open stamens downward when an insect visits the flower (see following page).

# LAMIACEAE

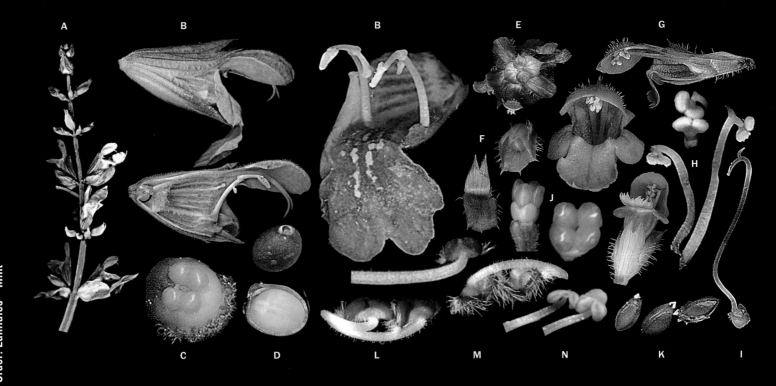

**A–D:** *Salvia officinalis.* A: Inflorescence. B: Flower; *upper left*, lateral/ *below*, longitudinal; *right*, frontal, upper lip removed. C: Ovary with nectary. D: Ripe mericarp; *above*, lateral; *below*, longitudinal.

**E–K:** *Prunella vulgaris.* E: Flower whorl, frontal. F: Calyx; *right*, in bud; *left*, flower parts removed and unfurled. G: Flower, frontal; *above*, longitudinal; *below*, from underneath. H: Stamen; *above*, from bud; *left*, lateral; *right*, from the front. I:

Gynoecium. J: Ovary; *left*, lateral; *right*, frontal. K: Mericarps.
**L:** *Lamium purpureum.* Stamens from both sides.
**M:** *L. album* stamens

**N:** *Origanum vulgare* stamens from bud from the front

## Mint family: function of "lips," stamens, and pollination | The

mint family plants (Lamiaceae) display special adaptations to their pollinators, most of which are bees or other insects, but can be birds. The upper lip, which is fused from two petals, often arches in a more or less galeate or helmet shape over the style/stigma and the didynamic stamens (fig. B, *left*). The lower lip (fig. B, *right*), grown from three fused petals, serves as a landing place for flower visitors; it protrudes forward, is more or less

wide, and often features visually conspicuous nectar guides that show the way to the nectar. The two filaments, of different lengths, sit on the inside of the corolla tube (fig. B, *right*) and may be equipped with a lever mechanism: the connective is divided into a long and a very short end. Only the long end supports the fertile half of an anther (theca). The short end has been transformed into a joint, the other anther half into a plate. The plates of both stamens meet in the middle. Since the anthers first present

their pollen (the flower is initially male), the stamens tilt when a flower visitor, on the way to the nectar, bumps its head against these plates and the animal gets its backdusted with pollen (the "turnpike mechanism"; fig. B, *right*). Only later, in the female blooming phase, does the style, which lies between the stamens, extend. Then, the two style arms are splayed out and can be pollinated; they accept pollen brought in by the insects. Self-pollination is prevented by the temporal separation of the male and

female phases. The **meadow sage** (*Salvia pratensis*) was used to create flower models for this structure, to be used pedagogically. But this elaborate mechanism also has its price: one theca per stamen is reduced; thus there are only two out of four pollen sacs available, which also reduces the amount of pollen. Other sage species display variations in the design of the lever. But rosemary and *Prunella* species (common self-heal, connective lever; fig. H) rely on the lever mechanism.

LARDIZABALACEAE

**A–D:** *Akebia × pentaphylla*. A: Leaf. B: Male flower, lateral. C: female flower, frontal. D: Ovary; *left*, transverse; *right*, longitudinal.
**E–J:** *Holboellia latifolia*. E: *Above*, male flower, frontal; *below*, longitudinal. F: From E; reduced gynoecium; *left*, lateral; *right*, frontal. G: Stamens from bud, frontal.
**H–J:** *Stauntonia hexaphylla*. H: Male flower. I: From H; reduced gynoecium. J: *Left*, stamens, lateral; *center*, open; *right*, splayed out.

**K–P:** *Decaisnea fargesii*. K: Male flower; *above*, frontal; *beneath it*, female flower, frontal. L: Androecium; *left*, lateral; *right*, splayed out. M: Calyx. N: Stigma. O: Young fruit; *left*, longitudinal; *right*, lateral. P: Fruit; *above it*, seeds, longitudinal; *right*, seeds with arils.
(2 genera in Chile, the others in Asia) indicates its great phylogenetic age.

**Genera** | 7–9; species: about 40
**Distribution** | Southeast Asia from the Himalayas to China-Japan, Chile
**Habit** | Lianas (*Akebia* and *Stautonia* climb counterclockwise), shrubs
**Leaves** | Alternate, compound, palmate, pinnate or trifoliate, partial leaflets entire; venation is mostly palmate (main nerves emerge from one point), leaf base may be swollen.
**Inflorescences** | Racemose
**Flowers** | Radial, rarely hermaphroditic; monoecious, dioecious, or polygamous-monoecious; female flowers (fig. C) with six staminodes; male flowers with reduced gynoecium (figs. F, I); nectar secreted from the perianth or androecium ("honey leaf"). Single flowers with or without bracts; small, fragrant, usually trimerous in two whorls (figs. E, H, K); three sepals, partially overlapping, occasionally petaloid; three petals, smaller than the sepals, may also be absent. There is often a double whorl of nectaries between petals and stamens. Androecium: usually six stamens in two whorls (figs. B, E, G, J, L) free or fused together, obdiplostemonous; usually three (6–15) carpels, apocarpous (fig. C), with many ovules.

**Fruits** | (Syncarpous) follicle fruit (fig. O), seeds with fleshy arils (fig. P)
**Use** | Because they grow rapidly, *Akebia* species are planted to create green facades (such as *A. trifoliata*, *A. inisignis*). The fleshy seed coats of the fruits of the **dead man's finger** (*Decaisnea fargesii*, *D. insignis*) and the **blue sausage vine** (*Akebia* sp.) are eaten as fruit. In Chile, the stalk fibers of *D. insignis* are used to make rope. The dried bark of the **chocolate vine** (*Akebia quinata*) is used as a diuretic in Japan. The **Japanese stauntonia vine** (*Stauntonia hexaphylla*) is used as an ornamental plant because of the rose-scented flowers and their decorative fruit.
**Characteristics** | The Lardizabalaceae family takes its name from the Mexican jurist and philosopher Manuel Miguel de Lardizábal y Uribe (1744–1820), a patron of the sciences. The English common name, "dead man's fingers," refers to the shape of the fingerlike fruits. The disjointed distribution area of this plant family (two genera in Chile, the others in Asia) indicates its great phylogenetic age.

A–K: *Machilus grijsii*. A: Opening bud. B: Flower, frontal. C: Flower, longitudinal. D: Flower from underneath. E: Unopened stamen from outer whorl. F: Stamen from inner whorl; *left*, unopened; *right*, next to it, with valves open. G: Staminode nectaries. H: The same, lateral, in flower cut longitudinally. I: Unripe fruit, frontal. J: Fruit, longitudinal. K: Fruit, transverse.

L–O: *Laurus nobilis*. L: Partial inflorescence. M: Flower, longitudinal. N: Ripe fruit, lateral. O: The same, longitudinal.

**Genera** | about 50; species: about 2,500

**Distribution** | Pantropical with concentrations in Central and South America, as well as in the Indo-Malaysian region; at times extends to the temperate regions

**Habit** | Trees (up to 50 meters tall), shrubs, hemiparasitic, perennials, herbaceous climbing plants. Buttress, aerial, and stilt roots all occur. Bark usually smooth, with many cork pores. All parts of the plant have an aromatic scent.

**Leaves** | Alternate, rarely opposite or in pseudo whorls; mostly evergreen, rarely deciduous; size varies greatly, from 1 to 60 cm long; shape is variable: lanceolate, circular, ovate, obovate, elliptic, rarely scale- or squamiform; leaf blade simple, entire, rarely lobed (sassafras), often leathery tough, rarely with domatia in the axils, stipules absent.

**Inflorescences** | In thyrses, panicles, racemose, or cymose umbels

**Flowers** | Radial, hermaphroditic or unisexual; in the latter, the species may be dioecious, monoecious, or polygamous-monoecious; single flowers relatively small, bimerous-trimerous (-tetramerous); there can be transitions between inflorescences and stamens (*Lindera*, *Litsea*); greenish, yellowish, or white; 8–12 stamens usually in 3 (–4) whorls, which open via valves (figs. F, H), sometimes with nectaries on the filament (fig. M), occasionally some reduced to staminodes; ovary usually superior (figs. B, C, J), consisting of only one carpel with an ovule.

**Fruits** | Berries, drupes (figs. N, O); pedicles or receptacle may help form the fruit.

**Use** | The fruits of the **avocado** (*Persea americana*) are usually eaten raw. High-quality avocado oil is pressed from particularly high-fat, overripe fruit. The **Ceylon cinnamon tree** (*Cinnamomum verum*) and the **bay laurel** (*Laurus nobilis*), which contain aromatic substances, are used as spices. Aromatics are extracted from the root bark of the **sassafras tree** (*Sassafras albidum*) for use in the perfume industry. The native North Americans used the bark to make chewing sticks. The substances in the bark are also used in toothpaste. The safrole contained in sassafras oil may cause contact allergies, and it is said to be liver toxic and a carcinogen. It serves as a basic material for making the drug Ecstasy, and therefore trading it is not allowed in the EU.

**Characteristics** | To prevent self-pollination, avocado trees display "synchronous dichogamy" in which two different types of pollination occur. Type A opens its flowers in the morning, and the stigmas can be pollinated. At noon, the flowers close. In the following afternoon they open again, when the stamens have opened. Type B opens its flowers in the afternoon, and the stigmas can be pollinated. Pollen presentation first occurs during the following morning.

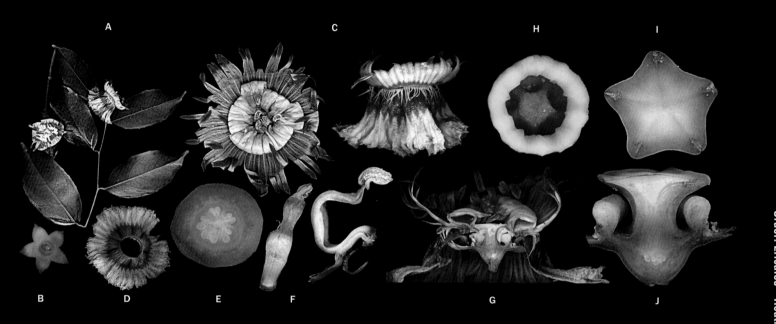

A–J: *Napoleonaea vogelii*. A: Leafy piece of branch with flowers. B: Calyx. C: *Left*, flower, frontal; *right*, lateral. D: Lower ring of the androecium. E: Ovary, transverse. F: Soliysty stamen. G: Flower, longitudinal. H: Nectary, frontal; transverse view of the ovary in the center of the upper part. I: Gynoecium, frontal; the stigmas are the small points on the 5 protrusions. J: Ovary with nectary, longitudinal.

**Genera** I 25; species: more than 300

**Distribution** I Pantropical

**Habits** I Trees, shrubs, rarely lianas, mostly evergreen. These plants grow in rainforests.

**Leaves** I Alternate, spiral or distichous arrangement; leaf blade simple, petiolate, with smooth or denticulate margins; stipules very small or absent

**Inflorescences** I Solitary, terminal, racemose, spikes (sometimes up to 1 meter long)

**Flowers** I Radial or zygomorphic, hermaphroditic, up to 10 cm tall, also fragrant, 4–6 (2–12) mostly thick sepals; 3–10 (–16) campanulate, petals yellow to red; corolla free or fused; 10–200 stamens in one, two, or more whorls, often fused with each other, basally or fused (or both) with the corolla; 2–6–8 carpels, fused with the receptacle or embedded in it; annular nectary (fig. H); style often short, stigma as a small strip-shaped area on the rays of the widened end of the style (fig. I)

**Fruits** I Pyxidium, the outside is usually fleshy and often red or woody, rarely berries, seeds mostly large and woody.

**Use** I The **Brazil nut tree** (*Berthollecia excelsa*) and **paradise nuts** (*Lecythis* species) provide seed fruit. Various species of *Eschweilera* supply wood. The crushed bark of the cauliflorous *Napoleonaea vogelii* is said to be used as a cough medicine in its African homeland. The **cannonball tree** (*Couroupita guianensis*) is very widespread in the tropics as an ornamental tree.

**Characteristics** I The German name for the Brazil nut, the *Paranussbaum*, is taken from that of the Brazilian state of Pará. Its flowers are pollinated by strong bees, which manage to force their way through the stamens to get at the nectar between the nectary and stigma.

The agouti, with its strong rodent teeth, is the only animal able to break open the hard shells of the Brazil nuts contained in the pyxidium fruit. Each time, they eat some of the seeds and then bury the rest as a food reserve. In this way, agouti contribute to the dispersal of the plants, because the animals do not find all the seeds again. It is known that the seeds of *Bertholletia* and *Lecythis* species accumulate selenium.

A–D: *Pinguicula* **sp**. A: Leaf rosette, about 15 cm in diameter. B: Flower, frontal. C: The same, longitudinal. D: Detail, stamens.

E–J: *Pinguicula moctezumae*. E: Flower, frontal. F: Bud, lateral, with spur. G: Calyx. H: *Right*, flower, longitudinal; *left*, detail. I: *Above*, stamens, frontal; *below*, from a bud, unopened, from underneath. J: Stamens and ovaries, longitudinal.

K–Q: *Utricularia calycifida*. K: Flower, frontal. L: Petal. M: Underside with spur; *below*, lateral. N: Ovary, lateral; *at right*, beside it, other side with stamens from above. O: Flower, longitudinal. P: Ripe fruit. Q: Bladder trap.

**Genera** I 3; species: more than 300
**Distribution** I Worldwide
**Habit** I Herbaceous plants, land or aquatic plants, can be epiphytic, sometimes with nodes
**Habitat** I In swamps or other damp habitats
**Leaves** I Alternate, often in compressed rosettes, simple, entire, sometimes covered with glandular hairs (butterworts, *Pinguicula* species) or with fine slits and bladder traps that catch animals (fig. Q)
**Inflorescences** I Racemose, spicate, single flowers
**Flowers** I Zygomorphic, hermaphroditic; the pentapetalous calyx with usually unequal-sized petals; the sometimes masked corolla is fused and bilabiate (upper lip: two petals; lower lip: three petals); the lower lip is enlarged or has a spur; two stamens with thecas that usually tilt toward each other; bicarpellate superior ovary with unequally two-lobed stigma.
**Fruits** I 2–4 valved capsules
**Characteristics** I All representatives are insectivores. The *Utricularia* species use suction traps formed of leaves or rhizoids where negative pressure prevails, to catch the smallest animals (such as water crayfish), algae, and unicellular organisms. The stimulus to open the trap is set off by trigger hairs, and the prey is suddenly sucked in.

**A–E:** *Tulipa gesneriana*. A: Habit. B: *Above*, flower, frontal; *below center*, longitudinal. C: Stigma. D: Ovary, transverse. E: *Above*, fruit, lateral; *beneath it*, frontal; *below*, transverse.

**F–I:** *Tricyrtis formosana*. F: *Above*, flower, frontal; *below*, longitudinal. G: Flower from underneath; the 3 spurs of the outer whorl of petals are visible. H: Stigma, lateral. I: Ovary; *left*, transverse; *right*, next to it, longitudinal.

**J–L:** *Tricyrtis hirta*. J: Habit. K: Flower, lateral. L: *Left*, outer tepal with basal spur, frontal, with yellow nectar guides; *right*, longitudinal.

**Subfamilies** | Lilioideae, Calochortoideae

**Genera** | 15; species: some 610. Well-known genera are *Lilium*, *Fritillaria*, *Tulipa*.

**Distribution** | Temperate latitudes of the Northern Hemisphere, especially East Asia and North America

**Habit** | Perennial herbaceous plants with bulbs or rhizomes as overwintering organs

**Leaves** | Alternate, spiral arrangement, distichous, leaf blade simple and undivided, linear, lanceolate to (broadly) ovate, smooth margins, rarely undulate, venation is parallel as a rule, sprout occasionally surrounded by a leaf sheath, rarely clasping the stem.

**Inflorescences** | Umbellate, racemose, corymbose, single flowers

**Flowers** | Radial to zygomorphic, hermaphroditic, trimerous, six tepals in two similarly structured whorls (perigone), mostly free, rarely fused; six stamens in two whorls of three, free; the superior ovary is fused from three carpels.

**Fruits** | Capsule, berry, seeds mostly flattened

**Use** | Many ornamental plants (*Erythronium*, *Gagea*, *Tricyrtis*), many tulip hybrids, preferably used as cut flowers. In China, starch is extracted from the bulbs of the **giant Himalayan lily** (*Cardocrinum giganteum*) to be used as food.

**Characteristics** | Many members of the lily family have contractile roots that help them anchor their bulbs in the best position deep in the soil. Some species develop bulbils for vegetative propagation; some also use the leaf axils for this propagation method, such as the **fire lily** (*Lilium bulbiferum*). A poisonous steroidal alkaloid (imperialin) is produced in the bulbs of the **crown imperial** (*Fritillaria imperialis*), which is a popular garden ornamental plant; this serves as a defense against herbivores. When eaten, it causes cardiovascular symptoms.

147

LINACEAE

**A–F:** *Linum usitatissimum*. A: *Above*, flower, frontal; *below it*, the underside. B: Gynoecium. C: Flower, longitudinal. D: Ovary, transverse. E: Ripe fruit, lateral. F: *Above*, seed lateral; *below*, longitudinal.

**G–J:** *Linum grandiflorum* **ssp.** *purpureum*. G: Flower, frontal. H: Flower, longitudinal. I: Stamens. J: Gynoecium with nectary.

**Genera** I 10–12; species: some 300
**Distribution** I Worldwide in the temperate zones
**Habit** I Shrubs, perennials, and herbaceous plants, as well as annuals
**Habitat** I Moorlands, dry turf, chalky soils, and at forest edges
**Leaves** I Alternate, rarely opposite, leaf blade simple, also glandular, stipules usually present
**Inflorescences** I Dichasia, scorpioid cymes, paniculate cymes, lower inflorescences also transformed into climbing spikes (*Hugonia*)

**Flowers** I Radial, hermaphroditic, tetramerous-pentamerous (figs. A, G); the free or fused sepals also ciliate at the margin (fig. C); the often-unguiculate, rapidly wilting petals often ciliate at the tip, also with ligulate appendages; 4–5–10 stamens, the filaments often broadened, basally united (fig. I) and often fused into a tube; the pentacarpellate ovary is superior (figs. B, C, J), with 1–2 ovules per locule; nectary scales usually develop beneath the base (figs. H, J); style more or less united, with

elongated or capitate stigmas at the end; can also be heterostylous.
**Fruits** I Capsules (fig. E), with five locules or up to ten locules due to false septums (fig. D), rarely drupes
**Use** I **Flax or linseed** (*Linum usitatissimum*) has been used and cultivated for thousands of years because of its oil-rich seeds and the flax fibers. The so-called press cake, which remains after the oil is extracted (linseed oil) from the seeds, is used as cattle feed. Also ornamental plants, such as the **biennial pale flax**

(*Linum bienne*), **scarlet flax** (*L. florum*), and **yellow flax** (*L. flavum*).
**Characteristics** I If flax seed is immersed in water, the seed coat swells up. This makes the seeds sticky, and they can, for example, be disseminated by attaching themselves to the hooves of animals. Flax seeds also swell up in the intestines and thus serve as fiber. In 2009, there were studies showing that the flax seed imported into the EU from Canada had been illegally genetically modified.

A–C: *Craterostigma plantagineum*. A: Habit. B: *Left*, flower, frontal; *center*, the same, lateral; *right*, the same, longitudinal. C: Opened capsule.

**Genera** I 13; species: more than 190
**Distribution** I Worldwide, tropical to temperate zones
**Habit** I Herbaceous plants, annuals to perennials, also trailing plants
**Leaves** I Opposite to decussate, as a result having a four-angled stem; also in rosettes

**Inflorescences** I Single, racemose, terminal, or in axils
**Flowers** I Zygomorphic, hermaphroditic, five fused sepals; five fused petals, also forming yellow scales in corolla throat, which make the corolla appear masked (fig. B, *right*); 2–4 stamens, in pair

arrangement; two carpels form the superior ovary; one style with penta-laciniate stigma (fig. B, *left*)
**Fruits** I Capsules, bivalved (fig. C)
**Use** I Ornamental plants, such as the **wishbone flower** (*Torenia fournieri*), are grown as a balcony plant.
**Characteristics** I Some species of

the genus *Craterostigma* are drought tolerant. The representatives of this family were formerly assigned to the figwort family (Scrophulariaceae). The families were separately classified after molecular investigation.

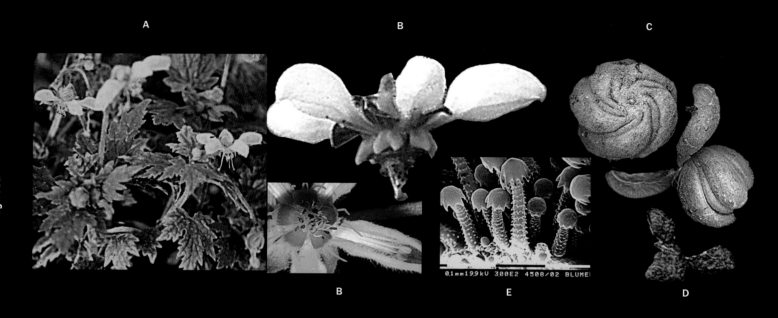

A · B · C

B · E · D

**A–D:** *Blumenbachia insignis.* A: Habit. B: *Above*, flower, lateral; *beneath it, center*, frontal. C: Ripe fruit; *above*, underside; right, beside it, lateral, partly opened. D: Seed. E: Stinging hair, SEM image

**Genera** | 14; species: over 260
**Distribution** | Predominantly the Americas; rarely Africa, Arabia
**Habitats** | From humid cloud forests to drylands
**Habits** | Most are herbaceous plants, rarely shrubby, *Blumenbachia* also climbing plants
**Leaves** | Alternate or opposite, mostly spiral arrangement; leaf blade mostly compound, simple, or lobed (fig. A)
**Inflorescences** | Cymes, capitiform
**Flowers** | Radial, hermaphroditic; the 4–5–7 sepals are usually fused into a tube, also fused with the ovary; 4–5 petals, also cymbiform (fig. B, *below*); usually five to many (50–100) stamens; pollen is also dispersed by explosion; flower interior can be transformed into nectary scales (fig. B: yellow), which can grow into a large nectary that is often of a contrasting color to the corolla; ovary more or less superior; the style is simple.
**Fruits** | Capsules (fig. C)
**Use** | Ornamental plants, in particular from the genera *Loasa*, *Blumenbachia*, and *Mentzelia*, such as the *Blumenbachia hieronymi* and the beautifully marked *B. insignis*.

**Characteristics** | The plants usually have stinging hairs (fig. E); hence the German name *Blumennessel* (flower nettle) for the loasa family.

A                    B              C          D              E                F    G

LOWIACEAE

**A–G:** *Orchidantha maxillarioides*. A: Habit; flowers with upper part of leaf. B: Central part of flower with tepal; *left*, lateral; *right*, frontal. C: Unripe androecium. D: Single stamen; *above*, rear side; *below*, front side. E: Ripe androecium and style/stigma; *left*, from the front; *right*, lateral. F: Style and stigma. G: Ovary, transverse.

**Genus** I 1; orchidantha; species: some 16
**Distribution** I Southeast Asia
**Habit** I Perennial herbaceous plants with rhizomes as overwintering organs and short stems
**Leaves** I Alternate, distichous, long leaf blade, long petiolate, simple, entire, usually linear-lanceolate, with a pronounced midrib and parallel lateral nervation

**Inflorescences** I A few with single flowers, cymose inflorescences, axillary, basal, or even underground
**Flowers** I Zygomorphic, hermaphroditic, trimerous; three sepals fused into a tube; three petals of different shapes; two small lateral bracts, inconspicuous; the median petal forms a labellum (fig. B, *right*), giving it an orchid-like flower appearance (hence the name!); five

fertile stamens (figs. C–E); three carpels are fused into an inferior ovary; long, thin style ends in a dorsiventral, zygomorphic trilobate stigma (figs. C, E, F), which has a species-typical structure (e.g., fringed, denticulate) and is considered to be a distinguishing feature from the related Zingiberales. Predominantly entomophily, primarily by *Dipterana* (such as flies)

**Fruits** I Three chambered, loculicidal capsules. Seeds with trilobatearil.
**Use** I Some are ornamental plants.
**Characteristics** I The plants have a secretory tissue called the "viscidium" (fig. E) at the base and ventral to the stigma lobes. Visitors to the flowers brush against the secretions with their backs, and the pollen then remains stuck there.

**A–C:** *Lythrum salicaria*. A: Inflorescence. B: Flower; *above*, longitudinal; *below*, frontal. C: *Above*, unripe fruit, transverse; *beneath it*, ripe fruit, frontal, opened transversely; *at the very bottom*, longitudinal.

**D–E:** *Lagerstroemia indica*. D: *Above*, flower, frontal; *below*, longitudinal. E: Fruit, longitudinal; *beneath it*, seeds

**F–L:** *Punica granatum*. F: *Left*, opening flower; *right*, frontal, petals fallen off; *beneath it*, flower, longitudinal. G: Bud, frontal. H: Style/stigma. I: Nectary in the hypanthium area. J: *Above*, ovary, longitudinal; *beneath it*, transverse. K: Fruit; *left*, lateral; *right*, next to it, longitudinal. L: *Left*, seed with aril; *right*, seed longitudinal.

**Genera** I More than 30; species: more than 600

**Distribution** I Worldwide, mostly in the tropics, also temperate regions

**Habit** I Trees, shrubs in tropical areas, herbaceous plants, perennials, aquatic plants in temperate zones

**Habitats** I Riparian zones, marshy meadows, low moors, stagnant water.

**Leaves** I Opposite, rarely whorled or spiral arrangement, leaf blade simple, stipules small or absent; the water chestnut (*Trapa natans*) has inflated petioles.

**Inflorescences** I Solitary, also axillary, racemose, panicular, cymes

**Flowers** I Radial, hermaphroditic; (3–) 4 or 6 (–16) sepals, more or less basally fused, also with outer calyx; four or six petals, also fused with the calyx; 8 or 12 (–100) stamens; the superior to inferior ovary, usually with 2 (–4–6) petals, has 2–6 locules. The style is simple, the stigma usually capitate. Nectar is secreted in the area of the hypanthium (figs. B, I).

**Fruits** I Capsules (figs. C, E), indehiscent fruits, nut fruits, dry berries

that open in the natural habitat (fig. K); the seeds have an aril (fig. L, *left*).

**Use** I The best-known representative of this family is the **pomegranate** (*Punica granatum*; figs. G–L); its arils (seeds) are eaten raw or used as to make juice (grenadine syrup). The leathery fruit peel is particularly rich in tannin and can be put to medical use. Many of the plants in the family are dye sources, such as **henna** (*Lawsonia inermis*); *Woodfordia fruticosa* leaves provide red dye, while the bark and wood of some *Lafoensia*

species produce a yellow dye. Ornamental plants, such as the **crape myrtle** (*Lagerstroemia indica*; figs. D–E) or *L. speciosa*.

**Characteristics** I The **purple loosestrife** (*Lythrum salicaria*) has styles of different lengths on a single plant (tristylous).

A–G: *Magnolia × soulangeana.* A: Flower, front petals removed. B: Androecium and gynoecium, lateral. C: Gynoecium, transverse. D: Single carpel, transverse. E: Ripe opened fruit. F: Seed with aril, longitudinal. G: Ripe seed without aril.

H: *Michelia skinneriana.* Androecium and gynoecium, longitudinal.

I–O: *Liriodendron tulipifera.* I: Flower, frontal. J: Gynoecium, longitudinal. K: The same, transverse. L: Solitary carpels. M: *Above,* ripe fruit, lateral; *below,* longitudinal. N: Ripe carpel, longitudinal. O: Seed.

**Genera** | 2: *Magnolia* with 225 species, *Liriodendron* with 2 species
**Distribution** | Temperate and tropical zones of Southeast and East Asia, temperate zones of southeastern North America, tropical South America as far south as Brazil
**Habit** | Trees, shrubs
**Leaves** | Alternate, spiral arrangement, evergreen or deciduous, leaf blade: simple or lobed (*Liriodendron*), large stipules
**Inflorescences** | Large single flowers (figs. A, I), terminal or axillary

**Flowers** | Hermaphroditic, all flower organs are arranged in spirals on the extended receptacle (figs. B, H); many free stamens; many free carpels with (1–) 2–12 (–16) ovules per carpel (fig. N). Nectar is secreted from the entire surface of the carpels. Pollination by pollen-eating beetles; the plants are reported to be thermogenetic.
**Fruits** | Follicles form one cone-shaped aggregate fruit (figs. E, M); seeds have an aril-like seed coat (figs. E, F); in fruits that open themselves, the seeds hang on an extended funicule (fig. E).

**Use** | Many **magnolia species** and hybrids, as well as the tulip trees (*Liriodendron tulipifera* and *L. chinense*) are cultivated as park and ornamental trees. In addition, the beautiful wood of the latter is very much in demand. The bark of *Magnolia officinalis* is used in traditional Chinese medicine; for example, as a sedative for anxiety and stress. Meanwhile, it is also used as an antioxidant and anti-inflammatory ingredient in cosmetics; it is said to slow down the aging of the skin. The two substances that produce this bioactive effect are the biphenols magnolol and honikiol.

**Characteristics** | The genus *Magnolia* was named in honor of Pierre Magnol (1638–1715), a French botanist and director of the Botanical Garden of Montpellier. The magnolia plants were widespread throughout the world during in the Tertiary period. The flowers of the representatives of this original family show few differentiated characteristics and have some of the simplest flower forms among angiosperms.

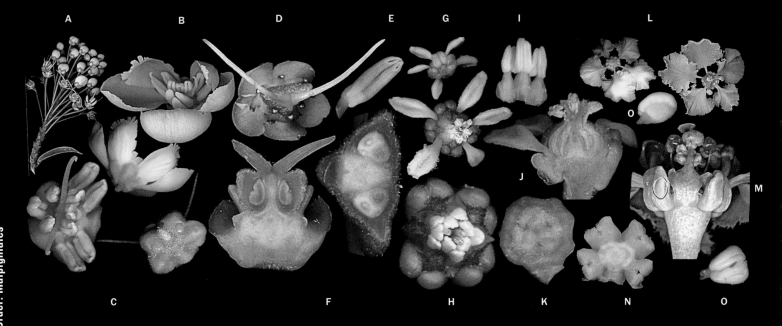

A B D E G I L

O

C F H K N O J M

**MALPIGHI FAMILY**
**Order: Malpighiales**

# MALPIGHIACEAE

**A–F:** *Acridocarpus smeathmannii.* A: Shoot with leaf and inflorescence. B: Flower; *above*, frontal; *below it*, lateral, from underneath. C: Androecium and gynoecium, frontal; *right*, the same from underneath, with a view of the 2 nectaries. D: Gynoecium and calyx, frontal. E: Anther with pore. F: *Left*, gynoecium longitudinal; *right*, transverse.

**G–K:** *Heteropteris* **sp**. G: *Above*, underside of flower; *below*, flower, frontal. H: Young flower, frontal. I: Stamens. J: Flower, longitudinal. K: Ovary, transverse.

**L–O:** *Stigmaphyllum ciliatum.* L: *Left*, underside of flower; *right*, frontal. M: Flower, lateral. N: Ovary, transverse; stamens with outward-facing thecas. O: Stamen; *above*, lateral; *below*, from the front.

**Genera** I 68; species: about 1,250
**Distribution** I Pantropical, especially in South America
**Habit** I Lianas, rarely trees, shrubs, half shrubs
**Habitat** I Often in tropical forests
**Leaves** I Mostly opposite, leaf blades simple, often hairy, can have stinging hairs, stipules present
**Inflorescences** I Terminal (fig. A) or axillary racemose
**Flowers** I Radial or zygomorphic (figs. B, G, L), mostly hermaphroditic, rarely male and female flowers on one plant,

calyx and corolla pentamerous; often the oil glands (epithelial elaiosomes, fig. M) alternate on the outside of the sepals (fig. C, *right*); calyx free or fused, also cordiform notched (fig. N); corolla often denticulate, fringed, or unguiculate (fig. L); 10 stamens, often with connective extensions, also basally fused (fig. I) and with pore-like opening (fig. E); (2–) 3 (–4–5) carpels form the superior ovary; each locule with one hanging ovule; style is free (fig. D).
**Fruits** I Three-segment schizocarpic

fruit, also winged fruit, drupes
**Use** I Some ornamental plants, some edible fruits in the *Malpighia* species, such as the **Barbados** or **acerola cherry** (*M. glabra*); these fruit have an especially high vitamin C content. Fibers from *Banisteropsis* species can be used to make ropes.
**Characteristics** I These plants often contain poisons; for example, in the leaves of *Banisteropsis caapi*, which are an ingredient of the drug called ayahuasca. Some of the approximately 950 Neotropic species have oil

flowers; solitary, oil-collecting female bees gather the fatty oil from the flowers. The bees do this by pressing their legs against the elaiophores (figs. M, N) in a stroking motion, whereby a thin spot in the cuticle tears open and a drop of oil swells out. The bees transport the fatty oil in their scopae (storage and transport apparatus on the hind legs) to their nest and feed it, mixed with pollen, into the brood cells as food for the larvae.

**A–C:** *Tilia plathyphyllos*. A: *Above*, flower, frontal; *below*, underside. B: Fruiting stage with winged leaf. C: *Left*, fruit, longitudinal; *right*, transverse.

**D–G:** *Gossypium herbaceum*. D: *Above*, flower, frontal; *below*, longitudinal. E: Calyx with outer calyx. F: Fruit, transverse. G: *Above*, hairy seed; *below*, seed.

**H–L:** *Althaea rosea*. H: *Above*, flower, frontal; *below*, longitudinal. I: Calyx with outer calyx. J: Androecium with protruding stigma. K: *Left*, gynoecium, lateral; *right*, transverse. L: *Above*, fruit, longitudinal; *center*, opened frontal fruit; *below*, lateral.

**M–Q:** *Malva sylvestris*. M: *Above*, flower, frontal; *below center*, longitudinal. N: Stigma. O: Underside of calyx. P: Androecium. Q: *Right*, fruit; *left*, seed.

**Genera** I Tilioideae: 3, with about 50 species; Malvoideae: 78, with more than 1,600 species
**Distribution** I Northern Hemisphere, temperate zones, Africa, Asia, Malaysia, Australia
**Habit** I Trees, shrubs, herbaceous plants, rarely lianas
**Leaves** I Usually alternate, simple to divided, palmate, lobed with smooth, notched, denticulate or serrated leaf margin; venation is also palmate. Stipules are present, also reduced.
**Inflorescences** I Cymose inflorescences; bracts may be present.
**Flowers** I Radial, rarely zygomorphic, the flowers can be asymmetrical,

usually hermaphroditic, rarely diclinous, monoecious or dioecious; 4–5 sepals and petals; sepals also fused and form nectar; can have outer calyx; 10 to many stamens, also in bundles, can be fused into a column around the style (Malvoideae); the superior ovary from one to many carpels; it may develop an androgynophore; usually many ovules, seeds can have an aril.
**Fruits** I Capsules, indehiscent fruits (may be winged), berries, drupes, nuts
**Use** I Many Malvaceae are ornamental plants, such as **hollyhocks** (*Alcaea* species), **vervain mallow** (*Malva alcea*), and **trailing abutilon**

(*Abutilon megapotamicum*). Fibers are harvested from the seed hairs of **Levant cotton** (*Gossypium herbaceum*) (fig. G) and from the stems of **jute plants** (*Chorcorus capsularis*, *C. olitorius*) and bast fibers of the **Congo jute** (*Urena lobata*). Kenaf fibers (*Hibiscus cannabinus*) can be used to make natural-fiber-reinforced plastics. The fleshy calyxes of the **roselle** (*Hibiscus sabdarffia*) are often dried to make fruit teas. **Okra** (*Hibiscus esculentus*) provides an edible fruit; the young fruit are eaten as vegetables. **Linden flowers** (*Tilia species*) can be used to make delicious jelly, and a tea helpful against fever

and cold symptoms; the soft wood is used for carving. Some barks are also used for rope making or braided items.
**Characteristics** I In woody species, the bark is often fibrous. The plants have mucous cells and stellate hairs, as well as extrafloral nectaries. The fruit is spread by means of various vectors.
**Notes** I The family of Malvaceae is today divided into nine subfamilies including up to 4,300 species; the four best known of these are presented here.

# MALVACEAE

**A–D:** *Pachira aquatica*. A: *Left*, flower, lateral; *right*, frontal. B: Stigma. C: Androecium, lateral. D: Ovary, transverse.

**E–G:** *Brachichiton bidwillii*. E: Flowers, frontal; *above*, male; *below*, female. F: Flowers, longitudinal; *left*, female; *right*, male. G: Carpel, longitudinal.

**H–I:** *Thomasia* **sp.** H: *Above*, flower, frontal; *below*, the underside, I: *Left*, ovary, longitudinal; *right*, transverse.

**J–N:** *Fremontodendron californicum*. J: *Above*, flower, frontal; *below*, longitudinal. K: *Above*, ovary, transverse; *below*, longitudinal. L: Androecium. M: *Above*, fruit lateral; *below*, splayed out. N: Seed.

**O–P:** *Cola acuminata*. O: Flowers; *left*, male; *right*, female. P: *Left*, androecium, lateral; *right*, stigma.

**Q–T:** *Theobroma cacao*. Q: *Right*, flower, lateral; *left*, cauliflory stem, dissected. R: *Left*, ovary, transverse; *right*, longitudinal. S: Stamen. T: Fruit, longitudinal.

**Genera** | 2; *Bombacoideae* with 120 species; *Sterculioideae* with about 400 species

**Distribution** | Tropics: Africa, South America, Australia, Madagascar

**Habit** | Trees over 50 meters tall, shrubs, herbaceous plants

**Leaves** | Alternate, simple, lobed, digitiform-pinnate, stipules slightly slanted

**Inflorescences** | May be cauliflorous (fig. Q, *left*), dichasial inflorescences

**Flowers** | Radial, rarely zygomorphic, hermaphroditic, Sterculioideae hermaphroditic or dioecious, pentamerous; sepals more or less fused; may have an outer calyx; five to many stamens, at times staminodes; 2–5 carpels form the superior gamosepalous ovary, which may also be apocarpous.

**Fruits** | Capsules, mericarps

**Use** | **Balsa** wood from *Ochroma pyramidale* is one of the lightest woods. **Kapok** fibers (*Ceiba pentandra*) are useful pericarp hairs that are used as packing material. The caffeine-containing seeds of **cola trees** (*Cola acuminata, C. nitida*, and *C. verticillata*) are used as a stimulant that drives away hunger, thirst, and fatigue. It is a flavoring used in soft drinks and chocolate. The **cacao tree** (*Theobroma cacao*) provides chocolate and cocoa butter, which is used to make high-quality cosmetics. The seed coats of the **durian** (*Durio zibethinus*) are considered a delicacy, although they stink terribly (you are not allowed to take durian on an airplane!).

**Characteristics** | The **baobab tree** (*Adansonia digitata*), which grows to be several hundred years old and is pollinated by bats, has a trunk that stores water. The trunk grows up to several meters in diameter, and thus it enables the tree to survive in dry habitats in Africa. The water stored in the trunk is used by the indigenous inhabitants and also by animals (elephants). The fruit flesh (which contains oil, vitamin B, and vitamin C) is edible. The local people often use the leaves as a medicinal plant for gastrointestinal complaints, as well as eating them as a vegetable. The baobab also plays a major role in popular belief.

**Comments** | Bombacaceae, Sterculiaceae, and Tiliaceae, earlier classified as autonomous families, are now classified as the subfamilies Bombacoideae, Sterculioideae, and Tilioideae. The first plate shows the linden and mallow family, and the second plate shows the kapok and cacao families.

**A–D:** *Maranta humilis*. A: Inflorescence, lateral. B: Flower, lateral, with bud. C: *Below*, asymmetrical flower, frontal; *above it*, center part, lateral. D: Stamen and stigma/style, lateral.

**E–L:** *Stromanthe lutea*. E: Inflorescence. F: Partial inflorescence, frontal. G: Bud. H: Two buds freed from sheath. I: Dissected bud. J: *Left*, gynoecium, stamen removed; *right*, with stamen. K: Young stamen. L: Bud, longitudinal.

**M–Q:** *Calathea lutea*. M: *Above*, flower, lateral; *below*, frontal. N: Ovary with nectary, longitudinal. O: Young stamen. P: Stigma/style. Q: Ovary, transverse.

**Genera** | 31; species: about 500
**Distribution** | Pantropical
**Habit** | Perennial herbaceous plants, often with rhizomes. Some are climbing plants.
**Leaves** | Alternate, basal or more or less distichous, leaf blade simple, entire, initially furled in conical shape, then ovate-oval, often with conspicuous patterns, pronounced midrib with air channels, with parallel, S-shape curved veins, which are netted together, one below the other. Characteristic is the so-called pulvinus, a joint between the petiole and leaf base, which is used to optimally direct the leaf toward the light in the shady undergrowth of the tropical rainforest.
**Inflorescences** | Terminal or lateral (figs. A, E), rarely growing directly out

of the rhizome; paniculate, capitiform, spicate, with two or many partial inflorescences (fig. F); their bracts are often conspicuously colored; the two uppermost flowers of the partial inflorescences grow as mirror images of each other.
**Flowers** | Asymmetrical, hermaphroditic, trimerous; three sepals, mostly free (fig. B); three petals with basally fused staminodes and style; only one of the inner whorl of stamens is fertile (figs. K, O), the other five mostly transformed into staminodes or absent; the three outer staminodes develop like petals (fig. C); the two inner whorls formed in different ways: one fleshy and thickened, the other cucullate or hooded, encasing the style (fig. D),

both often with appendages. Secondary pollen presentation; the ovary, grown from three fused carpels, is inferior (figs. L, N), ovules mostly reduced to one; septal nectaries; entomophily.
**Fruits** | Mostly fleshy capsule fruits, rarely berries or nuts, usually with only 1 (–3) seeds, with aril
**Use** | The taste- and odor-neutral starch called "arrowroot," which is harvested from the rhizomes of **arrowroot** (*Maranta arundinacea*), is used as a foodstuff. The term E957 is used to designate the natural sweetener thaumatin, which is harvested from the seed coat of **katamfe** (*Thaumatococcus daniellii*). This is a plant protein that is 2,000 times sweeter than sucrose, but

perception of the taste is delayed. *Calathea allouia* tubers ("sweetcorn root") are eaten cooked, as are the inflorescences. The long leaves of some **Calatheas** (*Calathea* sp.) were previously used to weave baskets, and the stems of *Schumannianthus dichotomus* were woven into mats. Some ornamental plants that are also popular as houseplants because of their leaf patterns or variegated leaves (such as *Calathea*, *Ctenanthe*, *Maranta*, and *Stromanthe* species).
**Other** | The Arawak, an indigenous South American people, used the starch harvested from **arrowroot** rhizomes to draw poison from poisoned arrows out of the body (hence the name!).

# MARCGRAVIACEAE

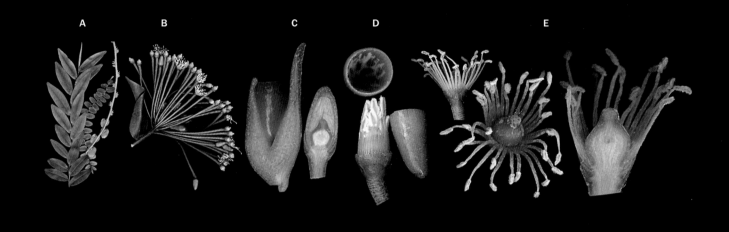

A  B  C  D  E

**A–E:** *Marcgravia umbellata.* A: Diversity of leaves and sterile climbing branch with aerial roots. B: Cymose umbel inflorescence with flowers and nectar containers or "jars" in the center. C: Nectar jar, lateral; *right*, longitudinal. D: Flower bud with cuculate sheath. E: Opened flower; *left*, lateral; *center*, frontal; *right*, longitudinal.

**Genera** I 5–7; species: over 120
**Distribution** I Tropical Americas
**Habits** I Woody plants, climbers or epiphytic
**Habitat** I Rainforests
**Leaves** I Spiral arrangement; leaf blade: simple, often heterophyllous (fig. A)
**Inflorescences** I Racemose, cymose umbellate or pseudo-spicate; flower ring around central nectar holders (fig. B)

**Flowers** I Radial, hermaphroditic, bracts often form nectar-producing containers or jars (fig. C); 4–5 sepals, free or fused at the base in cup shape; 4–5 more or less fused petals, petals also united into a self-unfurling bud sheath (fig. D); stamens in a single whorl; two, three, eight, or many carpels are fused to a multilocular ovary, which is superior or half inferior. One style with five-rayed stigmas or reduced to insignificant.

**Fruits** I Capsules that spring from the base in loculicidal form, sometimes berrylike; seeds can have reticulate testa and conspicuously colored pulp.
**Use** I Includes a few ornamental plants, such as *Norantea guianensis*, which has striking red-colored honey jars to attract birds for pollination
**Characteristics** I The bracts of the flowers are often united with the pedicle and form differently colored and shaped, mostly hollow, container-

like nectaries (hence the German family name, Honigbechergewächse, or "honey jar"!); bird pollination (ornithophily), but also bat (chiropterophily) and insect pollination (entomophily). The family's scientific name honors the German naturalist Georg Marckgraf (1610–1644).

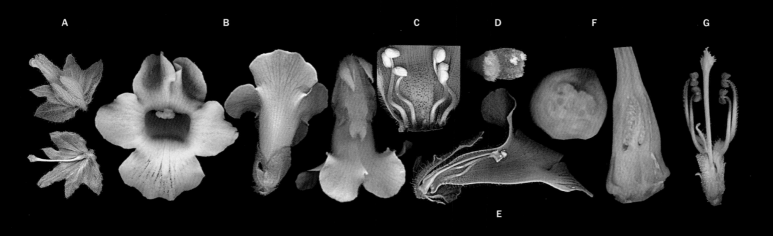

A–G: *Proboscidea parviflora*. A: Calyx; *above*, underside with 2 bracteoles; *below*, interior with gynoecium. B: *Left*, flower, frontal; *right*, next to it, 2 lateral views. C: 2 × 2 stamens in the opened corolla, the reduced fifth stamen in the center. D: Stigma, frontal. E: Flower, longitudinal. F: *Left*, ovary, transverse; *right*, the same, longitudinal. G: *Pterodiscus* sp.; 4 fertile stamens, the reduced fifth stamen in front of the ovary, perianth removed.

**Genera** I 4–5; species: about 15
**Distribution** I Neotropical
**Habitat** I Dry, near coastlines
**Habit** I Herbaceous plants, annuals to perennials, sometimes basally lignified
**Leaves** I Opposite, alternate, spiral arrangement; leaf blade simple petiolate, sticky hairs, mucous gland hairs

**Inflorescences** I Usually terminal racemose
**Flowers** I Zygomorphic, hermaphroditic; five free sepals, also with outer calyx-like bracts (fig. A); five fused petals, campanulate to funnel form; 2–4 stamens, splayed out thecas; one or two staminodes; the bicarpellate ovary is superior, basally surrounded by an annular nectary; one style with two stigma lobes that often are easy to stimulate.
**Fruits** I Capsules usually with a barbed style; outer wall often sticky
**Use** I Ornamental plants, such as the annual **cat's claw** (*Martynia annua*). Unripe fruits of *Proboscidea* species can be eaten when pickled.

**Notes** I The German name *Gämshorn* (chamois goat's horn) refers to the two barbed remnants of the style on the fruit. Some genera (such as *Ibicella*, *Pterodiscus*) have again been assigned to the Pedaliaceae.

MARTYNIACEAE

159

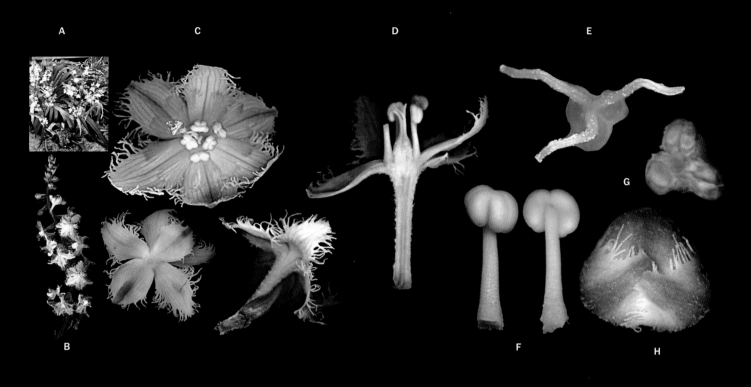

**A–H:** *Veratrum fimbriatrum*. A: Habit. B: Inflorescence. C: *Above*, flower frontal; *below left*, from underneath; *right*, beside it, lateral. D: Flower, longitudinal. E: Stigma. F: Stamen, front and rear side. G: Ovary, transverse. H: Bud, frontal.

**Genera** | About 17; species: 180. Well-known genera: *Paris*, *Trillium* (wakerobins), and *Veratrum* (false hellebores).

**Distribution** | Temperate latitudes of the Northern Hemisphere, concentrated in East Asia and North America

**Habit** | Perennial herbaceous plants with rhizomes, evergreen or deciduous, bulbs, rarely tubers

**Leaves** | Alternate, helical or in whorls; leaf blade: simple, undivided, lanceolate to ovate, entire, petiolate, usually parallel venation, occasionally reticulate

**Inflorescences** | Branched, spicate, racemose, paniculate or solitary

**Flowers** | Radial or zygomorphic, mostly hermaphroditic, usually trimerous (*Paris*: tetramerous to elevenfold); six tepals in two whorls of three (fig. C); tepals can have a different structure in the two whorls; tepals free or fused into a funnel-shaped tube (fig. D); six (4–11) stamens in two whorls of three (figs. C, F); three (4–11) carpels form the superior (fig. D), free or fused ovary; three styles (fig. E).

**Fruits** | Capsules, berries

**Use** | Some ornamental plants (*Trillium* sp., *Helonias bullata*, *Veratrum* sp.). The **white hellebore** (*Veratrum album*) is used as a homeopathic remedy for such symptoms as vomiting and poor blood circulation.

**Characteristics** | When it is in the vegetative phase, it is possible to confuse the **white hellebore** (*Veratrum album*) with the yellow gentian (*Gentiana lutea*), which is used for making schnapps. This can lead to fatal poisoning, since the white hellebore contains very toxic cardioactive steroidal alkaloids in all parts of the plant. These are also why the plant formerly was used as an arrow poison and for delousing; hence the German name *Lauswurz* (louse root). Today it is no longer used because the toxins can also enter the body through the scalp. Common beargrass (*Xenophyllum tenax*) is adapted to surviving recurring fires. Since it can survive with its rhizome, it is one of the first plants that can shoot up again after a fire.

**A–E:** *Melastoma candita*. A: Flower; *above*, frontal; *left, below*, lateral; *right*, longitudinal. B: Ovary, transverse. C: Stamens. D: Leaf. E: Fruit, longitudinal.

**F–K:** *Medinilla magnifica*. F: Inflorescence. G: Flower, frontal. H: *Right*, young flower, longitudinal, anthers are recessed; *above*, transverse view of bud in the area where the anthers are attached; *left*, ovary, transverse, in the same area.

I: Flower, longitudinal. J: Stamen, lateral and rear side. K: Partial inflorescence. **L–O:** *Calvoa orientalis*. L: *Above*, flower, frontal; *below*, longitudinal. M: *Left*, ovary, transverse; *right*, longitudinal. N: Stamens. O: Fruit; *above*, closed; *below*, open.

**P–R:** *Heterotis rotundifolia*. P: *Above*, flower, frontal; *below*, longitudinal. Q: Calyx. R: Ovary, transverse.

**Genera** | More than 180; species: more than 4,500
**Distribution** | Pantropical, rarely temperate latitudes, tropical and subtropical South America, center of diversity in Brazil
**Habit** | Small trees, shrubs, climbing plants, marsh plants, rarely epiphytes
**Leaves** | Often decussate (then four-sided stem), rarely alternate or whorled; leaf blade simple, characteristic are 3–9 arched veins, which unite at the tip (fig. D), without stipules, and can be hairy.
**Inflorescences** | Paniculate, corymbs, often with conspicuously

colored bracts (fig. F); can be cauliflorous.
**Flowers** | Radial to zygomorphic, hermaphroditic or dioecious, trimerous to pentamerous; calyx also with thistle-like glandular appendixes (fig. P); often twice as many stamens as petals, very variegated and conspicuously colored due to various connective formations (figs. C, J, P), often porous, protruding into small locules around the ovary in the bud (figs. H, P); there can also be differently shaped stamens in one flower; (1–) 3–5 (–14) carpels form the superior ovary, but usually an

inferior ovary due to fusion with the receptacle.
**Fruits** | Capsule (fig. E), berries, which will color your mouth dark after you eat them (hence the German name, Schwarzmundgewächse [black mouth family]!), such as of the genus *Miconia*
**Use** | Many ornamental plants from the genera *Melastoma* and *Tibouchina*, which are also cultivated as roadside trees in the tropics. The **showy medinilla** (*Medinilla magnifica*) is a popular container plant in cooler regions. Some species provide hardwood, such as **jongkong** (*Dactyloclados stenostachys*) or *Mouriri*

species. Black or yellow dyes, for example, can be obtained from *Memecylon edule*. The fruit of the **Singapore rhododendron** (*Melastoma malabathricum*) are edible. Despite the related name, it is not a rhododendron.
**Characteristics** | The special leaf venation and the stamens with their appendages are distinguishing features of the family. Bees use "buzz pollination" to extract the pollen from the pollen sacs by vibration. Many species can accumulate aluminum.

# MELIACEAE

**A–D:** *Azadirachta indica*. A: *Left*, just-opened flower; *right*, opened. B: flower, longitudinal. C: Stamens, top view. D: Ovary, transverse.

**E–I:** *Melia azedarach*. E: *Above left*, opening bud; *right*, next to it, already opened; *left*, beneath it, bud, longitudinal. F: Dissected bud, lateral. G: Fruit, lateral. H: *Above*, fruit, outer coat removed; *beneath it*, the same, lateral; *right*, next to it, longitudinal; *beneath it*, transverse. I: Seed.

**Genera** | More than 50; species: about 1,400
**Distribution** | Tropical: Asia, Africa, Australia, Malesia, Madagascar, Neotropics
**Habit** | Trees, shrubs, herbaceous plants
**Leaves** | Alternate, rarely opposite, predominantly (bi)pinnate, alternate on the midrib, no stipules

**Inflorescences** | Thyrses, rarely racemose, rarely spicate
**Flowers** | Usually dioecious, rarely monoecious; 3–6 sepals, free or fused into tube to cup shape; (3–) 4–5 (–6) petals, mostly free; 3–10 or many stamens, free or fused into a tube (fig. C), with paracorolla-like connective appendages (fig. A; fig. C; fig. E, *below*); 2–5 carpels are fused

into a superior ovary with one to many ovules per locule; style with a capitiform to disciform stigma.
**Fruits** | (Dry) berries, capsules, rarely drupes; seeds are winged or partially or completely encased in an aril, sarcotesta.
**Use** | Wood: **Big leaf mahogany** (*Swietenia macrophylla*), **West Indian mahogany** (*Swietenia*

*mahogani*), **African mahogany** (*Khaya* sp.), **neem tree** (*Azadirachta indica*). The **chinaberry tree** (*Melia azedarach*) has fragrant wood; oil from the seeds is used as a lubricant, and the seeds are made into chains for jewelry.
**Notes** | In general, all parts of the plants are poisonous!

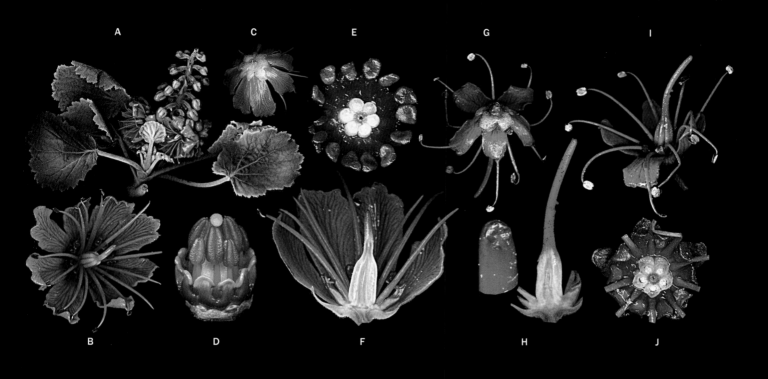

A–F: *Greyia sutherlandii*. A: Leafy branch with inflorescence. B: Flower, frontal. C: The same, underside. D: Opened bud, corolla removed, lateral. E: Ovary framed by staminodes, transverse. F: flower, longitudinal.

G–J: *Greyia radkoferi*. G: Flower from below. H: *Left*, stigma; *right*, gynoecium, longitudinal. I: Flower, lateral. J: Ovary, transverse; surrounded by filaments and nectar-producing staminodes.

**Genera** | 3; species: over 35

**Distribution** | Tropical and southern Africa

**Habit** | Small trees, shrubs, half shrubs, perennial herbaceous plants

**Leaves** | Spiral arrangement, alternate; leaf blades simple to mostly odd-pinnate, with or without denticulate stipules; underside can have hairs; leaf sheaths also fused with the shoot.

**Inflorescences** | Terminal and axillary racemose (fig. A)

**Flowers** | Radial (fig. B) to zygomorphic, hermaphroditic; 4–5 (–6) unsimilar, basally fused, as well as thickened sepals; usually there is a circular disc between calyx and corolla; additionally, may form conspicuous staminodes (figs. D, E); 4–5 petals, also unguiculate; 4–5 (6–10) stamens, free or basally fused within a disc, often with long filaments (fig. I); the (3–) 4–5 (–7) carpels are fused into a superior ovary, with one to many axile ovules (fig. J); one style with 4–5 stigma lobes; nectar may be produced from a disc.

**Fruits** | Capsule fruits with one-seed locules, loculicidal or septicidal, seeds with or without aril

**Use** | Strongly fragrant ornamental plants, such as *Greyia sutherlandii*. The flowers of the **honey bush species** (*Melianthus* sp.) secrete nectar in large drops that can be eaten, but the remaining parts of the plants are poisonous. Dye can be harvested from **giant honeybush** (*Melianthus major*) flowers. *Bersama abyssinica* is known for producing wood.

**Characteristics** | The roots, bark, and leaves of *Melianthus comosus* are used to treat snakebites.

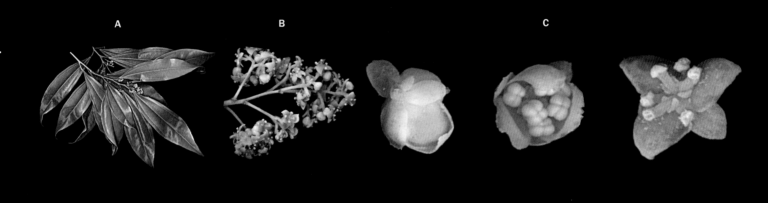

**A–C:** *Cocculus laurifolius*. A: Leafy branch with flowers. B: Male inflorescence. C: *Left*, underside of flower; *center,* opening male bud; *right*, opened male flower, frontal.

**Genera** | More than 65; species: more than 600

**Distribution** | Worldwide, primarily in the tropics and subtropics (pantropical)

**Habit** | Climbing plants, lianas, rarely shrubs, small trees or herbaceous plants, rarely stem succulents

**Leaves** | Alternate, whorled, leaf blade mostly simple, seasonally green, leathery, as a rule entire, the basal petiole is often swollen, palmate leaf venation (fig. A).

**Inflorescences** | Umbellate, cymose, capitiform, rarely thyrses

**Flowers** | Radial, unisexual, plants are dioecious; usually small flowers, usually trimerous; (1–3) 4 (6–8) sepals or sepals absent, free or fused; petals usually correspond to the number of sepals; seven flowers usually with six stamens (figs. B, C); occasionally with rudimentary ovaries; female flowers rarely with one carpel, usually with three or six or many; apocarpous, occasionally with remnants of staminodes.

**Fruits** | Drupes

**Use** | Many species produce toxic, often-psychoactive alkaloids, which in many cases act as neurotoxins in humans and are used medically. Examples include the roots of the **calumba** (*Jateorhiza palmata*), which is indigenous to tropical Africa; the stem and roots of the **Indian** or **fish berry** (*Anamirta cocculus*), as well as its seeds ("cockle-seeds"), also contain the toxic sesquiterpene lactone picrotoxin, which is used to treat Meniere's disease. The **curare vine** (*Chondrodendrum tomentosum*) is used to make a dart poison. *Stephania* species plant roots are used as a fish poison; they are also used in traditional Chinese medicine. In Madagascar, people take leaf or root extracts from *Strychnopsis thouarsii* to treat malaria, while in Nigeria and other countries, they take *Synclisia scabrida* extracts. **Guduchi** (= "that which protects the body"; *Tinospora cordifolia*) is one of the most important anti-aging plants used in India. These plants are used in Ayurvedic medicine to strengthen the body's defenses.

**Characteristics** | The crescent-shaped seeds of the moonseed plants gave the family its name.

A–B: *Menyanthes trifoliata*. A: *Left*, flower, frontal; *center*, the same lateral; *right*, the same, longitudinal. B: Ovary, transverse.

C–G: *Villarsia parnassifolia*. C: *Left*, flower, frontal; *center*, underside; *right*, longitudinal. D: Single petal. E: Stigma. F: Ovary, transverse. G: Androecium and gynoecium from bud.

**Genera** | About 5; species: about 40
**Distribution** | Worldwide
**Habitat** | Marshes, shore areas, stagnant waters
**Habit** | Perennial herbaceous plants, often with rhizomes or tufted rhizomes
**Leaves** | Alternate, basal; leaf blade simple and undivided, often with sheath at the base or ternate, without stipules
**Inflorescences** | In racemose panicles or paniculate, solitary
**Flowers** | Radial, hermaphroditic; calyx and white, yellow, or pink corolla are pentamerous; sepals may be slightly fused at the base; petals usually grow in a more or less tubular form; the tip of the free corolla can have long fringed margins. Long "fringed edges" may likewise grow on the upper side of the corolla (figs. A, C, D). The filament bases of the partially movable stamens are fused with the corolla. Usually, the two carpels form the superior ovary; the style is equipped with two style arms.

**Fruits** | Capsule fruits; the seeds can be winged.
**Use** | Ornamental plants, locally consumed food, and medicinal plants that contain substances such as menyanthin (lowers fever; hence the German name, Fieberkleegewächse [fever clover family]!). In Scandinavia, the leaves are also used to make tea and are even added to beer.
**Characteristics** | The seeds of **yellow floating heart** (*Nymphoides peltata*) are released into the water. Due to their shape and because they are equipped with air chambers, they remain buoyant a long time and can, for example, be dispersed in the plumage of waterfowl. The **buckbean** (*Menyanthes trifoliata*) is protected in Germany under the German Federal Species Protection Ordinance (Bundesartenschutzordnung); in Switzerland, the species is not endangered.

A B C D E

**A–E:** *Claytonia perfoliata (= Montia perfoliata).* A: Habit. B: Inflorescence on top of two fused bracts. C: *Left,* flower, frontal; *right,* underside. D: *Above,* ovary, longitudinal; *below,* transverse, E: *Above,* fruit, frontal; *below,* opened with 2 seeds.

**Genera** | 10; species: over 25
**Distribution** | Western North and South America, New Zealand, Caribbean islands, Subantarctic islands
**Habitat** | Waysides, dunes, brushwood; by streams, ditches, and damp fields
**Habit** | Herbaceous plants, annuals to perennials, rarely half shrubs
**Leaves** | Alternate, often in basal rosettes, often with base clasping the stem, hairless, covering of lammelate epicuticular wax
**Inflorescences** | Cymose and terminal, solitary and axillary; the bracts below the inflorescence are often fused (fig. B).
**Flowers** | Radial, hermaphroditic; two sepals (sepal-like bracts; fig. C, *right*); (4–) 5 (–9) petals; (3–) 5 (–100) stamens, sometimes basally fused; 2–3–8 carpels form the superior ovary, each with 4–7 ovules (figs. D–E).
**Fruits** | Capsule fruit
**Use** | The **moss rose** (*Portulaca grandiflora*) is a popular ornamental plant. **Common purslane** (*Portulaca oleracea*) is a vitamin-rich food plant. **Miner's lettuce** (also Indian lettuce, *Claytonia perfoliata*) originally comes from North America and has become a feral plant, especially from plant nurseries. The leaves can be eaten as salad.
**Characteristics** | Some species are succulents. Betalans occur as flower colorants in this family.

**A–E:** *Ficus benjaminii.* A: Inflorescence, frontal. B: Male and female flower, lateral. C: Inflorescence, longitudinal. D: Male flower. E: Female flower.

**F:** *Ficus carica* fruiting stage, longitudinal.

**G–L:** *Dorstenia foetida* **ssp.** *obovata.* G: Inflorescence, frontal. H: The same, lateral. I: Inflorescence, longitudinal. J: Unripe fruit, longitudinal. K: Ripe fruit with emerging seeds L: Ripe seeds.

**M–O:** *Morus alba.* M: Leafy branch with unripe fruit. N: *Above,* unripe fruiting stage, longitudinal; *beneath it,* lateral. O: Unripe single fruit, longitudinal; *beneath it,* the same, top view.

**Genera** I 40; species: about 1,000
**Distribution** I Worldwide, tropical, subtropical in both hemispheres
**Habit** I Trees or shrubs with milky sap
**Leaves** I Alternate, spiral arrangement or opposite. Leaf blade: undivided or lobed, palmate lobes, petiolate, also evergreen.
**Inflorescences** I Capitiform racemose (fig. N), flowers often enclosed by axial tissue with only one access (fig. C) or growing more or less crowded on a cup- to plate-shaped axis (figs. G, J)

**Flowers** I Unisexual, monoecious; the tetramerous perianth is usually inconspicuous, also becoming fleshy (figs. N, O); male flowers with 1–3–4 stamens. Cauliflory can occur.
**Fruits** I Fleshy multiple fruits, at times from fleshy tepals (fig. N)
**Use** I The leaves of the **white mulberry** (*Morus alba*) are used to feed silkworms. The clusters of **black** and **red mulberry** nut fruits (*M. nigra, M. rubra*) are eaten raw or dried to preserve them for a longer time. The **banyan tree** (*Ficus bengalensis*),

which grows in the tropics, initially grows as an epiphyte and forms aerial roots that grow to the ground. When these roots reach the ground, they become stronger and "strangle" the supporting tree.
**Characteristics** I Some ficus species, such as the **rubber fig** (*Ficus elastica*), the **fiddle-leaf fig** (*F. lyrata*), and the **weeping fig** (*F. benjaminii*), are grown as houseplants in apartments and are well known for decorating conference halls, shopping malls, or hotel lobbies. However, there

are many people who are allergic to the protein in the milky sap of the mulberry family ("latex allergy"). Therefore, it is not at all recommended that you place these plants in a closed room. The latex-containing milky sap of the weeping fig is also used to produce rubber.

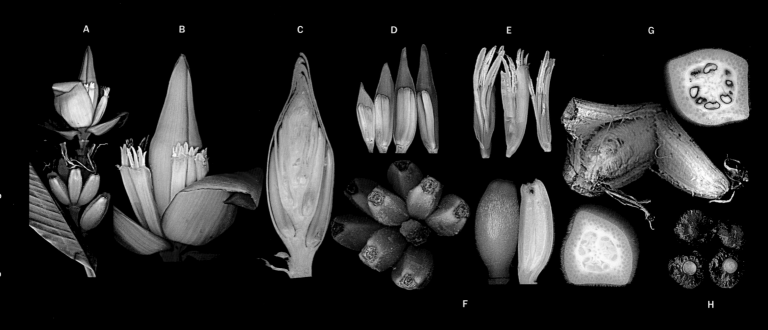

A B C D E G

F H

**A–H:** *Musa basjoo*. A: Part of a sprout with leaf; unripe fruit and flowers. B: Upper part of A; female flowers are visible under the outer bracts. C: Central bud from B, longitudinal: female and male flowers. D: Male flowers at various ages. E: Ripe male flowers. F: *Left*, unripe fruiting stage; *center*, single fruit, lateral and longitudinal; *right*, transverse. G: Opened fleshy capsule; *above*, transverse. H: Ripe seeds.

**Genera** I 3; species: about 40
**Distribution** I Originally from Africa, via tropical Asia to the Pacific. Today, due to the cultivation of bananas, this family is distributed worldwide in tropical and subtropical regions.
**Habit** I Perennials, perennial herbaceous plants with underground rhizomes, and "pseudo stem" of interleaved leaf sheaths, which can grow up to 12 meters tall
**Leaves** I Alternate, helical. Structure: leaf sheath, short petiole (except in the *Ensete*); leaf blade is very large, simple, linear, with a pronounced midrib and parallel lateral venation; entire; parallel to the lateral venation—however, often lacerated and thus apparently pinnapartite ("weathervane leaves").
**Inflorescences** I Terminal, rarely

lateral, upright to hanging, composed of several cymose partial inflorescences, which are in a spiral arrangement on a long axil. Groups of many small, yellowish single flowers grow in the axils of the coarse, red-violet bracts (fig. A).
**Flowers** I Monoecious, partial inflorescences, diclinous, with the lower bracts supporting female flowers, and the upper bracts male. Hermaphroditic flowers may grow in between, but only the female flowers develop further. Two whorls, each with three bracts, five of which are fused; one remains free, and this makes it possible for the corolla to appear bilabiate. Five to six free stamens (figs. D, E); occasionally a single staminode develops; the inferior ovary is fused from three carpels (fig. F, *right*);

10–100 ovules per each locule; the trichomes in the ovary later produce the fruit pulp. Septal nectaries, often having large amounts of nectar; pollination by bats, birds, insects.
**Fruits** I Fleshy capsule fruits that open when ripe (figs. F, G), usually mistakenly referred to as berry fruit, but these do not open by themselves. The wild species grow hard, dark seeds (fig. H); the hybrids produce fruit without fertilization (parthenocarpy = virgin production) and therefore do not grow any seeds. The brown small dots in cultivated bananas are the remnants of the ovules. Cultivated bananas are propagated by vegetative propagation.
**Use** I The **banana** (*Musa* × *paradisiaca*) is the most important representative, although it is a cross between *M. acuminata* × *M.*

*balbisiana*. There are over 1,000 different varieties. In Africa, plantains are eaten the way potatoes are eaten in Europe (i.e., boiled, fried, mashed). Banana flowers are eaten in Asia, and people wrap food in the leaves and then cook it. The **Ethiopian banana** (*Ensete ventriculosum*), which comes from central and East Africa, is sometimes cultivated as an ornamental plant. Manila hemp is harvested from the fibers of the vascular bundles that grow in the leaf sheaths of the **abaca** (*Musa textilis*).
**Characteristics** I Unripe fruits are not sweet, because the starch is converted into sugar only as the fruit ripens.

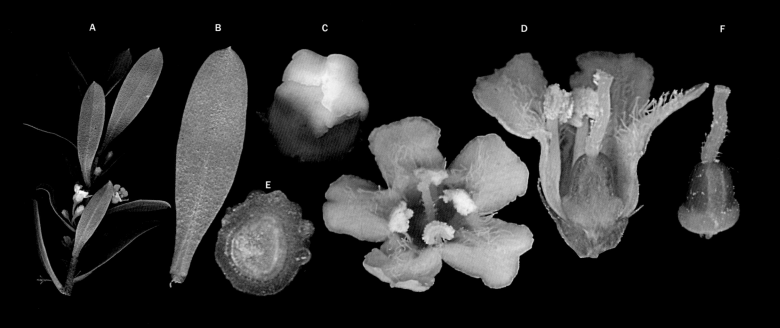

A–F: *Myoporum insulare*. A: Leafy branch with flowers. B: Leaf. C: Flower bud, frontal. D: *Left*, flower, frontal; *right*, the same, longitudinal E: Ovary, transverse. F: Ovary, lateral, with basal nectar ring.

# MYOPORACEAE

**Genera** | 3: *Myoporum, Eremophila, Diocirea*; species: almost 300

**Distribution** | Australia, the South Pacific, South Africa, East Asia, the West Indies, on rocky slopes and cliffs

**Habit** | Small trees, shrubs, also with glandular stems, also trailing plants

**Leaves** | Alternate, rarely opposite; leaf blade simple, sessile, dotted with glands (fig. B; hence the German name Lippenblütlerartige [lip-flowering]!); without stipules, often have glands, stellate or feathery hairs

**Inflorescences** | racemose, axillary, cymose, solitary

**Flowers** | Radial, hermaphroditic; 4–5 sepals, basally fused; five fused petals, funnel shaped or tubular, with colored nectar guides on top surrounded by fringes (fig. D, *left*); 4–5 stamens with kidney-shaped anthers, basally fused with the corolla (fig. D, *right*); can be in two pairs of unequal length; the bilocular superior ovary has a more or less hairy style with a smaller, bilobate stigma; the base of the ovary is surrounded by an annular nectary (fig. F).

**Fruits** | Drupes

**Use** | Ornamental plants in warm regions, such as the **spotted emu bush** (*Eremophila maculata*). *Myoporum insular* grows well in hedges and in windy regions; *M. acuminatum* can be planted in catchment areas for saline splash water. The indigenous Hawaiians used the wood of *Myoporum sandwicense* to build outrigger boats. Because of its fragrant wood, it is also called "false sandalwood."

**Characteristics** | The Myoporaceae family has also recently come to be regarded as a tribe of the Scrophulariaceae.

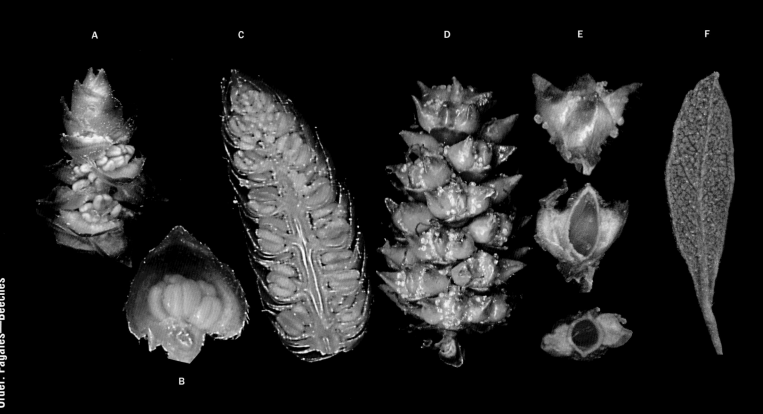

A–F: *Myrica gale*. A: Male inflorescence. B: Male flower. C: Male inflorescence, longitudinal. D: Female inflorescence, lateral. E: *Above*, female flower, lateral; *center*, the same, longitudinal; *below*, the same, transverse. F: Underside of foliage leaf.

MYRICACEAE

**BAYBERRY FAMILY**
Order: Fagales—Beeches

**Genera** | 3: *Canacomyrica*, *Comptonia*, *Myrica*; species: over 55
**Distribution** | Worldwide, except in Australia
**Habit** | Trees or shrubs
**Habitat** | Hill moorland and moorland
**Leaves** | Alternate, spiral arrangement; leaf blade simple, entire, or serrated; evergreen or deciduous; aromatic fragrance; often with scutate glandular hairs (fig. F); petiolate; stipules usually absent
**Inflorescences** | Catkins, spikes

**Flowers** | Mostly unisexual, monoecious or dioecious; male flowers usually solitary on the axil of a bract (fig. B) with (1–) 4–8 (–20) usually free or at most basally fused stamens; the female flowers grow solitary or in groups of 2–4 above a bract plus 2–4 bracteoles (fig. E); two carpels are fused into a unilocular ovary.
**Fruits** | Drupes, smooth or warty, sometimes encased in bracts or bracteoles
**Use** | People hang up bayberry or bog

myrtle twigs or put them in between linens or clothes because of the insect-repellent effect of the fragrant leaves. The plant was also used to brew beer and distill herbal liqueurs and myrtle schnapps. The dried leaves are used for seasoning and making perfumes. *Myrica rubra* fruit are eaten in Asia. The wax that is found on the outer skin of the fruit, such as on the **southern wax myrtle** (*Myrica cerifera*) and *M. pensylvanica*, can be removed by cooking the fruit. When the

fruit is subsequently cooled, the wax floats to the surface and can be skimmed off. Since the fruit are small, making candles from this wax takes a great deal of work!
**Characteristics** | Usually pollinated by wind (the pollen can cause allergies); root symbiosis with nitrogen-oxidizing bacteria of the species *Frankia alni*

170

**A–B:** *Anagallis arvensis*. A: *Above*, flower, frontal; *below*, longitudinal. B: Capsule; *above*, lateral; *center*, open; *bottom*, lid.

**C–F:** *Ardisia crenata*. C. *Left*, leafy branch with flowers; *right*, inflorescence. D: *Above*, flower, frontal; *below left*, from underneath. E: *Above*, calyx with ovary, transverse; *below*, flower, longitudinal; *right*, ovary, longitudinal. F: Fruit; *lower left*, longitudinal; *right*, seed.

**G–J:** *Lysimachia punctata*. G: *Above*, flower, frontal; *below*, from underneath. H: Stamens; *left*, lateral; *right*, frontal. I: Central part of the flower, longitudinal. J: Young capsule; *above*, lateral; *below*, transverse.

**K–N:** *Cyclamen hederifolium*. K: *Above*, leaf; *center*, flower, frontal; *below*, longitudinal. L: Stamens, lateral. M: *Above*, fruit; *below*, open capsule. N: Unopened fruit; *above*, lateral; *below left*, longitudinal; *right*, transverse.

**Genera** | More than 40; species: more than 1,400
**Distribution** | Pantropical, northern temperate latitudes
**Habits** | Small trees, shrubs, half shrubs, lianas, annual to perennial herbaceous plants
**Leaves** | Alternate, leaf blade simple, leathery (fig. C, *left*), dotted with glands or resin ducts, without stipules
**Inflorescences** | In tufts on short shoots, racemose or terminal panicles or cymes
**Flowers** | Radial, usually small, hermaphroditic or unisexual, then dioecious; the 3–6 sepals are free or (basally) fused, usually as many as the petals, fused in a wheel or plate shape; five (3–6) stamens, often epipetalous, free or fused, which often open inwardly through porous longitudinal lacerations (figs. E, I); the 4–6 locular ovary is superior or half inferior, one style with papillose stigma
**Fruits** | Fleshy drupes, berry fruits (fig. F) or multiseeded capsule fruits (figs. B, M)
**Use** | Some species are cultivated as ornamental plants, such as *Ardisia japonica* as a ground cover (although it is sensitive to frost), **moneywort** (*Lysimachia nummularia*), and other loosestrife species (*Lysimachia* sp.); the **hardy cyclamen** (*Cyclamen coum*) or the **Persian cyclamen** (*Cyclamen persicum* hybrids) as a houseplant.
**Characteristics** | The poisonous **scarlet pimpernel** (*Anagallis arvensis*) is an unpopular wildflower that is considered invasive. The female cuckoo bee (genus *Macropis*) is one of the oil-collecting bees, because in addition to the pollen, they also collect the fatty oil from the flowers of loosestrife species plants. There are oil glands on the outside of the stamen tube that secrete the fatty oil. Using the hairs on their fore- and middle legs, the females suck the oil from the glands and carry it to their nests in special oil-carrying "baskets" on their hind legs. Since the bees collect exclusively from loosestrife flowers (they are therefore oligolectic), they are thus dependent on how widely these plants are distributed; without them, they cannot care for their offspring.
**Notes** | The family of Myrsinaceae has recently also been classified as a subfamily of the Primulaceae.

MYRTACEAE

**A–B:** *Acca sellowiana*. A: *Above*, flower, longitudinal; *below*, from underneath. B: *Left*, fruit, lateral; *right*, transverse.
**C–D:** *Syzygium jambos*. C: *Above*, flower, longitudinal; *below at left*, calyx from underneath. D: *Above right*, fruit, transverse; *center*, frontal; *below*, longitudinal.
**E–I:** *Melaleuca diosmifolia*. E: Partial inflorescence. F: Leaf from underneath. G: Flower, lateral. H: Calyx, frontal. I: *Left*, ovary, transverse; *right*, flower, longitudinal.

**J–L:** *Chamelaucium unicatum*. J: *Above*, flower, frontal; *below*, from underneath. K: *Above*, bud, frontal; *below*, opened; *left*, longitudinal. L: Fruit; *left*, transverse; *right*, longitudinal.
**M–Q:** *Callistemon subulatus*. M: Inflorescence. N: Bud, frontal. O: Single flower, lateral. P: Flower; *center*, longitudinal. Q: *Left*, fruit, longitudinal; *right*, transverse; *center*, frontal.

**Genera** | More than 130; species: more than 4,500
**Distribution** | Tropical, subtropical, primarily in the Americas and Australia
**Habit** | Trees, shrubs, often small, can be creepers
**Leaves** | Opposite, rarely alternate; leaf blade often leathery and dotted with glands, which are globose oil holders (fig. F); simple and undivided, often evergreen, petiolate or sessile
**Inflorescences** | Racemose, cymes, panicles, dichasial, capitiform, often with two bracteoles
**Flowers** | Radial, predominantly hermaphroditic (trimerous-) tetramerous-pentamerous (-sexamerous); 4–5 sepals are free or fused, can be slanted in a cupped shape; 4–5 petals, usually fused;

colors range from white to yellow, pink to red. There is often one hypanthium; usually numerous stamens in groups or bundles, also basally fused in a whorl (fig. J); the connective often has an apical gland; staminodes may also be present; 2–3–5 carpels form the usually inferior, unilocular to multilocular ovary with mostly axile ovules; it may support a disc; the style is simple. Tufted flowers.
**Fruits** | (Pyxidium) capsule fruit (fig. Q), berry fruit; the seeds of *Eucalyptus* species may also be winged.
**Use** | Many of the myrtle family produce essential oils such as the *Melaleuca* species, from which we harvest cajeput oil (*M. cajeputi*) or tea tree oil (*M. alternifolium*). Eucalyptus oil is distilled from the branches and

leaves of various *Eucalyptus* species by means of steam distillation. The flower buds from the **clove tree** (*Syzygium aromaticum*) become the spice cloves, which also has an antibiotic effect (such as for toothache). Such plants as the **guava** (*Psidium guajava*), the **pineapple guava** (*Acca sellowiana*), and the **rose-apple** (*Syzygium jambos*) (fig. D) produce edible fruit. Honeybees produce high-quality manuka honey from the flowers of the **manuka** or **manuka myrtle** (*Leptospermum soparium*); this honey is said to have an anti-inflammatory effect. Flowering branches of *Chamelaucium uncinatum* (figs. J–L) or of *Thryptomene* species plants are often used to make bouquets. The northern

**rātā tree** (*Metrosideros* "iron-hearted" *robusta*) provides very ("iron") hard wood. Because of their striking reddish flowers, *Metrosideros* **trees** are also cultivated as ornamental plants in subtropical climates, such as the New Zealand Christmas tree or pōhutukawa (*M. excelsa*). Other ornamental plants include *Backhausia citriodora*, *Eucalyptus* and *Corymbia* species, **bottlebrushes** (*Callistemon* species; figs. M–Q), and the **common myrtle** (*Myrtus communis*), almost the only European plant in the family.
**Characteristics** | Bicollateral bundles: the phloem (which transports the nutrients) is inside the xylem.

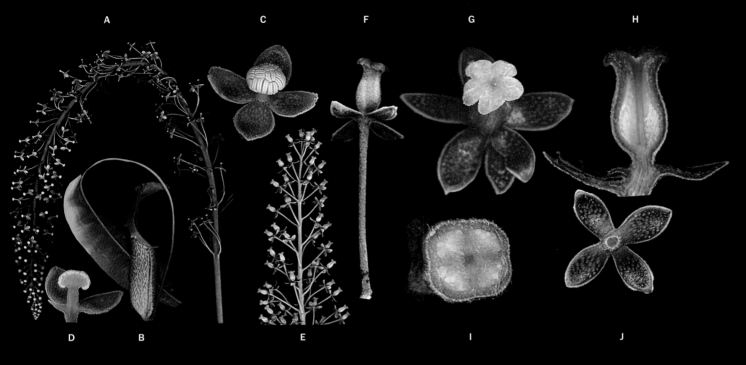

A–J: *Nepenthes dormesianum*. A: Maleinflorescence. B: Pitcher leaf. C: Male flower, lateral. M: The same, longitudinal.
E: Female inflorescence. F: Female flower, lateral. G: The same, frontal. H: The same, longitudinal. I: Ovary, transverse.
: Tepals of the female flower with nectar-producing glandular cells.

**Genus** | 1: Nepenthes; species: about 90

**Distribution** | Madagascar, Southeast Asia

**Habit** | Perennials, growing in rosettes

**Leaves** | Tubular, smooth interior, structured to trap animals

**Inflorescences** | Racemose

**Flowers** | Radial, dioecious, relatively long pedicillation (figs. A, E, F), tetramerous-pentamerous; the usually coarse bracts are dotted with glands on top: nectar glands; the anthers of the up to 15 stamens are arranged symmetrically on a capitate stem (fig. C); the ovary, fused from 4–8 carpels, is superior and has a flat, light-green disciform stigma with up to five rays (fig. G) on the very short style.

**Fruits** | Capsule fruit

**Use** | Like many insectivores, pitcher plants are popular ornamental plants.

In their tropical homelands, people drink the liquid from the pitcher leaves and use it for folk medicine remedies.

**Characteristics** | The long, petiolate pitfall traps protrude from the leaf blade, while the leaf base broadens out. An immobile display lid protrudes upward; the margin, which projects into the pitcher, is often brightly colored in tones of red. Toward the interior it becomes smoother; there are glands that produce digestive secretions on the inside margin of the tube. The trapped animals drown and are digested by means of enzymes. Usually the plants trap insects, but there are even some species with larger pitchers (which can have a volume of up to 4 liters), which can even trap and digest rodents. Many pitcher plants are endangered plants.

A–H: *Bougainvillea buttiana*. A: Inflorescence surrounded by 3 pink-colored bracts; *left*, lateral; *right*, frontal. B: Stem thorn. C: Single flower, lateral; stem with fused bracts. D: *Left*, flower, frontal; *right*, the same, longitudinal. E: Stamen; *above*, front side; *below*, rear side. F: Older flower, longitudinal; ovary on gynophore. G: Gynoecium, lateral; *right*, next to it, longitudinal. H: *Above*, flower, transverse; *beneath it*, ovary, transverse.

**Genera** I 30; species: 395
**Distribution** I Pantropical to warm temperate latitudes
**Habit** I Shrubs, climbing plants, annual or perennial herbaceous plants, rarely trees
**Leaves** I Mostly opposite, rarely alternate or spiral arrangement; petiolate leaf pairs can be of unequal size. Leaf blade: simple and herbaceous, also fleshy to succulent, smooth or hairy. Margin: smooth or notched, without stipules.
**Inflorescences** I Cymose, umbellate, racemose, single, and axillary; at times they grow conspicuous bracts (figs. A–C), so-called involucres.
**Flowers** I Radial, usually hermaphroditic, rarely unisexual, then monoecious; the perianth consists of a usually tube-shaped calyx (figs. A, D, F); corolla is absent; (1–) 3–5 (–30) stamens (fig. E), often basally fused; one carpel forms the superior, usually one-seeded ovary, with a thin style and a capitate or oblong papillary stigma. Nectary on the receptacle.
**Fruits** I Achene or nutlike fruit, encased in the leathery or fleshy calyx base; may also have winged fruits
**Use** I The **marvel of Peru** (*Mirabilis jalapa*) is a good subject for experiments on heredity. It is possible the plant was given this name because of the wonderful variety of colors displayed by its flowers. Since the flowers open in the afternoon, in English-speaking countries this plant is also called the "four o'clock" flower. The next day, the flower has already faded. These include many evening- or night-blooming flowers. *Bougainvillea spectabilis* and *B. glabra* and hybrids are popular ornamental plants.
**Characteristics** I The nodes can become thickened and thorny (fig. B). An abnormal secondary lateral growth may occur. The cut wood frequently oxidizes in the air and turns an orange-reddish brown.

A–G: *Nymphaea alba*. A: Flower, frontal. B: The same, longitudinal. C: *From left*, transition of stamens to petals. D: Fruit, transverse. E: Stigmas on fruit, frontal. F: Fruit, longitudinal. G: Ripe seeds; *above*, lateral; *below*, longitudinal.

H–J: *Nymphaea caerulea*. H: Blossom, longitudinal. I: Inside (*right*) to outside of stamens. J: Ovary, longitudinal.

K–N: *Nuphar lutea*. K: *Above*, flower, frontal, *below*, longitudinal. L: *Above*, young stamen; *beneath it*, ripe, lateral. M: Unripe fruit, transverse. N: Seed, longitudinal.

**Genera** I 6; species: 58–75. Well-known genera: *Barclaya*, *Euryale*, *Nuphar* (pond lilies), *Nymphea* (water lilies), *Victoria* (giant water lilies).

**Distribution** I Worldwide

**Habit** I Perennial, rarely annual herbaceous plants with creeping, upright, branched or unbranched rhizomes, at times bulbous and thickened; some species have runners. Freshwater aquatic plants are aerenchymatous.

**Leaves** I Alternate, long and petiolate, floating, submerged. Blade: cordiform to circular, peltate; leaf margin smooth or spiny and denticulate. Stipules may occur, reticulate venation, leaf underside is often spiny.

**Inflorescences** I Large, long, and pedicellate single flowers (figs. A, B, H)

**Flowers** I Radial, hermaphroditic. Flower organs: spiral arrangement (fig. A). Continuous transition from tepals to nectar leaves and stamens (figs. C, I); two whorls each containing 5– (20) –50 free, green, often-petaloid sepals; the 5–50 petals are white, yellow, pink, and purple to blue. Forty-eighty stamens, free, in spiral arrangement, centripetal; of these, 11–20 might be staminodes; stamens can occasionally have a connective appendage; ovary superior to half inferior (fig. B; fig. J; fig. K, *below*), from 5 to 35 partially or completely fused carpels (figs. D, M). The stigmas grow in a whorl directly on a disc (fig. E; fig. K, *above*). Thermogenesis is known to occur in some species. Cantharophily (pollination by beetles).

**Fruits** I Berrylike, fleshy fruits that often remain encased in the tepals (fig. F). Fleshy receptacle. Opens by swelling up. Seeds mostly with a small aril (*Nymphea*), which becomes buoyant by entrapping air (figs. G, N).

**Use** I In China, people eat the fruit of the **prickly water lily** (*Euryale ferox*), which becomes mushy. In Southeast Asia, the seeds are eaten roasted, and starch can also be harvested from these seeds. People eat the very young stems and rhizomes. Many ornamental plants.

**Characteristics** I The floating leaves of the **Victoria water lily** (*Victoria amazonica*) can grow up to 3 meters in diameter and weigh as much as 50 kg. Prominent ribs on the underside of the leaf support the large leaf pad. Together with the intercellular trapped air, these ensure that the leaf is able to float. The white flowers open in the evening and exude a beguiling fragrance that attracts beetles as pollinators. Then the flower closes for one day. The beetles remain trapped in their flower prison. While in captivity, the flower turns pink and the stamens open inside it, releasing the pollen on the beetles. The next evening, the now-scentless flower opens a second time. The beetles leave their prison to seek out the next white, fragrant flower. The play starts again from the beginning.

175

OLEACEAE

**A–C:** *Olea europaea*. A: Leafy branch with flowers and fruits; *below*, fruit, transverse. B: Flower; *above*, frontal; *center*, lateral; *below*, longitudinal. C: Fruit, longitudinal.

**D–F:** *Ligustrum vulgare*. D: *Left*, inflorescence; *right*, fruiting stage. E: *Above right*, flower, lateral; *below left*, frontal, with 3 stamens. F: Fruit; *above*, longitudinal; *below*, transverse.

**G–J:** *Syringa vulgaris*. G: Leafy branch with inflorescences. H: Flower, frontal. I: *Left*, bud, longitudinal; *center*, gynoecium, lateral; *right*, ovary, longitudinal. J: Fruit; *above*, longitudinal; *below*, lateral.

**K–O:** *Fraxinus excelsior*. K: Leaf. L: *Center*, partial inflorescence; *left*, flower; *right*, gynoecium, lateral. M: Young fruit, longitudinal. N: Fruiting stage. O: Seed.

**Genera** I 24; species: more than 600
**Distribution** I Worldwide, tropical and temperate zones
**Habit** I Trees, shrubs
**Leaves** I Opposite, leaf blade simple and undivided (figs. A, G) to single and pinnate (fig. K), entire, but also lobed, without stipules; at times can be evergreen (*Ligustrum vulgare*).
**Inflorescences** I Flowers in axils, panicles, or racemose, dichasias
**Flowers** I Radial, hermaphroditic,

rarely unisexual, at times appearing before the leaves (*Forsythia suspensa*); calyx usually tetramerous; corolla fourfold to twelvefold laciniate, also absent, gamosepalous, usually two stamens (figs. B, E); the bicarpellate ovary is superior, bilocular, often with two ovules per locule; one style with two papillary stigmas.
**Fruits** I Berry, loculicidal capsule, drupe, samara
**Use** I Wood from the **ash** species,

**olive trees** (*Olea europaea*). Olive oil is harvested from the fruit of the latter. There are some ornamental plants (such as forsythia hybrids). In Asia, the **sweet olive** (*Osmanthus fragrans*) is used to flavor tea and as a spice.
**Characteristics** I Some representatives are intensely fragrant (insect pollination): **common privet** (*Ligustrum vulgare*), **common lilac** (*Syringa vulgaris*), **manna ash** (*Fraxinus ornus*), and **common**

**jasmine** (*Jasminum officinale*), but they can be anemophilous (wind pollination) if there is a reduced corolla, such as on the **common ash** (*Fraxinus excelsior*; figs. K–O). In Nordic mythology, the latter was the tree of life, or "Yggdrasil."

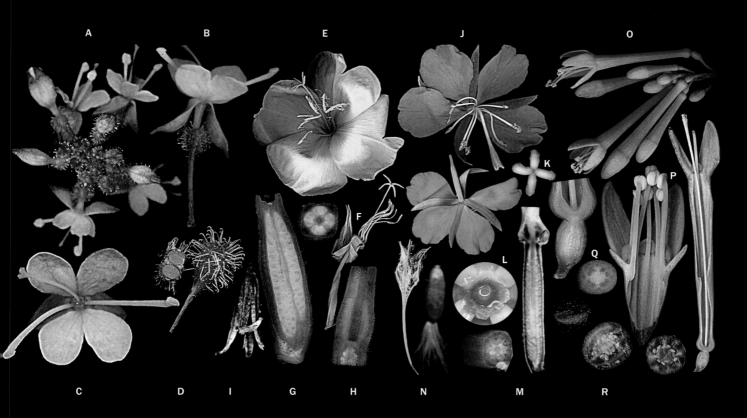

**A–D:** *Circaea lutetiana*. A: Partial inflorescence, frontal. B: Flower, lateral. C: The same, frontal. D: *Right*, fruit; *left*, transverse.

**E–H:** *Oenothera glazoviana*. E: Flower, frontal. F: Flower, lateral; crown removed, calyx visible. G: *Left*, ovary, longitudinal; *right*, transverse. H: Longitudinal section of hypanthium. I: Ripe, opened capsule.

**J–N:** *Epilobium angustifolium*. J: Flower, frontal; *below*, underside. K: Stigma. L: Nectar cover. M: *Left*, ovary, transverse; *right*, longitudinal. N: *Left*, ripe capsule; *right*, seed.

**O–R:** *Fuchsia decidua*. O: Partial inflorescence. P: *Right*, flower, longitudinal; *left*, detail of young flower with stamens. Q: *Left*, ovary, longitudinal; *right*, transverse. R: Fruit; *left*, lateral; *center*, longitudinal; *right*, transverse.

**Genera** I About 20; species: about 650

**Distribution** I Worldwide, predominantly in temperate latitudes

**Habitats** I Moorlands, clear-cut areas, ditches, rivers, damp (moorland) meadows; avoids calcareous soil, prefers silicate rock, areas of tall herbaceous vegetation, also shady humid forests, roadsides and waysides, dunes

**Habit** I Annual or biennial herbaceous plants or perennials, marsh or aquatic plants, with or without underground or aboveground runners

**Leaves** I Opposite, alternate, rarely spiral or whorled arrangement; petioles also hairy; leaf blade mostly simple, cordiform, ovate to linear; stipules are present or absent; the leaf margin is smooth to denticulate.

**Inflorescences** I With or without bracts, these also bristle shaped, racemose, panicular, spicate.

**Flowers** I Radial, rarely zygomorphic, hermaphroditic, double or simple husk, up to several centimeters in diameter, (bimerous-)tetramerous; 2–5 sepals (figs. B, F, J), petals also bifid (fig. C), can be unguiculate, sometimes shorter than the calyx; 2–4–8 stamens, often in two whorls, also strikingly colored short staminodes (fig. P, *left*); the tetracarpellate ovary is inferior, fused with a tubular or cup-shaped, often strikingly colored receptacle (fig. Q, *left*); usually four locules, more or less hairy; stigma is capitate or with four spikes/lobes (figs. F, K), nectary often in the area of the hypanthium (fig. H; fig. L; fig. Q, *left*).

**Fruits** I Capsules (fig. N), seed can have a hairy tuft (fig. N, *right*); nut fruits; berries (fig. R).

**Use** I **Fuchsias** (*Fuchsia magellanica* and hybrids) are popularly cultivated balcony and container plants. The berry fruits are edible. Evening primrose oil is harvested from the seeds of the **common evening primrose** (*Oenothera biennis*); the oil is rich in gamma-linolenic acid (an omega-3 fatty acid) and helps heal raw, sensitive skin, such as in cases of neurodermatitis. Evening primroses are also used as experimental plants in genetic investigations.

**Characteristics** I The flowers of the **evening primrose** (*Oenothera* sp.) open relatively quickly at dusk and are pollinated by moths. The evening primrose, which originated in America, was introduced into Europe in the 17th century and continued to develop there as an independent species. The fleshy root, which is harvested at the end of the first year, was especially appreciated as a vegetable in France. It turns pink when cooked; hence the German name *Schinkenwurzel* (ham root). Many **fuchsia** species are pollinated by birds in their natural habitat; some plants in this family are also wind-pollinated.

# ORCHIDACEAE

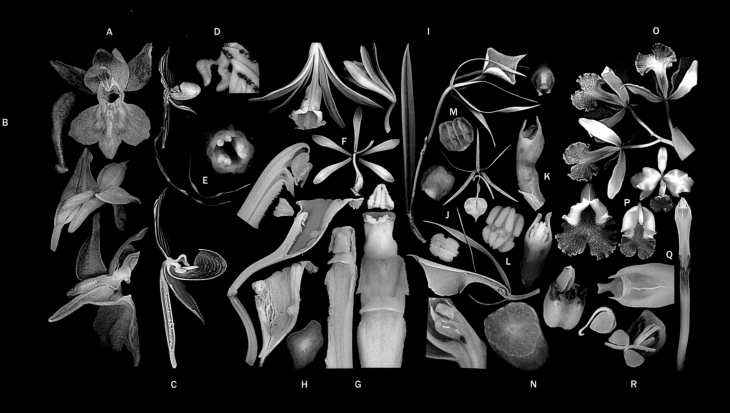

**A–B:** *Dactylorrhiza majalis*. A: *Above*, flower, frontal; *center*, rear side; *below*, longitudinal. B: Pollinarium.
**C–E:** *Paphiopedilum philipinense*. C: *Above*, flower, lateral; *below*, longitudinal. D: Staminode. E: Ovary, transverse.
**F–H:** *Vanilla planifolia*. F: *Left*, flower, frontal; *right*, lateral; *below*, dissected: *left*, gynostegium, longitudinal.

**G:** *Right*, the same, open, frontal; *center*, unopened; *left*, lower part of flower, longitudinal. H: Ovary, transverse.
**I–N:** *Brassavola nodosa*. I: Branch with flower. J: Laid-out petals. K: Gynostegium, lateral. L: *Right*, the same with pollinium; *left*, frontal; *far left*, from underneath; *below*, flower, longitudinal. N: *Right*, ovary, transverse; *left*, stigma area from L.

**O–R:** *Cattleya speciosissimum*. O: Partial inflorescence. P: *Right*, flower, frontal; *left*, labellum; *center*, upper part removed. Q: *Right*, ovary (green) with gynostegium; *left*, detail. R: *Left*, anther cap; *center*, pollinium; *right*, same as at left, from underneath.

**Genera** | More than 750; species: 18,000–24,000
**Distribution** | Almost worldwide, species diversity in the humid tropics
**Habit** | Perennials, rarely short-lived herbaceous plants with rhizomes or tubers, terrestrial; they can be epiphytes, lithophytes, rarely climbing plants. Autotrophic or mycotrophic. Basal internodes may be thickened by lateral growth into pseudo bulbils. Epiphytes with aerial roots that are encased in one or more layers of dead cells (*Velamen radicum*).
**Leaves** | Often distichous and alternate, rarely opposite, basal rosettes, stem leaves rarely stem-clasping; rarely small, reduced, parallel venation, often fleshy or leathery, frequently fleshy or leathery; most are smooth and without hairs.
**Inflorescences** | Lateral, terminal, racemose, spicate

**Flowers** | Zygomorphic, hermaphroditic, trimerous, two whorls of three tepals each; the outer and inner whorl is usually structured differently. The tepal, which faces the axis, is often more developed. Due to resupination, it tends to point downward and is referred to as the labellum (= lip); often has spurs, supports the nectaries, and serves as a landing place for pollinators. Many fragrant orchids offer perfumes for scent-gathering male orchid bees. Stamens: either one is present in the outer whorl or two in the inner whorl. Androecium, style, and stigma fused into a column (= gynostegium). The pollen is massed into round balls (= massulae); the pollen of one theca becomes stuck to a pollinium (figs. B, R), often on a stalk (stipe). The central stigma lobes form a projecting tissue (= rostellum), which separates stamens and stigma. The flower forms a retinaculum here; together with the stipe this becomes the pollinarium. It sticks to the pollinator by means of the basal sticky disc. Ovary is inferior, consisting of three fused carpels (fig. E). Entomophily, "lobster pot" traps, and sexually deceptive flowers occur.
**Fruits** | Capsule fruit
**Use** | Many hybrids are cultivated as ornamental plants, such as *Cattleya lueddemanniana* (figs. O–R). Capsule fruits (the vanilla "pod") of various species of the genus *Vanilla* (figs. F–H) are used as a flavoring after they have been fermented; for example, *V. planifolia*, *V. pompona*.
**Characteristics** | The seeds are the smallest (a fraction of a millimeter!) and the lightest (1 μg or microgram;

they are dispersed by wind!) in the plant kingdom. The plants have no nutritive tissue, which is why they are dependent on mycorrhizal fungi for germination and often remain dependent in the adult stage. Low germination rates require a high level of seed production, but this requires successful pollination (hence the pollinium structure). The targeted transmission of pollen is often done by only one species of insect. Plants of the genus *Orchis* form tubers that are reminiscent of testicles. Hence the German name *Knabenkräuter* ("boy herbs or boyworts") (Greek *orchis* = testicles). From ancient times until today, the nodes are sometimes used as aphrodisiacs.

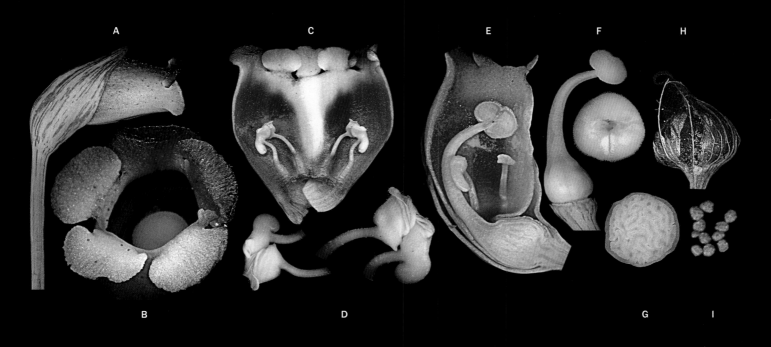

A–I: *Aeginetia indica*. A: Flower with bract, lateral. B: Flower, frontal. C: Unfurled corolla tube. D: Stamens from C, lateral.
E: Blossom, longitudinal. F: Gynoecium; *right*, stigma, frontal. G: Ovary, transverse. H: Fruit, lateral. I: Seed.

**Genera** I More than 100; species: more than 2,000. Well-known genera: cow wheat (*Melampyrum*), broomrape (*Orobanche*), louseworts (*Pedicularis*), and rattles (*Rhinanthus*).
**Distribution** I Worldwide
**Habit** I Root parasites; semi- and full parasites; only *Lindenbergia* not parasitic, often annuals

**Leaves** I If parasitic, then often leafless or few leaves; existing leaves may be undivided, pinnatifid, or pinnate.
**Inflorescences** I Racemose, spicate
**Flowers** I Zygomorphic, hermaphroditic, (tetramerous-) pentamerous, gamasepalous; four

stamens (fig. C); didynamia often occurs, the fifth often reduced to a staminode (fig. E); ovary superior, from 2 (–3) carpels with numerous ovules; one style with a capitate, slightly bilobate stigma. **Fruits** I Capsule fruit with very small seeds; it is often the case that they germinate only within the chemical sphere of influence of the host plant.

**Use** I **Eyebright** (*Euphrasia officinalis*) is used in homeopathy and folk medicine for eye diseases.
**Characteristics** I The **witchweeds** (*Striga* species) are parasites of important food grains such as millet, corn, or rice and are therefore feared as pests.

# OXALIDACEAE

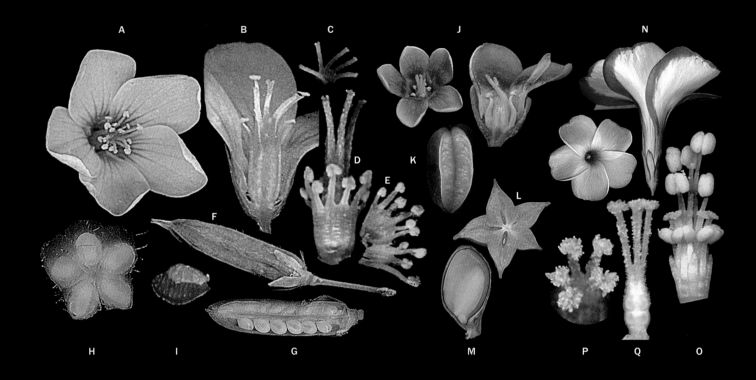

**A–I:** *Oxalis fontana.* A: Flower, frontal. B: The same, longitudinal. C: Stigma. D: Androecium with central gynoecium, perianth removed. E: Splayed-out androecium. F: Fruit, lateral. G: The same, longitudinal. H: Unripe fruit, transverse. I: Seed.

**J–M:** *Averrhoea carambola.* J: *Left,* flower, frontal; *right,* longitudinal. K: Fruit, lateral. L: The same, transverse. M: Seed, longitudinal.

**N–Q:** *Oxalis versicolor.* N: *Left,* flower, frontal; next to it, the same, lateral. O: Androecium and gynoecium, lateral. P: Stigma. Q: Ovary, longitudinal.

**Genera** | 6; species: over 750
**Distribution** | Worldwide, rarely in temperate regions
**Habit** | Rarely trees, shrubs, and lianas; primarily annual to perennial herbaceous plants
**Habitats** | Rainforests to deserts
**Leaves** | Basal, alternate, divided in whorls, blade usually articulated: digitate, ternate or pinnate, petiolate
**Inflorescences** | Umbellate, racemose, cymose, solitary in axils

**Flowers** | Radial, hermaphroditic, five usually free sepals, at most basally fused; five free or basally fused petals, can be unguiculate; usually two whorls of five different-length stamens, outside usually shorter (fig. O), also basally fused (fig. E); usually five carpels fused into one five-lobed superior ovary (figs. H, L), with usually 1–2 hanging ovules per locule; may be heterostylous; usually five free styles with capitate or bifid stigmas (figs. P, Q)

**Fruits** | Loculicidal capsule fruit, rarely berries
**Use** | The sour fruits of the **star fruit** (also **carambola**) (*Averrhoa carambola*) (figs. K, L) and the **bilimbi** (*A. bilimbi*) are used as food. The starchy stem tubers (called "oca") of the **oca** plant (*Oxalis tuberosa*) are an important food source in the Andes. Ornamental plants.
**Characteristics** | **Wood sorrel** (*Oxalis acetosella*), which has movable

leaflets ("joints"), also has fruits that sometimes eject the seeds when ripe; the fruit are "explosively" torn open and turned inside out, to fling away the fleshy outer cell layers. Oxalic acid, named after the genus *Oxalis*, occurs in all plants of this family.

A–I: *Paeonia cambessedesii.* A: Flower, frontal. B: The same, underside. C: Center of flower, longitudinal. D: Stigma. E: Carpel, transverse. F: The same, longitudinal. G: Fruit. H: Seeds without aril. I: Seed, transverse.

**Genus** | 1: *Paeonia*; species: 33
**Distribution** | Temperate and subtropical mountainous regions of Eurasia. Only two species in western North America.
**Habit** | Rarely half shrubs or dwarf shrubs, deciduous, mostly perennial herbaceous plants with thickened nodular rhizomes or roots as overwintering organs
**Leaves** | Alternate. Leaf blade: large, pinnate. Pinnate leaves more or less deeply divided, often narrowly lanceolate. Leaf margin denticulate or lobed, petiole present.
**Flowers** | Hermaphroditic, spiral arrangement; there can be a smooth

transition from foliage leaf to sepals. Large single flowers (up to 20 cm in diameter) grow on 1–6 bracts, usually from 3–5 free, green sepals; 5–10 (–13) free, spirally arranged petals that can be pink, red, white, or yellow in color and may be fragrant; many stamens (*dédoublement* or doubled up), spiral arrangement; 2–8 (–15) free, ampulliform or flask-shaped carpels form the superior ovary with a short style. Entomophily of pollen flowers.
**Fruits** | Follicles, seeds mostly black, occasionally sterile red ones in between them. Dispersal by birds.
**Use** | Ornamental plants: There are

many varieties of the **garden peony** (*Paeonia officinalis*), which is distributed throughout the Mediterranean region, commercially available, some also with filled flowers. The same is true of the **Chinese peony** (*Paeonia lactiflora*), which grows more than one flower on each stem. The **tree peony** (*Paeonia × suffruticosa*), which was created by cross-breeding various wild species, has also found its way into gardens as an ornamental plant. Although the plants are slightly poisonous due to containing glycosides, the root bark is used in China as anticonvulsant remedy. If taken internally, it can cause

vomiting and diarrhea.
**Characteristics** | In the Middle Ages, the **garden peony** (*Paeonia officinalis*) was used medicinally, including to treat gout; hence the German name *Gichtrose* (gout rose). However, the genus *Paeonia* is not related to the rose genus, even if peonies are part of Christian symbolism, as a "rose without thorns." The woody species lack trachea, which is considered a very original feature. The name *Paeonia* refers to Paean, the physician to the Greek gods.

# PANDANACEAE

A | B | C | E | F | H

D | G

**A–E:** *Freycinetia* **sp**. A: Part of a leaf and inflorescence. B: Female partial inflorescence from both sides. C: Female spadix, longitudinal. D: *Left*, gynoecium, lateral; *center*, frontal; *right*, spadix, transverse. E: *Left*, male spadixes at various ages; *right*, spadixes, longitudinal; *below*, transverse.

**F–H:** *Pandanus utilis*. F: *Left*, fruiting stage, frontal; *right*, next to it, fruit with front removed. G: *Left*, fruit, frontal; *center*, single fruit, longitudinal; *right*, transverse.

**Genera** | 4: *Freycinetia, Martellidendron, Pandanus, Sararaga*. More than 800 species.

**Distribution** | Tropical and subtropical regions of the Old World: Africa to Southeast Asia, Pacific islands

**Habit** | Woody trees or shrub-type plants, which, however, are not trees in the true sense, since as monocotyledons they do not exhibit any secondary lateral growth. In addition, can be lianas, rarely epiphytes. Many species grow adventitious roots (aerial or stilt roots) that help them grow in swampy soils or in shallow (salt) water. Treelike species usually grow dichotomous branches. Evergreen.

**Leaves** | Alternate, apparently helical, (distichous-)tristichous (or in 4) rows; leaf sheath open; leaf blade linear, lanceolate to scutate (fig. A), underside keeled, margin entire or margin can be spiny, frequently on the leaf midrib and tip

**Inflorescences** | Terminal or lateral, branched inflorescences with capitiform, spicate, racemose, or spadix-form partial inflorescences, surrounded by a usually colored spathe (figs. A, B). Inflorescences usually unisexual, differentiated between male (fig. E) and female (fig. C) inflorescences.

**Flowers** | Rarely hermaphroditic, dioecious or monoecious, perianth present or absent, male flowers with two to many stamens, which may be free or basally fused. Female flowers with one, two, or more, free to fused, superior carpels. Staminodes occur occasionally. Pollination mostly by wind, but also by insects, birds, bats.

**Fruits** | Multiple drupes (*Pandanus*; fig. F), compound berries (*Freycinetia*)

**Use** | The fruit of *Pandanus tectorius* are eaten fresh or as preserves. Flour is extracted from the fruits of various *Pandanus* species. The sweet, spadix-form compound berries of some *Freycinetia* species are edible. In Indonesia and Thailand, people wrap food in **pandan leaves** (*Pandanus amaryllifolius*) or cook them with the food. The vanilla-like nutty aroma flavors the food; the leaves themselves are not eaten. The leaves of various *Freycinetia* and *Pandanus* species, such as *P. utilis* and *P. tectorius*, are used for roofing and to supply fibers for weaving mats and baskets. The aerial roots serve as the binding material. In India, the fragrant male inflorescences of *P. odorifer* are distilled to obtain a fragrant oil, then used to produce an attar or perfume that is particularly in demand in Arab and Muslim countries. The byproduct is kewra water, which is used to flavor rice, sweets, and meat dishes.

**Characteristics** | The name "screw-pine family" comes from the seemingly helical or screwlike leaf arrangements on the *Pandanus* species.

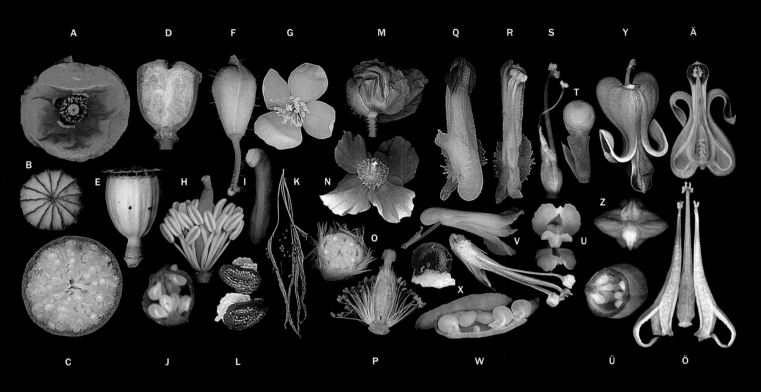

**A–E:** *Papaver rhoeas*. A: Flower, frontal. B: Stigma. C: Ovary, transverse. D: Ovary, longitudinal. E: Fruit, lateral.
**F–L:** *Chelidonium majus*. F: Bud in calyx, lateral. G: Flower, frontal. H: Androecium and gynoecium, lateral. I: Gynoecium. J: The same, transverse. K: Fruit. L: Seed with elaiosome.

**M–P:** *Meconopsis betonicifolia*. M: Bud, lateral. N: Flower, frontal. O: Ovary, transverse. P: Androecium and gynoecium, longitudinal.
**Q–T:** *Fumaria officinalis*. Q: Flower, lateral. R: The same, longitudinal. S: Gynoecium, 1 stamen. T: Fruit, longitudinal.

**U–X:** *Pseudofumaria lutea*. U: Flower, frontal. V: The same, lateral; *below*, longitudinal, without corolla. W: Unripe fruit. X: Seed with elaiosome.
**Y–Ü:** *Dicentra peregrina*. Y: Flower, lateral. Z: The same, underside. Ä: The same, longitudinal. Ö: Androecium and gynoecium. Ü: Ovary, transverse.

**Subfamilies** | Papaveroideae, Fumarioideae
**Genera** | More than 40; species: about 800
**Distribution** | Worldwide in northern temperate zones, southern Africa
**Habit** | Mostly annual, biennial, or perennial herbaceous plants with tubers
**Leaves** | Alternate, leaf blade pinnate or deeply divided
**Inflorescences** | Paniculate, racemose, but usually solitary
**Flowers** | Hermaphroditic, radial (subfamily Papaveroideae; figs. A, G, N), zygomorphic (subfamily Fumarioideae; figs. Q, U, V, Y). Doubled perianth: two sepals (fig. F), green or petaloid, usually fall off when the flower opens; four petals; many stamens (primary polyandry, Papaveroideae; figs. H, P) or four or six stamens (Fumarioideae); two to several carpels are fused to a superior ovary (figs. C, D, O); many ovules, parietal placentation (figs. J, Ü); the stigmas often form a so-called commissural stigma (fig. B).
**Fruits** | Usually capsule fruit that open through pores (fig. E) or valves, rarely pods (such as celandine; fig. K). Seeds with elaiosomes (dispersed by ants: corydalis, celandine; figs. L, X), otherwise dispersed by wind, burrs.
**Use** | The best known is the **opium poppy** (*Papaver somniferum*) because of the alkaloids contained in the milky sap, from which opium or morphine is harvested. Oil is extracted from its seeds, which are also used as a food in baked goods (rich in vitamin B and calcium). The young leaves and fruits of the **common poppy** (*Papaver rhoeas*; fig. C) can be eaten as a vegetable. Many ornamental plants, such as **Asian bleeding heart** (*Laprocapnos spectabilis*), **bleeding hearts** (*Dicentra* sp.), **corydalis** (*Corydalis* sp.), **blue Himalayan poppy** (*Meconopsis betonicifolia*), **California poppy** (*Escholtzia californica*), **Mexican prickly poppy** (*Argemone mexicana*), and **matilija poppy** (*Romneya coulteri*). The orange-colored milky sap of the **greater celandine** (*Chelidonium majus*; figs. F–L) is traditionally used as an external remedy for warts. The milky sap of the Persian poppy (*Papaver bracteatum*) contains the alkaloid thebaine, from which codeine, a painkiller and antitussive remedy, is made.
**Characteristics** | The milky sap contains alkaloids. Many poisonous plants; in the bleeding-heart subfamily, the underground tubers especially contain toxins, such as the **hollow corydalis** (*Corydalis cava*); these can cause muscle paralysis. The **yellow horned poppy** (*Glaucium flava*), an ornamental plant that is native to the Mediterranean region, is now found as a neophyte on almost all the coastlines in the world.

**A–D:** *Parnassia palustris*. A: *Left*, flower, frontal; *right*, underside. B: Older flower; petals and anthers have fallen; *left*, frontal; *right*, longitudinal. C: Staminode-like pseudo-nectary. D: Ovary, transverse.

**Genera** I 1–2; species: over 50
**Distribution** I Northern temperate regions
**Habitats** I On moors, moorland meadows, neglected grasslands
**Habit** I Mostly perennial herbaceous, up to 30 cm tall with rhizome
**Leaves** I Alternate, spiral arrangement, in rosettes, simple leaf blade. Cordiform leaf base, long and petiolate.
**Inflorescences** I —

**Flowers** I Single, radial, hermaphroditic, protandrous, pentamerous; the five sepals may be basally fused or free (fig. A, *right*); the five petals are free or may be absent; one whorl with five free stamens; in *Parnassia*, the second inner whorl is transformed into yellow-green sterile staminodes/nectar leaves (fig. B, *left*; fig. C); the (3–) 4 (–5) carpels form a superior or half-inferior ovary with parietal placentation (fig. D, *left*); the

usually short style normally has 3–4 stigma lobes of different sizes (fig. B, *left*).
**Fruits** I Capsules (fig. E), 3–4 locules usually with many winged seeds ("balloon flyer")
**Characteristics** I The yellow staminodes of the **marsh grass of Parnassus** (*Parnassia palustris*) have gland heads (fig. C) at their tips, but they do not secrete any nectar. They are interpreted to be mock stamens

and nectaries that have a visual impact on flies and are supposed to enhance attracting them to the flower. However, these are deceptive flowers, since they neither offer nectar nor any feigned abundance of pollen.
**Note**s I The family has recently been classified as the Parnassioideae subfamily of the Celastraceae family.

**A–F:** *Passiflora edulis f. edulis*. A: *Left*, flower, frontal; *right*, underside. B: Leaf with extrafloral nectaries and tendril; detail at left underneath. C: Flower, longitudinal. D: Ovary, longitudinal, with 2 stamens attached. E: Half of an ovary, transverse. F: Fruit, transverse; *above*, with seeds in aril; *below*, they have been removed.

**G–L:** *Passiflora mixta*. G: *Right*, flower, longitudinal; *left*, detail of the entrance to corolla tube. H: Leaf. I: Androecium and gynoecium, lateral. J: Basal area of flower with nectary, longitudinal. K: *Left*, gynoecium, lateral; *right*, ovary, transverse; *below the same*, longitudinal. L: Unripe fruit, transverse. M: Seed without aril.

PASSIFLORACEAE

**Genera** | 17; species: 670
**Distribution** | Worldwide in the tropical to warm temperate regions
**Habit** | Trees, shrubs, herbaceous plants; most climbing using stem tendrils, also xerophytes
**Leaves** | Alternate, leaf blade simple, ternate, rarely pinnate, stipules usually present; there are often extrafloral nectaries underneath the blade (fig. B).
**Inflorescences** | Solitary, racemose, cymose; often have bracts and bracteoles underneath them
**Flowers** | Radial, mostly hermaphroditic, calyx and corolla (trimerous-)pentamerous(-octamerous); often basally fused into a sometimes very long tube (fig. G, *right*), whereby the interior of the hypanthium functions like a nectary or one nectary can be

found there (fig. J). A paracorolla (= corona) in the form of striped fringes (fig. A, *left*), scales (fig. G, *left*), or the like is often present: androecium and gynoecium are often supported by an androgynophore, so that the stamens and ovary protrude from the corolla (fig. C; fig. G, *right*). Three (to five) fused carpels form the superior unilocular ovary with parietal placentation (fig. F, *below*). Solitary style, three-part stigma, usually capitate. Pollination by insects, hummingbirds (such as *P. mixta*), and bats.
**Fruits** | Capsules or berries often with fleshy pulp, which is grown from the juicy arils
**Use** | Ornamental plants. Fruit: the juicy arils of more than

50 species are edible, and those from some species are used to make juice (fig. F, *above*), such as **passionfruit** juice (also **purple passionfruit**, *Passiflora edulis*), **giant granadilla** (*P. quadrangularis*), **sweet granadilla** (*P. ligularis*), or **banana passionfruit** (*P. mollissima*). Passionflower herb contains alkaloids and is added to sleeping teas and calming teas. The essential oils from the leaves of the **damiana plant** (*Turnera diffusa*) are used in folk medicine.
**Characteristics** | The plants use stem tendrils (fig. B) to help them climb. In this family, pollination is by insects and birds. The name "passion" flower refers to the structure of its leaves and flowers. Christian believers

were said to have seen religious symbols of the crucifixion of Jesus Christ in the plant: the tripartite leaves (fig. H) as a symbol of the lance, the tendrils (fig. B) of the scourge, and the 10 petals representing the 10 apostles without Peter and Judas. The paracorolla (fig. A, *left*; fig. C) indicates the crown of thorns, the five stamens are interpreted as either stigmata or vinegar sponges, the pedicellate ovary (figs. C, G) as a symbol of the chalice, the three stigmas (figs. C, D, I, K) symbolize the nails used to nail Christ to the cross, and the white color of the sepals of the **purple passionflower** (*Passiflora incarnata*) as a sign of innocence.

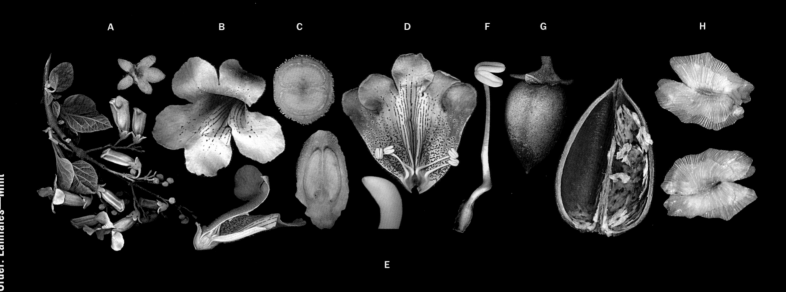

A–H: *Paulownia elongata*. A: Leafy branch with flowers and flower buds. B: *Left*, calyx; *right*, flower, frontal; *below*, longitudinal. C: *Above*, ovary, transverse; *below*, longitudinal. D: Corolla; *above*, opened and unfurled. E: Stigma. F: Stamen. G: *Left*, fruit, lateral; *right*, longitudinal. H: Seeds with winged edges from both sides.

**Genus** | 1: *Paulownia*; species: about 6–7
**Distribution** | East Asia
**Habit** | Trees
**Leaves** | Opposite, leaf blade simple, undivided or trilobate to quinquilobate, deciduous or evergreen, without stipules; leaves often have dense glandular hairs.

**Inflorescences** | Terminal, racemose to paniculate
**Flowers** | Zygomorphic, hermaphroditic, the single flowers are large (5–7 cm); calyx and corolla, pentamerous, gamosepalous; the calyx often has coarse leaves and dense hairs; the blue corolla with distinct nectar guides (figs. B, D), often several

centimeters tall; four stamens, the thecas often splayed out (fig. F); the superior ovary consists of two carpels; at its base is the whitish or yellowish nectar gland tissue, which is not further structured; one style with very small bifid stigma area (fig. E).
**Fruits** | Ovate schizocarp capsule fruit with many winged seeds (figs. G, H)

**Use** | The attractive **empress tree** (*Paulownia tomentosa*) is often cultivated as a roadside and park tree.
**Characteristics** | The name honors the Russian grand duchess and queen of the Netherlands Anna Pavlovna (1795–1865).

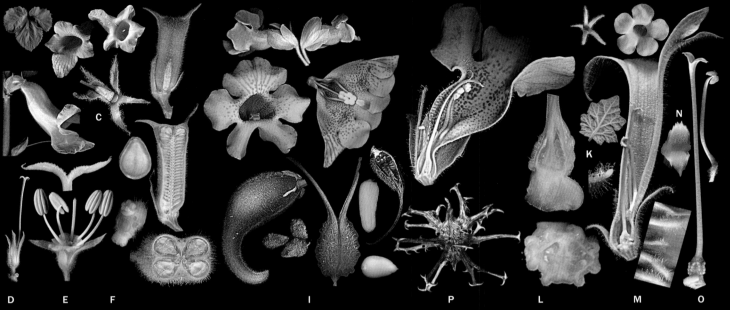

A B G H J

C

D E F I P L M O

K

N

**A–G:** *Ceratotheca triloba*. A: Leaf. B: Flower. C: Calyx, gynoecium, and nectary. D: Calyx, style/stigma, nectary on stem, right stigma. E: Flower without corolla, lateral. F: Nectary from D, frontal. G: *Above*, ovary, lateral; *center*, longitudinal; *left*, seeds; *below*, ovary, transverse.

**H–I:** *Ibicella lutea*. H: *Above*, 2 flowers, lateral; *beneath it at left*, flower, frontal; *right*, longitudinal; *center*, corolla unfurled. I: *Left*, unripe fruit, lateral; *center*, fruit, lateral; *right*, half fruit and seeds, longitudinal.

**J–O:** *Unkarina roeoesliana*. J: *Above*, calyx; *center*, flower, frontal; *below*, longitudinal. K: *Above*, leaf; *below*, leaf gland. L: *Above*, ovary, longitudinal; *below*, transverse. M: Filament attachment in corolla; *center*, staminode. N: *Right*, gynoecium; *left*, stigma, frontal. O: Stamen. P: Harpagophytum procumbens, fruit.

**Genera** I 12; species: about 150
**Distribution** I Tropics of the Old World
**Habit** I Annual and perennial herbaceous plants and bushes, often trailing, rarely shrubby
**Habitat** I Often in grassy or pasture areas passed over by herds of animals
**Leaves** I Opposite to spiral arrangement, leaf blade lobed, often with glandular hairs (fig. K, *below*)
**Inflorescences** I In upper axils, cymose

**Flowers** I Zygomorphic, hermaphroditic, pentamerous; the five sepals usually free; corolla is fused, can be enlarged, with distinct nectar guide; four stamens are fertile, with didynamia, the fifth reduced to a small staminode (fig M, *right*); the bilocular to tetralocular ovary, composed of two carpels, is superior; a nectary may be inserted toward the flower opening at the ovary base (fig. C, *yellow area*), but there are also so-called extrafloral nectaries below the calyx on both sides of the stem (figs. D, F). One style with two marginal papillary stigma lobes.
**Fruits** I Capsule, indehiscent fruit: grapple plants with pointed barbs (figs. I, P)
**Use** I **Sesame** (*Sesamum indicum*) supplies seeds for baked goods and for extracting oil, for cooking, as well as for making soap. People eat the leaves of some African species as vegetables (*Ceratotheca* species, *Pedalium* species). Extracts from the **devil's claw** (*Harpagophytum procumbens*), which comes from southern Africa, are used to treat rheumatic joint diseases.
**Characteristics** I The devil's claw got its name because of the clawlike growths on the fruit (fig. P). Grazing animals step on these grapple plants and drag them along for a while as the seeds fall out; thus the animals disperse this plant species (epizoochory seed dispersal).

# PENTAPHYLACACEAE

**A–H:** *Visnea mocanera.* A: Branch. B: Leaf margin. C: Flower, frontal. D: Calyx. E: Stamens/corolla. F: Ovary, transverse. G: Stamen. H: Ovary, longitudinal.

**Genera** I 12; species about 337. Major genera include *Anneslea*, *Eurya*, *Pentaphylax*, *Ternstroemia*, *Visnea*.
**Distribution** I Pantropical, in Asia from China to Sumatra, Africa, Canary Islands, Madeira
**Habit** I Small to larger trees, shrubs
**Habitat** I Mountain slopes, valleys, forests

**Leaves** I Alternate, often distichous, simple, leathery, usually no stipules
**Inflorescences** I Mostly solitary axillary (fig. A)
**Flowers** I Radial, hermaphroditic or unisexual, then dioecious, usually pentamerous; five free sepals; five petals; 5–30 free stamens, sometimes basally fused with the corolla (fig. E);

the 3–5 carpels are fused into a superior ovary; 3–5 free style arms.
**Fruits** I Berries, drupes, also woody capsule fruit; seeds can be winged.
**Use** I The Guanche people of Tenerife manufacture a kind of honey ("mocan") from the *Visnea mocanera*, which is anti-inflammatory and germicidal and has an analgesic effect. They ground

the roasted seeds to make flour ("gofio de mocan").
**Comments** I The family used to be called Ternstroemiaceae but was then assigned to the Theaceae family (camellia family) as the Ternstroemioideae subfamily.

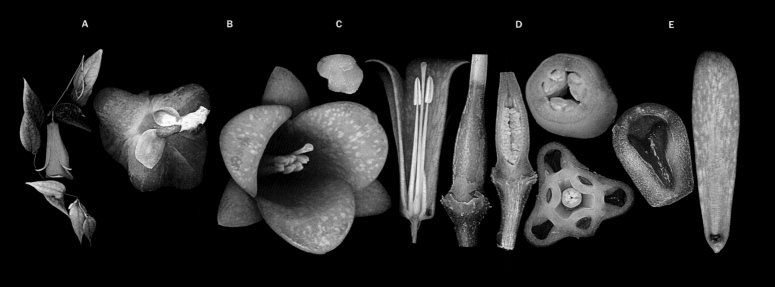

A–E: *Lapageria rosea*. A: Leafy branch with flower. B: *Center*, flower, frontal; *left*, underside; *right*, longitudinal. C: Stigma, frontal. D: *Left*, ovary, lateral; *center*, longitudinal; *above right*, transverse E: *Left*, cross section of flower; nectaries at the base inside on the outer petals; *center*, detail: nectary; *right*, 1 outer petal with basal nectary.

**Genera** | 2 with one species each: *Lapageria rosea* (Chilean bellflower) and *Philesia magellanica*
**Distribution** | Chile
**Habitat** | Temperate rainforests on the west coast of Chile
**Habit** | Evergreen lianas or shrubs
**Leaves** | Alternate, spiral arrangement or distichous. Leaf blade: simple, undivided, entire, linear, lanceolate to ovate.

**Inflorescences** | Solitary on short shoots or in the axils; 1–3 single flowers with short axis; bracts and bracteoles present (fig. B, *left*).
**Flowers** | Radial, hermaphroditic, campanulate, hanging (fig. A; fig. B, *center*), trimerous; six tepals in two whorls of three, free tepals; nectaries at the base of the tepals (fig. E); six stamens in two whorls of three, free or fused; poricidal anthers; superior ovary

consisting of three fused carpels (fig. D); the filiform style (fig. B, *right*) has a moist trilobate/capitate stigma.
**Fruits** | Berry
**Use** | Ornamental plants
**Characteristics** | The **Chilean bellflower** (*Lapageria rosea*) is the national flower of Chile. This plant secretes its nectar from chambers or locules (fig. E). Because the nectaries resemble the cartridge chambers in a

revolver, these flowers are also called "revolver flowers." The flower pollinators (hummingbirds) fly around the flower in such a way that they get maximum contact with the plant's sexual organs. The name *Lapageria* honors Napoleon's first wife, Josephine de La Pagerie.

# PHRYMACEAE

A—E: *Mimulus luteus*. A: Branch with leaves in opposite arrangement with 2 flowers, lateral view; *right*, next to it, detached corolla. B: Calyx, frontal, corolla removed; gynoecium is visible. C: *Above left*, flower, frontal; *beneath it*, lateral: underside; *right*, flower, longitudinal. D: Stigma; *left*, 1 style arm; *right*, lateral. E: Corolla with stamens grown onto the base, folded back. F: Ovary, transverse.

**Genera** | More than 180; species: more than 220

**Distribution** | Worldwide; concentration in western North America, Australia

**Habit** | Annual to perennial herbaceous plants or bushes, can have rhizomes, rarely half shrubs

**Leaves** | Opposite, leaf blade undivided, with coarsely denticulate margin, without stipules, often sessile (fig. A)

**Inflorescences** | Spicate racemose, axillary, or terminal

**Flowers** | Zygomorphic, hermaphroditic, pentamerous; the five sepals are fused (fig. A) and are often retained on the fruit; the five petals are fused, with distinct nectar guides (fig. E); in addition, there are papillae on arching-out parts of the petals, which also show visitors the way. The three lower petals are protruding: an optimal runway for landing (fig. C, *above left*).

Four fertile stamens; didynamia occurs; thecas may be spread apart. The superior ovary usually consists of two carpels, with one style and two leaflike style arms (fig. D). A small nectary is inserted at the base of the ovary.

**Fruits** | Capsule fruit

**Use** | Some are ornamental plants, such as *Mimulus* species and hybrids.

**Characteristics** | In the masked flowers of the **seep monkeyflower** (*Mimulus guttatus*), only strong visitors can force their way through the entrance to the flower. If they touch the bilabate stigma, the lobes clap together to get a tight hold on the pollen the insect brought along. This family formerly belonged to the Scrophulariaceae (figwort family).

A–C: *Phyllanthus arbuscula*. A: Inflorescences on sprouts broadened like leaves. B: *Left*, solitary inflorescence; *right*, next to it, inflorescence on common stem. C: *Left*, female flower lateral/underside; *center*, lateral; *right*, frontal.

**PHYLLANTHACEAE**

**Genera** I 59; species: more than 2,000
**Distribution** I Pantropical with concentration in Melanesia
**Habit** I Shrubs, half shrubs, herbaceous plants
**Habitat** I In swamps and sandy places
**Leaves** I Spiral arrangement, in two rows; leaf blade simple, can be variegated, can be reduced
**Inflorescences** I Racemose

**Flowers** I Diclinous, monoecious, rarely dioecious, 2–3–8 (–12) sepals; mostly (3) –5 petals; male flowers with 2–35 stamens, female flowers with 1–2–3–5 (–15) carpels that are fused to an ovary, with groups of different numbers of stamen-like nectar scales (fig C, *right*)
**Fruits** I Capsules with large seeds, can open by explosion
**Use** I The sour fruit of some species are edible, such as the **bignay**

(*Antidesma bunias*) and *Phyllanthus acidus* and *P. emblica* fruit. Some species are used to promote healing. All the parts of *Spondianthus preussi* are so extremely poisonous that they cannot be used for dart hunting, because the poison rapidly penetrates into the meat. Sap from the bark and the seeds in powdered form are used to poison rats. People used to use the poisonous fruit and seeds of such plants as the **giftboom** (*Hyaenanche*

*globosa*) to poison hyenas in South Africa. The bark is sometimes used to treat toothache and also for dyeing.
**Characteristics** I The flowers are often located on the margins of phylloclades (leaflike shoots; fig. A), and these plants accumulate aluminum ions. This family was previously classified as a subfamily of Euphorbiaceae (spurge family).

PHYTOLACCACEAE

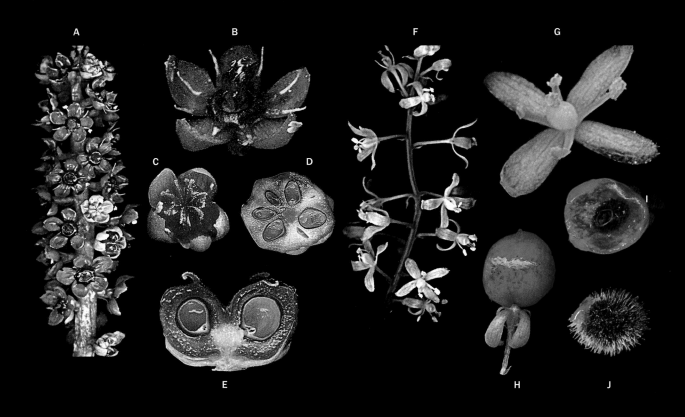

**A–E:** *Phytolacca octandra*. A: Inflorescence. B: Flower, lateral/frontal. C: Ripening fruit. D: The same, transverse. E: The same, longitudinal.

**F–J:** *Rivina humilis*. F: Inflorescence. G: Flower, frontal. H: Fruit, lateral. I: The same, transverse. J: Seed.

**Genera** I 18; species: 65
**Distribution** I Predominantly Neotropical, but also in tropical regions of Africa and Asia
**Habit** I Evergreen trees, shrubs, perennials
**Leaves** I Alternate; leaf blade: entire
**Inflorescences** I Terminal, racemose, paniculate, short, and pedicellate

**Flowers** I Radial, perianth is simple, tetramerous-pentamerous, colored green to reddish (figs. A, B); 6–16 stamens; 8–10 (–16) carpels, free or fused.
**Fruits** I Berrylike; in the *Phytolacca* they decompose into single fruits when ripe.
**Use** I The dioecious **pokeweed tree** (*Phytolacca dioica*) is a stately tree that

grows up to 15 meters tall. It is planted as a shade tree; hence the Italian name, *bella sombre* (= lovely shade).
The **American pokeweed** (*Phytolacca americana*) is occasionally cultivated as an ornamental plant.
**Characteristics** I The red pokeberries of the *Phytolacca americana* were formerly used to color red wine. This is prohibited today

because the fruits contain saponins and are poisonous.

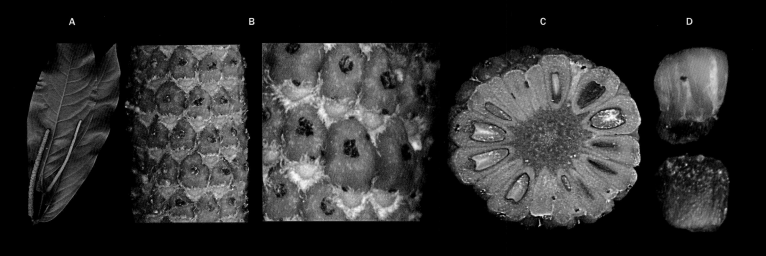

**A–D:** *Piper lanceolatum.* A: Leafy shoot with flower/fruiting stage. B: Detail of the flower/fruiting stage. C: The same, transverse with ripe seeds. D: Single gynoecium, lateral; *below*, seed, transverse.

**Subfamilies** I Verhuellioideae, Zippelioideae, Piperoideae
**Genera** I 5–8; species: some 2,500. Well-known genera include pepper (*Piper*) and *Peperomia*.
**Distribution** I Pantropical with concentration in tropical America and Asia
**Habit** I Trees, shrubs, lianas, annual or perennial herbaceous plants that grow tubers. Geobionts, epiphytes, some succulents.
**Leaves** I Alternate or opposite, leaf blade simple, entire, with oil glands that generate a spicy essential oil. Stipules present and often fused with the petioles.

**Inflorescences** I Terminal, axillary, or opposite a leaf; spadix-like, spicate; rarely umbellate or racemose inflorescences
**Flowers** I Hermaphroditic or unisexual, then dioecious; without perianth, small, usually sessile; 1–10 stamens, often two, then the flowers are monosymmetric, free; superior ovary; 2–5 fused carpels, unilocular, with one ovule (fig. D)
**Fruits** I Drupes
**Use** I **Black pepper** (*Piper nigrum*) is one of the world's most important spices. The various colors of peppercorns are due to different stages of ripeness and how the

peppercorns are treated. Green pepper consists of peppercorns harvested when still unripe. Because they oxidize rapidly, they are conserved in brine. Black pepper is also harvested when unripe and then takes on its black coloration and shrinks after being fermented and dried. White peppercorns are produced by peeling the ripe fruit. Dried ripe fruits appear pink; supplies are often made to go further by adding fruit from the **Brazilian pepper tree** (*Schinus molle*: Anacardiaceae), although this plant is not related to pepper. The roots of the **kava kava** (*Piper methysticum*) are consumed as stimulants: the

Polynesians use them to make an intoxicating drink. Since 2002, kava extracts have been used in Germany to treat mild anxiety. In Asia and Africa, people wrap betel nuts (the seeds of the **betel-nut palm**, *Areca catechu*) in **betel vine** (*Piper betel*) leaves and chew them, combined with other ingredients, as "betel nuts."
**Characteristics** I Fruits of *Piper* species from the Old World are dispersed by birds; New World species by fruit-eating bats.

A B C D F G H

E

J

**A–E:** *Pittosporum tenuifolium*. A: Flower, frontal. B: The same, lateral, husk removed. C: The same, longitudinal. D: Ovary, transverse. E: Opened fruit.

**F–J:** *Pittosporum tobira*. F: Leafy branch with flowers. G: *Above left*, underside of flower; *right*, frontal. H: Flower, longitudinal. I: Gynoecium and calyx. J: Ovary, transverse.

**Genera** I 9; species: over 200
**Distribution** I Old World tropics, Southeast Asia, Australia, Madagascar, New Zealand
**Habit** I Often evergreen trees, shrubs, half shrubs, lianas
**Leaves** I Alternate, also spiral arrangement, more or less whorled, often evergreen, leathery, entire, without stipules
**Inflorescences** I Umbellate, paniculate with bracts and bracteoles
**Flowers** I Radial, predominantly hermaphroditic; five mostly free sepals; corolla is free to fused into tube, can have unguiculate petals, white to yellow, red, or blue. Five stamens: in fused corollas, their filaments may be fused with the stamens; in some species, the stamens open via apical pores; (2–3)–5 carpels; superior multilocular ovary; simple style.
**Fruits** I Loculicidal capsule, berry. The frequently numerous, sometimes winged seeds are often covered with a sticky (also dark to black) slime (pulp) (in Greek, *pittos* means pitch; fig. E).
**Use** I Ornamental plants. These plants contain polyacetylenes.
**Characteristics** I Some species have a milky sap.

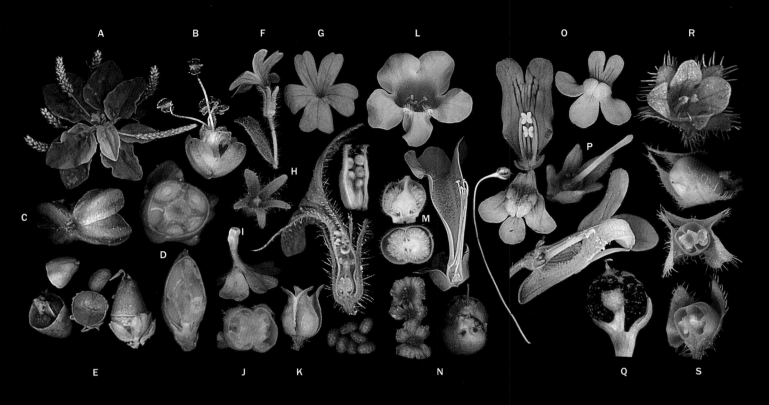

**A–E:** *Plantago major*. A: Habit. B: Flower, lateral. C: The same, underside. D: Ovary; *above*, transverse; *below*, longitudinal. E: Capsule; *right*, unopened; *left*, opened; *center*, lid from underneath.

**F–L:** *Erinus alpinus*. F: Flower, lateral. G: Flower; *above*, frontal; *below*, longitudinal. H: Calyx with gynoecium. I: Corolla. J: Ovary, transverse. K: Open capsule, lateral; *right*, seeds.

**L–N:** *Asarina erubescens*. L: *Above*, flower, frontal; *below*, longitudinal. M: *Above*, ovary, longitudinal; *below*, transverse. N: *Right*, fruit, frontal; *left*, seeds.

**O–Q:** *Cymbalaria muralis*. O: *Above right*, flower, frontal; *left*, opened. P: Gynoecium in calyx; *below*, flower, longitudinal. Q: Fruit, longitudinal.

**R–S:** *Veronica hederifolia*. R: Flower, frontal. S: Ovary; *above*, frontal; *center*, transverse; *below*, longitudinal

**Genera** I About 90; species: more than 1,700

**Distribution** I Worldwide

**Habit** I Rarely shrubs, mostly perennial herbaceous plants, also delicate aquatic plants

**Habitat** I On sandy waysides, in meadows and shoreline areas

**Leaves** I Opposite or alternate; if in basal rosettes, also spiral arrangement

**Inflorescences** I Axillary, spicate to racemose

**Flowers** I Radial to zygomorphic, free or fused, tetramerous-pentamerous calyx, with petals and corolla of the same size or different sizes; 2–4 stamens, can display didynamia. The superior ovary usually consists of two carpels; usually one style with a stigma. The stigma can also be slightly bilobate and usually distinctly papillose. The flowers can be wind-pollinated (*Plantago* species, except for *P. media*; fig. B) or insect-pollinated (figs. G, L, O, R); if the latter, the flowers are also equipped with nectar guides and papillae to "show the way" to the lower "landing zone," or they are even "masked" (fig. O, *right*).

**Fruits** I Capsule, with pyxidium (fig. E), pore capsule (fig. N), or loculicidal capsule; seeds also can have wing membrane (fig. N, *left*).

**Use** I Ornamental plants, such as **snapdragons** (*Antirrhinium majus*); the **Kenilworth ivy** (*Cymbalaria muralis*) (figs. O–Q) grows well in rockeries.

**Characteristics** I **Ribwort plantain** (*Plantago lanceolata*) has spread in the Americas after being colonized from Europe as a "footprint of the white man." **Butter-and-eggs** (*Linaria vulgaris*) has genuine masked flowers, in which the lower lip is attached to the upper lip, as if by a joint. Anyone who wants to get at the nectar in the spur, which is more than 11 mm long, must be able to forcefully push down the lower lip (a "power flower"). In our latitudes, as a rule, only bumblebees can do this. This family has been expanded on an enormous scale due to molecular-genetic outcomes; many of the former figworts now belong to the plantain family.

PLANTAGINACEAE

# PLUMBAGINACEAE

**A–D:** *Armeria maritima*. A: Habit. B: *Above left*, underside of the inflorescence; *right*, lateral, *underneath*, frontal. C: *Right*, flower, frontal; *left*, flower, longitudinal. D: *Left*, unripe fruit, lateral, front part of calyx removed; *right*, the same, longitudinal.

**E–F:** *Ceratostigma willmoottianum*. E: Flower, frontal, with protruding style arms; *right*, flower, longitudinal. F: Ovary, transverse.

**Genera** I 27; species: more than 835
**Distribution** I Worldwide; concentration in the Mediterranean region
**Habitats** I Steppes, semideserts, sea beaches
**Habit** I Perennial herbaceous plants, shrubs, rarely lianas or *Spreizklimmer* (incumbent climbers or ramblers), many xerophytes, some halophytes

**Leaves** I Mostly basal rosettes, leaf blade entire, often linear, lanceolate, grassy (fig. A), also fleshy, mucronate (has a prickly tip)
**Inflorescences** I Spicate, capitiform (fig. B), paniculate
**Flowers** I Radial, hermaphroditic; calyx and corolla usually pentamerous; sepals scarious or colored; petals fused at base or free; usually five

stamens with filamentous connective appendixes (fig. C, *left*); the filament may be hairy; the pentapetalous ovary contains only one basal ovule (fig. D); one style with five stigmas.
**Fruits** I Capsules or single-seeded nuts
**Use** I Dried inflorescences of **sea lavender** (*Limonium vulgare*) are used to make dried flower bouquets.

**Chinese plumbago** (*Ceratostigma willmottianum*) (figs. E–F) is an ornamental plant. In South Africa, people use the dark-gray sap of the **cape plumbago** (*Plumbago auriculata*) for tattooing.
**Characteristics** I The **sea thrift** (*Armeria maritima*) (figs. A–C) can accumulate lead and zinc.

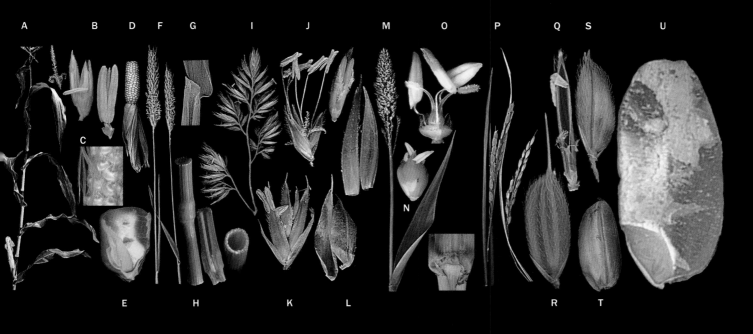

**A–E:** *Zea mays*. A: Habit. B: *Left*, male inflorescence; *right*, male flower. C: Detail of the female inflorescence. D: Spadix, husk folded down. E: Seed, longitudinal.
**F–H:** *Alopecurus pratensis*. F: Habit. G: Ligule. H: *Left*, stalk, lateral; *center*, longitudinal; *right*, transverse.

**I–L:** *Dactylis glomerata*. I: Inflorescence. J: *Left*, 3-flowered spikelet; *right*, flower above husk with stamens, stigma, and lodicula. K: 3-flowered spikelet glumes. L: *Above*, lemma and glume; *underneath it*, outer and inner glumes.

**M–O:** *Sorghum bicolor*. M: Habit. N: Single-flowered spikelet in sheath, below ligule. O: Androecium and gynoecium of a flower.
**P–U:** *Oryza sativa*. P: Flowers and fruiting stage. Q: Flower, lateral; *below*, ovary with stigma and lodicula. R: Single-flowered spikelet. S: Spikelet when fruit is ripe. T: Ripe achenes. U: Seed, longitudinal.

**Genera** | More than 650; species: more than 9,000
**Distribution** | Worldwide
**Habitats** | Dry steppes, semideserts, deserts, open areas **Habit** | Annuals and biennials or perennial plants, rarely woody (bamboo species), growing in tufts, in grassy form or solitary; vegetative propagation by runners, stolons, bulbils pseudovivipary); stem structured as a stalk that can grow from a few centimeters to 40 meters tall; round, mostly hollow (fig. H), with thickened nodes—above which lie the growth zones; the plants have a light structure since the stalks must grow as tall as possible because they are pollinated by wind. Exceptions: Corn, because the spadixes become heavy, and sugar cane, in which the stem serves to store sugar.

**Leaves** | Alternate, distichous, blade has a stem-clasping, mostly open leaf sheath; a membrane, the ligule (small scale or hairy; fig. G), is to be found there on the upper side of the leaf; parallel venation.
**Inflorescences** | Spikes, panicles (figs. I, M, P), spiciform or contracted panicles (fig. F). Flowers compounded into mostly multiflowered spikelets.
**Flowers** | Usually hermaphroditic. Partial inflorescence: spikelets (from base to top): outer, inner glumes (the spikelet covers = bracts of the inflorescence; fig. K); lemmas (= bracts of the flowers; often have bristles or awns on the rear side; fig. L); perianth reduced to a palea (the remnant of the outer whorl of the perigone); and lodicule (remnant of the inner whorl of the perigone). Three stamens (inner whorl fallen off); the stamens hang out on long filaments; superior ovary with one ovule, usually consisting of three fused carpels; two often-feathery style arms (figs. J, O).
**Fruits** | Usually caryopsis
**Use** | The most important plant family that supplies carbohydrates for human nutrition; the storage tissues of the seeds are consumed as grains: **rice** (*Oryza sativa*), **wheat** (*Triticum aestivum*), **corn** (*Zea mays*), **oats** (*Avena sativa*), **rye** (*Secale cereale*), **barley** (*Hordeum vulgare*), and **millet** (*Panicum, Setaria,* and *Teff* species). From the stalks of the **sugar cane** (*Saccharum officinarum*), the sweet juice is pressed and processed into table sugar. In Asia in particular, people consume **bamboo** species as vegetables and also use bamboo in building construction. **Miscanthus** (*Miscanthus* × *giganteus*) is used as a renewable resource for generating energy and producing paper and pulp.
**Characteristics** | The grasses use secondary anemophily (wind pollinated). In this way, they are able to colonize areas that were still free as ecological niches and are windy. Precondition for wind pollination: a large amount of smooth pollen, movable stamens, high population density, synchronous pollen dispersal, large stigmas to collect the pollen.

# POLEMONIACEAE

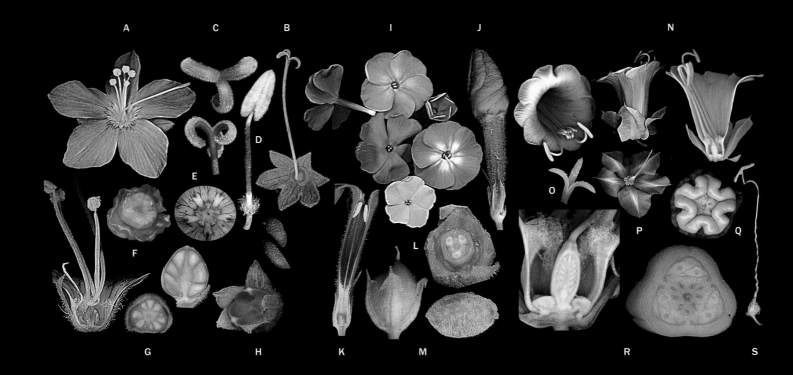

**A–H:** *Polemonium caeruleum*. A: *Above*, flower, frontal; *below left*, longitudinal. B: Calyx with gynoecium. C: Stigma; *above*, frontal; *beneath it*, lateral. D: Stamen. E: Marked nectar cover. F: Nectary around ovary, transverse. G: Ovary; *left*, transverse; *right*, longitudinal. H: *Below*, fruit; *above*, seed.

**I–M:** *Phlox maculata*. I: *Left*, corolla tube; *right*, next to it, variously colored flowers, frontal. J: Bud, lateral. K: Flower, longitudinal. L: Ovary, transverse. M: *Left*, fruit, lateral; *right*, next to it, seed.

**N–S:** *Cobaea scandens*. N: *Left*, flower, frontal; *center*, lateral; *right*, longitudinal. O: Stigma. P: Calyx. Q: Nectary. R: *Left*, central area of flower, longitudinal; *right*, transverse. S: Stamen.

**Genera** I 18; species: over 380
**Distribution** I Moderate regions of western North America
**Habit** I Rarely woody plants and climbing plants, perennials, herbaceous plants
**Habitats** I Meadows, fenlands, riverbanks, railway embankments
**Leaves** I Alternate, spiral or opposite arrangement, whorled, leaf blade simple or compound, petiolate or sessile, without stipules
**Inflorescences** I Cymose
**Flowers** I Radial to slightly zygomorphic, hermaphroditic, often fragrant (phlox, Jacob's ladder); 4–5 sepals, usually fused. Five petals fused in wheel, funnel, or trumpet shape (figs. A, I, N). Usually five stamens, also attached to the corolla. The ovary, fused out of (2–) 3 (–5) carpels, is superior, trilocular, with one to many ovules; surrounded by an annular to curved nectary (disc); one style with (2–) 3 (–4) stigma lobes (figs. C, O).
**Fruits** I Trilobate—pentalobate capsule fruit (fig. F); seeds are sometimes winged.
**Use** I Ornamental plants, such as **garden phlox** (also **perennial phlox**, *Phlox paniculata*) (fig. I), **cup and saucer vine** (*Cobaea scandens*) (figs. N–S). **Jacob's ladder** (*Polemonium caeruleum*) (figs. A–H) is a valuable food supply for bees.
**Characteristics** I Pollination by insects, birds, and bats; some species have a colored milky sap.

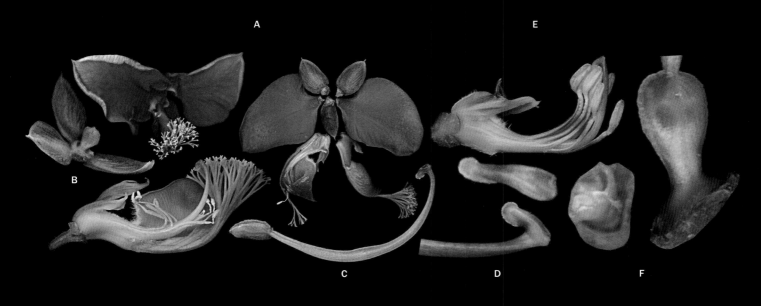

A–F: *Polygala myrtifolia*. A: *Left*, flower, frontal; *below*, longitudinal; *right*, dissected. B: Calyx with ovary. C: Gynoecium, lateral. D: Stigma; *above*, upper side; *beneath it*, lateral. E: Androecium. F: Ovary; *right*, lateral; *left*, transverse.

**Genera** I 20; species: over 1,000
**Distribution** I Worldwide except New Zealand and the islands of the South Pacific
**Habitats** I Dry grasslands, pine forests, poor pastureland, brushwood; avoids calcareous soil
**Habit** I Small trees, half shrubs, also climbing plants, herbaceous plants; stems can be runner-like trailers, rarely root parasites.

**Leaves** I Alternate, spiral arrangement, also whorled; leaf blade simple, rarely with stipules or spiny stipules, also evergreen
**Inflorescences** I Racemiform, spikes, panicles
**Flowers** I Zygomorphic, hermaphroditic, papilionoid (butterfly-like); (4–) 5 (–7) sepals, three of them usually small, two petaloid/petal-like; three or five petals, the anterior ones

carinate or keel-like, with fringed appendage (fig. A); usually 8 (–10) stamens, fused into a tube open at the top, the base often enveloped by an annular disc, and the stamens may open by means of pores; the bicarpellate ovary is superior, bilocular, with usually one hanging ovule; the style, which is often longer, bends again toward its end and supports a disciform, inward-directed stigma

(fig. D).
**Fruits** I Capsules, seeds sometimes have arils, also samaras, drupes.
**Use** I Ornamental plants; in North America, the indigenous population used some species to treat snakebites, such as *Polygala senega*. Some species provide dyes and fibers.
**Characteristics** I Some *Xanthophyllum* species accumulate aluminum ions.

# POLYGONACEAE

**A–E:** *Antigonone leptopus*. A: Flower, frontal. B: Stigma. C: Androecium from bud, frontal. D: Ripe fruit E: Flower, longitudinal.

**F–H:** *Fagopyrum esculentum*. F: Flower, frontal. G: The same, longitudinal. H: Seeds, lateral; *left*, longitudinal; *right*, transverse.

**I–N:** *Polygonum bistorta*. I: Stem with leaf and ochrea. J: Dissected flower, longitudinal. R: Flower, frontal. L: Fruit. M: The same, transverse. N: The same, longitudinal.

**O–U:** *Rumex acetosa*. O: Male flower, frontal. P: Female flower, frontal. Q: Ovary with 2 of 3 stigmas visible, lateral. R: Fruit. S: The same, frontal. T: The same, transverse. U: Ripe seed.

**Genera** I More than 40; species: 1,100.
**Distribution** I Worldwide.
**Habitats** I Mountain meadows, damp meadows, neglected grasslands, fields, brushwood, riverbanks, waste ground
**Habit** I Annual to perennial herbaceous plants; can be twining; rarely woody, thickened nodes
**Leaves** I Alternate, stipules envelope the vegetation point as ochrea; these are perfoliate and cover the internodes as a membranous sheath (fig. I).

**Inflorescences** I Spicate, spiciform paniculate, axillary cluster, paniculate
**Flowers** I Hermaphroditic or unisexual (figs. O–Q), calyx and corolla trimerous or pentamerous-sexamerous; 5–10 usually free stamens; in the knotweeds, the inner whorl of flowers is retained on the fruit as a dispersal organ (winged, burr, floating fruit; figs. S, T); the bicarpellate to quadricarpellate ovary, with only one ovule, is superior; the usually three styles are free (fig. J); the usually small stigma can be capitate disc-shaped (fig. B) or come to a very delicate tip (figs. G, J).
**Fruits** I One-seeded, two-to-three-edged nut (fig. H)
**Use** I **Buckwheat** (*Fagopyrum esculentum*) seeds (fig. H) as a source of starch; people eat the leaves of some sorrel species, such as **patience dock** (*Rumex patientia*), *R. acetosa* (sorrel), and *R. acetosella* (sheep's sorrel). Soon after it has started to sprout, **rhubarb** stalks (*Rheum rhabarbrum, R. raponticum*) can be made into preserves or juice. The **coral vine** (*Antigonon leptopus*) is cultivated as an ornamental plant and is now considered invasive in some areas.
**Characteristics** I Usually wind pollination

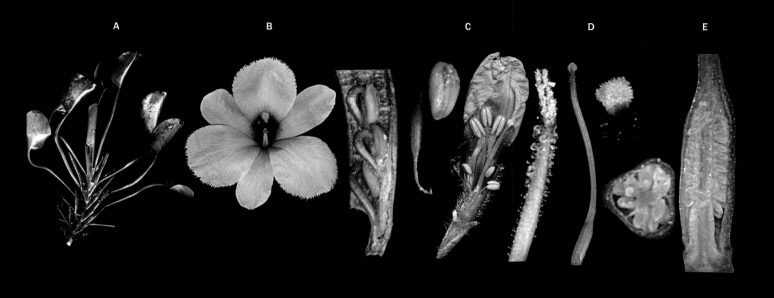

**A–E:** *Eichhornia azurea*. A: Habit. B: Flower, frontal. C: Stamens; *left*, in bud; *center*, single stamen from the front; *right*, the 2 whorls positioned on a petal; *far right*, opened stamen. D: *Left*, gynoecium; *above right*, stigma, frontal. E: Ovary; *left*, transverse; *right*, longitudinal.

**Genera** | About 6; species: about 30
**Distribution** | Almost worldwide, from the tropics into warm temperate zones; especially Neotropical
**Habit** | Annual or perennial herbaceous plants
**Habitats** | Water or marsh plants
**Leaves** | Alternate, spiral, or distichous, occasionally whorled arrangement; leaves simple, petiolate, with tubular leaf sheath; can have rhizomes, submerged or floating; parallel venation with a wide variety of leaf blade shapes.

**Inflorescences** | Thyrses of scorpioid cymes, racemose, solitary
**Flowers** | Mostly radial to zygomorphic, hermaphroditic, trimerous; six tepals in two whorls; tepals can be of similar or dissimilar type (fig. B), free or basally fused into a tube; (1–) 2 whorls, each of three free stamens (fig. C); 2–3 stamens may be transformed into staminodes; three carpels are fused to a superior ovary; style with three stigma lobes or capitate (fig. D). Pollination mostly by insects; cleistogamy does occur.

**Fruits** | Capsule or nut; they often ripen underwater (hydrocarpy).
**Use** | People use the dried stalks of the thick-stemmed **water hyacinth** (*Eichhornia crassipes*) to plait pieces for furniture. The ability of these plants to filter heavy metals out of water is exploited for water purification in India, where drinking water is heavily contaminated with arsenic. **Pickerel weed** (*Pontederia cordata*) is planted in ornamental ponds. Its young stems and seeds can be eaten both raw and cooked. **Stargrass** (*Heteranthera*

*zosterifolia*) is planted in aquariums.
**Characteristics** | *Eichhornia crassipes* is considered an invasive neophyte in many tropical areas because it has an extremely high vegetative propagation potential. In Africa especially, this plant often covers large areas of inland waters like a continuous plant carpet.

201

PORTULACACEAE

A   C   D   E

B

**A–B:** *Portulaca* **sp**. A: *Left*, flower, frontal; *right*, next to it, underside. B: Fruiting stage, capsule lids removed; seeds are visible.

**C–E:** *Portulaca pilosa*. C: Flower, frontal. D: Pyxidium (lid), lateral; *above right*, older pyxidium. E: Leafy part of a shoot.

**Genus** | 1: Portulaca; species: over 100
**Distribution** | Worldwide, mostly in the Americas
**Habit** | Annual to perennial herbaceous plants with thickened stems and succulent tubers
**Leaves** | Alternate, rarely opposite, decussed, sessile, usually thickened, flat to cylindrical; mostly without stipules, or these can be axillary hairs (fig. E).
**Inflorescences** | Cymose, paniculate, often with up to 30 sessile flowers; bracts present
**Flowers** | Hermaphroditic, rarely unisexual, then dioecious; the sepals are interpreted as being modified bracts, while the petals are considered to be displaced sepals; 4–6 (–100) stamens, also with sensory papillae on the sensitive filaments; ovaries inferior or half inferior; one style with five style arms.
**Fruits** | Unilocular capsules that open by a lid (fig. B), with many mostly colorful to shiny, black, spherical to kidney-shaped seeds (fig. B)
**Use** | *Portulaca oleracea* is eaten as a vegetable or salad and cooked as a soup green; also ornamental plants.
**Characteristics** | Betalains; because the flower of many species opens only in sunshine, these plants have been called "midday flowers." The outer seed coat surface is often used to define the species; these have a metallic shine and can have warty sculpting.

A–J: *Primula auricula*. A: Rosette plant with flowers. B: Foliage leaf with flower, lateral. C: Flower bud still furled. D: Calyx, frontal; stigma at the center. E: *Left*, flower with short style, frontal; *right*, longitudinal. F: *Left*, flower with long style, frontal; *right*, longitudinal. G: Ovary, longitudinal, with style and stigma. H: Ovary, transverse. I: Stigma, frontal. J: Unopened stamens from bud.

**Genera** I 9; species: more than 900
**Distribution** I Northern Hemisphere, temperate latitudes
**Habit** I Trees, shrubs, half shrubs, perennials, herbaceous plants, rosettes, also lianas
**Habitat** I Tall herbaceous vegetation, open forests, brushwood, forest edges, rock crevices, neglected grasslands
**Leaves** I Alternate, spiral arrangement or opposite, petiolate or sessile, usually simple; the leaf blades often display dark glandular points or lines.
**Inflorescences** I Solitary, umbellate, racemose, paniculate
**Flowers** I Radial, hermaphroditic; five usually fused sepals (fig. B); five usually fused petals (fig. E, *left*; fig. F, *left*); 5– (7–10) usually free stamens; the unilocular (fig. H) ovary is superior. The stylet may be heterostylous; that is, of various lengths, resulting in flowers with a style protruding from the corolla tube or a short style, which then causes the stamens to protrude from the corolla tube (fig. E, *left*).
**Fruits** I Capsules, often with 2 to more than 100 oil-containing seeds
**Use** I Ornamental plants
**Characteristics** I Rhizomes or tubers as overwintering organs; being heterostylous is common (figs. E, F). The benzoquinone derivative, primin, can cause skin irritation.
**Notes** I The Myrsinaceae and Theophrastaceae have meanwhile been classified as subfamilies of the primrose family.

PRIMROSE FAMILY
Order: Ericales—Heath

PRIMULACEAE

# PROTEACEAE

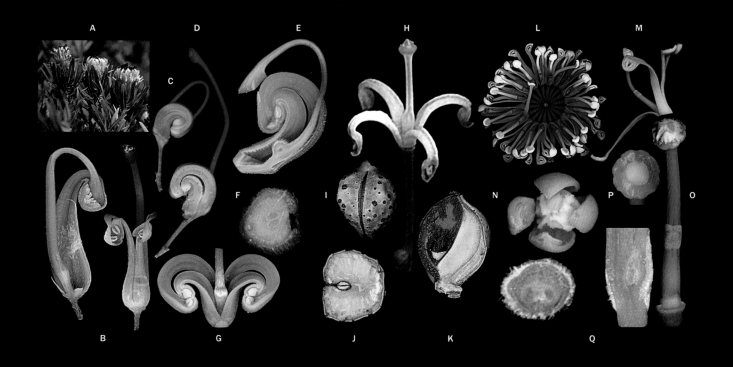

**A:** *Protea neriifolia* habit in its natural habitat
**B:** *Grevillea juniperina*. *Left*, flower, longitudinal, stigma still furled; *right*, next to it, flower, lateral, free stigma.

**C–G:** *Grevillea johnsonii*. C: Bud. D: Bud, free stigma. E: Flower, longitudinal. F: Ovary, transverse. G: Unfurled flower, stigma removed.
**H–K:** *Hakea drupacea*. H: Flower, lateral. I: Ripe fruit. J: Fruit, transverse. K: Fruit, longitudinal.

**L–Q:** *Stenocarpus sinuatus*. L: Inflorescence. M: Single flower, lateral. N: Opening flower, frontal. O: Ovary with deposited pollen. P: Young stigma from bud, frontal. Q: *Right*, ovary, longitudinal; *left*, the same, transverse.

**Genera** | About 80; species: about 1,700
**Distribution** | Disjointed distribution, mostly in the Southern Hemisphere: South Africa (Cape flora), southern India, southern China to Australia (largest diversity), South America
**Habit** | Trees, perennials, half shrubs, rarely herbaceous plants
**Leaves** | Alternate, crowded at end of the sprout, leaf blade pinnate in diverse ways, from simple and linear to fernlike; glabrous or covered with silvery, reflecting, silky hairs (hence the German name, Silberbaumgewächse [silver tree family]!), evergreen, often with forked venation, no stipules
**Inflorescences** | Simple or compound inflorescences, dense, floriferous, paniculate, racemose, umbellate (fig. L), cone shaped; bracts often of striking colors
**Flowers** | Radial or zygomorphic, usually hermaphroditic, functionally male or female, rarely monoecious or dioecious diclinous, simple perigone or doubly articulated in calyx and corolla; usually one whorl with four tepals, one whorl of mostly (3) –4 stamens (figs. B, G), usually fused with the tepals; often has secondary pollen presentation on the thickened style (fig. O); one superior carpel per flower (fig. H), often with a protruding style (figs. A–E, M); disciform nectary. Pollinators: birds, insects, marsupials (Australia), rodents (South America).
**Fruits** | Mostly follicles (fig. I), drupes, dry. One-seeded indehiscent fruits ("achenes"). Pericarp is often thick, woody.
**Use** | The only original Australian plant of supraregional economic importance is the **macadamia nut** (*Macadamia integrifolia*). The seeds in the follicles are encased in a particularly hard shell, which can be opened only by using a special nutcracker. The cotyledons are almost 80% oil and are made into spreads for bread, for example. The **king protea** (*Protea cynaroides*) is the national flower of South Africa; it is used as a cut flower. Some ornamental plants, such as the **firewheel tree** (*Stenocarpus sinuatus*; figs. L–Q), the **silver tree** (*Leucadendron argenteum*), or the **silky oak** (*Grevillea robusta*).
**Characteristics** | As an adaptation to recurring bushfires, these plants can be "pyrophytes" (= fire-tolerant plants); their fruit open only after contact with fire (such as *Banksia*, *Grevillea*, *Protea*). The so-called lignotubers are another adaption to fire: these are compressed, gnarled, and thickened stem growths with "sleeping" eyes that grow below to just above the ground surface and help the plant regenerate after a fire.

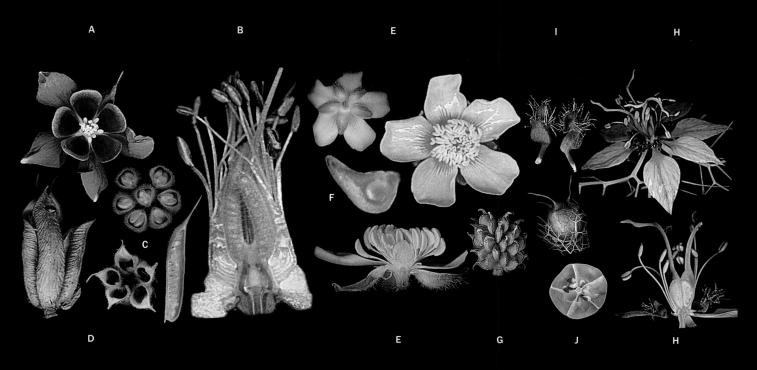

**A–D:** *Aquilegia vulgaris*. A: Flower, frontal. B: Central part of flower, longitudinal. C: Carpels, transverse; *underneath*, a solitary carpel, longitudinal. D: Fruit; *left*, lateral; *right*, frontal.

**E–G:** *Ranunculus repens*. E: *Above left*, underside of flower; *center*, flower, frontal; *below left*, flower, longitudinal. F: Solitary carpel, longitudinal. G: Fruiting stage.

**H–J:** *Nigella damascena*. H: *Above*, flower, lateral/frontal; *below it*, the same, longitudinal. I: Honey leaves. J: *Above*, fruit, lateral; *below it*, transverse.

**Genera** | About 60; species: more than 1,800

**Distribution** | Worldwide, especially in the temperate and cooler regions of the Northern Hemisphere

**Habit** | Most are perennial herbaceous plants, usually with rhizomes, also stem tubers as overwintering organs; rarely woody; climbing plants grow up to 15 meters tall (clematis).

**Habitat** | In moist locations (*Caltha, Ranunculus*), meadows, pastures

**Leaves** | Usually alternate, only opposite in the clematis, rarely basal; various leaf blades, with most pinnate, more or less distinctly segmented, palmate and divided, trilobate, rarely linear (*Myosurus*), often with leaf sheaths, without stipules

**Flowers** | Radial or zygomorphic, hermaphroditic, perianths of various types, often inarticulated; simple perigone or doubly articulated into calyx and corolla (fig. E). Varying numerical proportions in the perianth; flowers arranged in calyx and crown are mostly pentamerous; often transitions between perianth and bracts; large variety of different honey leaves (fig. I: such as a petallike spur), which can also grow between the tepals and stamens; large number of stamens (fig. E: free or fused together); one to usually many free carpels (figs. C, F), superior (figs. B, H); free style.

**Fruits** | Usually many-seeded follicle (fig. D) or single-seeded nut fruits (fig. G), rarely berries or poricidal capsule fruit (love-in-a-mist; fig. J)

**Use** | Many ornamental plants: for example, **Christmas rose** (Helleborus), **winter aconite** (Eranthis), **globeflower** (*Trollius europaeus*), **hepatical** (*Hepatica*). **Monkshood** (*Aconitum napellus*) forms one of the strongest toxins in the plant kingdom (aconitine), which can be absorbed through the skin if the plants are touched (florists should take care!). In the past, it was used as a dart poison and for various medical purposes, but today only in homeopathy. The **pasque flower** (*Pulsatilla vulgaris*) also supplies an important homeopathic remedy. **Black cumin** (*Nigella sativa*) supplies seeds with an antiflatulence effect, but they can be poisonous in large quantities.

**Characteristics** | All buttercup family plants form protoanemonin, which is toxic and irritating to skin and mucous membranes. The **black hellebore** (*Helleborus niger*) is in bloom at Christmas time, which is why the plant is also called the "Christmas rose." The climbing **common clematis** (*Clematis vitalba*) can cling to a support by using its petioles/rhachis. Unlike all other buttercup family plants, their flowers grow only four tepals. The name "buttercup" for these plants that grow in moist meadows during May refers to the earlier use of the yellow flowers to color butter because of their carotene content.

# RANUNCULACEAE

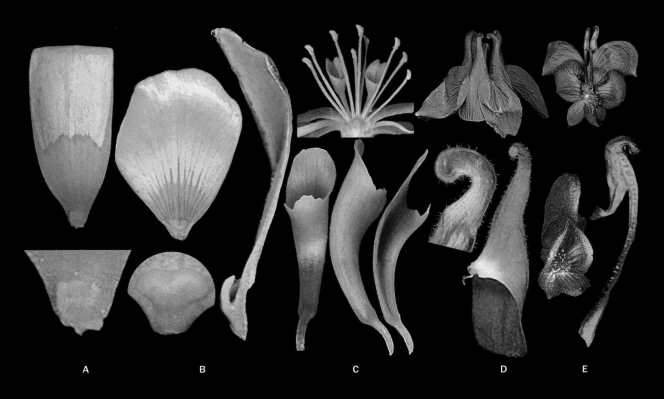

A          B          C          D          E

**A:** *Ficaria verna* honey leaf; *below*, detail.
**B:** *Ranunculus repens* honey leaf; *below*, detail; *right*, longitudinal.

**C:** *Helleborus niger* honey leaves between perianth and androecium; *below*, detail; *right*, longitudinal.

**D:** *Aquilegia vulgaris*. 5 spurs between the tepals; *below*, detail; *right*, spur, lateral, with the glandular area at the upper end already visible from outside; *left*, through the glandular zone, longitudinal.

**E:** *Aconitum napellus*. *Above*, unfurled hood: 2 spurs hidden underneath; *below left*, flower, lateral; *right*, solitary spur.

In the buttercup family, the plants often form nectar in special flower organs, which are likely derived from the androecium. These may be petallike "honey-leaves" that produce nectar in the axil between a basal scale and the large petallike area (figs. A and B). The flowers may also have small to larger spurs that can be hidden under a petal (such as in the **monk's hood**; fig. E). They can also be inserted in the open between the tepals (**common columbine**; fig. D) and in larger numbers as small tubular nectar sacs between petals and stamens (such as in the **black hellebore/Christmas rose**; fig. C). The nectar is produced in the spur itself, unlike, for example, in the violet family; in the latter, growths on the filaments protrude into the spur and secrete the nectar there.

**A–D:** *Reseda lutea.* A: Habit. B: *Left*, flower, frontal; *center*, underside; *right*, lateral. C: Flower, longitudinal. D: Single petal. E: *Above*, fruit, transverse; *below*, lateral.

**Genera** | About 5; species: more than 70
**Distribution** | Western Eurasia, Africa, North America
**Habitat** | Waysides, quarries, ruderal areas
**Habit** | Half shrubs, herbaceous plants, perennials

**Leaves** | Alternate, simple, and undivided, the upper leaves sometimes pinnatifid to divided
**Inflorescences** | Racemose, spikes with bracts, receptacle also emanating from a short androgynophore
**Flowers** | Zygomorphic, radial, hermaphroditic, tetramerous-

sexamerous(-septamerous); three or more stamens (also can be many); 2–6 carpels form the superior ovary with usually numerous ovules, which may open at the top when ripe; one style, usually absent.
**Fruits** | Capsules, berries

**Use** | Ornamental plants, often intensely fragrant, also a source of essential oils. **Dyer's rocket** (*Reseda luteola*) supplies the yellow dye luteolin (Dutch pink) and is used as a dye plant.

**A–F:** *Elegia capensis.* A: Habit. B: Leafy shoot. C: Sprout, transverse. D: Inflorescence. E: *Above,* female flower underside; *beneath it,* lateral with longitudinally sectioned ovary. F: *Above,* ovary, lateral; *left,* beneath it, the same, longitudinal; *right,* next to it, transverse.

**G–I:** *Leptocarpus similis.* G: Habit. H: Leafy sprout; beneath it, the same, transverse. I: Inflorescence.

**Subfamilies** | Anarthrioideae, Restionoideae, Sporadanthoideae, Centrolepidoideae, Leptocarpoideae
**Genera** | About 64; species: about 545. Well-known genera: *Desmocladus, Elegia, Restio.*
**Distribution** | In Southern Hemisphere warm temperate regions, especially in Australia, New Zealand, southwestern Africa, and South America. There they have the status that Poaceae, Cyperaceae, and Juncaceae have in the Northern Hemisphere.
**Habit** | Perennial herbaceous plants with grassy stalks (figs. A, G),

articulated into nodes and internodes
**Leaves** | Alternate, deciduous or evergreen, often reduced into a scale (figs. B, H); then the stem takes on the photosynthesis function. Some are xeromorphic.
**Inflorescences** | Male and female (figs. D, I) inflorescences have different structures and usually occur on different individual plants (dioecious).
**Flowers** | Radial to slightly zygomorphic; flowers small, usually unisexual, trimerous (figs. E, F), grouped in spikelets; three stamens, and the superior ovary usually consists of three carpels. Wind pollination.

**Fruits** | Capsules, nuts
**Use** | Some species were formerly used to make brooms and ropes (hence the name in Latin *restio* = rope maker) and as a building material. Some species are used as ornamental plants (not winter hardy in northern Europe).
**Characteristics** | Many species are adapted to recurring bushfires; the fruit survive the fires. Finds of fossilized pollen have demonstrated that this plant family has existed on the Earth for over 65 million years, when the original continent of Gondwana still formed a single landmass. The South

African "deceptive" plant *Ceratocaryum argenteum* has developed a special strategy to disperse its seeds. The seeds mimic the look and dung odor of antelope scat, thus attracting dung beetles, which roll the seeds away and bury them. Only when the beetles begin to eat the seeds do they realize that they have been deceived (fecal mimicry).

**A–C:** *Zizyphus jujuba*. A: *Above*, flower, frontal; *below*, longitudinal. B: Stem thorn, longitudinal. C: Unripe fruit; *left*, lateral; *right*, transverse.

**D–F:** *Frangula californica* **subsp.** *tomentella*. D: *Left*, young; *right*, older flower, frontal. E: Flower, longitudinal. F: Fruit; *above*, transverse; *below*, longitudinal. G: Seed.

**H–K:** *Phylica ericoides*. H: Branch with flowers. I: Leaf underside. J: Inflorescence, longitudinal. K: *Left*, fruiting stage; *right*, fruit, transverse; *center*, underside.

**L–N:** *Paliurus spina-christi*. L: Sprout. M: Flower, frontal. N: Fruit; *above*, frontal; *below*, from underneath; *left*, longitudinal.

**O–Q:** *Colletia hystrix*. O: *Above left*, stigma/stamens; *right*, flower, frontal; *below left*, longitudinal. P: Fruit; *above*, frontal; *below left*, transverse; *right*, longitudinal. Q: Stem thorns.

**R–T:** *Ceanothus oliganthus*. R: Flower, frontal. S: *Above*, fruit, transverse; *below*, longitudinal. T: Seeds.

**Genera** | 55; species: 900
**Distribution** | Worldwide, mostly tropical to subtropical
**Habitat** | Humid forests, moorlands, brushwood, rock crevices
**Habit** | Trees, shrubs, often with thorny branches; can climb with twining stems
**Leaves** | Opposite or alternate, spiral arrangement, simple, entire or serrated; most have small stipules.

**Inflorescences** | Cymose or racemose
**Flowers** | Radial, hermaphroditic or unisexual; hypanthium often present; tetramerous-pentamerous with disc or nectary in the hypanthium area (fig. E; fig. O, *below left*); calyx often multiply keeled inside (fig. A); small corolla, which may be absent; stamens open inwardly, 2–3–5 carpels form the medial to inferior ovary; one undivided style with bilobate-trilobate stigma (fig. D; fig. O, *above left*) or bifid-quinquefid.
**Fruits** | Drupe-like berry fruit, dry fruit
**Use** | Ornamental shrubs such as **California lilac** (*Ceanothus* species); various dyes from the fruit and bark of *Rhamnus* species, such as "sap green" from the fruit of the **European buckthorn** (*Rhamnus catarthicus*). The bark of the **alder buckthorn** (*Frangula alnus*) can be used to dye wool yellow, and it becomes reddish when subjected to light. The *Zizyphus jujuba* has edible fruits (jujube or Chinese date), and extracts from the leaves and bark are used for medicinal purposes (stimulants, laxatives).
**Characteristics** | Christ's crown of thorns was allegedly made from branches of the **crown-of-thorns** (*Paliurus spina-christi*) (figs. L–N).

# RORIDULACEAE

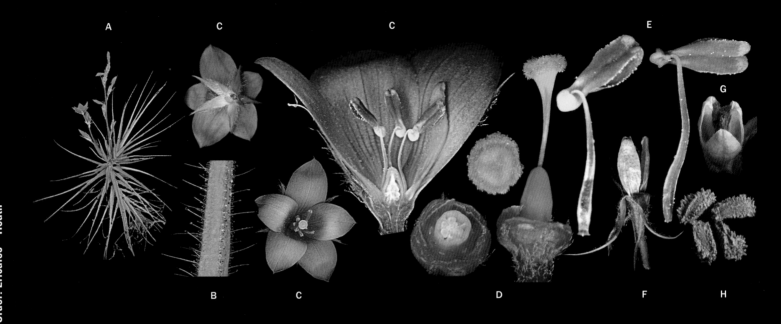

**A–H:** *Roridula gorgonias*. A: Habit. B: Leaf with glandular hairs. C: *Left*, underside of flower; *center*, flower, frontal; *right*, the same, longitudinal. D: *Right*, gynoecium; *above left*, next to it, stigma, frontal; *below left*, ovary, transverse. E: Stamen from both sides. F: Ripe fruit, lateral. G: The same, frontal. H: Seeds.

**Genus** I 1: *Roridula*; species: 2
**Distribution** I South Africa: the Cape region
**Habits** I Half shrubs growing up to 2 meters tall
**Habitat** I Mountains of the Cape region; fynbos region; foggy, marshy areas
**Leaves** I Spiral arrangement, alternate (figs. A, B), linear, with long, petiolate, and gummy (caoutchouc) glandular hairs (fig. B), without stipules; these plants trap insects. The young leaves are furled in a spiral (circinate venation: leaves furled from tip to base).
**Inflorescences** I Solitary, racemose
**Flowers** I Radial, hermaphroditic, pentamerous calyx (fig. C), which may be fused at the base; pentamerous corolla; five free stamens that open through apical pores; connective growths may contain nectar (fig. E); tricarpellate superior ovary with axile placentation; one style with disciform papillary stigma (fig. D, *right*).
**Fruits** I Loculicidal, trilocular capsule fruit (fig. G), smooth to cartilaginous, often with many seeds
**Characteristics** I The insects trapped by the gummy leaves are eaten by bugs or spiders that live on the plant; their excretions fertilize the plant. The plants are mostly self-pollinating. These plants are pyrophilous; that is, they are able to sprout after a fire, or the seeds can then germinate.

**A–D:** *Comarum palustre*. A: Flower, frontal. B: The same, underside. C: Leaf. D: *Above*, fruit, lateral; *below*, longitudinal.
**E–H:** *Prunus laurocerasus*. E: Leafy branch with inflorescence. F: Flower, frontal. G: The same, longitudinal. H: Fruit; *above*, lateral; *underneath*, longitudinal.

**I–K:** *Spiraea media*. I: Inflorescence. J: *Above*, flower, longitudinal; *below*, frontal. K: *Above*, fruit, frontal; *below*, longitudinal.
**L–M:** *Chaenomeles japonica*. L: *Above*, flower, frontal; *below*, longitudinal. M: Fruit; *left*, top view; *right*, next to it, transverse.

**N–P:** *Dryas octopetala*. N: Flower, frontal. O: Calyx with nectary/gynoecium, frontal. P: Leaf with stipules; *above*, upper side; *beneath it*, underside.

**Genera** I 100; species: 3,000
**Distribution** I Worldwide, mostly in temperate latitudes, very diverse distribution in the Northern Hemisphere
**Habitat** I Waysides, meadows, deciduous forests
**Habit** I Trees, shrubs, perennials, herbaceous plants; may have spines or thorns
**Leaves** I Alternate, spiral arrangement, with or without stipules, simple to tripinnate

**Inflorescences** I Panicles, cymes, racemose
**Flowers** I Radial, mostly hermaphroditic, perianth usually pentamerous, often cyclical; calyx can have outer calyx (fig. B); rarely 1–2 whorls with 1–5 stamens, usually 2–4 times as many as the petals through secondary growth; carpels: one to many, apocarpous or fused one below the other, often enveloped by the receptacle, inferior or sitting on the broadened receptacle, medial; nectaries often in the hypanthium; *Spiraea* have yellow nectar scales in front of the stamens (fig. J).
**Fruits** I Follicles, capsules; nutlets can have a style that grows feather-like for wind dispersal, or on a fleshy receptacle; drupes, berries, aggregate fruits.
**Use** I Ornamental plants: **roses**; fruit trees such as the various *Prunus* species: **sweet cherry** (*P. avium, P. cerasus*), **European plum** (*P. domestica*), **almond** (*P. dulcis*), **Armenian plum** (*P. armeniaca*), **peach** (*P. persica*), **apple** (*Malus sylvestris*), **medlar** (*Mespilus germanica*), **red raspberr**y (*Rubus idaeus, R. fruticosus*), **quince** (*Cydonia oblonga*). The wood is used, such as from cherry trees; rose oil and rose water from fragrant roses.

**A–C:** *Rubia tinctoria*. A: Partial inflorescence. B: *Above*, flower, lateral; *below*, frontal. C: Fruit; *above*, longitudinal; *below*, transverse.
**D–F:** *Coffea arabica*. D: Flower, frontal. E: Bud, longitudinal. F: Fruit; *above*, lateral; *center*, transverse; *below*, longitudinal. G: Seeds.

**H–J:** *Galium odoratum*. H: Whorl of leaves. I: *Above*, flower, frontal; *below*, longitudinal. J: Fruit; *above*, lateral; *below*, transverse.
**K–P:** *Psychotria erithrocarpa*. K: *Above*, flower, frontal; *center*, lateral; *below*, longitudinal. L: Stigma. M: Nectary. N: Ovary, transverse. O: Fruit; *above left*, lateral; *below*, transverse; *right*, longitudinal. P: Seed.

**Q–U:** *Pogonopus speciosus*. Q: Partial inflorescence. R: Flower, longitudinal. S: *Above*, androecium; *below*, stamen. T: Stigma, lateral. U: *Above*, fruit, longitudinal; *below*, transverse.

**Genera** | More than 600; species: more than 10,000
**Distribution** | Almost worldwide
**Habits** | Trees, shrubs, perennials, herbaceous plants, also lianas and aquatic plants
**Habitats** | Waysides, meadows, also in deciduous forests and rainforests
**Leaves** | Opposite, decussate, simple leaf blade; stipules often like foliage leaves, creating the impression of leaf whorls/verticils (fig. H); leaves can be leathery.
**Inflorescences** | Loose to capitate thyrses, paniculate, whorled, also capitiform to globose

**Flowers** | Radial, rarely zygomorphic, hermaphroditic, tetramerous-pentamerous, fused; calyx often short or absent; corolla mostly of 4–5 fused leaves, more rarely 3–8–10, with short to long tubes; 4–5 stamens, can open through pores, the bicarpellate (rarely up to nine-carpellate) ovary is inferior.
**Fruits** | Schizocarps/mericarps, berries, drupes, capsules, often with hooked hairs (fig. J), so that dispersal can also be by epizoochory (on an animal's exterior)
**Use** | The roots of many of the bedstraw or madder family are used for red dyes, such as **dyer's madder**

(*Rubia tinctorum*) as well as various **bedstraw** species; in the latter, the resulting red has a characteristic more yellowish/brownish color. The seeds of **coffee plants** (*Coffea arabica* [fig. G, *left*], and *C. canescens*) are roasted. The fleshy husk of the "coffee cherries" (a drupe) is used to make a refreshing drink called "cascara," which is drunk cold or as a "coffee tea"; a single glass of cascara contains up to eight times more caffeine than a cup of coffee. In Germany, the **woodruff** (*Galium odoratum*) is used to flavor Maibowle ("May bowl": flavored white wine).
**Yellow bedstraw** (*Galium verum*)

contains the enzyme rennet, which can be used to clot milk for cheese making; today, however, cheese is usually made using biotechnology processes. Many people have ornamental plants of the poisonous *Cubanola* species on their terraces.
**Characteristics** | The foliage leaves may contain raphides; the plants may contain alkaloids, coumarins (**woodruff**), and saponins.

**A–C:** *Ruta graveolens*. A: *Left*, flower, frontal; *right*, from below. B: Androecium. C: Fruit; *left*, longitudinal; *right*, transverse. **D–E:** *Murraya paniculata*. D: *Left*, flower, frontal; *right*, lateral. E: *Above left*, fruit, lateral; *right*, longitudinal; *below*, transverse.

**F–I:** *Esenbeckia grandiflora*. F: *Above left*, flower, frontal; *beneath it*, lateral; *above right*, underside; *beneath it*, flower, longitudinal. G: Nectary. H: Young fruit; *left*, transverse; *right*, longitudinal. I: Fruit; *left*, frontal; *right*, lateral.

**J–N:** *Poncirus trifoliata*. J: Opened bud. K: *Left*, bud, longitudinal; *below*, frontal; *above right*, from underneath. L: Calyx. M: Flower, longitudinal. N: *Left*, fruit, longitudinal; *center*, frontal; *right*, transverse.

**O:** *Agathosma foetidissima*. *Left*, inflorescence, frontal; *right*, habit.

**Genera** | More than 160; species: more than 1,800

**Distribution** | Worldwide, subtropics, tropics, a few species in the northern temperate latitudes

**Habit** | Trees, shrubs, half shrubs, rarely herbaceous plants, deciduous, evergreens

**Habitat** | Dry forests, also in calcareous soils

**Leaves** | Primarily alternate, spiral arrangement, rarely opposite, leaf blade dotted with oil glands, simple, trimerous or pinnate, without stipules, sometimes reduced to spines

**Inflorescences** | Rarely solitary, dichasias

**Flowers** | Radial, rarely zygomorphic, hermaphroditic, can be diclinous, monoecious or dioecious; bimerous-pentamerous, and sometimes terminal flowers are pentamerous, lateral flowers tetramerous; calyx free or basally fused, also reduced; 4–5 petals are free or fused; 2–3–5–10–20–60 stamens; filaments free or can be basally fused one below the other; intrastaminal disc; the 1–4–5 free or fused carpels form the superior ovary; rarely half inferior, can be lobed; the sturdy style ends in a papillary stigma.

**Fruits** | Capsules, drupes, berries

**Use** | Ornamental and medicinal plants; the citrus species especially are consumed as fruit, juice, preserves, etc. The **common rue** (*Ruta graveolens*), a winter-hardy, evergreen perennial, has long been cultivated as a medicinal plant. Bergamot essential oil from bergamot oranges is also used in making perfumes. The fruit pulp of the citrus species consists of so-called juice vesicles.

**Characteristics** | Leaves and stems have lysigenous oil glands. Essential oils in different parts of the plants.

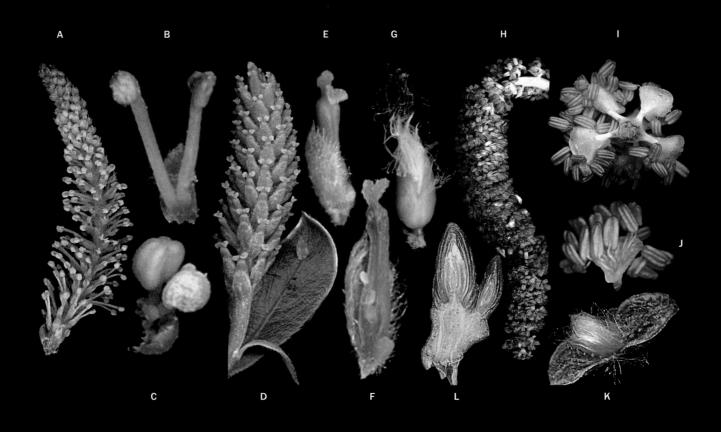

A B E G H I

C D F L K

J

**A–G:** *Salix alba*. A: Male inflorescence. B: Male single flower. C: Young male single flower. D: Female inflorescence. E: Female single flower. F: The same, longitudinal. G: Opened capsule with seeds.

**H–L:** *Populus tremula*. H: Male inflorescence. I: Four male flowers, undersides. J: Male flower, lateral. K: Open capsule with seeds. L: Bud, longitudinal, with female inflorescence in the center.

**Genera** I 55; species: more than 1,000
**Distribution** I Worldwide, Arctic to temperate latitudes
**Habit** I Trees, shrubs, also thorny stems
**Habitat** I Pastures, often grow in ground with more or less high groundwater levels, riparian areas, riparian forests
**Leaves** I Usually alternate, rarely opposite, also spiral arrangement, simple, usually have stipules, deciduous, can be evergreen, simple
**Inflorescences** I Catkins (figs. A, H), spikes (fig. D), flowers often in the axils of bracts, bundles, cymens
**Flowers** I Unisexual, dioecious, perianth often absent or usually simple; male flowers with two to many stamens, in the axils of bracts (figs. B, C, J) or with simple pentamerous hull; female flowers in the axils of bracts with bicarpellate superior ovary, often contains many hairy seeds in a cup-shaped receptacle; style short to long; stigma bilobate-trilobate; the very reduced female flowers of Salix alba contain one nectar scale positioned in front the ovary base (fig. F).
**Fruits** I Capsules, seeds have hairy tufts (figs. G, K).
**Use** I The wood is used to make paper, and the basket willow is used for weaving (e.g., baskets); some ornamental plants. Willows are important bee pastures in the spring, and some solitary bee species collect pollen exclusively from willows.
**Characteristics** I The plants bloom before the leaves unfurl: pussy willow.
**Notes** I Because of their different features and distribution, the Flacourtiaceae, meanwhile a subfamily of Salicaceae, is discussed separately; see there.

A–B: *Osyris alba*. A: Male flower, frontal. B: Male flower, longitudinal.

C–J: *Viscum album*. C: *Above*, habit; *beneath it*, branch with male flowers. D: Male flower, lateral. E: Male single flower, frontal. F: Female flower, lateral. G: The same, frontal. H: Female flower, longitudinal. I: Ripe fruit; *below right*, 1 seed. J: Fruit, longitudinal.

**Genera** I More than 40; species: more than 900
**Distribution** I Worldwide
**Habitat** I Parasite on roots of other plants or on stems
**Habit** I Trees, shrubs, rarely herbaceous plants; most are semiparasites.
**Leaves** I Alternate or opposite, spiral arrangement, simple and undivided, leathery, mostly light green; leaves conduct photosynthesis, without stipules.
**Inflorescences** I Racemose, paniculate, cymes, spikes, capitiform
**Flowers** I Radial, hermaphroditic or unisexual, then usually dioecious, in single whorls; 3–6 tepals, petaloid or bract-like; corolla and stamens fused; same number of stamens as petals; the ovary is superior or inferior with nectar glands, unilocular; the style is simple.
**Fruits** I Sticky berries often with only one seed (bird dispersal), nut fruit, berrylike drupes
**Use** I **Sandalwood** (*Santalum album*), which contains essential oils, is used for body care and for making soap and perfume as well as incense sticks; the wood is used for carving. Some species also produce edible fruits and tubers.
**Characteristics** I The leaves have cells containing silicic acid. Hardwood mistletoe (*Viscum album* **ssp.** *album*) never grows on beech trees and only rarely on oaks; the fir mistletoe (*V. album* **ssp.** *abietis*) grows on fir trees, and the pine tree mistletoe (*Viscum laxum*) on pines.

SANTALACEAE

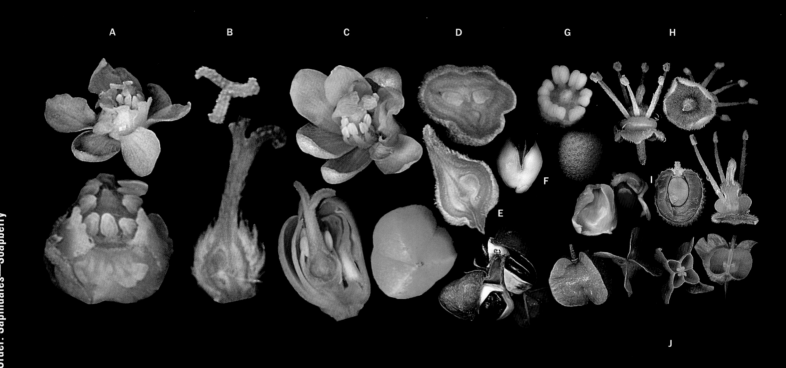

**A–B:** *Paulinia mamarae.* A: *Above,* flower, lateral; *below,* young opened flower. B: *Above,* stigma, frontal; *below,* ovary, longitudinal.

**C–F:** *Paulinia cupana.* C: *Above,* flower, frontal; *beneath it,* bud, longitudinal. D: Young fruit; *above,* transverse; *beneath it,* longitudinal. E: *Left,* fruit, frontal; *right,* opened. F: Seed with aril, lateral.

**G–I:** *Litchi sinensis.* G: Opened bud. H: *Left,* flower, lateral; *right,* underside; *beneath it,* flower, longitudinal. I: *Left,* fruit, lateral; *right,* longitudinal; *left,* next to it, seeds with arils.

**J:** *Dodonaea ptarmicifolia. From left:* fruit, lateral; *center left,* frontal; *center right,* transverse; *far right,* longitudinal.

**Subfamilies** I Aceroideae (110 species, *see below*), Hippocastanoideae (4 genera, 130 species, *see below*), Sapindoideae (135 genera, 1,185 species), Dodonaeoideae (20 genera, about 161–167 species), Xanthoceroideae (1 genus, 1 species)

**Genera** I About 135, with about 1,185 species (Sapindoideae)

**Distribution** I Pantropical, especially in the tropics and subtropics of South America, Africa, and Asia, as well as Australia, New Zealand, and Oceania; only a few in the Northern Hemisphere (*Acer*)

**Habit** I Trees, shrubs, lianas, herbaceous climbing plants. Evergreen or deciduous.

**Leaves** I Alternate, spiral arrangement, or rarely opposite, foliage leaves are petiolate. Leaf blade: rarely simple and undivided, most are compound, then palmate and lobed, digitate or pinnate.

**Inflorescences** I Paniculate, racemose, bundled or solitary, in axils, terminal, pseudoterminal, cauliflorous or ramiflorous

**Flowers** I Mostly small, (tetramerous-)pentamerous (fig. B); sepals free or basally fused (fig. C; Aceraceae); petals whitish or greenish yellow, usually with an adaxial appendage (fig. A); hermaphroditic, but mostly androgynous, since functionally unisexual; usually with disc (fig. H), (3–) 5–8 (–30) stamens; superior ovary fused from (1–) 3–8 carpels (fig. E, fruit habit), carpels with 1–2 (rarely many) ovules.

**Fruits** I A great variety, such as capsules (*Aesculus, Koelreuteria, Dodonaea*; fig. J), drupes, schizocarps (*Acer*; fig. G in Aceraceae), samaras (*Dipteronia*); seeds often have an aril or sarcotesta.

**Use** I The juicy arils of various species are edible, such as **ackee** (*Blighia sapida*), **lychee** (*Litchi chinensis*) (fig. I), **longan** (*Dimocarpus longan*), and **rambutan** (*Nephelium lappaceum*). The caffeine-containing seeds of **guarana** (*Paulinia cupana*; figs. C–E) are marketed as a dietary supplement due to their stimulating and hunger-suppressing effects and are added to energy drinks. There are well-known ornamental plants in several genera (*Koelreutheria, Dodonaea, Xanthoceras*).

**Characteristics** I The transition from insect to wind pollination is associated with a tendency to develop unisexual and severely reduced flowers. The common feature of all Sapindaceae is that originally they grew a disc at the base of the flower. It is absent in the species that use secondary wind pollination. The four subfamilies are distinguished by the structure of the ovary: Sapindoideae with one, Hippocastanoideae with two, Dodonaeoideae with two to several, and Xanthoceroideae with 6–8 ovules per carpel.

**Notes** I The maples and horse-chestnut family were formerly classified each as their own family (Aceraceae and Hippocastanaceae), but in accordance with APG III, both are now classified as a subfamily.

**A–D:** *Acer platanoides.* A: Leafy shoot with young fruits. B: Flower, frontal. C: Flower, underside. D: Flower, longitudinal.

**E–F:** *Acer platanoides* **f.** *ruburum*. E: Young flower, husk removed. F: Ovary, longitudinal.

**G–I:** *Acer platanoides.* G: Fruit. H: Single fruit section, longitudinal. I: *Left*, seedling, lateral; *right*, frontal.

**Genus** I Aceroideae 1, species: approx. 110
**Distribution** I Northern temperate regions
**Habit** I Trees, shrubs
**Habitat** I Riparian forests, sunny rocky slopes, lower elevations, open deciduous forests
**Leaves** I Opposite, simple, palmate and lobed

**Inflorescences** I Paniculate, corymbose, racemose
**Flowers** I Radial, hermaphroditic, tetramerous-pentamerous; five sepals, more or less freely attached to the receptacle; five mostly free petals; 6–7–8 free stamens (fig. E); 2–3 carpels form the fused superior ovary, which may be enveloped by a broad, annular nectary (figs. D, E); one style

with two distinct style arms (figs. B, E). Tendency to grow unisexual and at times greatly reduced flowers in the transition from insect to wind pollination.
**Fruits** I Winged schizocarp fruits (fig. G); the wings are horizontal or at a sharp/blunt angle.
**Use** I **Maple** species as ornamental roadside trees

**Notes** I Aceraceae (maple family) and Hippocastanaceae (horse-chestnut family) were formerly separate families and have now been assigned to the Sapindaceae.

SAPINDACEAE

SOAPBERRY FAMILY (including Aceraceae • MAPLE FAMILY and Hippocastanaceae HORSE-CHESTNUT FAMILY)
Order: Sapindales—Soapberry

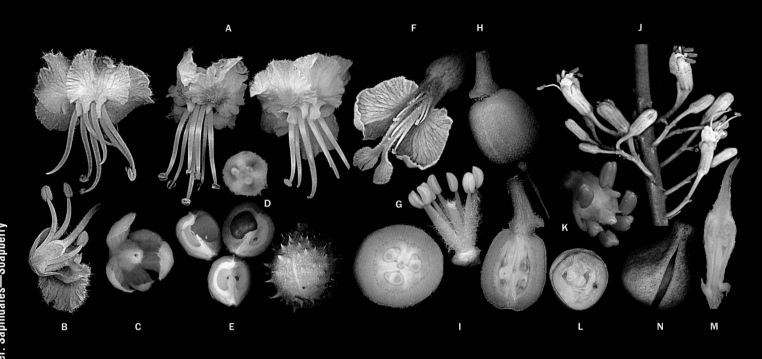

**A–E:** *Aesculus hippocastanum.* A: Three flowers of various ages from an inflorescence; youngest at left, the oldest flower at center. B: Flower, longitudinal. C: Calyx and ovary. D: Ovary, transverse. E: Fruit; *left*, open; *right*, lateral.

**F–I:** *Aesculus flava.* F: Flower, frontal. G: Androecium and ovary. H: Young fruit. I: The same; *left*, transverse; *right*, longitudinal.

**J–N:** *Aesculus parviflora.* J: Partial inflorescence. K: From a bud: Androecium and gynoecium. L: Ovary, transverse. M: Ovary, longitudinal. N: Fruit, lateral.

**Genus** | 1, Hippocastanoideae; species: about 13

**Distribution** | Northern temperate regions

**Habit** | Deciduous trees, shrubs, open deciduous forests

**Habitats** | Riparian forests, sunny rocky slopes, such as in mountains of the Balkan Peninsula

**Leaves** | Opposite, simple or compound, quinate-nonate digitate, palmate and pinnate; leaflets are 8–35 cm long, stipules absent.

**Inflorescences** | Paniculate, racemose

**Flowers** | Radial to zygomorphic, hermaphroditic, also unisexual, dioecious, tetramerous-pentamerous; five sepals, attached more or less freely to the receptacle; five usually free unguiculate petals of unequal length; 6–7–8 free, usually long projecting stamens; three carpels form the fused, superior ovary, which may be enveloped by a broad, annular nectary; one style with a small capitate stigma or two distinct style arms (Aceraceae).

**Fruits** | Capsules, up to 7 cm long, coarsely or lightly spiny

**Use** | Ornamental and roadside trees: the **red horse-chestnut** (*Aesculus × carnea*). The **red buckeye** (*Aesculus pavia*), native to North America, is poisonous and has no sticky buds.

**Notes** | Aceraceae (maple family) and Hippocastanaceae (horse-chestnut family) were formerly separate families and have now been assigned to the Sapindaceae.

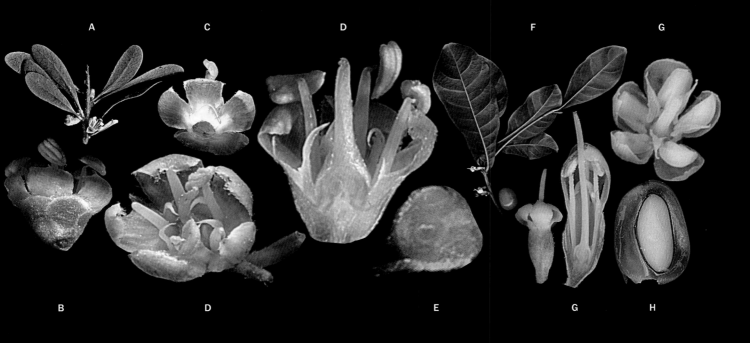

A  C  D  F  G

B  D  E  G  H

**A–E:** *Argania spinosa.* A: Leafy branch with flowers. B: Flower, lateral. C: Detached corolla lateral from underneath. D: *Left*, flower, frontal; *right*, next to it, the same, longitudinal. E: Ovary, transverse.

**F–H:** *Synsepalum dulcificum.* F: Leafy branch with flowers and 1 fruit. G: Flower; *left*, lateral; *center*, longitudinal; *right*, frontal. H: Fruit, longitudinal.

**Genera** I More than 50; species: more than 1,100

**Distribution** I Pantropical, possibly originating from Southeast Asia

**Habits** I Usually evergreen woody plants

**Habitat** I Lowland and mountain rainforests

**Leaves** I Mostly spiral arrangement, alternate, rarely almost opposite, simple, entire, with or without deciduous stipules; the petiole, often with channels or cavities, can be winged.

**Inflorescences** I Flowers often in axillary tufts (fig. A), also cauliflorous

**Flowers** I Radial, hermaphroditic, rarely unisexual; 4–6 (–8) sepals often in two whorls, rarely spiral arrangement, often fused at the base; the corolla, which is usually fragrant, of 4–8 (9–18) also divided petals, is fused; stamens in 1–3 whorls to 4–5, usually six times as many stamens as petals; the outer ones can be transformed into staminodes; 4–12 carpels form the locular superior ovary; simple style; stigma is unremarkable.

**Fruits** I Berries (fig. F), rarely leathery and bursting open; drupes, capsule fruits with usually large black-brown shiny seeds (fig. H)

**Use** I Gutta-percha, harvested from the latex of the **gutta-percha tree** (*Pala quin gutta*), is used for medical purposes, but also to insulate cables; latex from the **sapodilla tree** (*Manilkara zapota*) is used to make chewing gum (chicle), and the tree also provides edible fruit, as does the **star apple tree** (*Chrysophyllum cainito*) or the **mamey sapote** (*Pouteria sapota*). The trees are also used as a wood source, such as *Sideroxylon* sp. ("ironwood"). The oil-containing fruit of the **argan tree** (*Argania spinosa*) provide an edible oil that is laboriously produced by Moroccan women by

hand. The seeds of the **shea butter tree** (*Vitellaria paradoxa*) are the source of shea butter; it is edible but is also used to make cosmetics.

**Characteristics** I Hairs have two arms; the flowers of many species open at night: bat pollination can occur. The fruit of the **miracle fruit** (*Synsepalum dulcificum*; figs. F, H) produce the glycoprotein miraculin. It influences the perception of taste, so that something acid is perceived to taste sweet.

SARRACENIACEAE

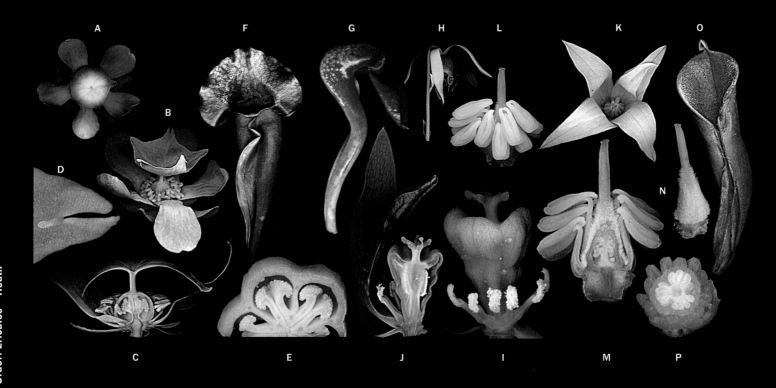

A B C D E F G H L K O J I M P N

**A–F:** *Sarracenia purpurea.* A: Flower, frontal. B: Flower, lateral. C: The same, longitudinal. D: Stigma. E: Half ovary, transverse. F: Pitcher leaf.

**G–J:** *Darlingtonia californica.* G: Pitcher leaf. H. Flower, lateral. I: Androecium and gynoecium, lateral. J: The same, longitudinal.

**K–O:** *Heliamphora pulchella.* K: Flower, frontal. L: Androecium and gynoeceum, lateral. M: The same, longitudinal. N: Gynoecium, lateral. O: Pitcher leaf.

**P:** *Heliamphora minor* ovary, transverse

**Genera** | *Heliamphora, Darlingtonia, Sarracenia*; species: 15–20
**Distribution** | North America to northern South America; *Sarracenia* has been naturalized in Switzerland.
**Habit**s | Mostly perennials, herbaceous plants, also basal rosettes
**Habitat** | Moorland
**Leaves** | Alternate, tubular, short-stemmed leaves without stipules, to trap insects (figs. F, G, O), with a thickened, specially structured margin (peristome, with internal "slipping-down zone") and a hoodlike "lid," which is usually attractively patterned and colored to attract insects. The upper inner side of the pitcher leaves may be equipped with honey glands, while the deeper part is provided with protease-secreting glands, which are used to digest trapped insects. There can be one vertical flange (ala) running along the side facing the axis; it can be doubled.
**Inflorescences** | Solitary or racemose
**Flowers** | Radial, hermaphroditic, 6–3 often-retained sepals; five or no petals; from 12 to many stamens, free or in groups (figs. L, M); five or three (fig. P) carpels are united in the superior ovary; the style is simple, either short with a fringed stigma, with five star-shaped stigmas (figs. B, D), or as a scutate structure. Prophylls are found in *Heliamphora*.
**Fruits** | Loculicidal capsule fruit usually with many seeds, which can be winged
**Characteristics** | Insect-trapping pitcher leaves; the plants may contain the alkaloid sarracenin.

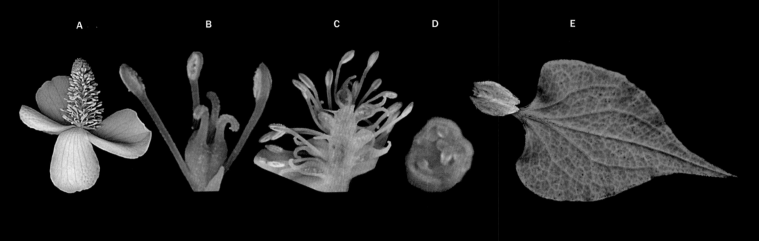

A–D: *Saururus cernuus*. A: Inflorescence with bracts, lateral. B: Single flower, lateral. C: Inflorescence, longitudinal. D: Ovary, transverse. E: Foliage leaf with fused stipules.

**Genera** I 5; species: 6. Well-known genera are *Anemopsis*, *Gymnotheca*, *Houttuynia*, *Sauurus*.

**Distribution** I Holarctic in South and Southeast Asia and North America

**Habit** I Biennial or rhizome-forming, perennial herbaceous plants

**Leaves** I Alternate or distichous, leaf blade simple, entire, also very fleshy, aromatic. Leaf base: cordiform or rounded; stipules present, fused with the petioles (fig. E)

**Inflorescences** I Terminal or racemose. Colored, petaloid bracts underneath the inflorescence serve to attract visitors (fig. A).

**Flowers** I More or less radial, hermaphroditic (fig. B), small, without perianth, mostly sessile; three, six, or eight stamens (one whorl of three, or two whorls of 3–4); androecium is either completely or partially fused with gynoecium, sometimes not fused (figs. B, C); ovaries mostly superior (inferior only in *Anemopsis*), 3–4 (–5) carpels, mostly free or fused, unilocular, (1–) 2–9 (–12) ovules per carpel.

**Fruits** I Follicle fruits, capsules, fleshy aggregate fruits (*Saururus*)

**Use** I A variegated variety of the chameleon plant (*Houttuynia cordata*) is cultivated as a garden plant, with the German name *Buntblatt* (colored leaf); "chameleon plant" in English; it is used especially as a ground cover. In East Asia, where these plants originated, the fruit, rhizomes, and leaves are eaten. Due to the aromatic substances they contain, people also use the leaves as a spice. There are supposed to be different "chemical species" that generate a wide variety of flavors, from that of fish to coriander (from China to Vietnam) to orange (from Japan).

**Characteristics** I The **lizard's tail** (*Saururus cernuus*), which comes from eastern North America (figs. A–E), is used as a marsh plant in aquaristics. Due to their robustness and qualified winter-hardiness, the species is also planted in garden ponds; as a result, this plant is considered a neophyte in Italy.

# SAXIFRAGACEAE

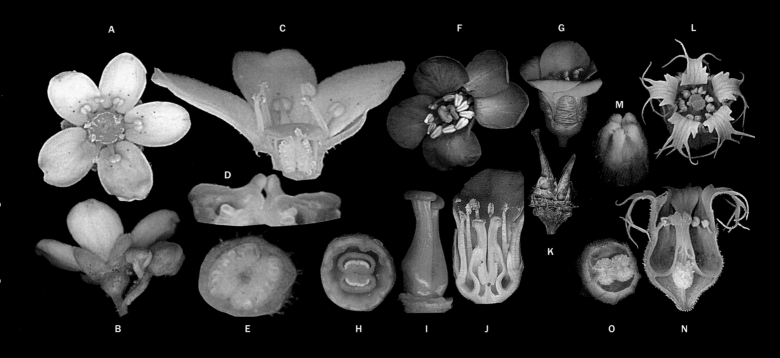

**A–E:** *Saxifraga paniculata*. A: Flower, frontal. B: Flower and buds, lateral. C: Flower, longitudinal. D: Detail: stigma and nectary, longitudinal. E: Ovary, transverse.

**F–K:** *Bergenia cordifolia*. F: Flower, frontal. G: Flower, lateral. H: Ovary, transverse, with receptacle-nectary. I: Gynoecium, lateral. J: Flower, longitudinal. K: Fruit, lateral.

**L–O:** *Tellima grandiflora*. L: Flower, frontal. M: Bud with sepals. N: Flower, longitudinal. O: Ovary, transverse.

**Genera** I 33; species: about 600
**Distribution** I Moderate regions of the Northern Hemisphere
**Habitat** I Mountain plants, also tropical mountains, Arctic. About 40 saxifrage species in the European Alps.
**Habit** I Mostly perennial herbaceous plants, rarely annuals or biennials, usually with rhizomes. Can be succulent-leaf cushion plants.
**Leaves** I Usually alternate, rarely opposite; leaf blade: simple or pinnate, petiolate or sessile; leaf margin: varies from entire margin to lobed, notched or denticulate; hydathodes frequently occur on the leaf margin; no stipules present.

**Inflorescences** I Paniculate, racemose or cymose
**Flowers** I Radial, hermaphroditic, usually pentamerous (figs. A, F, L); simple or double perianth; five sepals (figs. B, G); five petals, colored white, red, yellow, or greenish; ten stamens in two whorls; the ovary consists of two carpels, fused at the base (figs. E, H, O); however, usually free above it (fig. I, J), superior to inferior, often with disc nectary (figs. D, H); entomophily.
**Fruits** I Mostly septicidal capsules. Seeds are flung out as rain "ballistae" or are rainborne by drops of water or washed out; dispersal by animals, or can be dust seeds.

**Use** I Many ornamental plants, such as the **heart-leaved** and **leather bergenia** (*Bergenia cordifolia, B. crassifolia*), **coral bells** (*Heuchera* sp.), **rodgersia** (*Rodgersia* sp.), **foamflowers** (*Tiarella* sp.), **umbrella plant** (*Darmera peltata*), and **Chinese astilbe** (*Astilbe chinensis*). The leaves or young fruit of some poplar species are eaten or used as a tea substitute. The leaves of **lettuceleaf saxifrage** (*Saxifraga micranthidifolia*) are said to be edible raw and cooked.
**Characteristics** I The name "saxifrage" goes back to Pliny, who had already observed that some

species grow in rocky crevices, and he may therefore have thought that these plants can "break stone." As a result, the saxifrage species were also used as a remedy for bladder stones, according to the doctrine of signatures. The **golden saxifrages** (*Chrysoplenium* sp.) were used, according to this doctrine, as a remedy for diseases of the spleen, since their leaves are spleen shaped.

**A–F:** *Illicium floridanum*. A: Flower, frontal. B: Flower from underneath. C: Flower, longitudinal. D: Detail from C: carpels, longitudinal. E: Detail from A: stigma ready to be pollinated; stamens still closed. F: Detail of flower center: stamens are opened.

**G–I:** *Illicium verum*. G: Ripe fruit from underneath. H: Ripe fruit, open, from above. I: Ripe seeds; *left*, longitudinal; *right*, lateral.

# SCHISANDRACEAE

**Genera** | 3: *Schisandra, Illicium, Kadsura*, with 92 species; the best known is the star anise (*Illicium verum*).

**Distribution** | Southeast Asia, southeastern North America, Mexico

**Habit** | Trees, shrubs, lianas

**Leaves** | Alternate, evergreen, herbaceous plants, leathery or papery; leaf blade: simple and undivided, leaf margin entire or denticulate, stipules absent.

**Inflorescences** | Rarely 2–3 in the axils, or compactly clustered, usually single flowers (fig. A)

**Flowers** | Hermaphroditic or unisexual, monoecious (*Katsura, Schisandra*) or dioecious (*Illicium*). Flowers greenish, white, yellowish to reddish; 7–33 tepals, outer ones narrow, bract-like (fig. B), becoming larger toward the interior; petaloid, 4–40 stamens, free (figs. E, F) or fused together; ovary superior, of 5–21 carpels, free, arranged in a whorl (*Illicium*; figs. C–F), or of 12–300 in helical arrangement, with 1–2 ovules each. Thermogenesis may occur.

**Fruits** | Aggregate follicle fruit (figs. G, H), (aggregate) berries. The *Illicium* follicle fruit, which are fused at the base in a star shape, open in an explosion and fling out the seeds (fig. I). The red berry fruits (*Kadsura, Schisandra*) are possibly dispersed by birds.

**Use** | The **five-flavor fruit** (*Schisandra chinensis*) is used in traditional Chinese medicine. The essential oils are used in perfume making. The ripe fruits are called "five-flavor fruit" because they taste sweet, sour, bitter, spicy, and salty. The fruit of *Kadsura coccinea* are edible. The entire fruit of the **star anise** (*Illicium verum*) is used as a spice, since the pericarp is spicier than the seeds. The taste is sweetish and like licorice. Because it contains anethoil, star anise dissolves mucus and works as an expectorant.

**Characteristics** | Sometimes the fruit of the **Japanese star anise** (*Illicium anisatum*) is added to genuine star anise. The latter are poisonous because they contain shikimi toxin and may cause such diseases as kidney or liver damage.

SCHLEGELIACEAE

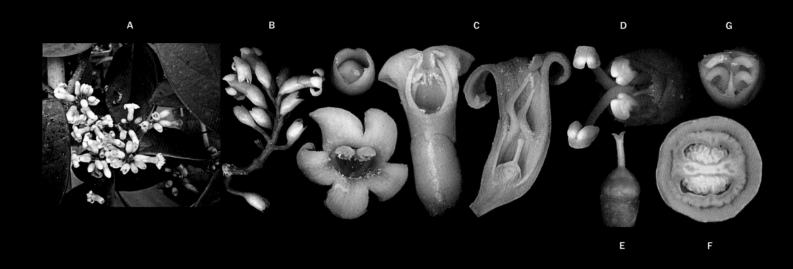

**A–G:** *Schlegelia fuscata*. A: Leafy shoot with inflorescence. B: Partial inflorescence. C: *Above left*, calyx, frontal; *beneath it*, flower, frontal; *center*, flower, lateral, parts of the corolla removed; *right*, flower, longitudinal. D: Stamen from bud. E: Gynoecium, lateral. F: Ovary, transverse. G: The fifth, reduced stamen in front of the filaments of the fertile stamens.

**Genera** I 4; species: 28
**Distribution** I Mexico to tropical South America
**Habit** I Shrubs, half shrubs, lianas
**Leaves** I More or less opposite, simple, rarely trifoliate, petiolate, entire to finely serrated, can be leathery, with pinnate venation; the veins on the underside may be slightly hairy, stipules absent.

**Inflorescences** I Solitary, cymose, racemose (fig. B), rarely in tufts
**Flowers** I Bilateral, more or less radial, pentamerous; there are five sepal lobes, which can be irregular; these are retained on the fruit; the five petals are fused into a tube or funnel shape (figs. B, C); four stamens (fig. C, *left*; fig. D), in pairs, of unequal length; filaments fused with the corolla tube,

the fifth stamen reduced to a staminode (fig G, *above*); bicarpellate ovary is superior and has many ovules; one style with simple stigmas.
**Fruits** I Many-seeded berries
**Characteristics** I Species of the genus *Schlegelia* often use their roots to climb; they can be epiphytic.

**A–E:** *Buddleja davidii.* A: Inflorescence. B: Flowers, frontal, various cultivated forms. C: Stamen. D: Gynoecium. E: Fruits, lateral; *below,* seeds.
**F–I:** *Scrophularia nodosa.* F: *Above left,* flower, frontal; *center right,* longitudinal; *below,* opened flower: gynoecium and androecium. G: Calyx and nectary, frontal. H: *Left,* gynoecium, lateral; *right,* ovary, longitudinal; *above it,* transverse. I: Capsule: *left,* lateral; *center,* seeds; *right,* fruit, lateral.
**J–L:** *Verbascum sinuatum.* J: *Left,* flower, frontal; *right,* underside; *below,* flower, longitudinal. K: Corolla, underside. L: Fruit; *left,* longitudinal; *above right,* frontal; *beneath it,* seeds.
**M–N:** *Verbsacum nigrum.* M: *Above,* flower, frontal; *below,* lateral. N: Bud, longitudinal.

**Genera** | More than 60; species: more than 1,900
**Distribution** | Worldwide
**Habit** | Herbaceous plants, perennials, shrubs
**Leaves** | Opposite, rarely alternate, leaf blade simple, undivided
**Inflorescences** | Racemose, panicles, dichasia
**Flowers** | Radial to zygomorphic, hermaphroditic; 4–5 sepals mostly free; 4–5 petals, fused, also with nectar guides (fig. B); 4–5 stamens; the filaments may have hairs of a contrasting color to the corolla (fig. J); the superior ovary is fused out of two carpels; one style with two style arms; the nectary usually grows an inconspicuous, more or less small swelling around the base of the ovary (fig. G).
**Fruits** | Capsule fruit
**Use** | Some **mulleins** (*Verbascum* species, such as great mullein, *V. thapsus*) are used as medicinal plants; their mucilage is said to be a remedy for coughs, bronchitis, and asthma.
**Twinspur** (*Diascia varieties*) and **blue bird** (*Nemesia fruticans*) are often grown as deciduous bedding plants and balcony plants or in hanging baskets.
**Characteristics** | The **butterfly bush** (*Buddleja davidii* hybrids) is cultivated as a shrub that is very attractive to insects. In some areas, however, it is spreading uncontrollably and is considered an invasive neophyte.

SCROPHULARIACEAE

225

**A–D:** *Simmondsia chinensis.* A: Leafy branch with male inflorescences. B: Partial male inflorescence. C: Foliage leaf with bud. D: Male flower; *left*, frontal; *right*, underside.

**JOJOBA FAMILY**
**Order: Caryophyllales—Carnations**

# SIMMONDSIACEAE

**Genus** I 1; species: 2; *Simmondsia californica, S. chinensis*
**Distribution** I Southwestern North America
**Habitat** I Deserts, semideserts
**Habit** I Evergreen shrub that can grow to be over 200 years old, with taproot
**Leaves** I Opposite, short petiole, simple and leathery, entire, without stipules, hairy (fig. C)
**Inflorescences** I Male flowers mostly terminal (fig. A); female flowers mostly solitary and axillary
**Flowers** I Diclinous, dioecious, male flowers with pentapetalous green husk (fig. D, *left and right*); the (4–) 5 (–6) free yellow stamens are often arranged in two whorls; the light-green female flowers have a superior, trilocular ovary of three carpels with one hanging ovule per locule.
**Fruits** I Capsule fruit
**Use** I Seeds contain jojoba oil, which contains the provitamins A and E and is used to produce cosmetics. The plants are cultivated in hedgerows several meters apart; 5% of the plants should be male; first crop after 3–5 years.
**Characteristics** I Simmondsin, which is contained in the seeds, is banned as a food additive because of its toxic effect.

A–D: *Smilax aspera*. A: Leafy, thorny branch with flowers. B: Leaf. C: Partial inflorescence. D: *Left*, male flower, frontal; *right*, two male flowers on branch, lateral; *left*, flower, longitudinal.

**Genera** | 2: *Heterosmilax*, *Smilax*; species: about 350

**Distribution** | Worldwide in the tropics and subtropics, only a few species in temperate latitudes

**Habit** | Evergreen, woody or herbaceous plants; stems often armed with thorns (*Smilax*; fig. A) and climbs as an "incumbent climber" or rambler, with rhizomes or tubers as overwintering organs.

**Leaves** | Alternate, petiole present; there can be tendrils attached to the base; leaf blade: simple, undivided, entire, linear, lanceolate to ovate, occasionally spiny (fig. B).

**Inflorescences** | Lateral (fig. C), paniculate, racemose, spicate, addorsed (back to back); bracteole can occur, also single flowers.

**Flowers** | Radial, unisexual, mostly dioecious, small single flowers, trimerous; six tepals in two whorls of three, tepals of the same or a different structure, free or more or less fused; male flowers: usually six stamens in two whorls of three, free (fig. D); female flowers with staminodes; the superior ovary usually consists of three fused carpels; style is free or fused; three stigmas. Entomophily.

**Fruits** | Berry

**Use** | The rhizomes of various *Smilax* species were formerly used to treat syphilis. Today it is occasionally still used in homeopathy under the names "sarsaparilla / Sassaparilla officinalis" and taken in the form of globules to treat such problems as bladder infections.

**Characteristics** | The German name for the greenbrier family, Stechwinden, or "twining stingers," comes from the thorny, stinging stems of many species. The presence of saponins is a family characteristic.

# SOLANACEAE

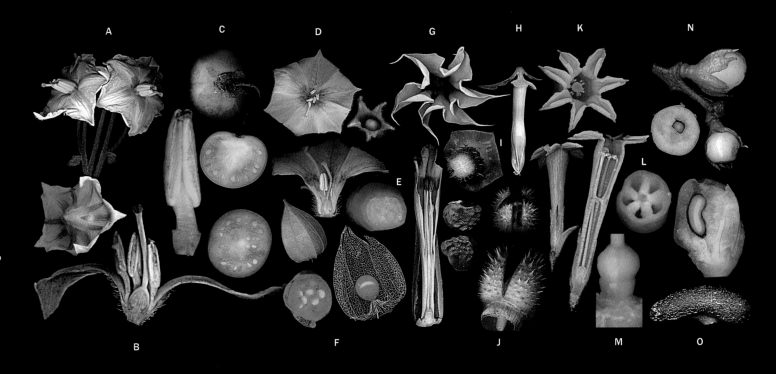

A B C D E F G H I J K L M N O

**A–C:** *Solanum tuberosum*. A: *Above*, flowers, lateral; *center*, from underneath; *below*, longitudinal. B: Porate stamen. C: *Above*, fruit. *center*, longitudinal; *below*, transverse.

**D–F:** *Physalis alkekengi*. D: *Above*, flower, frontal; *below*, longitudinal; *right*, calyx with ovary. E: Ovary, transverse. F: *Above left*, fruit in a calyx; *below*, transverse; *right*, in remnant of calyx.

**G–J:** *Datura stramonium*. G: *Above*, flower, frontal; *beneath it*, longitudinal. H: Bud, lateral. I: Ovary in the calyx, transverse. J: *Above right*, fruit, frontal; *below*, lateral, left seeds.

**K–O:** *Cestrum angustifolia*. K: *Above*, flower, frontal; *left*, lateral; *right*, longitudinal. L: Corolla with "entry barrier." M: Ovary/nectar ring. N: *Above right*, fruits; *left*, transverse; *below*, longitudinal. O: Seed.

**Genera** I More than 100; species: more than 2,400
**Distribution** I Worldwide; concentrated in Central and South America
**Habit** I Herbaceous plants, perennials, rarely woody plants
**Leaves** I Alternate, undivided, without stipules
**Inflorescences** I Scorpioid cymes or single flowers
**Flowers** I Mostly radial, hermaphroditic; calyx and corolla usually pentamerous (fig. D); the stamens open through apical pores ("poricidial anthers"; fig. B); ovaries usually of two carpels (fig. C, *below*).
**Fruits** I Berries, capsule fruits
**Use** I **Tomatoes** (*Solanum lycopersicum*), **eggplant** (*Solanum melongena*), **potatoes** (*Solanum tuberosum*), **peppers** (*Capsicum annuum*), **tobacco** (*Nicotiana tabacum*), the **Peruvian groundcherry** (*Physalis peruviana*). Ornamental plants, such as the Chinese lantern (*Physalis alkekengi*).
**Characteristics** I Many wild species are highly toxic because they contain phytochemicals (such as steroids, alkaloids) that are highly poisonous. These plants include **black henbane** (*Hyoscyamus niger*), **tobacco** (*Nicotiana tabacum*), **belladonna** (*Atropa belladonna*), **daturas** (*Datura* sp.), **angel's trumpet** (*Brugmansia* sp.), **shoofly plant** (*Nicandra physalodes*), and **mandrake** (*Mandragora officinarum*). They have often been used as herbs for witchcraft and can have a hallucinogenic effect; any inexact dosage can easily be fatal. In the **Chinese lantern** (*Physalis alkekengi*), the calyx grows larger as the fruit ripens and turns a bright red (fig. F, *above left*).

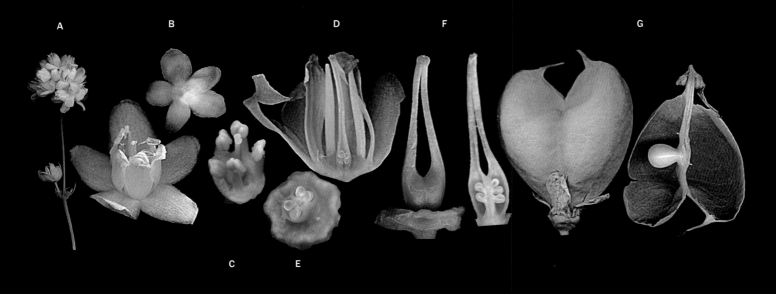

**A–G:** *Staphylea pinnata.* A: Inflorescence. B: Flower, frontal; *right*, above it, underside. C: Young androecium from a bud around style/stigma, frontal. D: Flower, longitudinal. E: Ovary, transverse, with surrounding nectary. F: *Left*, gynoecium, lateral; *right*, next to it, the same, longitudinal. G: Fruit; *left*, lateral; *next to it at right*, the same, longitudinal.

**Genera** | 3 (2–5); species: about 45–60
**Distribution** | Worldwide
**Habit** | Shrubs
**Habitat** | Waysides
**Leaves** | Opposite or alternate, tripinnate to multiply pinnate, with stipules in pairs
**Inflorescences** | Racemose panicles, at times with long petioles

**Flowers** | Radial, hermaphroditic or sometimes unisexual, pentamerous; the five sepals are often petaloid; the five free petals can grow like a tube around the pentamerous androecium; 4–3–2 carpels form the superior, more or less fused ovary, with one to several ovules per locule on axile placentas; each carpel with style and stigma more or less fused in the upper area or can

be free (fig. F). An undulated glandular tissue around the base of the ovary generates the nectar (fig. E).
**Fruits** | Follicles, which can be more or less basally fused, (inflated) capsule, indehiscent fruit; the seeds have an oily endosperm and can grow an aril.
**Use** | Ornamental plants; the fruit are used locally for medical purposes. The fruit of *Euscaphis japonica* are also

used as a drug.
**Characteristics** | The plants can accumulate calcium oxalate crystals; alkaloids are often present. The German name for the bladdernut species (*Staphylea* sp.), *Pimpernuss*, comes from the plants' "pimples."

STRELITZIACEAE

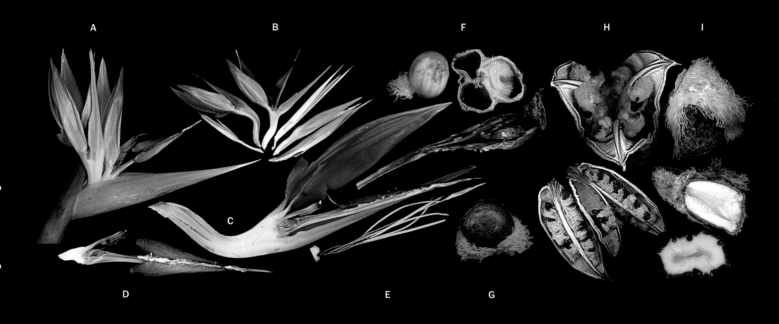

A–G: *Strelitzia reginae*. A: Inflorescence, lateral. B: The same, dissected into parts. C: Single flower, longitudinal. D: Inner blue perianth whorl: *left*, a bract covers the entryway to the nectar; the two at right are sagittate and fused and envelope the stamens and style. E: Stamens. F: *Below*, fruit, lateral; *above it*, transverse; *left*, next to it, seeds with aril. G: Ripe seed with aril, lateral.

H–I: *Strelitzia nicolai*. H: Opened capsule; *below*, open, longitudinal. I: *Above*, seed with aril; *center*, longitudinal; *below*, transverse.

**Genera** I 3: *Phenakospermum, Ravenala, Strelitzia*; species: 7
**Distribution** I Tropical South America (*Phenakospermum*), Madagascar (*Ravenala*), both monotypic genera; eastern South Africa (*Strelitzia*, 5 species)
**Habit** I Perennials, multiannual herbaceous plants with underground rhizomes; at times, treelike "giant perennials" that grow up to 15 meters tall (*Ravenala*), but not lignified.
**Leaves** I Alternate, distichous; structure: leaf sheath, longer petiole, leaf blade very large, banana-like, simple, linear, with a thick midrib and lateral nervation, entire
**Inflorescences** I Terminal or lateral, scorpioid cymes with cymbiform bract

(fig. A) with several single flowers growing in its axil
**Flowers** I Zygomorphic, hermaphroditic; trimerous—two whorls with three involucral bracts each, free in the outer whorl, with the same or a different structure, the two lateral ones of the inner whorl modified into a hastate hull around the style or also the stamens (in *Strelitzia*) (fig D). Two whorls with originally six fertile stamens (*Ravenala*); all the others have only five (fig. E); no staminodes; the inferior ovary is fused from three carpels; many ovules per locule, axile, with septal nectaries. Pollination by birds (*Strelitzia*), bats (*Phenakospermum*), lemurs (*Ravenala*).
**Fruits** I Woody, loculicidal capsule

(figs. F, H), seeds with colored arils (*Strelitzia*: yellow orange [figs. G, I]; *Phenakospermum*: red; *Ravenala*: blue). Dispersal by birds.
**Use** I The unripe seeds of the **white bird-of-paradise tree** (*Strelitzia nicolai*; fig. F) and the **traveler's tree** (*Ravenala madagascariensis*) are edible; the seeds can be made into flour. People eat the young leaves of the latter, while older leaves are used for roofing. Both species, as well as other *Strelitzia*, are cultivated as ornamental plants in tropical and subtropical gardens. The folding mechanism of the **bird-of-paradise** (*S. reginae*) flowers became the model for a bionic invention: a nonhinged sunshade or blind system.

**Characteristics** I The name *Strelitzia* refers to Queen Charlotte, a native of Mecklenburg-Strelitz and the wife of King George III. The name "**bird-of-paradise flower**" refers to the flower's colors. Water accumulates in the narrow, boat-shaped leaf bases of the **traveler's tree**; thirsty travelers were said to pierce the leaf base to get at the water so they could drink it. The fact is, however, that protozoa and other dead animals also live in this water. Therefore, drinking this water is not recommended.

A–F: *Stylidium debile (= Candollea debile).* A: Habit; *left*, lateral; *above right*, leaf rosette, frontal. B: Flower, lateral; *center*, flower, frontal; *right*, rotated 90°. C: Bud; *left*, frontal; *right*, longitudinal. D: Flower, frontal, gynostemium with stigma. E: Calyx with ovary, transverse. F: Gynostemium underside with anthers.

**Genera** | 6; species: about 240
**Distribution** | Australia, New Zealand, South America, sometimes Southeast Asia
**Habit** | Rarely shrubs, usually annual to perennial herbaceous plants
**Habitats** | Some are adapted to drier locations but also can be moorland plants.
**Leaves** | Alternating, basal rosettes (fig. A, *above*: plant about 25 cm tall), leaf blade simple and undivided, without stipules

**Inflorescences** | Racemose to paniculate
**Flowers** | Zygomorphic, hermaphroditic or unisexual, monoecious, dioecious; calyx is more or less bilabiate (fig. E) and corolla mostly pentamerous, with one of the petals very small and pointing downward (fig. B, *right*); nectar guides present. Calyx and petals may be externally covered with capitate glandular hairs (fig. B, *right*); 2 (–3) stamens, often united with the style

into a column-like unit (gynostemium; fig. B), with the anthers pointed up and the undivided or bilobate, papillose, hairy stigma pointing down. The inferior ovary consists of two fused carpels and has many ovules.
**Fruits** | Bivalved capsules
**Use** | Ornamental plants
**Characteristics** | The **triggerplants** (*Stylidium* sp.) use their gynostemium to "strike" visitors to the flower. The column is touch-sensitive: as soon as a visitor lands on

the flower in the male stage, within milliseconds the gynostemium is "shot," with the pollen, onto the insect's body. If the flower is already in its female phase, the stigma has grown out of the column and can accept pollen that an insect has brought to it.

**A–G:** *Tacca integrifolia*. A: Habit with filiform elongated bracts. B: Foliage leaf. C: Flower, frontal. D: Stamens; *above*, longitudinal; *below*, frontal. E: *Left*, flower, longitudinal; *center*, ovary, transverse; *right*, beside it, flower and bud, lateral. F: Fruit; *above*, longitudinal; *below right*, transverse. G: *Left*, seeds, lateral; *right*, longitudinal.

**Genus** | 1: *Tacca* (occasionally the monotypic genus *Schizocapsa* is separated from *Tacca* because of the different fruit morphology and the anatomy of the stomata); species: 31

**Distribution** | Subtropical, tropical (tropical Asia, Africa, Madagascar, Melanesia)

**Habit** | Perennial herbaceous plants with starchy rhizomes

**Leaves** | Basal, alternate, spiral arrangement; leaf blade: entire, simple and undivided or compound—if simple, then lanceolate to ovate (fig. B), and if divided, then pinnatipartite or palmate, petiolate

**Inflorescences** | Terminal, umbellate, consisting of groups of scorpioid cymes, with up to 18 single flowers, surrounded by (1–) 4 (–12) leaflike bracts, several of which are conspicuously long and filiform (fig. A)

**Flowers** | Radial (fig. C), hermaphroditic, trimerous; six tepals in two whorls; campanulate perigone tube, green, purple, brown; six fertile stamens in two whorls or three outer fertile stamens and three inner staminodes, diplostemonous; stamens in the lower section are fused with the tepals (fig. D); the inferior ovary is from three carpels (fig. E); one style, short with three petaloid stigma lobes. Entomophily, pollination by flies or autogamous.

**Fruits** | Capsule, berry (fig. F)

**Use** | The stem tubers of some species are used for their starch content, such as **Polynesian arrowroot** (*Tacca leontopetaloides*), **white batflower** (*T. integrifolia*), and **black batflower** (*T. chantrieri*). However, since they contain a large amount of bitter substances, these tubers must first be washed in water repeatedly. In addition to being used as bread flour, they also used supply laundry starch.

**Characteristics** | The Italian architect and sculptor Pietro Tacca (1577–1640), who created the first equestrian statue with a rearing horse (Phillip IV, Madrid), gave these plants his name. The plants contain the steroid saponins (diosgenin), flavonoid glycosides, and tropane alkaloids.

A–F: *Talinum* **sp**. A: Dichasial inflorescence; *below left*, leaves. B: *Left*, flower, frontal; *right*, the same, longitudinal.
C: Underside of flower. D: Stigma, frontal. E: Gynoecium, lateral. F: Ovary; *above*, longitudinal; *below*, transverse.

**TALINACEAE**

**Genera** I 3; species: more than 25
**Distribution** I Neotropics, Africa, Asia, Madagascar
**Habit** I Shrubs, half shrubs, annual to perennial herbaceous plants, also climbing species; can have root tubers

**Leaves** I Alternate, often slightly fleshy, two scales per axil, ± deciduous
**Inflorescences** I Dichasial
**Flowers** I Radial, hermaphroditic; usually two sepals (fig. C); five free petals (fig. B); 5–15 stamens; the usually tricarpellate ovary is superior,

unilocular, with central placenta (figs. E–F); the stylet spreads apart at the top into three style arms (fig. D).
**Fruits** I Capsule fruit
**Characteristics** I Some species are CAM plants, other C3 plants. Tannin-containing cells are present.

**Comments** I Until 2001, the family belonged to the portulaca family (Portulacaceae).

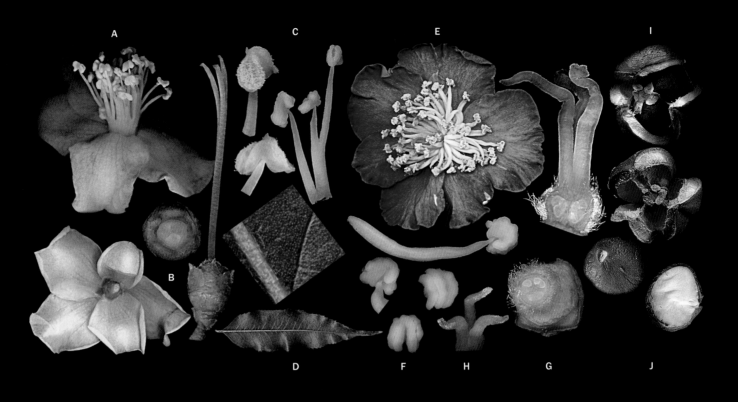

**A–D:** *Camellia tsai*. A: *Above*, flower, lateral, underside beneath it. B: *Left*, ovary, transverse; *right*, lateral, with calyx. C: Opened and unopened stamens. D: *Below*, foliage leaf, detail above it.

**E–H:** *Camellia sasquana*. E: Flower, frontal. F: Stamens. G: *Above*, ovary, longitudinal; *beneath it*, transverse. H: Stigma.

**I–J:** *Camellia japonica*. I: *Above*, open fruit with seeds, emptied below. J: Seed; *left*, lateral; *right*, longitudinal.

**Genera** I 7; species: more than 190
**Distribution** I Southeast Asia, tropical and subtropical zones of the Americas
**Habits** I Often evergreen trees, shrubs, rarely climbing plants
**Habitat** I Often mountain forests, undergrowth
**Leaves** I Usually alternate, often evergreen, leathery, rarely deciduous, leaf margin often serrated, without stipules
**Inflorescences** I Solitary in leaf axils, 1–4 in short shoots, rarely paniculate, also with bracts
**Flowers** I Radial, hermaphroditic, tetramerous-septamerous; 4–7 sepals, free or basally fused; between four and very many petals, but mostly five, free or basally fused, whorled to spiral arrangement; the 10 or more (at times very many) stamens are free or basally fused (figs. D, E); the superior ovary consists of 3–5 (–10) carpels, often fused only at the base; style free or fused with three style arms (fig. B, *above*; fig. F; fig. G, *above*).
**Fruits** I Capsules (fig. H), drupes, berries; seeds can be winged.
**Use** I The leaves of *Camellia sinensis* supply tea; other species also harvested for edible oils; many camellia species are planted as ornamental shrubs.
**Characteristics** I Bark and leaves often have branched or rounded sclereids. Sepals and petals can merge with each other. The leaves may accumulate aluminum ions.

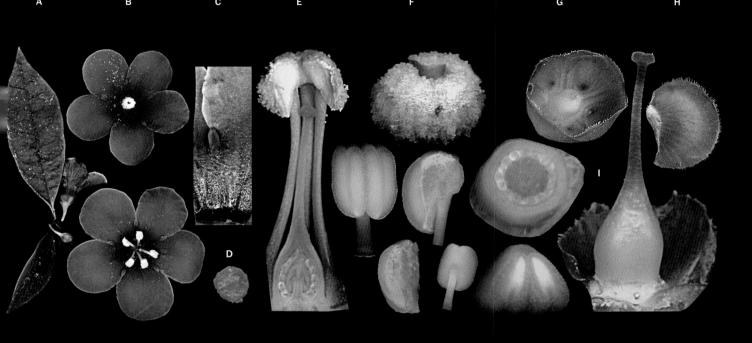

**A–I:** *Deherainia smaragdina.* A: Leafy branch with flowers, lateral. B: Flower; *above*, male phase; *below*, female phase, C: Staminode in the petals' growth area. D: Stigma, frontal. E: Androecium and gynoecium, longitudinal. F: *Above*, anthers with several different pollens; *center left*, stamen from the front; *right*, next to it, longitudinal; *beneath it at left*, anther longitudinal; *right*, next to it, rear side; *far right*, frontal; view of superior, still-closed pollen sacs. G: Calyx; frontal with gynoecium in the center. H: Single detached sepal. I: *Right*, gynoecium, lateral; *left*, ovary, transverse.

**Genera** I About 6–9; species: more than 100

**Distribution** I Tropical Americas, West Indies, Hawaii

**Habits** I Small trees, shrubs, also tall, mostly woody plants

**Habitat** I Usually in coastal habitats

**Leaves** I Rarely opposite, often crowded in tufts at the ends of the branches, simple (fig. A), often with subepidermal sclerenchyma, often dotted with glands

**Inflorescences** I Racemose, corymbose, scorpioid cymes, paniculate, rarely cauliflorous

**Flowers** I Radial, hermaphroditic or unisexual, can be protanderous; five sepals are free or basally fused; five petals fused into a wheel-, funnel-, or urn-shaped corolla; 5–10 stamens, which can open inward; often also five staminodes as episepalous staminode whorl.

**Fruits** I Berries, mostly dry, rarely drupes, but can be five-valved capsules, often with large yellow or orange-red seeds.

**Use** I Some species of *Jacquinia* are used as fish poison; others are considered to be characteristic sandy ocean beach plants in the Antilles; ornamental plants.

**Characteristics** I Capitiform glandular hairs. The stamens of the **emerald flower** (*Deherainia smaragdina*) have pollen sacs with extra chambers; the upper release white pollen, while the lower ones release yellow pollen during different phases (figs. B, E–F). Using a magnifying glass, you can recognize subepidermal fibers in the dried foliage leaves.

**Notes** I The Theophrastaceae have meanwhile been assigned to the Primulaceae family as a subfamily.

THYMELAEACEAE

**A–D:** *Phaleria capitata.* A: Leafy branch with inflorescence and 1 fruit. B: Partial inflorescence, lateral. C: *Above*, flower, frontal: *below*, longitudinal. D: *Left*, ripe fruit; *right*, next to it, longitudinal; *below*, seeds.

**E–H:** *Passerina filiformis.* E: Leafy branch with flowers. F: Partial inflorescence. G: *Left*, flower, frontal; *right*, next to it, lateral; *above*, underside of calyx. H: Stamens from bud.

**I–L:** *Edgeworthia chrysantha.* I: Inflorescence, longitudinal. J: *Left*, flower, frontal; *right*, the same, longitudinal. K: Unfurled corolla with 2 whorls of stamens. L: *Left*, gynoecium, lateral; *center*, ovary, transverse; *right*, the same, longitudinal.

**Genera** I More than 45; species: more than 750

**Distribution** I Worldwide, temperate subtropical regions in Australia and Africa

**Habitat** I Rocky, dry soil; calcareous soils; mountain forests

**Habit** I Shrubs, rarely herbaceous plants, rarely lianas

**Leaves** I Alternate, opposite, whorled, simple and undivided; can be leathery, linear, evergreen or deciduous

**Inflorescences** I Axillary, racemose, terminal, and capitiform; also, cauliflorous (*Phaleria*) bracts may be present.

**Flowers** I Radial, hermaphroditic or unisexual, monoecious or dioecious, tetramerous-pentamerous; tubular receptacle; petaloid calyx; merging with the hypanthium at the base; petals absent or reduced to scales; 4–5 (–11–35) stamens, often in two whorls, attached to the corolla tube at the base; the unilocular ovary is superior; disc.

**Fruits** I Nut fruit, drupe, berry

**Use** I Ornamental plants, such as **February daphne** (*Daphne mezereum*), which blooms before the plant starts to leaf. For harvesting wood, incense.

**Characteristics** I The **daphne** is poisonous! The plants often have an aromatic fragrance. Its flowers grow directly from the stem.

A                    B                                                              C

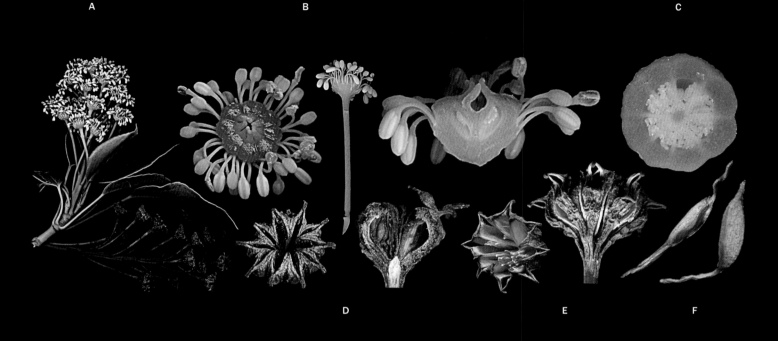

D                                        E              F

**A–F:** *Trochodendron aralioides*. A: Leafy branch with flowers and fruiting stage. B: *Left*, flower, frontal; *center*, the same, lateral; *right*, longitudinal. C: Ovary, transverse. D: *Left*, opened fruit, frontal; *right*, longitudinal, with seed. E: *Left*, fruit, frontal, after winter; *right*, next to it, lateral. F: Seed.

**Genera** | 2; with 2 species: *Tetracentron sinense, Trochodendron aralioides*
**Distribution** | Laurel forests of Asia
**Habit** | Trees or shrubs, up to 15 meters tall
**Leaves** | Alternate; in *Trochodendron*, tufted at the end of the shoot, deciduous or evergreen, leaf blade entire, ovate to cordiform or obovate, base wedge-shaped or cordiform, leathery, leaf margin denticulate, long and petiolate; reticulate venation, stipules present (*Tetracentron sinense*) or absent (*Trochodendron aralioides*)

**Inflorescences** | Terminal, cymosee to racemose (fig. A; *T. aralioides*) or catkins (*Tetracentron sinense*)
**Flowers** | Radial, hermaphroditic or unisexual, *T. aralioides* can be androdiecious (there are hermaphroditic and male flowers); 1–2 mm (*T. sinense*) or 1 cm (*T. aralioides*) in diameter; long and petiolate; free perianth (composed of four small, narrow bracts/tepals [*T. sinense*]) or absent (*T. aralioides*); nectaries present, four (*T. sinense*) or many (40–100; *T. aralioides*); stamens free, spiral, in *T. aralioides* arranged on a broad, greenish disc (fig. B); four (*T. sinense*) or (4–) 6–11 (–17) (*T. aralioides*) carpels, apocarpous or syncarpous (laterally fused at the base); superior ovary; marginal placentation (fig. C); 5–6 (*T. sinense*) or many (*T. aralioides*) ovules per carpel. Entomophily.
**Fruits** | (Syncarpous) follicle fruit in *T. aralioides*, with the receptacle fused into an aggregate fruit (figs. D, E). Flattened seeds (fig. F).
**Use** | The **wheel tree** (*Trochodendron aralioides*) and the **tetracentron** (*Tetracentron sinense*) are occasionally cultivated in arboretums as rare specimens.
**Characteristics** | The wood of these plants lacks the trachea that are the typical water-conducting structures in most other angiosperms. Because the flowers of the wheel tree look similar to those of some of the *Aralias*, these plants were given the specific name *aralioides*. The fruit, which look like the spokes of a wheel, is the source of its common name.

TROPAEOLACEAE

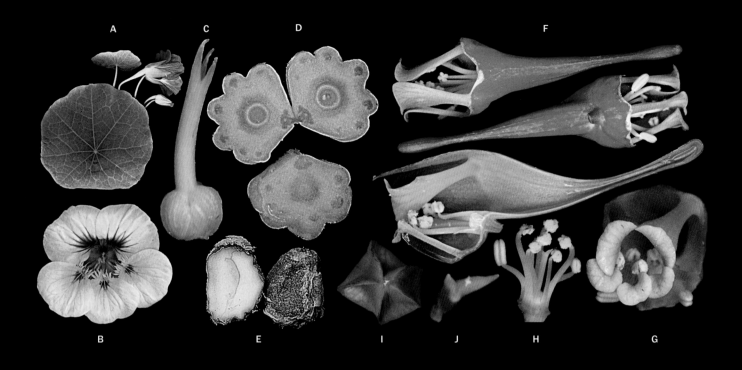

**A–E:** *Tropaeolum majus*. A: Scutate leaves and shrubs, lateral. B: Flower, frontal. C: Gynoecium, lateral. D: Ovary, transverse. E: Seed; *left*, longitudinal; *right*, lateral.

**F–J:** *Tropaeolum tricolor*. F: Upper side of flower; *center*, underside; *beneath it*, longitudinal. G: Blossom, frontal. H: Androecium. I: Bud, frontal. J: Stigma.

**Genus** I 1: Tropaeolum; species: 95
**Distribution** I The Americas
**Habitat** I Mountains
**Habit** I Herbaceous plants, also trailing or climbing, at times with root tubers
**Leaves** I Alternate, can be opposite in lower part, scutate (fig. A), also divided in "pseudowhorls," palmate and cleft; the petioles of the twining species can be touch-sensitive; stipules absent.
**Inflorescences** I Solitary in leaf axils
**Flowers** I Zygomorphic, hermaphroditic, with spur (figs. A, F); mostly with five free sepals, one of which forms the spur; five free, often-unguiculate petals of differing sizes, with the upper ones usually smaller; eight stamens; three fused carpels form the superior ovary; one style with three stigma tips (fig. C).
**Fruits** I Schizocarp fruit in three single-seeded indehiscente fruits (fig. D)
**Use** I All parts of the **nasturtium** (*Tropaeolum majus*) are edible: it tastes like horseradish (glucosinolates); unripe fruits can be preserved in brine as a substitute for capers. Worldwide as ornamental plants.
**Characteristics** I As happens on lotus flowers, water forms drops or "beads" on the surfaces of the leaves ("lotus effect"). For the nasturtium, however, this is only because of the leaves' waxy surface, while lotus flowers have additional nobby structures.

**A–E:** *Ulmus laevis.* A: Inflorescences. B: *Left and below*, flower, lateral; *center*, with calyx removed; *right*, gynoecium. C: Asymmetrical foliage leaf. D: *Above left*, fruit, longitudinal; *center*, lateral; *below*, transverse; *below*, seeds. E: Leaves growing from a bud.

**Genera** | More than 6–7; species: more than 30

**Distribution** | Worldwide, northern temperate latitudes, tropical and subtropical latitudes

**Habitat** | Lowlands, riparian forests, forests

**Habit** | Woody plants without milky sap

**Leaves** | Opposite or alternate, distichous, asymmetrical, simple, serrated leaf margin, caducous stipules, deciduous but also evergreen

**Inflorescences** | Umbellate, tufted

**Flowers** | Radial, hermaphroditic or unisexual, the (2–) 4–5 (–9) petalled perianth simple, usually small, often fused (fig. B); (2–) 4–8 (–15) free stamens; (1–) 2 (–3) carpels form the fused superior ovary with a very short style and reddish stigma (fig. B).

**Fruits** | Winged nut fruit (= samara), may have cilia along the edge; wind dispersal

**Use** | Ornamental trees such as **Japanese zelkova** (*Zelkovia serrata*). The often-water-resistant hardwood in used especially to make plywood, while the mucus-containing bark of *Ulmus rubra* is used as a healing agent.

**Characteristics** | At the beginning of the 20th century, the elm fungus *Ophiostoma ulmi* was imported from Asia to Europe. Unlike their Asian relatives, the European elms are not resistant to this fungus. European elm bark beetles (*Scolytus* sp.) transport the fungal spores when they drill brood galleries in the bark and petioles of the elm trees. The infection causes the trees' water-conducting structures to close up, leaving the elms to dry out.

A–E: *Urtica dioica*. A: Partial inflorescence on opposite-leafed stem. B: Underside of male flower. D: Male flower, frontal. D: Female flowers. E: Ripe fruit.

F–H: *Parietaria officinalis*. F: Male flower, frontal. G: Female flower, frontal. H: Seed.

**Genera** | More than 55; species: more than 2,500

**Distribution** | Worldwide, northern temperate latitudes, tropical, subtropical latitudes

**Habitat** | Waysides, ruderal areas

**Habit** | Trees, shrubs, herbaceous plants, annuals to perennials, can be succulent, perennials with stinging hairs, rarely lianas

**Leaves** | Opposite or alternate, mostly simple and petiolate, stipules often present, also half fused, evergreen or deciduous, epidermis with cystolites, stinging hairs

**Inflorescences** | Paniculate, spiciform-paniculate, capitiform, capitiform cymes, clusters

**Flowers** | Radial, rarely zygomorphic, unisexual, monoecious or dioecious; simple (bimerous-)tetramerous-pentamerous (sexamerous) perianth; male flowers usually have (2–) 4–5 (–6) stamens; the unilocular ovary is superior and has one style; wind pollination.

**Fruits** | Nut fruits, fleshy single-seeded drupes

**Use** | The fibers, which are usually long, are used to make clothing. The leaves of some species can be eaten raw or cooked: *Girardinia, Laportea, Urtica*. The fruit of the *Cecropia* and *Pourouma* species are also edible.

**Characteristics** | The stamens are often "explosive"; in this case, the stamens in the bud are crooked inward and when the flower blossoms they quickly bend back, so that the pollen is flung out. When the capitula on the nettles or stinging hairs, especially on the **stinging nettle** (*Urtica dioica*), are touched, the tip breaks off and the hair releases acetylcholine, histamine, and serotonin, which all can cause more or less intense itching and swelling. The stinging-nettle leaves provide food for the caterpillars of many butterfly species (such as the peacock butterfly). These plants rarely have spines. Sometimes the plants develop an aqueous milky sap.

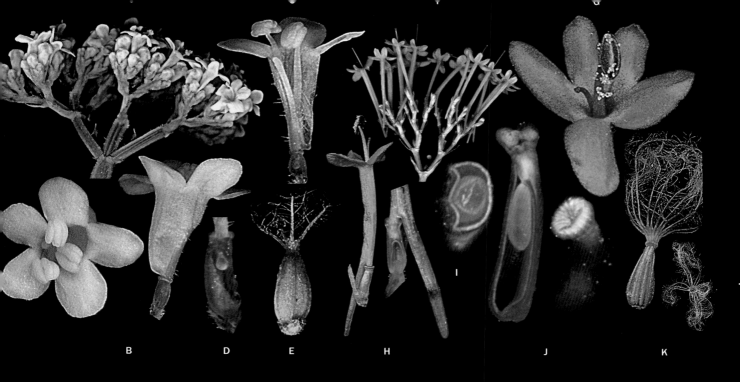

B   D   E   H   J   K

VALERIANA

**E:** *Valeriana officinalis*. A: Partial inflorescence, lateral. B: *Left*, flower, frontal; *ot*, lateral, with view of spur. C: Flower, longitudinal. D: Ovary, longitudinal. ..lmost ripe fruit.

**F–K:** *Centranthus ruber*. F: Thyrse partial inflorescence. G: Flower, frontal. H: *Left*, flower, lateral; *right*, ovary and spur, longitudinal. I: *Left*, ovary, transverse; *right*, longitudinal. J: Unripe fruit. K: Ripe fruit with "flight apparatus"; *right*, next to it, frontal.

**nera** | 13; species: more than 110
**stribution** | Northern Hemisphere, th America
**bitat** | Mountains, moorland adows
**bit** | Annual to perennial shrubs, e rarely (also evergreen) shrubs, n containing essential oils
**aves** | Opposite, basal, without ules, simple or pinnatipartite
**prescences** | Cymose

inflorescence, thyrses (fig. F)
**Flowers** | Radial to asymmetric, mostly hermaphroditic; the usually five-lobed calyx is membranous or bristly, still furled at blossoming time (figs. D, I–J), and often it unfurls only when the fruit is ripe (figs. E, K) and when used for wind dispersal as a pappus (hair, wings, hook); corolla usually pentamerous (trimerous-tetramerous); often with a weakly to

strongly developed spur; gamosepalous (1–) 4 (–5) stamens, at times protruding a long way out of the corolla (figs. F, H); the stigma is small and capitate; inferior ovary, often single seeded with hanging ovule (figs. D, J).
**Fruits** | Nutlike achenes
**Use** | The roots of the garden heliotrope (*Valeriana officinalis*) are used for healing; they contain valeric

acid and essential oils. The roots of valerian spikenard (*Valeriana celtica*) are used to make perfumers. Valerians (*Centranthus* species) are also used as ornamental plants.
**Notes** | The Valerianaceae family has meanwhile been assigned to the Caprifoliaceae as the Valerianoideaea subfamily.

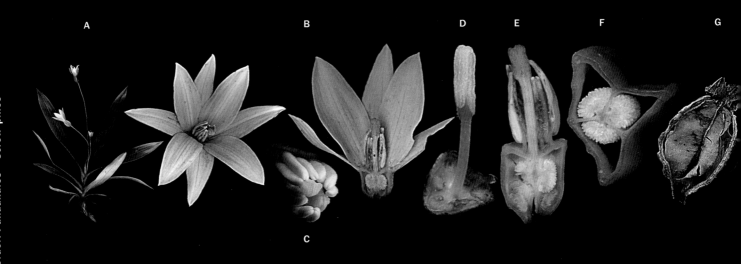

**A–G:** *Barbacenia elegans*. A: Habit. B: *Left*, flower, frontal; *right*, longitudinal. C: Androecium around bud stigma, frontal.
D: Style and stigma on receptacle. E: Androecium and gynoecium, longitudinal. F: Ovary, transverse. G: Fruit, lateral.

**Subfamilies** I Vellozioideae,
Acanthochlamydoideae
**Genera** I 10; species: 250.
Well-known genera are *Barbacenia*
and *Vellozia*.
**Distribution** I Subtropics and
tropics, the Neotropical and
Palaeotropical regions, concentration
in South America
**Habit** I Shrubby with adventitious
roots that grow through the perennial

"stem"; also herbaceous plants
**Leaves** I Alternate, tristichous or
spiral arrangement, tufted at the end of
the shoots, evergreen, leaves of many
species (especially of inselberg
species) are xerophytic, coarse. Blade:
simple, linear. Leaf margin: smooth
(fig. A) or studded with spines.
**Inflorescences** I Terminal or often
axial, often has just one flower
**Flowers** I Radial, hermaphroditic,

grows a hypanthium; six more or less
large, free tepals in two whorls of
similar structure; normally trimerous
(however, see fig. B, *left*); 1–8 cm long;
perigone often purple, white, yellow,
blue, orange, red, to greenish; 6 (–66)
stamens per flower (fig. C); the inferior
ovary consists of three fused carpels
(fig. B, *right*; figs. E, F); the one style
with three style arms serves flower
visitors as a landing platform

starchy seeds
**Use** I Some species of the genus
*Vellozia* are used as ornamental pla
(*V. candida*, *V. squamata*).
**Characteristics** I The family hon
the Portuguese Franciscan priest ar
botanist José Mariano da Conceiçã
Velloso (1742–1811). The flowers li
a particularly long time and can stay
open for several days.

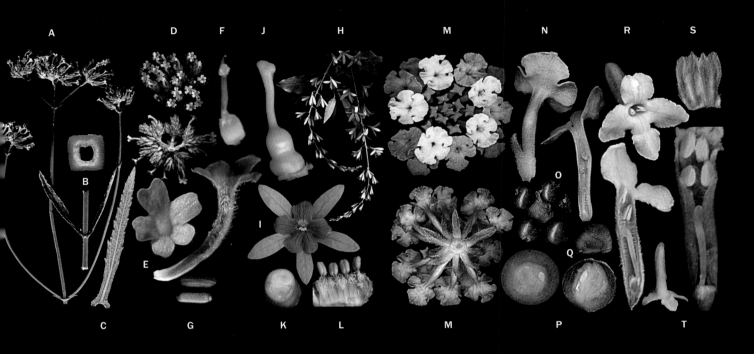

**A–G:** *Verbena bonariensis*. A: Inflorescence. B: Sprout with leaves; *above*, transverse. C: Underside of leaf. D: Partial inflorescence, from above and below. E: *Left*, corolla, frontal; *below*, longitudinal. F: Gynoecium, lateral. G: Seed.

**H–L:** *Petrea volubilis*. H: Inflorescence. I: Flower, frontal. J: Gynoecium, lateral. K: Ovary, transverse. L: Stamens.

**M–Q:** *Lantana carnara*. M: *Above*, inflorescence, frontal; *below*, underside. N: *Left*, flower, lateral; *right*, longitudinal. O: Ripe berry fruits. P: *Left*, unripe fruit, transverse; *right*, the same, longitudinal. Q: Seed.

**R–T:** *Aloysia citriodora*. R: *Above*, flower, frontal; *beneath it*, longitudinal; *right*, lateral. S: Splayed-out calyx. T: Opened bud with stamens and style.

**Genera** I More than 30; species: more than 1,100

**Distribution** I Worldwide

**Habitat** I Shorelines, waysides, ruderal meadows

**Habit** I Herbaceous plants, perennials, rarely trees or lianas

**Leaves** I Opposite, without stipules, sessile, notched to pinnatifid, often fragrant (essential oils)

**Inflorescences** I Spicate, racemose, cymose

**Flowers** I Zygomorphic, rarely radial, hermaphroditic, almost bilabiate; calyx and corolla (tetramerous-)pentamerous(-octamerous), gamosepalous; in some species the lobes may also be deeply bifid; usually (2–) 4 (–5) stamens, often of unequal length; the bicarpellate ovary is superior, may be divided by a false septum into four locules; one style usually with two stigma lobes.

**Fruits** I Four single-seeded nutlets

**Use** I The lemon-scented leaves of **lemon verbena** (*Aloysia citriodora*) are used as a spice in food and beverages. The **Aztec sweet herb** (*Lippia dulcis*) contains sesquiterpene hernandulcin, which tastes much sweeter than sugar does. The herb's bitter aftertaste and the fact that the plants lose their sweetness when dried has prevented any wider use of it as a sweetener.

**Characteristics** I The **lantana** (*Lantana camara*), which is native to the American tropics, is cultivated as an ornamental plant but has meanwhile become an invasive neophyte in other tropical and subtropical countries.

243

**A–H:** *Viola odorata*. A: *Left*, flower, frontal; *right*, lateral. B: Flower, longitudinal. C: One of the two stamens, with a nectar-producing appendage that protrudes into the spur. D: *Above left*, ovary, transverse; *right*, gynoecium, lateral. E: Underside of calyx. F: Open fruit. G: Seed with elaiosome. H: Leaf with stipules.

**I–N:** *Viola canina*. I: Flower, frontal. J: Petal with spur. K: Calyx. L: Androecium and gynoecium in calyx. M: Gynoecium, longitudinal. N: *Left*, stamen without appendage; *center and right*, with appendage.

**O–R:** *Viola arborescens*. O: Flower, frontal. P: *Above*, gynoecium, lateral; *below*, frontal. Q: Stamen. R: Androecium and gynoecium in calyx, corolla removed.

**Genera** I 23; species: 800
**Distribution** I Worldwide
**Habit** I Small trees, half shrubs, perennials, herbaceous plants, annuals to perennials, also lianas
**Habitat** I Light riparian, deciduous/oak forests, also on chalky soil, in dry grasslands and moorland meadows, tall herbaceous vegetation
**Leaves** I Spiral arrangement, also rosettes, simple and petiolate with more or less large, fringed stipules (fig. H)
**Inflorescences** I Solitary, often long and petiolate, drooping, racemose, spicate, panicular
**Flowers** I Zygomorphic, rarely radial, hermaphroditic, pentamerous; the five usually free or at most basally fused sepals are often of unequal size (fig. E), with basal appendages; the front one (lowest, largest) of the five free petals forms a spur (figs. A, B, J) that protrudes into the appendages on the two anterior stamens and secretes nectar (figs. B, C); five stamens; three (rarely 2–5) carpels form the superior ovary (fig. D, *left*); usually one style with oblong cordiform and shallow stigma (fig. P).
**Fruits** I Capsule, seed with elaiosome (dispersal by ants; figs. F, G), rarely nut fruits or berries

**Use** I Ornamental plants; the flowers of some fragrant species such as the **violet** (*Viola odorata*) can be candied or used for extracting essential oils. The roots of some species are also used for healing. In East Asia, people eat the slimy leaves of *Viola verucunda*.
**Characteristics** I The flowers are usually enveloped by two bracts.

A–E: *Vitis vinifera*. A: Leafy shoot with stem tendrils. B: Paniculate inflorescence. C: *Left*, opening flower; *center*, underside of detached perianth; *right*, side view of flower as it opens. D: *Left*, flower, frontal; *right*, longitudinal. E: *Left*, various ripe fruits; *right*, berry, longitudinal.

**Genera** | About 14–16; species: about 900

**Distribution** | Pantropical, warm temperate latitudes

**Habit** | Climbing shrubs/lianas with dichotomous stem tendrils (fig. A), with or without adhesive discs, shrubs, rarely succulents

**Leaves** | Alternate, distichous, leaf tendrils opposite the leaves, leaf blade is notched lobed, palmate and divided, digitate or pinnate; stipules present, deciduous or evergreen.

**Inflorescences** | Branched panicles (fig. B) or golden umbels

**Flowers** | Radial, hermaphroditic (fig. D), polygamo-monoecious or -dioecious, tetramerous-pentamerous(-septamerous); one whorl with four, five, or rarely seven stamens; two carpels form the superior ovary (fig. D); disc nectary present

**Fruits** | Berries (fig. E)

**Use** | The grapes of the **grapevine** (*Vitis vinifera* ssp. *vinifera*) are consumed as fresh fruit or dried as raisins/sultanas/grapes/currants and processed into juice or wine. The pressed, fermented pomace from wine making is distilled to make grappa. Pressing 40 kg of grape seeds will yield about 1 liter of grapeseed oil; this oil is used to dress salads or to make cosmetics. Phytochemicals contained in the kernels (oligomeric procyanidins = OPC) have antioxidant effects. They are available as a dietary supplement. The grape skins contain a phytoalexin, resveratrol, which has antioxidant properties and is used as antiaging agent in cosmetics. The fruits of *Ampelocissus africana* and the **frost grape** (*Vitis vulpina*) are also edible. The North American **riverbank grape** (*Vitis riparia*) is resistant to grape phylloxera and powdery mildew, and therefore it is preferable to use this species as a rootstock in vineyards. In Africa, people eat the leaves of such plants as *Cayratia gracilis* as vegetables in times of need. In China, people apply the leaves of *Ampelopsis japonica* to ease pain. Some *Cissus* species are used medicinally. The self-climbing **thicket creeper** or **woodbine** (*Parthenocissus inserta*) is often grown to create green building facades. Some garden plants, park plants, and houseplants (*Cissus* and *Cyphostemma* species; *Tetrastigma voinierianum*).

**Characteristics** | The vine tendrils react to touch and their growth is negatively geotropic, that is, away from the light. Even if grape vines are designated as *Trauben* in German, in botanic terms the inflorescences are not *traubig* (racemose) but, rather, panicular (fig. B). By the mid-19th century, phylloxera (*Dactylosphaera vitifolii*) had been introduced into Europe from America; the epidemic destroyed extensive areas of vineyards, because these grape varieties were not resistant to the louse. Since then, the tasty noble European varieties have been grafted onto resistant rootstocks.

A–G: *Drimys winterii*. A: Leafy branch with inflorescence. B: Underside of flower. C: Flower, frontal. D: Flower, longitudinal. E: Androecium and gynoecium, lateral. F: Stamen. G: Carpel, longitudinal.

**Genera** I 4–7; species: about 60–90
**Distribution** I Temperate regions, tropical mountains in Southeast Asia, New Zealand, eastern Australia, Central and South America, Madagascar
**Habit** I Evergreen trees, shrubs
**Leaves** I Alternate, spiral arrangement, rarely whorled, petiole present; leaf blade: simple, entire, soft leaved, or leathery; aromatic due to the essential oils in the leaves (peppery), stipules absent
**Inflorescences** I Cymose inflorescences (fig. A) or solitary
**Flowers** I Radial (fig. C),

hermaphroditic, spiral arrangement (figs. C, D), no set number of perianths, double perianth; 2–4 (–6) sepals in one whorl (fig. B), fused, at least at the base; (2–) 5–50 petals in 1–3 whorls, with outer whorl sometimes fused to a flower husk or otherwise free; 15–100 stamens in 2–5 whorls, free (figs. E, F); pollen usually in tetrads, rarely solitary; the ovary is superior (figs. C–E), comprising (1–) 3–20 carpels in one whorl, mostly apocarpous (fig. D) or syncarpous; carpels may not be completely closed; up to 100 ovules per carpel (fig. G). Anemophily, entomophily (that is, by thrips, small

beetles).
**Fruits** I Berrylike follicles or capsules, also aggregate fruits. Ornithochory.
**Use** I *Drymis winteri*, commonly known as **South American winter's bark**, is used as a medicine. The dried fruits and leaves of **Tasmanian mountain pepper** (*Tasmannia lanceolata*) first taste sweet, then spicy, and finally leave your mouth feeling numb. The fruit especially are much spicier than pepper. In Japan, people season wasabi with this spice. The fruits are supposed to have an antibiotic and antioxidant effect.

**Characteristics** I A very primordi family that existed by the lower Cretaceous period. The wood contai only tracheids, but no trachea. The family is named after John Wynter, captain of the sailing ship the *Elizabeth*, who was one of the men who circumnavigated the globe with Sir Francis Drake on the famous voyage of 1577–1580. The genus *Wintera*, which gave the family its name, now belongs to the genus *Pseudowintera*.

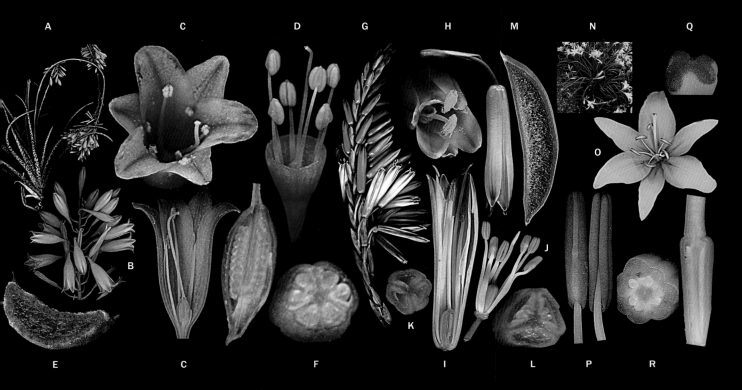

**–F:** *Aloe perryi*. A: Habit. B: Inflorescence. C: Flower; *bove*, frontal; *below*, longitudinal. D: Open bud with oung stamens, style/stigma. E: Leaf, transverse. : *Left*, fruit, longitudinal; *right*, transverse.

**G–M:** *Aloe succotrina*. G: Inflorescence. H: *Left*, flower, frontal; *right*, next to it, lateral. I: Flower, longitudinal. J: Androecium and gynoecium from bud, lateral. K: Part of basal ovary with incipient nectary, transverse. L: Ovary, transverse. M: Leaf, transverse.

**N–R:** *Hemerocallis hybrids*. N: Habit. O: Flower, frontal. P: Stamens from both sides. Q: Stigma, lateral. R: *Left*, ovary, transverse; *right*, longitudinal.

**Subfamilie**s I Asphodeloideae, Hemerocallidoideae, Xanthorrhoeoideae

**Genera** I 35; species: some 900. Well-known genera: *Aloe, Asphodelus, Eremurus, Gasteria, Haworthia, Hemerocallis, Kniphofia, Xanthorrhoea.*

**Distribution** I Worldwide. Asphodeloideae in the Old World, primarily Mediterranean to central Asia, Africa (concentration: South African Cape region). Hemerocallidoideae: almost worldwide; Xanthorrhoeoideae: tropical and subtropical Australia.

**Habit** I Perennial herbaceous plants with rhizomes or root tubers, some succulents, some treelike with anomalous lateral growth

**Leaves** I Alternate, spiral arrangement, rarely distichous (fig. N) arranged in basal (fig. A) or terminal or tufted rosettes; leaf blade: linear-lanceolate, simple, usually sessile, occasionally succulent (figs. E, M, N), parallel venation.

**Inflorescences** I In racemes (figs. A, B, G), spikes, or single flowers

**Flowers** I Radial to slightly zygomorphic, trimerous in two whorls; tepals free or fused, usually two whorls with three stamens each (figs. C, D, J); superior ovary (fig. C, *below*; figs. I, O) comprising three fused carpels (figs. F, K, L, P).

**Fruits** I Mostly capsules, berries (*Dianella*)

**Use** I The leaves of *Aloe vera* contain resin ducts that run longitudinally under the epidermis; if the leaf is cut into, the ducts release a yellow resin that serves the plant as a defense against herbivores. It used to be taken as a drastic laxative. *Aloe vera* gel is better known; this serves as a water reservoir in the succulent leaves of the plant. It works to cool skin, especially if the skin is sun-damaged, and is said to have a wound-healing effect ("wound cactus"). The leaf fibers of **New Zealand flax** (*Phormium tenax*) are used to manufacture ropes, fabrics, and paper. The **orange day-lily** (*Hemerocallis fulva*) is a popular ornamental garden plant; its tubers are also said to be edible.

**Characteristics** I In their Australian homeland, the **grasstrees** (*Xanthorrhoea* species), are able to survive the frequently occurring bushfires (fire ecosystems). Parts of the dead leaves remain on the plants and form a shell-like husk, which serves as insulation and thus protects the plant from the heat. This process protects the apical meristem, which is sunk deep within the stem, in particular; the meristem is capable of division and is the tissue from which the plant regenerates. After a fire, the stems are charred black, which is why the plants are called "black-boy." Since the plants are fostered by fire, they belong to the so-called pyrophytes. The family name (Greek *xanthos* = yellow, *roea* = flow) refers to the acaroid resins that are secreted in the leaf bases of the grasstree plants; Australian Aborigines used the resin as an adhesive.

# ZINGIBERACEAE

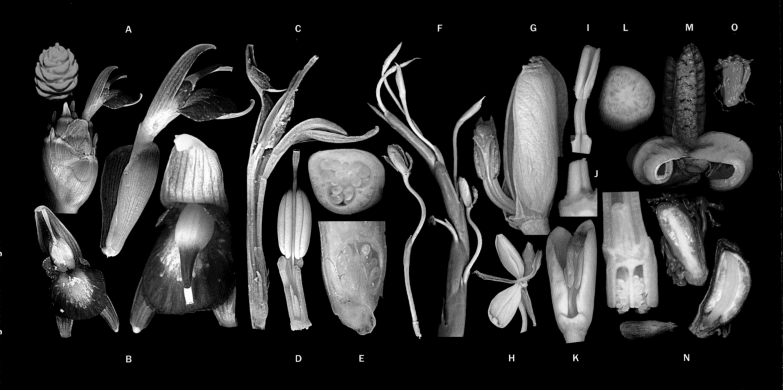

A    C    F    G    I    L    M    O

B    D    E    H    K    N

**A–E:** *Zingiber officinale*. A: *Above*, inflorescence, frontal; *below*, lateral, with flower. B: *Left*, flower, frontal; *center*, with bract, lateral; *right*, frontal. C: Flower, longitudinal. D: Stamen with style/stigma. E: *Above*, ovary, transverse; *below*, longitudinal.

**F–O:** *Brachychilum horsfieldii*. F: Partial inflorescence; *left*, flower, lateral. G: Upper part of the flower with stamen and style/stigma. H: Flower, lateral. I: Stamen. J: *Left*, nectary; *right*, upper part of the flower, longitudinal, with nectary on the ovary. K: Upper part of the flower with stamen and style/stigma. L: Ovary, transverse. M: Capsule. N: *Left*, seed with aril, longitudinal; *right*, without aril; *below*, left seed, lateral. O: aril.

**Genera** | More than 50; species: more than 1,200

**Distribution** | Pantropical, especially in Southeast Asia

**Habit** | Perennial evergreen herbaceous plants with underground rhizomes and short stems; they grow psuedostems.

**Leaves** | Alternate, distichous, leaves sessile or petiolate, simple, linear, entire, furled when in the bud (*convolute vernation*); marked midrib, parallel lateral nervation, lower leaves often reduced to a leaf sheath

**Inflorescences** | Terminal (fig. A) or growing directly from the rhizomes, often spicate thyrses or cymes, with strikingly colored bracts

**Flowers** | Zygomorphic, hermaphroditic, trimerous; the three sepals fused on one side in a tube sheath in one whorl; three petals basally fused in one whorl; two whorls with originally six stamens; only one is fertile (figs. D, I, K), and the others reduced or absent; the two lateral staminodes of the inner whorl transformed into a conspicuous petallike labellum (fig. B, *below*) (characteristic of the family) and often fused with the two lateral staminodes of the outer whorl (if present); inferior ovary fused from three carpels (figs. E, L); the thin style grows in a groove in the anther (fig. C); the stigma lies above the anther (figs. D, K); a large amount of nectar (fig. J). Entomophily or ornithophily.

**Fruits** | Dry or fleshy capsules (fig. M), berries. Seeds have an aril (figs. N, O).

**Use** | Rhizomes contain essential oils in excretory cells; the plants produce many spices; can be medicinal plants.

**Ginger** rhizomes (*Zingiber officinale*) have an intense taste due to the ginger oil; ginger has an antibacterial and anti-inflammatory effect. The rhizomes of the **galanga** (*Kaempferia galanga*) are used as a spice and in traditional medicine. The rhizomes of the **lesser galangal** (*Alpinia officinarum*, *A. galanga*) are used to make cordials and are an ingredient in curries. The bright-yellow-colored rhizomes of **turmeric** (*Curcuma longa*) are used as food coloring and are a main ingredient in curries. **Grains of paradise** are the seeds of the *Aframomum melegueta*. They add a savory spiciness to meat dishes. The capsules or seeds of the **cardamom** (*Elettaria cardamomum*) are an ingredient for making Indian masala dishes, and a spice used in sausage and gingerbread; also used to remedy digestive complaints. In Southeast Asia, people eat young inflorescences of **torch ginger** (*Ettlingera/Nicolaia elatior*) as salad.

**Characteristics** | The **kahili ginger** (*Hedychium gardnerianum*), which comes from Southeast Asia, was brought to the Azores, Hawaii, and New Zealand as an ornamental plant. There it became an invasive neophytes and is a threat to natural habitats (such as the remaining laurel forests on Sao Miguel).

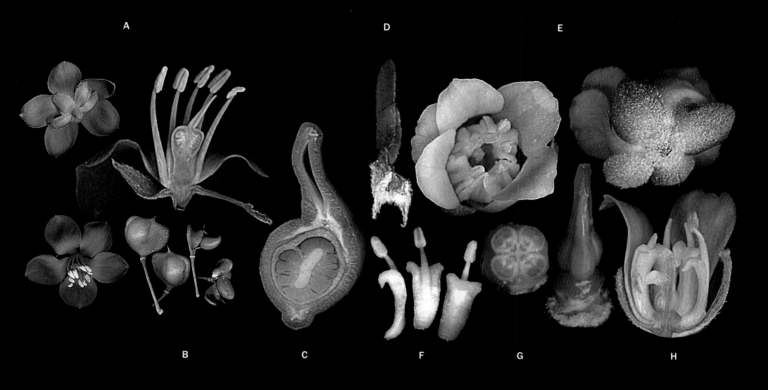

**A–C:** *Guaiacum officinale*. A: *Above*, underside of flower; *center*, flower, longitudinal; *below left*, frontal. B: *Left*, unripe, and *right*, ripe open fruits, with seeds growing out of them. C: Fruit, longitudinal.

**D–H:** *Poliera hygrometra*. D: Pinnate pair of leaves furled together, E: *Left*, flower, frontal; *right*, underside. F: Stamens from all sides. G: *Left*, ovary, transverse; *right*, gynoecium, lateral. H: Flower, longitudinal.

**Genera** I 26; species: 285

**Distribution** I Pantropical, mostly in arid areas, occasionally on saline soils

**Habit** I Usually trees, shrubs, half shrubs, rarely annual or perennial herbaceous plants. Xerophytes may occur.

**Leaves** I Usually opposite, usually abruptly pinnate, petiolate, often fleshy, stipules present, may be transformed into spines

**Inflorescences** I Solitary, terminal or axillary, racemose or cymose

**Flowers** I Mostly radial, usually hermaphroditic, (tetramerous-) pentamerous (figs. A, E); sepals and petals with 4–5 free stamens, which are often covered with scales at the base (fig. F); (2–3) 4–5 carpels are fused to a superior ovary (fig. A, *center*; fig. H).

**Fruits** I Usually capsules (fig. B), drupes, or schizocarpic fruits. The fruits of the genus *Tribulus* are an exception; these can have false septums.

**Use** I The **lignum-vitae tree** (*Guaiacum officinale*) has one of the hardest woods that exists. Commercial use of this protected tropical timber is subject to authorization, because the plant is listed in Annex II of the Washington Convention on International Trade in Endangered Species of Wild Flora and Fauna. *Guaiacum* resin (such as from *G. sanctum* and *G. officinale*) is used as an agent to detect blood in stools, since guaiaconic acid turns blue with oxidizing agents (such as hydrogen peroxide) and thus makes a quick test possible. It is also used as an ingredient in smoked fish and meat products and in herbal liqueurs.

**Verawood** is another hardwood but comes from the *Bulnesia arborea*. The leaves of the **creosote bush** (*Larrea tridentata*) were formerly added to foodstuffs as an antioxidant. However, it has been linked to liver and kidney damage, so its use is limited today. The fruits of the **desert date** (*Balanites aegyptica*) are edible. The flower buds of the **Syrian bean-caper** (*Zygophyllum fabago*) can be preserved and eaten like capers.

**Characteristics** I The German name *Pockholz* (pock wood) comes from the earlier assumption that the resinous wood chips would help heal smallpox. The **bindii** (*Tribulus terrestris*) is said to enhance testosterone secretion. Although it was not possible to prove in any studies, the plant is sometimes used as an ingredient in muscle-building preparations and taken to an unreasonable extent by some bodybuilders ("testosterone boosters"). *Porlieria* (*Porlieria hygrometra*) folds down the pinnate leaflets at night (fig. D).

APPENDIX

**abaxial:** Used in reference to the leaf surface facing away from the stem (leaf underside)

**achenes:** Single-seeded indehiscent fruit, in which the seed and fruit skin are fused together (Asteraceae: daisy family)

**adaxial:** Used in reference to the leaf surface side facing the stem (leaf upper side)

**addorsed bracetole:** A bracteole that has its rear side oriented to the principal axis. Typical of monocotyledon plants.

**aerenchyma:** (Greek: *aer* = air; *enchyma* = filling). Tissue for aeration, characterized by large intercellular spaces. This occurs predominantly in marsh and aquatic plants and serves aeration in order to increase interchange of gases. Aerenchyma generates buoyancy in aquatic plants. In the rushes (*Juncus* sp.), it grows in a star shape in the leaf blade.

**alates:** Winged, the two lateral petals in the butterfly bush. **allorhizous:** Root system. The radicle becomes the primary root; the first, second, etc. order is formed by the lateral roots (most of the dicotyledons).

**alternate:** Alternating

**androecium:** Totality of male flower organs (stamens)

**androgynophore:** Androecium and gynoecium are supported by an additional stalk.

**androphore:** The androecium is supported by an additional stalk.

**anemochory:** Fruits are dispersed by the wind.

**anemophily:** Wind pollination

**anisophyllous:** When leaves are of unequal size

**anomalous secondary lateral growth:** In monocotyledon plants, there is no secondary lateral growth as there is in dicotyledons, because monoctyledons lack a divisible tissue between the xylem and the phloem. In some taxa, however, a secondary cambium grows in the bark layers, so that there can be a limited amount of lateral growth.

**anther:** All the pollen sacs of a stamen (usually four)

**apocarpous:** *See* choricarpous.

**areolea:** Sprouting area on cacti; here the leaves emerge, which are reduced to spines (usually also hairs).

**arid:** Annual precipitation does not exceed the potential evaporation (evaporation capacity of the atmosphere).

**aril:** (Usually fleshy) seed coat, which grows out from the funicules (seed stalks) and usually completely covers the seed.

**bicollateral vascular bundles:** In the vascular bundle, xylem (water-conducting tissue) and phloem (nutrient-conducting tissue) are separated by a divisible tissue (cambium). Another part of the phloem is attached to the xylem, but without a cambium in between.

**bifacial:** Leaves with an upper side and different underside

**bifid:** Leaf blades cleft in two parts

**bilateral symmetry (disymmetric):** Only two vertical symmetry axes perpendicular to each other when looking frontally at the flower

**bipinnate leaves:** Doubly pinnate leaves

**botryoid:** (= grape-like). Special form/reduction of a panicle. The terminal flowers show that this is a panicle, but with only a few branches, so it looks like a bunch of grapes. (Grapes, however, do not have the terminal flower.)

**bristles:** Bristle-like growths on leaves such as on the husks of the grasses

**bulbil:** (Greek *bulbos*, Latin *bulbus* = bulb). Small bulbs for vegetative propagation.

**C3 plants:** Normal case of photosynthesis. Plants absorb and fix $CO_2$ during the day. The resulting intermediates have three carbon atoms; hence the name C3 plants.

**calyx:** Calyx

**CAM plants:** Plants that display the special acid metabolism of Crassulaceae (crassulacean acid metabolism). In the process, the plants open the stomata on their leaves at night and absorb $CO_2$, which is stored as malic acid. During the day, the stomata remain closed, and the $CO_2$ is dissolved out of the acid and further processed into carbohydrates. Advantageous in dry locations: less water is lost through transpiration through the stomata.

**cambium:** Cell layer usually arranged annularly in the cross section of the stem axis and capable of division

**carina:** A keel, the two smallest of the five petals of a papilionaceous flower, which more or less envelop the androecium and gynoecium

**carpel:** Carpel

**carpophore:** Fruit holder, such as growing between the double achenes of the Umbelliflorae

**caruncle:** Elaiosome (seed outgrowth)

**caryopsis:** Nut fruit growing from a superior ovary with one seed; the seed and fruit skin are fused together. Fruit of the grass family.

**cauliflory:** Stem-flowering; flowers grow on woody stems or branches (such as *Theobroma cacao*—cocoa)

**choricarpous:** The carpels are fused only with themselves and not with others (the resulting fruits are follicle fruits).

**cleistogamous:** Nonopening hermaphroditic flowers that pollinate themselves.

**clone:** Plant that grows from vegetative propagation

**coevolution:** Common development of various groups of living organisms over long periods of their tribal history **conduplicate:** Petals are furled together in the bud.

**commensural stigmas:** Stigmas that correspond to the margins or sutures of each carpel, such as in the oriental poppy

**connective:** (Sterile) center part of an anther (continuation of the filament)

**corolla:** All the petals

**costapalmate leaf:** A digitate leaf, in which the petiole continues into the leaf blade

**cotyledon:** Primary embryo leaf

**cremocarp:** Schizocarp fruit of the Umbelliflorae

**cryptophytes:** Habit in which the overwintering organs are buried, such as in the earth (geophytes)

**cyathium:** Partial inflorescence typical of *Euphorbia*: many male flowers with only one stamen envelop a female flower with a petiolate ovary.

**cymes, cymose:** Partial inflorescence of a thyrse; its axis supports only 1–2 bracteoles and ends in a flower. Branching can continue from the bracteole axils.

**cymes 2:** Inflorescence, the individual flowers of which lie approximately along one plane, as in a umbel, but the flower stems do not emanate from one point.

**cystolith:** (Greek *kystis* = sac, *lithos* = stone). Deposits are formed by accumulation of silicic acid and calcium carbonate.

**decussate leaf arrangement:** When opposite leaf pairs rotate each time by 90° from node to node (usually results in a four-edged shoot)

**dichasia:** A terminal flower with two bracteoles grows each time in turn from the bracteole axils of the terminal flower.

**dichotomous branching:** Similar, forked branching **didynamic:** Two pairs of usually different-length stamens

**dicotyledons:** Plants with two cotyledons in the seed

**dioecious:** Male and female flowers growing on separate plants

**diplostemonous flower:** Androecium that consists of two whorls of stamens. The outer whorl is borne by the sepals (episepalous); the inner above the petals (epipetalous).

**disc:** Usually a disciform nectary (which can be supported on the inferior ovary)

**doctrine of signatures:** A way of thinking that was assumed by antiquity, but later also in the Middle Ages, that everything is connected in nature, and thus a plant characteristic (such as smell, form, or color) can indicate, as if by a divine sign, how they can be used medically. For example, the flower colors of the lungwort, which appear red when young and later appear blue violet, could be interpreted as a sign that this plant would help heal lung diseases, since the changes in color showed a relationship to the human lung (in the lung, the oxygen-depleted blood is loaded with oxygen and thus changes color).

**domatium, domatia:** Hollows in the angles of the protruding veins on a leaf underside, often enclosed by hairs and inhabited by insects or mites

**elaiosomes:** (Greek *elaia* = oil tree, *soma* = body). Oil or protein-containing tissue appendages on seeds. They help seed dispersal, because ants carry off the seeds and eat the food particles.

**endocarp:** Innermost layer of the pericarp

**ensiform leaves:** Sword-shaped, flattened on the sides, and their narrow side faces the stem (on the iris); outside there is only the epidermis on the leaf underside (with stomata, the actual upper side is confined to a small triangular area in front of the suture)

**entomophily:** Pollination by insects

**epiphytes:** Plants that grow on other plants but do not penetrate into their support

**epithelial elaiosomes:** Oil glands in which the oil is hidden under a cuticle bladder

**equifacial:** Leaves with only one leaf side

**extrafloral:** Outside the flower

**filament:** Filaments

**funicules:** Connector between ovule and placenta

**funnel-shaped panicle:** Panicle in which the basal lateral branches are markedly elongated, so that the flowers in their entirety are arranged in a funnel form. The terminal flowers are located at the base of the funnel.

**generative propagation:** Sexual reproduction

**gynoecium:** The entire female part of a flower: ovary with placenta and ovules on the funiculus (stalk), style, and stigma

**gynophore:** The gynoecium is supported by a stalk.

**gynostegium:** (Greek *gyne* = woman; *-stemon* = support/chain on a loom). Also called a column or style column, since it is a column-like structure that grows from the union of style and stamens (such as in the Asclepiadaceae).

**gynostemium:** Column in the Orchidaceae

**halophytes:** Salt-tolerant plants

**hapaxanth plants:** Flower and fruit only once; they die after the seeds form.

**haplostemonous flower:** Greek *haploo* = simple, *sporos* = germ. Androecium that consists only of one whorl of stamens.

**haustoria:** Absorbing organs of parasitic plants, often transformed roots, which the plants use to penetrate the host plant

**hemiparasite:** Partially parasitic plants that can independently photosynthesize but depend on the host plant to supply water, nutrients, or both.

**hermaphroditic flowers:** Both sexes occur in one flower.

**heterostyly:** Styles of different lengths and different insertion of the stamen (above or below the style) in the same kind of flowers, such as primroses

**holarctic distribution:** Northern temperate latitudes

**homorhizous:** The radicle is replaced by similar roots (in most monocotyledons).

**humid:** Annual precipitation exceeds the potential evaporation (evaporation capacity of the atmosphere).

**husks:** Involucral bracts of grasses

**hydathodes:** Water fissures that serve for active, drop-shaped discharge of water. They are often found on leaf tips or in serration on leaf margins.

**hydrochory:** (Greek *hydor* = water, *choirizein* = detach). Dispersal by water.

**hypanthium:** Flower cup (Greek *hypo* = under, *anthos* = flower). By this we understand a tubular fused area between the ovaries and the other flower organs (usually calyx, corolla, filaments).

**imbricate bud cover:** On the bud, the leaves cover each other with edges overlapping like roof tiles.

**incumbent climber or rambler:** With the help of long, slender shoots or with spines or thorns pointing backward, these climbers can hook fast to supports and grow toward the light.

**internode:** Stem area between two nodes

**involucre:** Calyx hull on capitiform or basketlike inflorescences, such as Asteraceae

**labellum:** The rear petal in orchid flowers

**lamina:** Leaf blade (expanded area of the leaf)

**laminar placentation:** The ovules are attached to the surface of the carpel.

**lenticels:** Corky warts (such as grow on many stems)

**ligule:** Usually scales that grow additionally at the base on leaf organs, such as on grasses: scales on the transitional area between open leaf blade and leaf sheath; on petals mostly on the inner base

**lithophytes:** (Latin *litho* = stone, *-phyton* = plant). Plants that grow on stones.

**locules:** Cavity in a fruit

**loculicidal:** Cleft opening (of fruits)

**lodiculae:** (Latin: underscale). Swellings that cause grass flowers to open; when the flowers bloom, they swell up above the small scales inserted over the lemmas.

**mamillate:** Cactus stems having wartlike growths where the areoles are located

**mimicry:** Imitation of an appearance

**monocotyledons:** Plants with a single cotyledon in the seed

**monoecious:** Male and female flowers growing on one plant

**mucronate leaves:** Ending in a point

**mycoheterotrophic nutrition:** Plants without chlorophyll, which depend completely on being fed by fungi

**mycorrhizal fungi:** (Greek *mykes* = fungus, *rhiza* = root). Symbiosis between fungi and seed plants. The fungus hyphae can grow among the plant root cells (ectotrophic mycorrhiza) or penetrate the cells (endotrophic mycorrhiza). They supply the plants with water and dissolved minerals and replace the absent root hairs. In return, they get carbohydrates from the plants.

**mycotrophic:** (Greek *mykes* = fungus, *trophein* = nourish). Plants that nourish themselves with the aid of fungi, either temporarily or permanently

**neophytes:** (Greek *neos* = new; *-phyton* = plant). Species that have become established after 1492 in an area where they are not native, with or without human intervention.

**Neotropics:** The New World (Americas)

**nodus:** nodes, stem tubers

**obdiplostemonous:** Flowers with two whorls of stamens, where the outer whorl is above the petals, the inner stamen whorl above the sepals

**opposite:** Same position: opposite

**ornithophily:** Bird pollination

**ovarium:** Ovary: the ovule-bearing part of the carpel **palaeotropics**: The Old World (Africa, Asia)

**palmate leaves:** In divided leaf blades, these are palmlike, hand-shaped fan leaves. In leaves with palmate venation, the leaf nerves grow from a common point, the petiole, and fan out in a hand shape.

**panicle:** Inflorescence that resembles a multibranched bunch of grapes

**pantropical distribution:** Tropical and subtropical areas of all continents

**parietal placentation:** The placentas with the ovules are inserted on the sides of the carpels.

**peltate:** Stalk attached on leaf underside

**perianth:** Double-whorled flower envelope of calyx and a different corolla

**perigone:** Two-whorled perianth, from the same involucral bracts

**petals, petalum:** Petals of a perianth

**phylloclades:** (Greek *phyllon* = leaf, *klados* = branch, sapling). Short shoot structured like a leaf. These broadened, flat and green shoots take over photosynthesis.

**pinnate leaves:** "Feathered" leaves with separate leaflets

**placentation:** Describes the arrangement of the ovules in a carpel or in the ovary

**pollen, pollen grains:** Male microspores

**pollinium:** Pollen mass: all the pollen grains cohering together into a single body, which is transported as a whole. The pollinia are connected by a stalk with a viscidium; this helps them get stuck to the flower visitors.

**polygamo-monoecious:** Transition between monoecious and dioecious. Besides the flowers of the dominant sex, also have hermaphroditic flowers or flowers of the opposite sex: plants with male, female, and hermaphroditic flowers.

**prickle:** A sharp outgrowth usually grown from the epidermis and a few layers below it; it is not connected to the vascular bundles.

**protandry, protandrous:** The stamens ripen before the stigmas.

**pseudo-vivparity:** This is a form of vegetative reproduction in which daughter plants of the same heredity grow in flowers instead of in seeds; these fall to the ground and can grow into new plants.

**pyrophytes:** "Fire plants"; plants whose growth is promoted by fire, either directly (such as fruits that open only after great heat) or indirectly (the competitors burn and supply nutrients from their ashes)

**racemose:** Inflorescence in which pedicellate flowers grow (from the axils of a bract) along the unbranched main axis

**rachis:** Axis of a pinnate leaf

**radial symmetry (polysymmetric, actinomorphic):** Many levels of symmetry through the central point. Visible in a frontal view of the flower.

**resupination:** (Latin *resupinatio* = bending back, inversion). This is understood to mean the rotation of flowers; through this process, parts originally located on the upper side (adaxial) are turned downward and thus grow into an abaxial position. In orchid flowers, for example, the ovary is often rotated in a helical or coiled form.

**rhizome:** The stem grows horizontally in the ground, forming roots that grow downward and leaves and flowers that grow upward—usually at the tip.

**sapromyiophily:** Pollination syndrome by carrion / dung flies

**scape:** An inflorescence stem without nodes (such as on the common dandelion—*Taraxacum officinale*)

**schizogenous excretory ducts:** Excretory tissue in plants. The divergence of cells creates intercellular spaces that often contain essential oils, resins, or balms. These often serve to close wounds.

**sclereids:** Sclereid cells

**scorpioid cyme:** Monochasial branching in the inflorescence area

**SEM:** Scanning electron microscope

**sepalum, sepals:** Sepal, sepals

**septal nectaries:** Nectar-producing glands that grow between the septum of the ovary

**septicidal:** Fruit that open through the walls/sutures in the carpels

**spadix:** Inflorescence with sessile flowers growing directly on the thickened axis (from the axil of a bract)

**spikes:** Unbranched inflorescence with sessile flowers growing directly on the axis (also from the axil of a bract)

**spines:** Pointed, stiff formations that grow from the transformation of branches, leaves, and lateral roots; they are connected to vascular bundles in a different way than thorns are.

**stamen, stamens:** Stamen, stamens

**stigma:** *Stigma* = receptive; area of the gynoecium that can be pollinated, usually with external pollen of the same species

**stipules:** Stipules

**stolons:** Aboveground runners

**style:** Style

**subdioecious:** In addition to the flowers of the dominant sex, also have hermaphroditic flowers or flowers of the opposite sex

**submerged:** Plants that live underwater

**succulent:** Water-storing (mostly in special water storage tissues).

**synandrium:** Fused stamens, either the filaments or the anthers

**synocarpous:** (Greek *syn* = together, *karpos* = fruit). Having a multilocular ovary grown by the fusion of several carpels.

**tepal, tepals:** Tepals, tepals of a perigone.

**terrestrial:** Growing on the ground

**testa:** Seed coat

**theca:** One-half of the anther, usually two out of four pollen sacs pointing to one side, forming a chamber that tears open in the middle

**thyrse:** Inflorescence with partial inflorescences branching from the axils of the bracteoles

**trichome:** Hair

**trimerous:** Tripartite; a whorl consisting of three parts

**turions:** (Latin *turio*, *-onis* = underground stem bud, shoot). Vegetatively grown overwintering organs. Distinguished as hibernaculum in aquatic plants (Latin *hibernaculum* = winter quarters). They grow in the autumn and sink to the bottom of the water. In the spring they reach the water surface and sprout into new plants.

**utricule:** Small bladder or tube

**vegetative propagation:** Propagation from nonsexual parts of plants

**vexillum:** The uppermost, usually vertical petal of the papilionaceae (Fabaceae)

**viscin threads:** Thin threads of sporopollenin, which bind pollen grains together (such as in Onagraceae, Ericaceae)

**viviparity:** Bearing live young; here this means that the seedling germinates on the mother plant (such as on mangroves)

**whorl:** Circles or whorls (such as in flowers)

**xerophytes:** Plants that are adapted to extremely dry conditions. Some show a special form of metabolism (CAM—crassulacean acid metabolism, C4 syndrome). In order not to allow the precious water to evaporate through the stomata on the leaves, many of these plants have a reduced leaf blade, especially the case for cacti. Other adaptations include having a thickened epidermis, thick wax deposits, or hairs that reflect radiation.

**zoochory:** Fruit dispersal fruit by animals, either by passing through the intestinal e (= endozoochory) or on the animal's exterior (epizoochory)

**zygomorphic symmetry:** Only one axis of symmetry, visible in a frontal view of the flower

SOURCES

Angiosperm Phylogeny Group. *"An Update of the Angiosperm Phylogeny Group Classification for the Orders and Families of Flowering Plants."* **Botanical Journal of the Linnean Society** 161, no. 2 (2009): 105–21.

Blanke, R. *Farbatlas exotische Früchte* ["Color atlas of exotic fruits"]. Stuttgart: Ulmer, 2000.

Bresinsky, A., C. Körner, J. W. Kadereit, G. Neuhaus, and U. Sonnewald. *Straßburger Lehrbuch der Botanik* ["Strasbourg textbook of botany"]. 36th ed. Heidelberg, Germany: Spektrum Akademischer Verlag, 2008.

*Code of Botanical Nomenclature.* Utrecht, The Netherlands, 1952.

Denffer, D. von, F. Ehrendorfer, K. Mägdefrau, and H. Ziegler. *Straßburger: Lehrbuch der Botanik.* 31st ed. Stuttgart and New York: Gustav Fischer Verlag, 1978.

Düll, R., and H. Kutzelnigg. *Taschenlexikon der Pflanzen Deutschlands* ["Pocket dictionary of the plants of Germany"]. 7th ed. Wiebelsheim, Germany: Quelle & Meyer Verlag, 2011.

Engler, A. *Syllabus der Pflanzenfamilien* ["Syllabus of plant families"]. Berlin: Gebrüder Borntraeger, 1964.

Erbar, C. "Nectar Secretion and Nectaries in Basal Angiosperms, Magnolids and Non-core Eudicots and a Comparison with Core Eudicots." *Plant Diversity and Evolution* 131, no. 2 (2014): 63–143.

Frey, W., ed. *Syllabus of Plant Families: Adolf Engler's Syllabus der Pflanzenfamilien. Vol. 4, Pinopsida (Gymnospers), Magnoliopsida (Angiosprems) p.p. Subclass Magnoliidae.* 13th ed. Stuttgart: Gebrüder Borntraeger Verlagsbuchhandlung, 2015.

Fuchs, E. J., and J. L. Hamrick. "Genetic Diversity in the Endangered Tropical Tree, *Guaiacum sanctum (Zygophyllaceae)." Journal of Heredity* 101, no. 3 (2010): 284–91.

Grow, S., and E. Schwarztman. "The Status of *Guaiacum* Species in Trade." *Medical Plant Conservation* 7 (2001): 19–21.

Heywood, V. H. *Blütenpflanzen der Welt* ["Flowering plants of the world"]. Stuttgart: Birkhäuser Verlag, 1982.

Kadereit, J. W., and C. Jeffrey, eds. *The Families and Genera of Vascular Plants.* Flowering Plants 8: Dicotyledons: Asterales. Berlin and New York: Springer, 2007.

Kadereit, J. W., C. Körner, B. Kost, and U. Sonnewald. *Straßburger Lehrbuch der Botanik.* 37th ed. Berlin: Springer Spectrum, 2014.

Kubitzki, K., ed. *The Families and Genera of Vascular Plants. Vol. 3, Flowering Plants: Monocotyledones; Lilianae (except Orchidaceae).* Berlin and New York: Springer, 1989.

Kubitzki, K., ed. *The Families and Genera of Vascular Plants. Vol. 4, Flowering Plants: Monocotyledones; Alismatanae and Commelinanae (except Gramineae).* Berlin and New York: Springer, 1989.

Kubitzki, K., ed. *The Families and Genera of Vascular Plants. Vol. 6, Flowering Plants: Dicotyledons; Celastrales, Oxalidales, Rosales, Cornales, Ericales.* Berlin and New York: Springer, 2004.

Kubitzki, K., ed. *The Families and Genera of Vascular Plants. Vol. 9, Flowering Plants: Eudicots; Berberidopsidales, Buxales, Crossosomatales, Fabales p.p., Geraniales, Gunnerales, Myrtales p.p., Proteales, Saxifragales, Vitales, Zygophyllales, Clusiaceae Alliance, Passifloraceae Alliance, Dilleniaceae, Huaceae, Picramniaceae, Sabiaceae.* Berlin and New York: Springer, 2007.

Kubitzki, K., ed. *The Families and Genera of Vascular Plants. Vol. 10, Flowering Plants: Eudicots; Sapindales, Cucurbitales, Myrtaceae.* Berlin and New York: Springer, 2011.

Kubitzki, K., and C. Bayer, eds. *The Families and Genera of Vascular Plants. Vol. 5, Flowering Plants: Dicotyledons; Malvales, Capperales and Non-betalain Caryopyllales.* Berlin and New York: Springer, 2003.

Kubitzki, K., and J. W. Kadereit, eds. *The Families and Genera of Vascular Plants. Vol. 7, Flowering Plants: Dicotyledons; Lamiales (except Acanthaceae including Avicenniaceae).* Berlin and New York: Springer, 2004.

Kullmann, F., D. P. Banks, G. Bryant, C. Jennings, D. Jones, I. La Crois, M. S. Light, N. Nash, R. Parsons, A. Perkins, and J. Tanaka. *Die Kosmos Enzyklopädie der Orchideen* ["The Cosmos encyclopedia of orchids"]. 2nd ed. Stuttgart: Franck-Kosmos Verlag, 2011.

Lieberei, R., and C. Reisdorff. *Nutzpflanzenkunde* ["Botany of useful plants"]. 7th ed. Stuttgart: Thieme Verlag, 2007.

Neinhuis, C., D. Roth, and W. Barthlott. "*Aristolochia arborea:* The Biology and Thread of a Remarkable Rain Tree from Central America." *Der Palmengarten* ["The palm garden"] 58, no. 1 (1994): 15–19.

Oxelman, B., and M. Lidén. *"The Position of Circaeaster*—Evidence from Nuclear Ribosomal DNA." *Plant Systematics and Evolution* [Supplement] 9 (1995): 189–93.

Schenek, A. *Naturfaserlexikon* ["Dictionary of natural fibers"]. Frankfurt: Deutscher Fachverlag, 2000.

Schmeil, O., and J. Fitschen. *Die Flora Deutschlands und angrenzender Länder* ["The flora of Germany and neighboring countries"]. Edited by G. Parolly and J. G. Rohwer. Wiebelsheim, Germany: Quelle & Meyer Verlag, 2011.

Vogel, S. "Von Ölblumen und Parfümblumen" ["On oil flowers and perfume flowers"]. In *Blütenökologie faszinierendes Miteinander von Pflanzen und Tieren* ["Flower ecology fascinating coexistence of plants and animals"]. Edited by G. Zizka and S. Schneckenburger, 82–83. Kleine Senckenberg-Reihe [Short Senckenberg Series] 33. Frankfurt: W. Kramer, 1999.

Vogel, S. "Von Ölblumen und ölsammelnden Bienen" ["On oil flowers and oil-collecting bees"]. *Tropische und Subtropische Pflanzenwelt* ["Tropical and subtropical plant life"] 7 (1974): 1–267.

Wagenitz, G. *Wörterbuch der Botanik* ["Dictionary of botany"]. Jena, Germany: Gustav Fischer Verlag, 1996.

## Internet Sources

Chapman, G. P., and Y.-Z. Wang. "The Plant Life of China: Diversity and Distribution." 2013. www.researchgate.net/publication/259795544_The_Plant_Life_of_China_Diversity_and_Distribution_by_G_P_Chapman_Y_Z_Wang. Accessed on Feb. 17, 2017.

Greenpeace. "Illegale Gen-Leinsamen in Lebensmitteln" ["Illegal genetically modified flaxseed in foods"]. 2009. www.greenpeace.de/sites/www.greenpeace.de/files/fs_genleinsamen_update_30.09.02009.pdf. Accessed on Jan. 25, 2017.

Horres, R. "Untersuchungen zur Systematik und Phylogenie der Bromeliaceae unter besonderer Berücksichtigung molekularer Merkmale" ["Studies on the systematics and phylogeny of Bromeliaceae, with special emphasis on molecular characteristics"]. Dissertation. 2003. http://publikationen.ub.uni-frankfurt.de/frontdoor/index/index/docld/2314. Accessed on Jan. 19, 2017.

Midgley, J. J., J. D. M. White, S. D. Johnson, and G. N. Bronner. "Faecal Mimicry by Seeds Ensures Dispersal by Training Beetles." *Nature Plants* 1, no. 10 (2015): 15141. www.researchgate.net/publication/282618768_Faecal_mimicry_by_seeds_ensures_dispersal_by_dung_beetles. Accessed on Jan. 19, 2017. mobot.org/MOBOT/Research/APWeb/orders/. Accessed on Dec. 10, 2016. nature.com/articles/nplants2015141. Accessed on Feb. 6, 2017. pflanzenforschung [plant research].de/de/journal/journalbeitrage/die-perfekte-taeuschung-mistkaefer-vergraebt-samen-weil-10508. Accessed on Feb. 13, 2017.

Mori, S. A., and G. T. Prance. "2006 Onward: The Lecythidaceae Pages." New York Botanical Garden, New York. http://sweetgum.nybg.org/science/projects/lp/?irn=23835. Accessed on 03/01/2017.

Springer Science & Business Media. https://books.google.de/books?id=eafvCAAAQBAJ&dq=Circeaster+agrestis&hl=de&source=gbs_navlinks_s. Accessed on Feb. 13, 2017.

Stevens, P. F. "2001 Onwards." Angiosperm Phylogeny website.version 13. www.mobot.org/MOBOT/Research/APweb/Vogel, S. "Malpighiaceen und ihre Bestäuber" [Malpighiaceen and their pollinators"]. Film segment, Ed. IWF, Göttingen. http://dx.doi.org/10.3203/IWF/W-7047#t=09:53,09:55. Accessed on March 1, 2017.

Wang, X., P. Zhang, Q. Du, H. He, L. Zhao, and Y. Ren. "Heterodichogamy in Kingdonia (Circaeasteraceae, Ranunculales)." *Annals of Botany* 109, no. 6 (2012): 1125–32. https://doi.org/10.1093/aob/mcs041. Accessed on Feb. 17, 2017.

Watson, L., and M. J. Dallwitz. "1992 Onwards: The Families of Flowering Plants; Descriptions, Illustrations, Identification, and Information Retrieval." Version: Oct. 19, 2016. http://delta-intkey.com/angio/.

## Acknowledgments and Thanks

I would like to thank all those who have been involved in the creation of this book, directly and indirectly; first and foremost, of course, the Greenhouse directors: Kerstin Arendt, Katrin Baumgärtner, Susanne Bösader, Tobias Brose, Sabine Herrmann, Bernd Lohse, and Christian Werner, but also Ingo Kaczmarek and Philipp Bornemann.

Thanks also to teachers and colleagues, some of whom are no longer with us: Dr. Friedel Feindt, Privatdozent (PD), Dr. Heidrun E. K. Hartmann, prof. emeritus Dr. H.-D. Ihlenfeldt, and Dr. Carsten Schirarend, for the references on rare plants. I thank Prof. Dr. Norbert Jürgens for allowing me to use the first "service scanner," the same device that I also had at home, and I thank Prof. Dr. Med. Jens Rohwer for his willingness to be of help in the attribution of many plants and terms.

My special thanks also go to Angela Niebel-Lohmann, who was so immediately and spontaneously ready to work on the text.